What Made Cinema?

What Made Cinema?

Visual Culture and Early Film

Selected Essays Volume 1

Ian Christie

Sticking Place Books
New York

© Sticking Place Books 2025

www.stickingplacebooks.com

Designed by Goran Tovilovic

All rights reserved.

No part of this book may be reproduced, stored in or introduced into a retrieval system, or transmitted, in any form or by any means (electronic, mechanical, photocopying, recording or otherwise) without the written permission of the publishers, except in the case of brief quotations embodied in critical articles or reviews.

ISBN ISBN 978-1-942782-84-1

In memory of

Richard Brown, Stephen Herbert,
Paul Spehr and Roland-François Lack.

Devoted scholars who opened
new vistas on the birth of cinema,
and from whom I learned much.

Contents

Introduction: Back to the Future — 1

Mixed Media

1. Toys, Instruments, Machines:
   Why the Hardware Matters — 7
2. Moving Picture Media and Modernity: Taking
   Intermediate and Ephemeral Media Seriously — 23
3. Not Only 'King of the Vast':
   John Martin and 19th-Century Visual Spectacle — 41
4. Screening the City: The Long History of
   London Screen Entertainment — 51
5. The Anglo-Boer War in North London:
   A Micro-Study — 67
6. The Ghosts of Cinema Past:
   Screen Heritage in Australia — 75

Revisions: Getting the Story Straight

7. The Tarnished Myth of British Precedence:
   Friese-Greene, Paul and Will Day — 87
8. 'Everyday Life' in Early Cinema — 99
9. 'Something to Look At':
   On the Disappearing History of Lantern Slides — 113
10. A 'Stagey Marvel':
    The Genealogy of an Early Trick Film — 121
11. Now You See It... From 'Tricks' to 'Effects' — 133

Structuring a New Industry

12. Staffing an Early Film Studio — 145
13. The Lost World of
    Early North London Filmmaking — 155
14. 'Fumbling Towards Some New Art':
    The Structure of Cinema Programmes c.1909-13 — 169

15.	'What is a Film?' Legal Controversy and Cases Before 1910	183
16.	Measuring Early Screen Stardom in Europe	191

Sounds Familiar

17.	Early Synchronised Pictures	207
18.	'Suitable Music': Silent-Era Accompaniment Practices	217

Time and Space Machine

19.	Bringing the Empire Home: Imperial Spectacle in Early Cinema	235
20.	Ancient Rome Revisited: Classical Subjects and Cinema's Expansion after 1910	251
21.	A 'Theatre of Memory'? Screening Historic Literary London	267
22.	Who Needs Film Archives? Notes Towards a User-Centred Future	295

Pivotal Portraits

23.	'A Very Wonderful Process': Queen Victoria, Photography and Film	309
24.	Thomas Edison: The Media Wizard of Oz	327
25.	Robert and Ellen: Inventing Cinema	339
26.	Fred Karno's Fun Factory	349

What Cinema Made of Us

27.	New Windows on the World	357

Epilogue

28.	Strange Meeting: *They Shall Not Grow Old*	383

Endnotes	387
Index	439

Introduction

Looking back at essays written across nearly thirty years has taught me some interesting lessons. It seems that I've been pursuing two preoccupations during this time which might appear contradictory. One has been exploring the drive towards creating forms of spectacular entertainment – immersive, we would say now – that first became an obsession during the last decades of the 18th century, and has returned in different forms ever since. I've written recently about this 'long history' of immersive entertainment, summarising what was explored in more detail in a number of the pieces reprinted here, especially in the 'Mixed Media' section.[1]

The other preoccupation has been to identify the combination of drives, discoveries, social and psychological factors that coalesced to create what became 'cinema' around 1912 – initially known in America as 'photoplays' and eventually 'motion pictures' or movies. What initially prompted this pre-occupation was a realisation around 1990 that the 'centenary of cinema' was fast approaching, whether this was to be celebrated in 1993, 1994, 1995 or 1996, according to different national narratives.

I was working at the British Film Institute at this time, overseeing film distribution, and had recently launched video publishing via the Connoisseur VHS label, in partnership with the great French producer Anatole Dauman. While home video was thought to be accelerating the decline of cinema audiences, these had been steadily falling around the world, with television and now video seemingly set to take over as the main channels for satisfying audiovisual appetites. The potential of digital media to rescue cinema was not yet apparent – indeed was being trenchantly resisted in many quarters before the arrival of *Avatar* in 2009. So I suggested that we should try to celebrate what might turn out to be the medium's last big birthday.

In Britain, two 'centenary' projects took shape. One was an exhibition about how film related to contemporary art, which eventually emerged as *Spellbound: Art and Film*, co-curated with Philip Dodd at the Hayward Gallery in 1996.[2] The other was a kind of dramatised archaeology of the explosion of entrepreneurial invention that produced the first film shows in the 1890s, weaving together themes and figures which were rarely considered part of a history that I felt had become much too focused on mechanism and a handful of 'inventors'. Yet our title might have suggested otherwise: according to the great avant-garde filmmaker, Hollis Frampton, film was 'the last machine', the last device whose operation and function was visible and widely understandable before the age of electrical media.

Fortunately, our pitch appealed to Michael Jackson at BBC2, who commissioned *The Last Machine*, although I later heard that he was surprised by the amount of Victoriana that we managed to assemble at Pinewood Studio. But through the efforts of John Wyver, Richard Curson Smith, Jeff Baynes, Paul Cheetham and their teams, with a versatile cast headed by Terry Gilliam, we pulled off a five-part series that was broadcast on Saturday evenings in 1994 – something I still find hard to believe. The BBC never retransmitted the series, although it was shown in many other countries and happily uploaded to YouTube from Australia.[3]

Researching the series involved visits to many archives and collections around the world, especially the Library of Congress in Washington, the French CNC's Archive at Bois d'Arcy, and the Nederlands Film Museum, and brought me into contact with many remarkable scholars and collectors, some happily still good friends, including Kevin Brownlow, Paolo Cherchi Usai, Tom Gunning, Peter Jewell, Charlie Musser and Yuri Tsivian. An unforgettable visit to the Edison Historical Site at Orange, New Jersey, prompted the essay included here.

But writing and co-producing *The Last Machine* left me with many unanswered questions and lines of inquiry I wanted to pursue. One of these was the mystery of Robert Paul, an English pioneer we had featured, but about whom so little was known. It would be nearly twenty years before I managed to complete a book – *Robert Paul and the Origins of British Cinema* – containing all I had managed to discover about Paul and his fellow pioneers. In the process, I learned much more about the context in which Edison, Paul and the Lumières created the first decade of moving picture entertainment, some of which informs the rest of essays in this collection.

During the time I was working on *The Last Machine*, London enjoyed the world's first interactive museum devoted to the origins of cinema and related media: the British Film Institute's Museum of the Moving Image. Created by David Francis, Leslie Hardcastle and David Robinson, with funding found by Tony Smith, this opened in 1988, ingeniously housed under Waterloo Bridge. Although not directly involved in its creation, I contributed to the programme and its dramatised, hands-on approach undoubtedly influenced *The Last Machine*. The BFI's deplorable and unjustified closure of MoMI in 1999 deprived Britain of a major asset, and despite efforts to continue its inspirational example with the London Film Museum at County Hall and in Covent Garden, when I worked with David Robinson and the Leslie Hardcastle, this absence continues to be felt in Britain.

Another source of inspiration for much of what appears here was a programme at Birkbeck College, University of London, where I have taught since 2000. Started as The London Project in 2004, part of the AHRB Centre for British Film and Television Studies, with Luke McKernan and Simon Brown as research fellows, this would eventually lead to a London Screen Studies programme of exhibitions, such as *Moving Pictures Come to London*, screenings and courses offered in London Screen History between 2007 and 2014.[4] None of these survived the impact of major reorganisation at Birkbeck forced by government cuts, but some traces certainly appear in the essays gathered here.

During the decades over which the contents of this book were written, cinema itself has changed massively, having embraced digital technology after the global success of *Avatar*, and been largely domesticated by a combination of streaming and large-scale home displays. In many ways, I would argue that we now live in a post-cinema era, even if the forms and traditions of early 20th-century cinema still inform digital production and consumption on many platforms and devices.[5] Which is indeed rather similar to the experience of our ancestors, when stage melodrama, the variety theatre and projected spectacle shaped the early film experience. Yet even as we see the parallels, we also need to understand the specificity of the many forms and 'machines' that have preceded our own equally ephemeral present, which is a recurrent theme here.

Most of these essays are reprinted substantially as they originally appeared, with some minor editing to eliminate excessive repetition and update references. Many were called into existence by the biennial conferences of Domitor, the international association for the study of early cinema, which I have been involved with over many years, before a recent stint serving as co-president with Tami Williams. Most of this work would have been impossible without the encouragement and support of Patsy Nightingale, who also shared Paul Cronin's belief that they deserve another outing in compact form. I am hopeful that their appearance will stimulate readers to make their own discoveries and connections, and to cherish collections that still offer access to the material history of what was cinema, such as the Bill Douglas Museum at Exeter University, the Eye Museum in Amsterdam, the Cinémathèque française in Paris, the Museo Nazionale del Cinema in National Museum of Cinema in Turin and others.

While digital media greatly extend our reach, with online resources such as the Media History Digital Library and Dartmouth College's Early Cinema Compendium, as well as many online national newspaper libraries, they also distance us from the fabric and machinery of spectacle. Finding a balance seems to be increasingly the challenge – but also, as never before, an opportunity.

Counterfactual History: A note about the cover illustration
The event pictured so vividly on the cover never took place. It is a painting made by Roy Carnon for an advertisement by the Reed Paper Group in 1952. No doubt aiming to liven up the subject of papermaking, Reed had their illustrator work up a scene dated 1895 that supposedly coincided with Albert E. Reed starting his business near Maidstone. Reed, we are told, was 'one of the purposeful men who made the 1890s a period of promise unique in our history' – just like Robert W. Paul. In Carnon's illustration, a remarkably convincing Paul is seen projecting 'strange new pictures on a magic lantern screen' in his Hatton Garden workshop. The audience of three or four viewers look more 1952 than 1895, but the machine Paul is cranking is clearly modelled accurately on his Theatrograph projector of 1896. And if Paul hadn't yet created his projector in 1895, he and Birt Acres had shot their first film, outside Clovelly Cottage in Barnet, and run it on one of Paul's Kinetoscopes at his workshop in Hatton Garden, making enough noise to attract the attention of local police. This became the basis of a celebrated scene in the Boultings' film *The Magic Box*, made for the Festival of Britain in 1951, but there attributed to William Friese-Greene.

Possibly Carnon's illustration was intended as a correction to the once widespread belief in Britain that Friese-Greene was the unacknowledged 'inventor of kinematography', as his grave in Highgate Cemetery still proclaims. But if so, by whom? For details and analysis of this confusion, see Chapter 7, 'The Tarnished Myth of British Precedence'. The painter Roy Carnon, incidentally, would go on to become a noted concept artist in cinema, creating the iconic circular space station for Kubrick's *2001: A Space Odyssey* in 1968 and contributing to many other notable films. History, like cinema and painting, has strange ways of mingling truth and myth. Or as Walter Benjamin put it more poetically: 'the historian is the herald who invites the dead to the table'.[6]

Mixed Media

1.
Toys, Instruments, Machines: Why the Hardware Matters

> A machine was a thing made up of distinguishable 'parts', organised in imitation of some part of the human body. Machines were said to work'.
>
> Hollis Frampton.¹

What were moving pictures for? I raise the question in order to explore a theme which is in danger of being obscured by the obvious fact that moving-picture apparatus quickly became the means to fulfil a number of purposes: to produce entertainment and to a lesser extent instruction. In this sense, it joined the ranks of machines, 'apparatuses with a definite function' (according to part of the *Oxford English Dictionary* definition, of which more later) – and became correspondingly invisible. Or, rather, the history of cameras, projectors and sound recorders became a matter for connoisseurship or engineering history, rather than one likely to interest historians of the medium of cinema, whether aesthetic, social or ideological. What does it matter how the image is produced and delivered, once it has been sufficiently standardised to attract no interest in itself, except perhaps when it malfunctions?²

If we believe this, then collecting historic cinema apparatus or the various optical instruments, gadgets and toys that preceded and accompanied its rise to dominance is merely antiquarian. However curious or valuable they may be as objects, they will not tell us anything about the experience of cinema. However, I want to argue against such an idealist position, and to assert a materialist history based on taking into account the machinery and its discursive presentation, as well as its products; and on seeing cinema as part of a continuing tradition of spectacle and illusion, rather than as a separate art with a 'pre-history'. Part of my argument will take the kaleidoscope as an example of an instrument which appears, to us at least, to have no 'purpose'.³

But let us return to the question of what moving pictures were 'for'. The simplest answer is that they demonstrated the successful achievement of animated photography. They were self-referential or reflexive, in the way that the phonograph or electrical lighting was primarily the demonstration of an achievement before it was a means to some end.[4] Such expectations are clear from the terms of press reports during the early months of projected film shows:

> THE CINÉMATOGRAPHE, which is the invention of MM. A. and L. Lumière, is a contrivance belonging to the same family as Edison's Kinetoscope and the old Wheel of Life, but in a rather higher state of development. The spectator no longer gazes through a narrow aperture at the changing picture, but has it presented to him full size on a large screen. The principle, however, is much the same, consisting simply of passing rapidly before the eye a series of pictures representing the successive stages of the action or the changing scene that has to be reproduced.[5]

> Edison's beautiful optical instrument, the kinetoscope, has now become known to most people through its exhibition in various large towns.[6]

> Animated lantern pictures are still the rage, for not only are there four different machines or projection apparatus being publicly exhibited at the present time in London, but these are being duplicated at the east and west ends, besides arrangements being in progress for provincial exhibitions.[7]

Another reason for paying close attention to such early reports is to note their terminology. The terms used by both the non-specialist and professional press of 1896 range across 'invention', 'contrivance', 'instrument', 'machine' and 'apparatus'. They are evocative of a period of intense development or 'perfecting' (a favourite Edison term) of basic mechanisms in order to fulfil their aim or potential.[8] There was indeed considerable contemporary amusement at the proliferation of pompous terminology, as evidenced in another 1896 press report that spoke of 'the new thing with the long name and the old thing with the name that isn't much shorter',[9] while the many variations on '…graph' already seemed absurd to the *British Journal of Photography* by the summer of that year. There would also be commercial considerations relating to proprietary names and legal ones relating to patented principles. But was there any significance in something being described as an 'instrument' or a 'machine' rather than a 'toy', as *The New York Times* called Edison's first projector in April 1896? 'The new thing at Koster and Bial's last night was Edison's vitascope, exhibited for the first time. The ingenious inventor's latest toy is a projection of his kinetoscope figures in stereopticon fashion, upon a white screen in a darkened hall'.[10]

In the turn-of-the-century worldview, an instrument had a purpose. According to the 1910 edition of the *Oxford English Dictionary*, it is a material thing designed for the accomplishment of some mechanical or other physical effect, which stands somewhere between a 'tool... used by a workman or artisan' and a machine, distinguished from this by 'having less mechanism'; although, as the dictionary warned, 'the terms over-lap'.[11]

This ambiguity could equally apply to the status of moving picture devices in 1896. Lacking as yet any established use, these were exhibited for the entertainment and instruction of spectators, just as a long line of optical devices known as optical toys had been throughout the 19th century and earlier. However, by the end of the century, 'toy' was already restricted to the juvenile or trivial connotations we know today. Webster's definition in 1913 was 'a plaything for children... A thing for amusement, but of no real value';[12] while the 1910 *OED* offered among 'concrete senses': 'a material object for children or others to play with (often an imitation of some familiar object)... something contrived for amusement rather than practical use', noting that 'this is now the leading sense, to which others are referred'. It had not always been the leading sense; and the possibility of tracing shifts in the usage of this and other words was the result of another quintessentially Victorian enterprise, the study of the history of language, as part of a general preoccupation with classification which would serve the new sciences of the era.[13]

The 1910 *OED* history of the word 'toy' is revealing. Not only is the word's origin uncertain, but after a single recorded use in 1303, it seems to 'disappear for two centuries, and then all at once burst into view with a wide sense-development.[14] This explosion of use in the 16th century ranges across 'fantastic acts and practices, jests and jokes, lively phrases of melody and odd conceits' – all of which indicate how central concepts of fantasy and play were to Elizabethan culture. Equally central, and related, was a fascination with magic; and the distinction between supernatural and natural forms of magic, although insisted on by such practitioners of the latter as Giambattista della Porta, was often hard to maintain. According to della Porta's bestseller, *Natural Magick*: 'There are two sorts of Magick; the one is infamous, and unhappy, because it has to do with foul Spirits, and consists of incantations and wicked curiosity; and this is called Sorcery; an art which all learned and good men detest; neither is it able to yield a truth of reason or nature, but stands merely upon fancies and imaginations... The other Magick is natural; which all excellent wise men do admit and embrace, and worship with great applause'.[15]

Despite the protestations of della Porta and many other Renaissance scholars, such distinctions would remain hard to maintain, not least because of the fascination of the infamous magic; and since the pioneering work of Frances Yates on the Elizabethan magus John Dee and on Giordano Bruno, it has become commonplace to acknowledge the continued cohabitation of magic and early science.[16]

Something of this fascination was surely present in the following century's preoccupation with what became known as 'philosophical toys'. The most celebrated of these took the form of ingenious machines, initially imitating animals, as in the gardens of the Villa d'Este at Tivoli and the Villa Pratolino near Florence, where an early 17th-century English traveller described how 'the birds do sing, sitting upon twigs, so naturally, as one would verily think they were all quick and living birds... and, when they are in the midst of their best singing, then comes an owl flying: and the birds suddenly, all at once, are still'.[17] The birds' mechanical nature was dramatically revealed by their sudden immobility. Later mechanical marvels would aim at a more integral emulation of living behaviour, as in the celebrated excreting duck made by Jacques de Vaucanson and various humanoid automata such as Vaucanson's flautist, Pierre Jaquet-Droz's automatic writer and his son Henri-Louis' harpist, whose eyes 'followed' the music.[18] In Vienna, Wolfgang von Kempelen created two of the marvels of the age in his talking machine and chess player of 1783.

What gave this range of ingenious machines their scientific or 'philosophical' status was the speculation among such philosophers as Hume, Descartes and Bayle on whether animals, or even human bodies, could be regarded as machines, uniquely animated in the latter case by the possession of a soul. The ability of man-made automata to reproduce animal and human behaviour made this seem more likely, and helped to focus such debates on devices which were also entertaining and costly. Derek Price was one of the first scholars in the history of science and technology to argue that these mechanical marvels, like their ancestors in the ancient world, were not intended to be 'practical' or even strictly illusory.[19] Their appeal was rather aesthetic, or exemplary. They demonstrated principles and possibilities, such as those first proposed by the Greek philosopher and scientist Hero in his *Pneumatics*, which was widely studied as both a work of early physics and a guide to 'natural magic', which included phenomena relating to magnetism, change of state and optical illusion. Daniel Tiffany has summed up this complex of ideology and practice in his wide-ranging study of 'materialism and modern lyric', *Toy Medium*, arguing that the tradition of 'philosophical atomism' or materialism had long made use of a discourse of automated and spectacular 'proofs'.[20]

By the 19th century, such proofs had begun to assume more modest and didactic forms, and 'toy' was moving closer to its modern sense of something manual which is played with. The sequence of specifically kinetic optical toys, as distinct from the essentially static images of the magic lantern and the peep show,[21] is usually traced from the launch of the thaumatrope and the phenakistoscope in the 1820s. Both of these were inspired, or at least explained, by Peter Mark Roget's 1824 paper 'Explanation of an optical deception in the appearance of the spokes of a wheel seen through vertical apertures', and by Michael Faraday's subsequent demonstration of the consequences of afterimages, or the persistence of vision, with what became known as 'Faraday's wheel'.[22] All of these followed from the fundamental studies of vision initiated by Newton, Goethe and others, concerned with questions about how physiology conditions what we see. Human vision had become a form of 'apparatus', with specific limitations and properties, which were demonstrated by the paradoxes of the thaumatrope and phenakistoscope.

Charles Wheatstone, perhaps best known today as the pioneer of stereoscopy, was the inventor of another such device, the kaleidophone, and defined the rationale of the modern philosophical toy in 1827: 'The application of the principles of science to ornamental and amusing purposes contributes, in a greater degree, to render them extensively popular; for the exhibition of striking experiments induces the observer to investigate their causes with additional interest, and enables him more permanently to remember their effects'.[23]

Wheatstone's instrument, or 'toy', which traced illuminated figures in space, was named after the recent and highly successful kaleidoscope; and I want to focus on this because it is something we now hardly think of as an instrument at all. If an instrument has by definition a purpose, a use, then it is difficult to see what this could be in the case of the kaleidoscope with its display of ever-changing abstract patterns.

NATURAL MAGICK

BY

John Baptista Porta,

A NEAPOLITANE:

IN

TWENTY BOOKS:

1 Of the Causes of Wonderful things.
2 Of the Generation of Animals.
3 Of the Production of new Plants.
4 Of increasing Houshold-Stuff.
5 Of changing Metals.
6 Of counterfeiting Gold.
7 Of the Wonders of the Load-stone.
8 Of strange Cures.
9 Of Beautifying Women.
10 Of Distillation.
11 Of Perfuming.
12 Of Artificial Fires.
13 Of Tempering Steel.
14 Of Cookery.
15 Of Fishing, Fowling, Hunting, &c.
16 Of Invisible Writing.
17 Of Strange Glasses.
18 Of Statick Experiments.
19 Of Pneumatick Experiments.
20 Of the Chaos.

Wherein are set forth
All the RICHES and DELIGHTS
Of the
NATURAL SCIENCES

LONDON,
Printed for *Thomas Young*, and *Samuel Speed*; and are to be sold at the three Pigeons, and at the Angel in St. *Paul's* Church-yard. 1658.

John Baptista Porta (Giambattista della Porta),
Natural Magick in Twenty Books:
Wherein are set forth All the Riches and Delights of the Natural Sciences.
London: Thomas Young and Samuel Speed, 1658.

Tabletop kaleidoscope, c.1850.
Courtesy of the Bill Douglas Cinema Museum, University of Exeter.

Chronologically, the kaleidoscope pre-dates the other 19th-century devices, having been invented in 1815 by the Scottish natural philosopher David Brewster. Brewster was working on optics and crystallography, and his interest in angles of refraction and mirroring would lead him to anticipate the development of the Fresnel dioptric lens, which became standard equipment in lighthouses. As he noted in his 1819 treatise on the kaleidoscope, the device emerged by chance from his experimental practice: 'The first idea of this instrument presented itself to me in the year 1814, in the course of a series of experiments in the polarisation of light by successive reflections between plates of glass'.[24]

Brewster realised that this could become a device that would produce an infinite range of symmetrical aesthetic patterns, and named it from a combination of the Greek words *kalos* (beautiful), *eidos* (form) and *skopeo* (to look). He proceeded to patent and develop it, while admitting that in its simplest form it 'could not be considered as a general philosophical instrument of universal application'. But it caused a sensation when marketed in 1816 and Brewster felt able to declare it a 'popular instrument for the purposes of rational amusement'. He also argued that it had many practical applications, such as producing patterns for tiles, carpets and other forms of interior decoration. 'The Kaleidoscope will assume the character of the highest class of machinery, which improves at the same time as it abridges the exertions of individuals... it will create in an hour what a thousand artists could not create in a year'.[25]

Here is a striking case of terminological slippage, from 'philosophical' to 'popular instrument', and to 'machine' – all referring to the same device considered within different frames of reference. Yet the kaleidoscope is hardly a machine in the modern sense, lacking even the mechanism of the phenakistoscope or later, more complex, optical devices. It is strictly personal, activated by handling, and belongs to the object-type or instrument family that includes the telescope and the microscope.[26] Somewhat like the latter, the kaleidoscope 'reveals a microcosmic world' to the viewer, even if it is an artificial one.

Jonathan Crary has claimed, in his influential *Techniques of the Observer*, that Brewster's justification for marketing the kaleidoscope was 'productivity and efficiency', since it offered a mechanical means for the reformation of art according to an industrial paradigm'.[27] But a reading less influenced by Foucault's preoccupation with mechanisms of coercion and modernisation might acknowledge Brewster's utilitarian rationalisation, while noting his equal emphasis on 'amusement' and instruction. From his research in crystallography and physiology, Brewster was well aware of nature's underlying symmetry, as revealed by the microscope and now simulated by the kaleidoscope. He stood on the threshold of the era when machinery was expected to be labour-saving and profitable. And as a Scot, his hopes for the kaleidoscope as a pattern generator reflect the importance of textile weaving and carpet making in Scotland in the early 19th century, with the recent innovation of the Jacquard loom making pattern variety both possible and commercially vital.[28] But Brewster also had his roots in the tradition of the philosophical toy as a precision instrument designed to impress with its craftsmanship and ingenuity, while demonstrating some basic principles which might be scientific but also – in the language of the era – 'moral'.

Helen Weston has shown how another key optical device, the magic lantern, could signify either illusion or illumination, depending on the political context, and how it stood for both during the French Revolution.[29] The kaleidoscope similarly became a polemical figure for Marx and Engels, in their critique of Saint-Simon in *The German Ideology*, as 'a kaleidoscopic display… composed entirely of reflections of itself'.[30] For the poet Charles Baudelaire, however, it offered an emblem of modernity, a trope for the dandy's experience of urban life: '[The dandy] moves into the crowd as though into an enormous reservoir of electricity. He, the lover of life, may also be compared to a mirror as vast as this crowd; to a kaleidoscope endowed with consciousness, with which every one of its movements presents a pattern of life, in all its multiplicity'.[31]

Not only did Baudelaire link the kaleidoscope with the newer technology of electricity, but he postulated a purposeful 'conscious' instrument which might represent a 'pattern of life'. There is a strong temptation to read this as an anticipation of cinema's ability to represent the crowd; and yet it is equally important to resist that if we want to understand the *mentalité* of the mid-century and the place of optical toys within it.[32] In a slightly earlier essay, Baudelaire described at length the effect produced by the phenakistoscope with its decomposed images of a dancer or juggler which unite into one moving figure.[33] Such 'scientific toys', he observes, can develop in the child's brain a taste for marvellous and surprising effects'.

In spite of Brewster's hopes for the kaleidoscope as an aid to industry, there is little evidence that it became so. However, it did not disappear – despite Crary's assumption to the contrary – but joined the stereoscope, which enjoyed an even greater popular success in the 1850s, as a staple 'toy' continuing to be produced in a vast range of variations up to the present day.[34] But if Crary is clearly right that we cannot 'know what the stereoscope looked like to a nineteenth-century viewer', can we still recover the fascination that remains in diluted form today in our very different sensory world? In part, we may be able to do so when the conjunction of apparatus and image is sufficiently unusual to short-circuit the sense of condescension that often accompanies such exercises.

I can vividly recall seeing a series of stereo views of Western Front trenches in a Somme battlefield museum in France, which made me feel 'closer' to the experience than anything I had seen in any other medium or format. However, in the absence of such personal experience, we may have to resort to collecting written evidence. One such account of the kaleidoscope is particularly valuable in challenging our sense that it offers only fleeting diversion. In his autobiography, André Gide recalled his fascination with 'that worker of marvels called a kaleidoscope', which would have been in the 1870s (Gide was born in 1869).[35] He describes how the shifting of the patterns 'filled me with unspeakable delight', and lists the colours and shapes, before drawing a distinction between how his girl cousins used the toy, shaking and turning it 'to get a complete change', while he preferred to turn it slowly and savour the process of change. Gide also recounts how his fascination led to his taking the kaleidoscope apart, removing some of the pieces of glass, and replacing them with objects such as a nib, a fly's wing and a blade of grass, which produced a duller picture but one that still had some 'geometrical interest'.

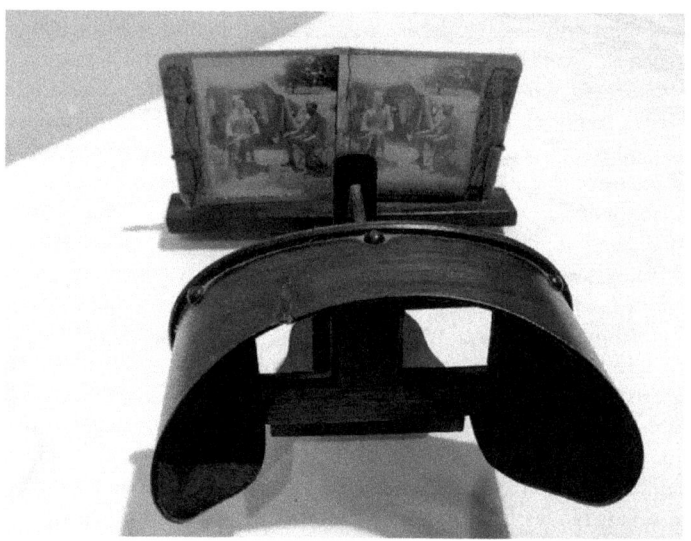

Holmes type stereoscope.

Gide's recollection of passing 'hours and days over this amusement' valuably restores a temporal as well as a haptic or experimental dimension to the enjoyment of the kaleidoscope. Reading his account, written nearly fifty years after the experience, and in an era already saturated with photography and film, we can understand better the kind of response evoked by Brewster and Baudelaire. But harder to appreciate are the spatial, material and contextual dimensions, when we know these devices only in museum collections. How did kaleidoscopes, stereoscopes and the other optical toys fit into the drawing rooms, smoking rooms, studies and nurseries that were their natural habitats? While there is some evidence that can be deduced from the elaborate panoply of 'optical' allusions in such authors as Proust and Joyce, it must be admitted that the detailed contextualisation of 19th-century optical devices still awaits serious study.[36] A model for the kind of exploration required might be Dolf Sternberger's chapter 'The Domestic Interior' in his *Panorama of the Nineteenth Century*, which traces the theme of light gradually entering this originally dark and densely cluttered space of the home.[37] The brightly coloured vignettes offered by the kaleidoscope and the stereoscope need to be imagined against contemporary wall-coverings and furnishings, and mediated by the transition from candles to gas lamps and finally electricity.

We can find a wider frame of reference for the consider-ation of instructive illusion in another of Brewster's texts, his *Letters on Natural Magic*, addressed to his famous fellow-countryman Sir Walter Scott in 1832. Here Brewster, who was also a pious churchman, set out to expose how corrupt governments throughout history had 'maintained their influence over the human mind' by cynically exploiting natural phenomena as 'magic'. An example of this from Brewster's own era was the mission undertaken by the magician Jean-Eugène Robert-Houdin in 1856 at the request of the French state, to help suppress an uprising in Algeria by demonstrating superior European magic.[38] Another important theme of much later 19th-century illusionism was the performance of magic as an 'antidote' to superstition and especially the growing Victorian fascination with spiritualism. By showing that furniture could mysteriously move and apparitions appear at the behest of skilled magicians, it was claimed that the credulous would realise how they were deceived by fraudulent mediums. In his dramatic monologue, *Mr Sludge, 'The Medium'*, Robert Browning would lay bare the tricks of the medium's trade, while allowing his subject, Mr Sludge, to indict the 'curious gentlefolk' who have encouraged him to make a living by satisfying their desire for signs and wonders.[39]

In a similar vein, Nevil Maskelyne's avowed intention in his Egyptian Hall magic shows was to unmask fraudulent spiritualists such as the Davenports by replicating their effects. Behind such conspicuous professions of rationality and responsibility, we may suspect some form of over-compensation at work, perhaps related to the apparent self-deception in responses to the 18th-century

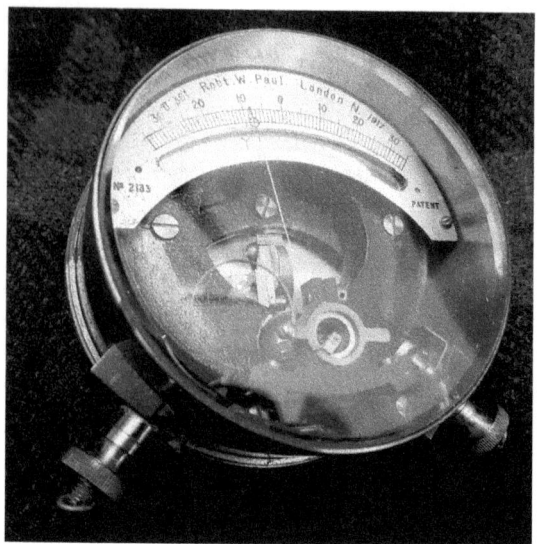

Robert Paul's Unipivot Galvanometer.

automata. We might further suspect – although there is no space to explore this further here – a connection with the source material of Freud's essay 'The Uncanny': namely the suggestion that 'uncertainty over whether a figure in a story is a human being or an automaton' induces the feeling of uncanniness.[40]

Many early modern media proposed what may seem today to be either fraudulent or at best utopian fantasies of empowerment. Others claimed seemingly practical, instrument-like capabilities which also seem like fantasies within the technological capability of the time, such as the idea of a phonograph to take messages at the front door, or to fill an opera house; or a moving image so 'real' that it compels viewers to dive for cover, or to doubt their spouses' fidelity.[41] Here instrument history may help to explain how these conform to a general historical pattern. Derek Price's study of *parerga*, or ancient ornamental devices, led him to conclude that 'the most ingenious mechanical devices of antiquity were not useful machines but trivial toys. Only slowly do the machines of everyday life take up the scientific advances and principles used long before in despicable playthings and overly ingenious, impracticable scientific models and instruments'.[42]

Moving pictures emerged from the profusion of optical toys and devices to become 'machines of everyday life'; and in doing so their apparatus became invisible, while this institutionalisation perhaps served to 'infantilise' their forerunners, making them imperfect approximations to the apparently achieved illusion of cinema.

Robert Paul's Theatrograph no. 2, as presented by him
to the Science Museum in 1913.

However, this repression of the instrumental is worth probing further. The first successful manufacturers of moving-picture apparatus were necessarily precision engineers and instrument makers, such as Jules Carpentier, responsible for fabricating the Lumières' first *cinématographes*, and Robert Paul, who made replica kinetoscopes for the British market before producing his own camera and projector. Paul was an instrument maker when he entered the moving-picture business in 1894, to become Britain's leading producer and leader of the film industry over the next fifteen years, before concentrating solely on instrument making after 1910.[43] These have sometimes seemed to be incompatible careers, as if Paul were distracted or seduced into becoming a purveyor of risqué jokes, ghost stories and travelogues, before returning to his 'true' vocation. But within the perspective outlined here, instrument makers had long been in the business of illusion and demonstration. When Paul branched out from electrical instruments in 1894, he became central to a new conjunction of engineering, electricity and chemistry in moving pictures. But he never abandoned instrument making, and his kinetoscopes, cameras, projectors and other related machines were in the tradition of the philosophical toy, later adapted to the growing demand for science teaching.[44]

Initially, they had no immediate function except to satisfy curiosity – while certainly covering their costs – and they could also serve to demonstrate new principles and discoveries, as when Paul produced animated illustrations of magnetic fields for lectures by the director of the Royal Institution, Professor Sylvanus Thompson, in the early 1900s.[45] By the same token, Paul continued to work on other types of instrument. In 1902, at the height of his moving-picture success, he patented the 'unipivot' galvanometer, as a portable, accurate means of measuring current. Earlier, Carpentier had produced a pioneering extended-scale galvanometer in 1889, in response to the demand for such new instruments that had been stimulated by new developments in telegraphy after the laying of the first transatlantic cable in 1858, and by the rise of electrical power distribution in the 1880s.[46]

Classical film theory fetishised an idealised institution that functioned between approximately 1939 and 1959, neglecting the burgeoning process of technological development which long preceded (and followed) the hallowed threshold of 1894-96. It was helped in doing so by a largely uncritical acceptance of André Bazin's 'myth of total cinema', which claimed that the pioneers of cinema were aiming at an 'integral illusion' which was more or less achieved at an early stage, even in advance of incremental improvements through the addition of synchronised sound, colour and stereoscopy.[47] The fundamental axiom of this paradigm became 'the impression of reality' regarded as cinema's distinctive feature, distinguishing it from all other forms of artistic representation and creating automatically, as Christian Metz describes it, a mechanism of affective and perceptual participation in the spectator.[48] Yet moving-image media have always been hybrid, and constantly engaged in the 'spectacular demonstration' of their own premises, as evidenced in the cinema industry's relentless marketing of innovation.

The argument against Bazin's myth has been put most persuasively by Laurent Mannoni, outlining the scope of what he calls deceptive art. According to Mannoni, it is thanks to collectors such as Werner Nekes – and we might certainly add Bill Douglas and Peter Jewell, as well as William and John Barnes – that the 'vastness, beauty and complexity' of the history of deceptive art is beginning to be realised.[49] However, we are enjoined not just to admire, but to recognise that cinema remains an art of illusion, 'not merely a mechanical transfer of the exterior world onto the screen', and that deceptive art should be treated as an autonomous current of aesthetic and technical questing', of which cinema is just one strand. Instead of seeing the kaleidoscope as merely a decorative digression in the history of toys, or the stereoscope as (teleologically) an anticipation of cinema's immersive effect, we would do better to regard these as having their own identity, albeit within a constantly shifting and evolving tradition of 'illusion' wherein today's 'plaything' or 'overly ingenious instrument' may indeed become tomorrow's 'machine of everyday life', like so many of its forerunners.

Preserving these, as the Bill Douglas Museum and many other collections do, remains vital – but only if they are displayed in ways that help us see them in their original context, and can stimulate us to reflect on the material underpinning of 'the art of illusion' and the part it continues to play in our lives today, albeit through devices that we can no longer consider 'machines' in the sense that Frampton invoked. And discourse has also continued to evolve, always unavoidably out of step with what it describes, but equally important in how we characterise and understand the devices of our everyday life.

Originally a chapter in James Lyons and John Plunkett, eds., *Multimedia Histories: From the Magic Lantern to the Internet* (University of Exeter Press, 2007).

2.
Moving Picture Media and Modernity: Taking Intermediate and Ephemeral Media Seriously

> Somewhere between live media and dead media is ephemeral media, something that might deserve a passing comment, if only to contrast it to the really dead stuff.
>
> Stefan Jones,
> 'Dead medium: Children's Dead Media'[1]

In 1994, I was working on a television series and book, *The Last Machine*, subtitled 'early cinema and the birth of the modern world', which tried among other things to locate moving pictures in a wider cultural and technological field than was normal at the time.[2] But in wanting to rescue this history from a merely technicist or 'pioneer' account, based on inventions and scientific principles, there was a danger of going too far in the opposite direction, paying excessive attention to ancestry and context. To say, as others did at this time of celebrating the centenary of cinema, that late 19th-century culture was '"cinematic" before the fact', so that 'the emergence of cinema was both inevitable and redundant', does not actually explain very much, even if it provides a capacious platform for the exploration of retrospectively 'cinematic' qualities in other media.[3] The original rallying cry of the new historians of early cinema had been 'against teleology': rejecting a selective account of the early period that identified 'primitive' techniques and forms as pointing towards the achievement of true cinema, in favour of an unprejudiced survey of all early forms of film in order to identify the full range of intermedial influences and connections from which the institution of cinema would emerge.

In the same year as *The Last Machine*, Tom Gunning published one of his key papers on this same theme, 'The Whole Town's Gawking', with a subtitle coincidentally similar to mine, 'Early Cinema and the Visual Experience of Modernity'.[4] In this sequel to his influential earlier paper on 'the cinema of attractions',[5] Gunning began by restating the case against the *telos* of narrative, before suggesting that 'attractions' not only open up the study of distinctive forms of reception and exhibition of early cinema, but also provide 'the key for exploring what a primarily German tradition describes as 'modernity'.[6] And from this he moved beyond the historiography of early cinema itself to consider environmental and psychological features of the world in which the first films were made and seen.

It was such claims, by Gunning, myself and others, that led David Bordwell to question this equation between the characteristic forms of moving pictures and modernity in his historiographic book *On the History of Film Style*.[7] But despite such scepticism, it must be admitted that the attractions–modernity thesis has become something like received opinion.[8] The 'pull' of this equation is understandable, in a culture that has fetishised 'modernity' and made 'Modernism' its correlate, even if Bordwell's critique of the explanatory value of 'modernity' remains hard to answer on his terms. What I want to do here is backtrack from this apparent impasse, and consider some other implications of disavowing the teleological inevitability of cinema. Certainly, it is clear that the mass viewing of projected narratives became a major leisure activity for an increasing number of 20th-century citizens around the world. But it is also becoming clear that many factors over and above the visual organisation of these narratives contributed to this outcome – economic, social and psychological factors, that 'delivered' the mass audience, which then subjected early moving pictures to modification by means of customer feedback. These are the lessons of the new spectator-based approaches to cinema history.[9]

Another consequence of rejecting teleology is to call into question the 'succession' thesis, whereby optical toys 'led to' the first viewing apparatuses, which were then superseded by projected pictures.[10] If the history of modern media tells us anything, it is surely that very few if any of these media have ever died out. On the contrary, they have existed in an ongoing ensemble, with frequent revivals and repurposings, and of course technological upgrades. So instead of a succession model, we need some other way of conceptualising what I am calling the ensemble of visual media. And if we succeed in this, we might also want to confront the edifice that 'modernity' has become – questioning its explanatory or even descriptive value.

Dead Media?
There is or was a website devoted to commemorating 'dead media'.[11] Ironically, this became something of a dead medium in its own right, having been created in the late 1990s and since abandoned to float in cyberspace. Two apparently contradictory propositions lay behind this quixotic initiative. One was the claim that few media ever truly 'die': instead they 'jostle around' and often reposition themselves in relation to a newer medium; or they may shrink back into a 'protective niche'.

But the same manifesto also noted that many media forms have proved temporary, and in effect died, and the website was intended to gather information about these as a collective endeavour. The primary impulse behind its accumulated archive of 'working notes' was clearly the meta-history of media that began to emerge in the 1960s, originally inspired in large part by Marshall McLuhan and later by Friedrich Kittler, but now boasting its own eclectic history of speculation and even its own folklore.[12] Another impulse, perhaps equally strong, was the alliance that has grown up between specialist antiquarians and internet enthusiasts, making the web a vast archive of personal collections and research about these – and of course a global marketplace for collector-scholars of every kind of apparatus and ephemera. Thanks to such intensive activity, there are few kinds of collectible artefact that lack visibility on the web, and it is surely this burgeoning virtual presence that has boosted awareness of 'dead media' beyond anything previously achieved by traditional museum displays.[13]

Such displays were invariably chronological and supported an implicitly teleological account of how optical toys and devices 'led to' the climactic achievement of photog-raphic moving pictures in the mid-1890s.[14] What was readily apparent, however, was that the successful pioneers of moving pictures – Thomas Edison, the Lumière brothers, Birt Acres and Robert Paul – had little involvement with such 'pre-cinema' devices. Their skills were essentially mechanical and/or photographic, even if their machines exploited various principles involved in other optical devices. Moreover, much of what subsequently consolidated the appeal of moving pictures came from quite different cultural sources: from the variety theatre and the lantern lecture. So the idea of a genealogy or a chain of invention could hardly be proved, and perhaps was never intended as an explanatory argument, but rather more of a presentational convenience for organising a selection of otherwise heterogeneous material. For the sheer profusion of devices and entertainments that could be drawn into even a loose association was vast, as has become apparent in the different kinds of presentation that have emerged since the late 1990s. In the displays mounted by the Bill Douglas Museum (in situ and online), and in many national cinematheques, as well as the Getty Museum's Devices of Wonder exhibition and touring exhibitions based on Werner Nekes' collection, there has been a sharply diminishing concern with placing these devices in relation to the institution of cinema, and a corresponding interest in displaying their diversity and intrinsic appeal.[15]

This may correspond to a wider shift towards a 'new antiquarianism', which values historic items of many kinds for their individuality, and for their rarity, rather than as precursors of modern instances. The internet has undoubtedly facilitated access to this history, and allowed a closer engagement with individual objects than traditional glass-case static display, but paradoxically it is no substitute for being able to 'use' such devices either manually or optically.

The 'deadness' of such media, together with their quaint names and rarity, may have appealed to the self-styled 'necronauts' of the Dead Media website, but the key research issues for many of us are to revise the taxonomy of such media, and to determine the extent of their contemporary appeal and the significance of their diverse lifespans. Ever since McLuhan provocatively expanded the range of what might be considered a 'medium' to include modes of transport, power sources and tools, we have become accustomed to considering a wide range of technologies and forms as media – and indeed to McLuhanesque claims about their psychological and social influence.[16] But such claims normally relate to the major media that shape an era – print, telegraphy, photography, cinema, broadcasting – and have little to say about minor media. If it is implausible that a minor recreational device or 'medium' should exert wide influence, what can we say about the significance of such products? If they do not determine or shape a culture, are they symptomatic of aspirations, widely shared interests? Might they point to what Noël Burch called a 'collective drive'?[17] And deserve rescuing from a cinematic version of what the historian E. P. Thompson called 'the enormous condescension of posterity' in cinema history?[18]

Three 'Dead' Media: Praxinoscope, Kinetoscope and Flip-book
I want to consider here three examples of what might normally be termed ephemeral media (or perhaps 'intermediate technology') and explore the implications of taking these seriously *as* media forms, not as stepping stones 'towards' cinema proper but as devices

which were developed, launched and marketed – all apparently with some success – during the same period of fascination with kinetic images that saw projected pictures emerge.

The first of these is the Praxinoscope, patented in 1877 in France by Emile Reynaud.[19] This was a development of two earlier optical toys, the Phenakistiscope, launched in 1833 by Joseph Plateau, and the Zoetrope, developed from the Phenakistiscope by William Horner in 1835 and often known in Britain by the less classicised name of 'wheel of life'. Both of these were effectively means of viewing a series of sequential images so that these would merge into a single, apparently moving figure. The Phenakistiscope was in the form of a flat disc, viewed through another slotted disc, while the Zoetrope was a cylinder with perforated slots, which could be viewed by more than one spectator. Reynaud retained the cylinder and introduced a mirror and a central candle, making his device a self-contained table-top means of viewing animated pictures. He would go on to create two main variations on this device: the Praxinoscope-Théâtre in 1879, with a second strip of images which provided a changeable static background to the performing figure, framed by a miniature proscenium, and then a Projecting Praxinoscope, capable of throwing its images onto a wall.[20]

In 1888, Reynaud devised the Théâtre Optique, using a belt of images passed before a lantern, and exhibited it at the following year's Exposition Universelle, where the Lumière brothers and Edison may well have seen it. The Théâtre Optique was eventually installed at Paris' famous waxworks and palace of curiosities, the Musée Grevin, in 1892, where Reynaud performed under the title 'Pantomimes Lumineuses' and steadily added new subjects over the subsequent eight years.

All of this is now relatively well known, and has become part of the familiar 'story of moving pictures', first mentioned in passing by Bardèche and Brasillach in 1935, then firmly inserted into the lineage of moving pictures in the mid 1960s.[21] The shape of Reynaud's story is also very familiar: how he battled against the success of the Lumière Cinématographe after 1896, but was eventually forced out of his Musée Grevin residency in 1900 and later destroyed much of his apparatus in despair, before dying in poverty in 1918 – a martyr to the mechanisation of spectacle that the Cinématographe inaugurated. The problem here, I suggest, is partly one of narrative. Reynaud has become more important as an emblematic figure – prefiguring the tragic story of Georges Méliès, forced into obscurity and poverty during the 'teens and

'20s – than as the creator of highly successful series of devices. In fact the Praxinoscope received awards at both the 1879 and 1889 Paris expositions and its box lid boasted of 100,000 sold, while the Théâtre Optique was seen by 500,000 spectators during its eight years at the Musée Grevin.[22]

Reynaud's Projecting Praxinoscope.

To modern eyes, the Praxinoscope seems so limited in what it offered – no more than a few seconds of moving image – that it can only be regarded as a toy, with the implication that it is therefore *only* distracting or diverting. And yet, the optical toy had inherited the tradition of the 'philosophical toy' of the 18th century, whose purpose was by no means merely to entertain children.[23] These 'toys' of the Enlightenment were in effect demonstration apparatuses, revealing the principles of 'natural magic', that is to say of anatomy and physics. Their successors were increasingly aimed at children, and marketed as 'educational' in an era when self-improvement was paramount. But it was the poet Charles Baudelaire – otherwise hardly a follower of Samuel Smiles' doctrine of useful knowledge – who observed in his 'Morale du joujou' that such devices as the Phenakistiscope would develop in the child 'a taste for marvellous and surprising effects' – as had indeed happened to him, after he received a Phenikisticope at the age of twelve.[24]

> Each little figure [on a strip of twenty] benefits from nineteen others. On a circle, she turns, and the speed makes her invisible; in the mirror, seen through the turning window,

she appears immobile, carrying out all the movements distributed across the twenty figures. The number of pictures that can be created in this way is infinite.

Like Robert Louis Stevenson's later account of the charm and suggestiveness of the toy theatre, this communicates an experience which we can no longer have.[25] And the Praxinoscope seems to have belonged to that same tradition, offering a table-top world of remediated popular entertainment – through the many printed strips available for it, of clowns, jugglers, fairy tales, children playing – in an elegant form which was also, incidentally, a demonstration of the persistence of vision. To subordinate it to the *telos* of cinema is to abstract it from a context in which it marked a real and lasting achievement, well suited to both the market and the *mentalité* of its era. The Théâtre Optique was indeed superseded by the Cinématographe and other public moving-picture shows, but the Praxinoscope was arguably followed by the 'toy projector', a domestic version of the public film show, and in fact continued to be widely sold well into the cinema era.[26]

The second device to discuss here is the Kinetoscope, patented in March 1893 by Thomas Edison, and probably much better known to almost everyone with even a passing knowledge of cinema history. For much of the 20th century, the Kinetoscope seemed to belong firmly to the category of primitive forerunners, part of the vast lumber-room of 'pre-cinema' devices that preceded the real thing. But now that the 'real thing' has itself splintered into so many different forms of delivery, from giant IMAX screens to mobile phone displays, we can perhaps look afresh at the Kinetoscope and appreciate what an important achievement it marked in its own right. For three years, between 1894 and 1896, this was widely hailed as the marvel of the age. It was not yet the forerunner of projected pictures, which only existed fitfully in the workshops and dreams of a few scattered experimenters. It *was* moving pictures, and remained the benchmark when projection first appeared. Many 'first encounter' reports of projected pictures invoked the familiar Kinetoscope experience to explain that this was the same, only now thrown on a screen, which of course linked it with the already even more familiar magic lantern experience.

Like other devices that exploited scientific principles and new technologies, it still enjoyed an ambiguous status, part 'demonstration' and part novelty, waiting to see if there was a market. Edison spoke of his doubts that it had a commercial future in some early interviews,²⁷ and the fact that he did not seek patent protection beyond the United States has often been interpreted as due to his lack of belief in the Kinetoscope's market potential. However, since he had already spent many years and expended much staff time on it, another explanation is that he would have realised some of its features would not be patentable abroad, where other moving-picture devices already used perforated translucent strips and intermittent illumination.²⁸

Kinetoscope Parlor on Broadway at 28th Street, New York City, c.1895. With fashionable women prominent among customers and bust of Edison.

Whatever the reservations about its potential or parentage, the Kinetoscope made its commercial debut in a special 'parlour', or arcade, on Broadway on 14 April 1894. With ten machines, each offering a different subject, the Holland Brothers' venture proved an immediate success, leading them to open similar parlours in Chicago and San Francisco within six weeks. Unlike much of the subsequent history of moving pictures, the economics of this first phase of exhibition are largely known. The Hollands paid $300 for each machine to the Kinetoscope Company, which in turn bought them for $200 from Edison. Against this relatively high outlay, and the high cost of viewing – 5 cents for less than 30 seconds – they apparently grossed an average of $1,400 per month for the first year, which translates into an average of 1,000 customers per day.²⁹ Other companies sprang up to open Kinetoscope shows in many cities around the world – one of which was London, where the first parlour opened on Oxford Street on 17 October. Before long, there would be at least six venues in London, including one (or two) operated by Demetrius Georgiades and George Trajidis.[30]

A typical Kinetoscope Parlour in 1895. As it was a single-viewer coin-operated device, operators needed to invest in as many as possible to maximise income.

No doubt, what drew such crowds at the beginning was literally novelty – to be able to see fragments of 'life' in action, through the addition of movement to normal 'still' photography. Edison had worked hard to establish his name as a brand, promising endless new marvels, and was already associated with the lifelike recording of sound.[31] But the choice of subjects photographed for the first Kinetoscope loops was also shrewd. Six of the ten were variety acts of the kind that might be seen on the vaudeville or music hall stage (two featuring Ena Bertholdi, a British-born contortionist; a *Highland Dance*; Sandow the strong-man posing; trapeze and wrestling acts). Two others were typical genre scenes, *Blacksmiths* and *Horse Shoeing*, that might have been the subject of photographs or prints, but were now in natural motion. *Barber Shop* was a physical comedy, a cartoon subject brought to life.

And *Cock Fight* was a sporting scene, albeit of a sport which was then banned in both the US and Britain.[32] We might say their main appeal lay in demonstrating movement – which is to insert them in the 'media succession' tradition – but they also offered a varied bill of attractions, based on the variety theatre, while gesturing in other potential directions.

Discovering who attended the Kinetoscope parlours is inevitably somewhat speculative. Anecdotes recorded in newspapers during 1894 and 1895 turned on how rapidly word of this wonder had spread and the impact it had on the unsuspecting. A Syracuse newspaper declared in December 1894 that 'everyone knows that the kinetoscope is the device by which a prize-fight, a family row, skirt dancer… can be reproduced pictorially'.[33] And a March 1895 account of the first encounter is already patronising the inexperienced:

> The expression on the customer's face undergoes a swift change… He gazes at the picture in rapt amazement, as if he expected the figures in it to speak. Before he recovers from his surprise the vivid scene is blotted out in a snap.
>
> He lifts his astonished eyes from the picture, and looking up exclaims:
> 'By gosh, I've allus heard tell that them livin' pictures was great'.[34]

Accounts would also vie to convey its life-likeness, as exemplified by the anecdote of a boxer watching the Corbett-Courtney fight on a Kinetoscope on Broadway and bragging that, on the basis of what he'd seen, he 'could punch [Corbett's] head off'.[35] However, one of the few available photographs of a parlour with people present, from San Francisco, shows two women at the back of the row of machines, where three men pose stiffly (probably the proprietors). And in a promotional illustration of the period, published in New York, a fashionable lady is placed prominently in the foreground. An advertisement from Bradford in December 1894 spoke of 'expressions of astonishment at the wonders which the instruments reveal. It is undoubtedly the duty of everyone who is interested in the progress of events of who wishes to be thoroughly 'up-to-date' to visit this scene of attraction. Not that the Kinetoscope, any more than the phonograph, is exclusively of scientific interest. It is also a means of entertainment'.[36]

All of this circumstantial evidence points to the Kinetoscope attracting, or at least intending to attract, a mixed clientele of men and women, and also suggests a transition underway from the educational dimension of new technology displays towards a more frankly entertainment goal.

Edison's original large Kinetograph camera required a stable mounting and electrical supply, with strong lighting of its subjects and a black background to provide the maximum contrast between brightly lit performers and black drapes, producing 'the singular distinctness of the 'kineto strips' described by Edison's assistant W. K. L. Dickson, which ensured these remained legible when viewed in the Kinetoscope. These factors may not have wholly determined what Dickson and his colleagues chose to film. But their choices *did* serve to attract the first audiences. And what happened next was something like a rehearsal of the course of cinema itself, all compressed into less than eighteen months. Soon after the first variety subjects came multi-part pictures, with a boxing match specially staged for the Kinetograph in June, so that it could be shown, round by round, on a row of Kinetoscopes. Next, a range of dancers offering ever more alluring images of the scantily dressed female body, and by December, the grand finale of a full-scale Broadway musical, Hoyt's *The Milk White Flag*, with 'thirty-four persons in costume'. During the next year, the repertoire would broaden even more dramatically, as independent manufacturers entered the field outside the United States and also became producers of films for their Kinetoscopes. The largest body of these are the Paul-Acres films, but others were active as well, even if their efforts are now lost.[37]

Mainstream cinema history has traditionally assigned the Kinetoscope to a minor and transient role in the develop-ment of moving pictures, but this is to fall into the trap of thinking that media evolve sequentially, with each replacing its predecessor. We should not forget that all the films first shown on screens, other than those of the Lumières, were originally made for Kinetoscope use, and that almost all of the first generation of moving picture makers and spectators began with the Kinetoscope. Less obviously, it has left its own cultural trace, in such classics as H. G. Wells' *The Time Machine* and Marcel Proust's *À la recherche du temps perdu*, and in many lesser known works.[38] Nor did it simply disappear in early 1896, when the first screen projection began in Europe. Again the traces are scant, but there is evidence that Kinetoscopes continued to be operated until the end of the decade (certainly in Australia); and its direct descendent, the robust Mutoscope, using single cards instead of a filmstrip, would continue to provide popular entertainment well beyond the middle of the 20th century.

We might say that, from a non-teleological point of view, projected moving pictures were a hybrid of two existing types of optical entertainment: the long-established magic lantern and the recent moving-picture Kinetoscope device. But the Kinetoscope was also imbricated in two other systems. It belonged to the tradition of optical toys, like the Praxinoscope, with the added attraction of using electricity for both motion and illumination. And as a coin-operated machine – at least in some markets – it belonged to a new form of retailing-cum-entertainment. The single viewer paying for a brief glimpse of 'living pictures' fitted well with a new business model, as automatic vending and gambling machines began to make their appearance on both sides of the Atlantic. Being part of this new wave of mechanisation no doubt contributed to its popularity.

The first such machine is usually credited to an English publisher and bookseller, Richard Carlisle, who began selling postcards automatically in London in the 1880s. Near the end of the decade, the Adams Gum company installed machines to sell its Tutti-Fruiti chewing gum across the New York subway system and Charles Fey in San Francisco produced the first Liberty Bell gambling machine, with a lever to spin its three drums. By 1891, Sittman and Pitt's similar machines were common in New York bars, suggesting a kind of forerunner of the Kinetoscope parlour, with its brief bursts of kinetic excitement. In Germany in 1892, Ottomar Anschütz's electric 'Schnellseher' (literally 'Rapid Viewer') showed images on a celluloid disk and was coin-operated. All of the new American devices used nickels, which presumably guided the Edison laboratory's decision that the Kinetoscope should take the same coin. And the link between early moving pictures and automated confectionary sales would continue. The British pioneer (and Paul's temporary partner) Birt Acres was hired in 1895 by the German chocolate company Ludwig Stollwerck to make films for its Kinetoscope parlours;[39] while in 1897 another American gum company would introduce animated figures as an extra attraction on its vending machines, as if acknowledging Edison's success.

But the Kinetoscope was not only part of the latest thing in vending; it was also a precursor of what would soon be known as 'automatic' or 'electric vaudeville', a condensation of the variety theatre or vaudeville experience, realised in an amusement arcade. One of the most famous of amusement arcade proprietors was Marcus Loew, the future cinema magnate – which again, of course, draws us into the fast-forward effect of teleological history. Yes, Loew saw the writing on the wall (or screen) and moved into cinema, but the amusement arcade survived, and flourished, later to become the seed-bed of video gaming. So rather than a succession model, we have here a network or rhizome model. What we don't need – as Tom Gunning said in his 1994 article – is a biological schema, and certainly not a Darwinian one of survival of the fittest.

My third and final instance of an apparently ephemeral medium or form is the Filoscope. This followed the pattern we have already seen in the Phenakisticope-to-Praxiniscope series. It was a commodified and improved version of the traditional flip or flick-book, with a batch of printed sequential photographs in a metal casing, moved by means of a lever. To the moving picture or optical toy historian, this belongs in the series of devices which includes the Lumières' Kinora and Herman Casler's Mutoscope – all using the product of the film camera as a basis for a paper-based moving picture experience, derived from the earlier drawn images of the flip-book.

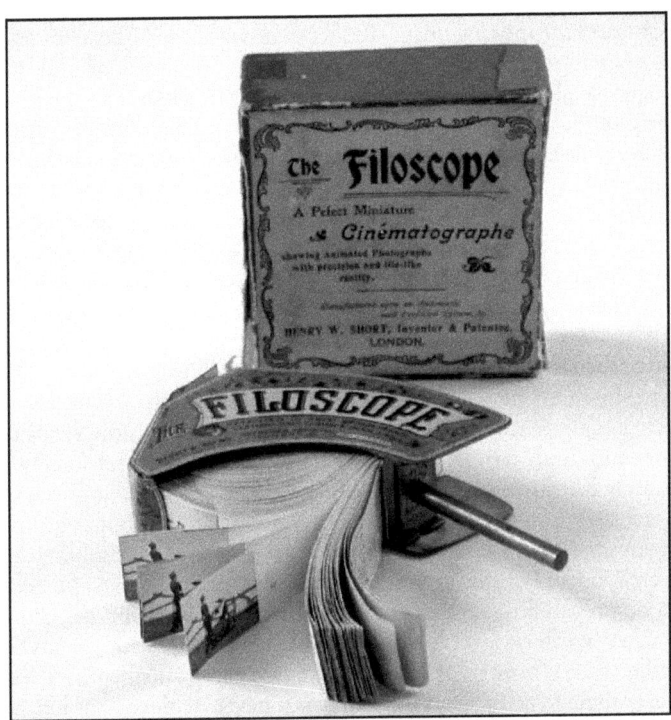

Henry Short's Filoscope.

This new improved flip-book was patented by Henry Short, who had played a momentous part in moving image history in Britain, first by introducing the Kinetoscope entrepreneurs Georgedis and Trajedis to Robert Paul in 1894, then by introducing Paul to Birt Acres, which led to the development of the first successful moving picture camera in Britain, producing films for the Kinetoscope. Short also took the first major foreign series of films for Paul, in Spain and Portugal, in 1897. These achievements have naturally rather overshadowed his invention of the Filoscope, launched in 1898, and of the three devices discussed here, this probably had the least impact, despite being marketed by the grandly named Anglo-French Filoscope Company. In fact, according to the historian of flip-books, Pascal Fouché, Short's invention was only one of a forest of similar devices launched between the 1880s and 1900s, with another British patent granted only months before his, in 1897.[40]

What Fouché's research points to, from the media historian's perspective, is a relationship between two sequential forms – the book and the moving image. Rather than see Short's Filoscope and its contemporaries as curiosities, or mere by-products of film, we ought to take a longer view and recognise that there is a very long interaction between one of the most successful and durable forms of portable entertainment – the book – and the moving image, in its various forms of support, from cardboard and celluloid to digital displays on plasma and LED screens. And thanks to modern optical-to-digital technology, we can use the surviving Filoscopes to recreate otherwise lost films originated on celluloid by Robert Paul, in an operation that has some parallels with archaeology.[41]

What then is 'the moral of these toys', to paraphrase Baudelaire? For repentant film scholars or born-again media historians, it is of course very simply that we need to get out more, to look at more kinds of apparatus and learn from those who do this more professionally – namely instrument historians. It is also that we need to be aware of other histories, not merely in an opportunistic way, but engaging seriously with the history of the book, of science and technology, of recreation and of the domestic interior. And crucially, that we need to be prepared to renounce finally the grandiose vision of André Bazin's 'myth of total cinema', recognising it as, precisely, a myth, rather than a history or a blueprint.[42] What we called cinema was never unitary, but always hybrid. It was never 'achieved', or indeed 'classical', but existed in a constant state of development and flux, and it always belonged to a long history of what Laurent Mannoni has persuasively called 'deceptive art' (in his contribution to the catalogue for *Eyes, Lies and Illusion*, the magnificent exhibition drawn from Werner Nekes' collection).

Looking at the devices lovingly collected, first by Will Day and Henri Langlois, then by John and William Barnes, Bill Douglas and Peter Jewell, we can begin to appreciate the range and complexity of the art of illusion. We might agree with Mannoni that this should be regarded as 'an autonomous current of aesthetic and technical questing', but not one divorced from wider tendencies. The Praxinoscope, the Kinetoscope and the Filoscope could be regarded as symptoms of Burch's 'collective drive', not initially 'to extend the "conquest of nature" by triumphing over death through an ersatz of Life itself',[43] but to satisfy social and economic motives. Two of these were the instrumentalisation of leisure, especially for children, and the commodification of time.

As the distinctive patterns of middle-class society emerged during the 19th century, childhood increasingly came to be seen as a period of instruction and formation for adult life. In Britain, Thomas Arnold of Rugby initiated a reform of the public school curriculum, introducing elements of science, history and modern languages into a previously classical domain.[44] Science made slow progress within the school system, but the traditional retailers of technical toys, opticians, began to add to their range of steam engines, magic lanterns and building blocks such novelties as the kaleidoscope and the zoetrope and their successors.[45] A key feature of these instructive new toys was that they would also appeal to adults, fostering a bond between parent and child. So an advertisement for the Praxinoscope states that 'this instrument provides an interesting recreation for adults which is also attractive to children', while the most famous illustration of the Praxinoscope-Théâtre in use shows an older male and a young girl, both fascinated by its display.[46] Time, as Alice is rudely reminded in Lewis Carroll's *Through the Looking Glass*, 'is worth a thousand pounds a minute'.[47]

Back to 'Modernity'
Finally, does this have any bearing on 'modernity' and Bordwell's critique of the 'history of vision' and other culturalists' theses? Certainly he was right to question the idea of a single experience of modernity, which a crude invocation of the 'cinema of attractions' might imply. What the actual spectatorial experience of c.1897-1917 offered was an irregular series of shifts and conflicts within the field of projected collective entertainment, and it was this very heterogeneity that constitutes a part of the experience of 'modernity' reflected in the rise of cinema, as Virginia Woolf

recorded in her retrospect on the experience of early cinema.[48] Cinema, as it emerged, could embrace an extremely diverse range of kinds of entertainment, from short slapstick comedies, through actualities about the 'wonders of the world' (a genre that has been consistently ignored, yet remained present in cinema programming until, probably the 1960s) to emerging forms of immersive drama. Sometimes these emerging forms of long drama included 'internal' diversity, as in D. W. Griffith's *Intolerance*, Thomas Ince's *Civilisation* and Cecil B. DeMille's flashback and parallel stories (such as the 1923 *Ten Commandments*).

But their spectators were, in any case, living in a world that included much more than cinema, where the cinema experience was embedded in a whole culture of optical and visual forms: stereoscopes, comics, fan magazines, picture postcards, cigarette cards, a mass of 'ephemera' that continued unabated. Some of these had preceded cinema, but came to refract it; others, like the Filoscope and Mutoscope, stemmed from it, and continued in parallel. These testify to a persistence of novelty, of a taste for visual distraction which 'normalised' cinema, however successful in other respects, did not satisfy. The dominant history of cinema that is still widely reproduced not only ignored the variety of spectatorship and exhibition, but has concentrated almost exclusively on the normalised film experience, dismissing such 'distractions' as colour inserts, 3-D glasses, trailers, posters, etc.[49]

Bordwell was surely right to say that culturalist/modernity arguments do not challenge, or explain, the *stylistic* history of what became cinema, which is largely a history of filmmakers 'replicating, amplifying, or synthesising schemas' that enable them to pursue their commercial and artistic goals.[50] But many would argue that the modernity hypothesis operates at a different level – initially referring to the turn of the century bricolage that includes early screened moving pictures, and later to the avant-garde assault on precisely those synthesised schemas that had become narrative cinema – Fernand Léger's celebrated 'revenge of the poets and painters' on conventional cinema.[51]

But another reason for the apparent impasse between Bordwell and the advocates of history of vision/modernity surely stems from confining attention to the normalised mainstream of cinema, which did indeed allow a critical mass of filmmakers and film viewers to pursue apparently convergent goals. A history of cinema focused on the evolution of narrative form and style works to minimise, if not completely erase, 'extraneous' aspects of cinemagoing and moving-image consumption. Yet we know that such factors were an intrinsic part of 'cinema', almost certainly looming larger than the experience of the film itself, which is arguably a retrospective construct made possible by the non-theatrical technologies of 16mm, video and digital that have been central to academic film study. Equally, it is now apparent that the received history of cinema largely ignored the procession of novelties that characterised cinema, such as the addition of live and recorded sound, colour, widescreen and super-size formats, and 3-D, which continue to this day. And, of course, the theatrical model also suppressed recognition of the continuity of domestic and portable forms (miniature formats, television, recorders, handheld devices).

Yuri Tsivian has argued persuasively against attempts to unify the histories of cinema and film around single organising concepts or substances, proposing instead that these are, respectively, a 'multiple, nonunifiable' object and process.[52] The 'nonunifiable process' must surely be expanded and revised to include the many moving image cognates, of which I have considered just three, and also to counteract that 'enormous condescension' which cinema effectively directed towards ephemeral and minor media. In an age of rapidly proliferating media, many of which may prove much more ephemeral than the flip-book, it is surely time to democratise our media history.

First appeared in a special issue of *Comparative Critical Studies* 6.3, October 2009; then as a chapter in the collection edited by Jeffrey Gaiger and Karin Littau, *Cinematicity in Media History* (Edinburgh University Press, 2013).

3.
Not Only 'King of the Vast': John Martin and 19th-Century Visual Spectacle

The early 19th century saw a fashion for enormous paintings, and artists including John Martin, Benjamin Haydon and Francis Danby showed their huge pictures to a largely adoring public. These painters lived in a newly competitive age of showmanship and spectacle, apparently boosted or at least accompanied by the panoramas that flourished in the late Georgian and Regency period. But Martin's *Joshua Commanding the Sun to Stand Still upon Gibeon* (1816) at 2.34 metres wide, or Benjamin Haydon's *Christ's Triumphal Entry into Jerusalem* (1820) at 4.5 metres, both long regarded with embarrassment or outright scorn by art historians, have recently seemed more deserving of attention. This is not to say that all such monsters would benefit from the turnabout in taste (to borrow William Vaughan's useful phrase) that rescued late Turner from critical oblivion in the early 20th century.[1] No doubt there was considerable bemusement among visitors to Tate Britain's 2011 exhibition *John Martin: Apocalypse*, a rare opportunity to see one of the leading 'Kings of the Vast'. But equally many would have encountered this forgotten phase of British art for the first time – or rather, would be seeing it in its original spectacular form, rather than reproduced as 'illustration' in religious or fantasy contexts.

Could this new-found ability to contemplate such acres of canvas with more equanimity have something to do with our expanded sense of image scale – from IMAX cinemas and giant public LED displays? Like Martin and his early 19th-century contemporaries, we are living in a new age of spectacle, and of course there are as many sceptical voices as there were in Martin's own lifetime. That contemptuous phrase 'King of the Vast' appeared in *Blackwood's Magazine* while Martin was at the height of his fame, and his near-contemporaries Haydon and Francis Danby were engaged in what seemed to some a contest in sheer scale.[2] Martin had launched his career in London in 1812 with a commanding upright picture, *Sadak in Search of the Waters of Oblivion*, measuring 1.83 by 1.31 metres, and just seven years later, Constable decided to work on a similar scale, with the first of his 'six-footers', *The White Horse* in 1819, followed by the now celebrated River Stour series. Throughout this period, Haydon laboured on his *Christ's Entry*, finally displaying it at the Egyptian Hall in Piccadilly in 1820, where it hung in the Great Room for seven months, bringing the penniless Haydon final receipts of over £1,500, meaning that some 40,000 had had paid to see this huge canvas.[3] Among the celebrity visitors recorded were Sir Walter Scott, already famous for his novel *Waverley*, who sat on the hall's steps before it opened, and the famous actress Mrs Siddons who, when asked if she 'liked the Christ', was reported to have replied 'in a deep, loud, tragic tone, "It is completely successful"'.

Did the fact that Haydon's long-gestating work was not shown in a 'proper' exhibition hall but among the freak shows and novelties of what would later be known as 'England's home of mystery' diminish its cultural status? On the contrary, Haydon's success and the even greater success of Géricault's *Raft of the Medusa*, shown simultaneously at the Hall in 1820, helped confirm it as very much the 'chief London hall for the temporary display of pictures' over the next forty years, according to Richard Altick in his magisterial *The Shows of London*.[4] At this time, London had many exhibition rooms, while the establishment of a National Gallery still lay in the future, as did the Royal Academy's takeover of Burlington House, to create the hierarchy that would become familiar during the following century.

John Martin, *Belshazzar's Feast* (1820).

In fact, while Haydon experienced both his climactic success and his final humiliation at the Egyptian Hall, John Martin exhibited there rarely. His *Destruction of Pompeii and Herculaneum* was shown in 1822, as part of a kind of retrospective, which however did not include his major early success, *Belshazzar's Feast*.[5] This had been exhibited at the British Institution in Pall Mall in 1821, a more exclusive venue, where it proved so popular that it had to be roped off to keep back the numbers of spectators, and the show extended for an extra three weeks.[6] But what happened next is instructive, if we want to understand more precisely the interplay between 'old' and new media in the early 19th century. *Belshazzar's Feast* transferred to the Strand premises of Martin's former employer, the glass and ceramics merchant William Collins, who had bought it for 800 guineas. Five thousand more people paid to see it there, along with a copy of the picture painted on glass by Martin and set into the wall of the shop, so that, according to a witness, 'the light was really transmitted through the terrible handwriting'.[7] What *Belshazzar's Feast* depicted was the Biblical scene in which the Babylonian king's feast is disrupted by a divine hand prophesying his doom in an inscription which is interpreted by the prophet Daniel.[8] The scene is probably more familiar from the 'close-up' painted by Rembrandt in the 1630s, now in the National Gallery, and from this we can perhaps form a better idea of what Martin's glass picture may have been like, presumably either backlit by daylight or lamplight.

Altick suggests that 'never had the fine arts and the diorama drawn closer together', apparently forgetting that Daguerre's Diorama would not reach London until two years later. However, when it did arrive and proved wildly popular in a number of locations, Martin would find himself the victim of unauthorised and, he claimed, inept copying. In 1832, Thomas Hamlet's British Diorama at the Royal Bazaar on Oxford Street departed from its normal menu of romantic views and ruins to show a 190-m² version of *Belshazzar's Feast*, advertised as 'occupying in magnitude the space of Four Dioramic Views'.[9] Martin tried, unsuccessfully, to shut down this display with a court order, complaining that 'it was a most infamous piece of painting... ruining my reputation, and at the same time taking from me what ought to be my copyright.[10] Altick lists three other instances of Martin paintings being reproduced on glass, apparently all with his consent if not involvement, which was an early indication that he was actively involved with this lesser-known branch of Victorian 'new media'.

More recently, Sally Rush has reopened the subject of Martin's relation to glass painting, in a polemical article that takes issue with earlier accounts, including its treatment in the major 2011 Tate exhibition.[11] Her main contention is that 'Georgian glass painting is a fundamentally different thing to a Victorian stained-glass window and was concerned more with expanding the aesthetic limitations of easel painting than with the revival of medieval tradition'. Accordingly, she attacks the claim made by the Tate curators, Martin Myrone and Anna Austen, that the glass version of *Belshazzar's Feast* belongs to the 'visual techniques of popular entertainment', tracing this to his working-class background and early apprenticeship to Collins, as well as to 'interdisciplinary writing on "pre-cinema"', which she clearly considers ill-informed, at least on the issue of Georgian glass painting and its 'aesthetic significance'.[12]

Rush maintains, convincingly I think, that amid the confusion over what was exhibited by Collins in 1821 and the surviving glass version of *Belshazzar's Feast*, executed by George Hoadley and Anthony Oldfield in 1828, apparently with Martin's full approval, what has been lost is appreciation of 'the contemporary interface of science and art where optically assisted viewing and the harnessing of real light formed part of serious aesthetic experiment'.[13] Crucial for her argument is the set-up in which the glass paintings were viewed, which appears to have involved a magnifying glass: 'at least when exhibited to the public before sale, these versions were set within a box behind a partition wall, backlit, and viewed through an aperture fitted with a magnifying lens. So, beyond issues of scale, the viewing of the glass paintings and the original oil paintings were fundamentally different experiences'. She cites Jonathan Crary's influential *Techniques of the Observer* and his claim that 'the reorganisation of the observer' required 'modulation between eye and optical apparatus',[14] to justify claiming that 'in the case of the glass paintings after Martin, viewer immersion allowed the imagination to lose itself in magnified vastness and obscurity'. Hoadley and Oldfield were also responsible in 1837 for other glass versions of Martin subjects, *Joshua Commanding the Sun to Stand Still* and *The Fall of Nineveh*, along with a version of Francis Danby's *Opening of the Sixth Seal*, all clearly with the artists' support and seen in a setting 'far removed from crowded exhibition rooms'.

This is not the occasion to follow Rush's detailed analysis of the fundamental difference between the work of Martin's and other 'panoramic' contemporaries viewed at exhibition scale and through lenses in 'cabinet conditions'. Suffice to say that she makes a strong case for Martin and others being well aware of this difference, and valuing the latter more highly in aesthetic terms – with the large canvases perhaps serving to advertise their subjects, before their appearance in other media, including of course prints. But it may be worth noting also that the panorama tradition, as initiated by Thomas Barker and family and his successor at the Leicester Square rotunda, Robert Burford, was by no means wholly despised by cognoscenti. The *Athenaeum* magazine might mock, commenting in December 1849: 'There is a perfect battle of *B*'s with new panoramas to catch the holiday people of London and the country visitors of this festive period of the year. We have Burford, Banvard, Brees and Bonomi, all catering successfully for the amusement and instruction of the public'.[15]

Yet one of the most stringent arbiters of taste, John Ruskin, drew a distinction between the 'stupid and vulgar panorama painters' and 'the real old Burford's work [that] was worth a million of them'. Barker, himself a painter, had insisted that the panorama represented 'AN IMPROVEMENT ON PAINTING, which relieves that sublime Art from a Restraint it has ever laboured under'. Much more than simply working on a larger scale, it was conceived as a carefully controlled experience, with light entering the rotunda from above and a viewing platform placing spectators at mid-height 'in' the picture, at a predetermined distance.

Likewise, as Rush notes, contemporaries were well aware of the difference between the original Diorama of Daguerre, with its meticulous painted scenes, and the many inferior imitations which followed. Both 'panoramic' and dioramic' would indeed become derogatory as well as descriptive terms, but the initial success of both forms of exhibition was born of considerable artistic ambition, and recognised as a fundamental restructuring of the visual and experiential field.

Martin and the 'Mighty Milton'

Martin would return to epic-scale painting for his last works, the 'Judgement' trilogy, *The Plains of Heaven*, *The Great Day of His Wrath*, and *The Last Judgement*. But before this, in the mid-1820s, he began work in another medium and on a very different scale that would perhaps ultimately reach a much larger public. In 1824, he was commissioned by an American publisher, Septimus Prowett, to produce a set of mezzotint illustrations for Milton's *Paradise Lost*. Mezzotint collecting was becoming popular, especially in Britain, and the plan was to produce 48 prints in total,

24 in octavo size and 24 for a larger *de luxe* portfolio. Subscribers would receive prints regularly until 1827. The idea of illustrating Milton's *Paradise Lost* was hardly novel – Blake had made a series of watercolours in 1807 and Gustave Doré would produce a set of engravings in 1866. But Martin's approach was unusual, in that he undertook the work on the plates himself, apparently working without prior sketches. He was also one of the first to use steel rather than copper plates, which would enable more impressions to be made. No doubt this drew on his early craft experience in china and glass painting, and it produced impressive results. When he exhibited a selection at the Royal Society of British Artists in 1825, the response was enthusiastic: 'we know of no artist whose genius so perfectly fitted him to be the illustrator of the mighty Milton… and he has more than realised the highest of our hopes. There is a wildness, a grandeur and a mystery about his designs which are indescribably fine'.

What is striking about these illustrations is Martin's ability to simplify dramatically, doing almost the opposite to his panoramic paintings, with their massive detail and legions of figures. The *Paradise Lost* images are mostly of single figures or pairs, starkly deployed in fantastic chiaroscuro settings. Here his vision thrived, with greater intensity than in the large paintings and with a rare delicacy. When a selection of the mezzotints was shown as part of the 2011 Tate exhibition, Laura Cumming was duly impressed, although not immune to hinting at modern parallels:

> These little prints are more amazing than the grand machines – Satan holding court in what looks like a solo performance in the Albert Hall (decades in advance); imaginary cities stretching away into the misty air that look remarkably like mezzotints, or even sepia photographs, but turn out to be tiny watercolours.
>
> You see Martin dreaming up, on a delicate scale, all sorts of things he had never seen: Asian peaks, Egyptians, ziggurats, the stones of Avebury when it was first built, exotic trees, volcanic eruptions, even dinosaurs (is he the first dinosaur artist?) – and in each case the quick intimacy matches the potent vision.[16]

Once again, as with Rush's strictures on recent writers about the glass paintings, we might see a straining to justify Martin as anticipating more modern graphic forms, such as comic-book or science-fiction art, once again removing him from the category of fine art.

John Martin, Satan Presiding at the Infernal Council. *Paradise Lost* (1824).

The other danger in 'reading him forward' is to remove him from his immediate context: the era of revolution and of Romanticism. A modern gallery selling the *Paradise Lost* mezzotints usefully emphasises how these

> depict a war between light and darkness, and leave us always with the memory of the light shining in the darkness that cannot extinguish it. Martin's mezzotints on *Paradise Lost* and on *The Last Judgment* are justifiably famous as monuments to the visionary strain of Romantic art, conveying an impression not unlike that described in Mary Shelley's *Frankenstein* – written just a few years before Martin's mezzotints were made – in which Victor Frankenstein takes comfort in the landscape of the Alps the moment before his creature comes bounding to confront him: 'The immense mountains and precipices that overhang me on every side, the sound of the river raging among the rocks, and the dashing of waterfalls around spoke of a power mighty as Omnipotence – and I ceased to fear or to bend before any being less almighty than that which had created and ruled the elements, here displayed in their most terrific guise'.[17]

In his 2009 book *The Prometheans*, which predated the Tate exhibition, Max Adam comprehensively allied Martin with a generation of revolutionaries in different spheres: cultural, technical and political. Not only the Shelley of *Ozymandius* (1818) and *Prometheus Unbound* (1821) but the post-apocalyptic novel by the poet's widow, Mary Shelley, *The Last Man* (1826), although Martin's 1833 print and 1849 painting refer to Thomas Campbell's 1823 poem of the same name – 'last men' were a popular theme from the 1820s up to H. G. Wells' dramatic updating of the theme in his *The Time Machine* of 1895.

D. W. Griffith, *Intolerance* (1916).
Babylon sets were influenced by Martin's *Belshazzar's Feast*.

Emphasising the aesthetic quality of Martin's mezzotints, and indeed his many other prints, as well as elucidating his relationship with glass painting helps to identify him as a true early Victorian multimedia artist. But recognising the reproducibility of his fantastic worlds, and how these have influenced later artists striving for an 'apocalyptic sublime' in modern media, should not, as it seemingly has so often, lead to a downgrading of his work. And here the reflex references to spectacular cinema have undoubtedly worked against Martin's reputation. To link him with D. W. Griffith and Cecil B. DeMille, some of whose work undoubtedly drew on his images – as well as those of many other 19th-century painters, notably Alma-Tadema, Gérôme and Tissot – should not count against any of these artists. And yet it seems that it has, no doubt due of a lack of first-hand acquaintance with many of the relevant films but also an ambient condescension towards cinema and its scenography.

Nothing that I can write or present is likely to change these dismal obstacles on the road towards a wider understanding of how the 'minor' or 'subaltern' arts have played a major part in creating the visual and material world we inhabit today. Cinema continues to play a large part in this, as its entire history becomes accessible online. Might one of William Vaughan's 'turnabouts in taste' reverse the direction of judgement, so that instead of seeing the great peplum spectacles of Italian and American cinema as debased echoes of 19th-century art, we take pleasure in detecting the sources?[18] I'm not holding my breath.

This essay first appeared in very different form in *Tate Magazine*, September 2011, accompanying the *John Martin: Apocalypse* exhibition. It has been substantially revised to make a broader and more up to date argument about Martin's reputation, not only in relation to the popular 'new media' of the panorama and the Diorama, but also taking account of his work in glass painting and mezzotint, as well as the recurrent issue of his influence on 'blockbuster' cinema.

4.
Screening the City: The Long History of London Screen Entertainment

What does or could 'screen history' cover?[1] It must certainly be expanded beyond the era of cinema *per se*, since the work of several generations of historians of pre- and early cinema has demonstrated clearly that almost all the elements of a 'cinematic experience' were in place before the actual mechanisms of moving pictures appeared at the 'eleventh hour' of the 1890s.[2] It could more properly be considered a branch of entertainment history, with a particular emphasis on exploiting the illusory potential of the two-dimensional image. Such a definition would encourage thinking about the variables of such presentations – issues of location, competition, pricing – and the fact that although each strand has its own diachronic history, these were, and are, experienced synchronously by audiences. Screen history cannot therefore be confined to the cataloguing of various devices and 'shows', but should attempt to engage with the dynamic processes of production and consumption within the city.[3]

The projecting lantern in its earliest, essentially domestic form, must be considered the starting point of a tradition of screened entertainment in the 17th century. Samuel Pepys wrote in his diary in August 1666: 'comes by agreement Mr. Reeves... he bringing me a frame he closes on, to see how the rays of light do cut one another... He did also bring a lanthorne with pictures in glasse, to make strange things appear on a wall, very pretty [...] and do like my glasse very well, and did even with him for it and a little perspective and the Lanthorne that shows tricks, altogether costing me £9 5s.0d'.[4]

The collection of optical devices that Pepys bought from Robert Reeves included a telescope and a prism, as well as the 'lanthorne' that showed 'pretty pictures' and 'tricks'. These instruments would have been fashionable in the circles that Pepys frequented, shortly after a group of natural philosophers had founded the Royal Society of London for Improving Natural Knowledge.[5] Indeed, we can trace a continuous tradition of use of the projecting lantern in scientific demonstration from the 17th century, after Christiaan Huygens and Athanasius Kircher first published accounts of its principles, up to the present, when digital projection continues to fulfil essentially the same purpose.[6]

Various forms of lantern have also been more or less continuously used for domestic entertainment from Pepys' time until recently, although largely supplanted by electronic displays. But my concern here is with forms of display intended for the public: a tradition of 'screen entertainment' that depends on some degree of spectacle, on showmanship and on a potential paying audience.

Just over a century after Pepys' account, we find a remarkable succession of commercial displays that can be considered the foundation of London's public screen entertainment between the 1780s and the 1820s. Chronologically, the first of these was Philippe de Loutherbourg's Eidophusikon, presented at various venues between 1781 and 1786. De Loutherbourg had trained as a painter in his native France before coming to England in 1771 and starting to work for the actor-manager David Garrick at the Drury Lane theatre. Here he soon developed a reputation for remarkable lighting and scenic effects, which eventually led to the model theatre that he named Eidophusikon.[7] In its first commercial presentation, in Lisle Street, this miniature theatre enabled an audience of up to 130, seated on benches in a darkened room, to view through a proscenium aperture about two metres by three, painted tableaux animated by shining light through taffeta, apparently including movable miniature models and accompanied by sound effects and music. Among the popular subjects were the recent wrecking of a merchant ship, the *Halsewell*, and the Pandemonium scene from Milton's *Paradise Lost*.[8]

De Loutherbourg described his entertainment as 'movable paintings' and press advertisements referred, for the first time, to 'moving pictures'. Clearly the Eidophusikon represented an attempt to develop the painterly mise-en-scène that De Loutherbourg had pioneered on stage (itself carrying forward the work of Inigo Jones for the Jacobean masque), miniaturising and mechanising such effects. In this, he might be seen as linking the slightly earlier passion for mechanical simulation through automata[9] with the emerging aesthetic of Romanticism, to which he also contributed with his spectacular landscape paintings, such as *Coalbrookdale by Night* (1801).[10]

A decade after De Loutherbourg's first presentations, another painter, the Irish-born Robert Barker, opened his Panorama in

Leicester Square in 1793. This contained large paintings, up to 1,100 sq. metres, displayed within a cylindrical rotunda structure, with light entering from above.[11] Spectators were accommodated centrally on a viewing platform, and because of its size, the effect became 'immersive'. Including three-dimensional elements in the foreground was later found to help create the illusion of a panoramic reality, and the viewer's ability to move around the platforms and walkways, sometimes with a guide, and even the provision of telescopes, also contributed to the sense of 'visiting' the scene portrayed.[12] Barker's Panorama building with its entrance in Cranbourne Street, on the north corner of Leicester Square, could accommodate both a large and a smaller painting simultaneously, and his early subjects included a View of the Grand Fleet and a View of London and Westminster. Naval and military scenes would remain popular throughout the life of the original Panorama, which remained in business under various proprietors until 1863. But despite Barker's patent, imitations had appeared as early as 1796, with the Great Room in Spring Gardens and the Lyceum in the Strand popular London panorama venues. The idea quickly spread and during the following decades panoramas were constructed in most European cities and toured to many provincial towns.

Viewing the Eidophusikon. Watercolour by Francis Burney, 1782.

The Eidophusikon and panoramas had created a taste for dramatic visual spectacle, which must have paved the way for Paul de Philipsthal, also known as Philidor, to bring his Phantasmagoria to London in 1801 for a two-year run. Essentially an elaborate magic lantern show based on Gothic themes and using a movable lantern hidden behind the screen, this was first presented in Paris in 1792 by Philipsthal, and further developed by his rival Etienne-Gaspard Robert (also known as Robertson) before Philipsthal revived it in London. The lanternist and historian Mervyn Heard described its effects as including 'ancillary auditorium-based projections, thunder and lightning effects, ventriloquism, spine-tingling glass harmonica music, electric shocks, shadow-show effects, life-size masked figures, incense, smoke and... sensory deprivation'.[13]

Philipsthal would later also show musical automata at the Lyceum Theatre, where he was joined in 1802 by Marie Tussaud, who had brought her collection of wax figures from Revolutionary France. Tussaud's wax museum would tour Britain and Ireland for the next thirty years, before establishing a permanent exhibition on Baker Street in London in 1835, which would prove to have a longer life than the Phantasmagoria and become a permanent feature of London entertainment.

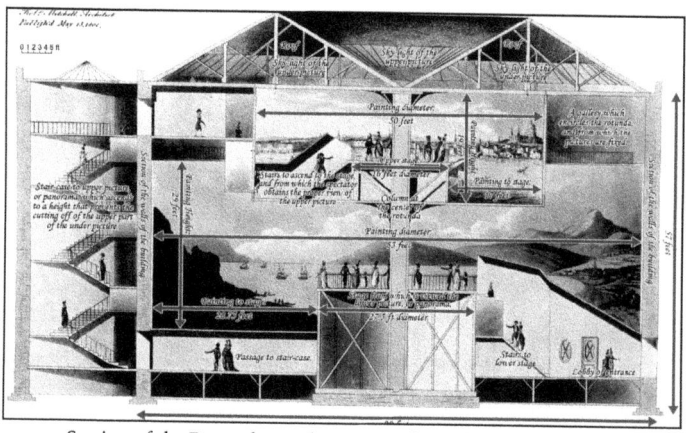

Section of the Rotunda, on the corner of Cranbourne Street and Leicester Square, where Robert Barker opened his Panorana in 1793 with great success.

Throughout the 19th and 20th centuries, Leicester Square and the surrounding areas of Haymarket, Strand and Soho would remain central to large-scale and innovative screen entertainment. In 1851, the many established and ephemeral entertainments of Leicester Square were joined by Jonathan Wyld's Great Globe, sixty feet in diametre and built in the centre of the square. Wyld had initially proposed his structure to the organisers of the Great Exhibition, but when it was rejected, he went ahead with it as a free-standing spectacle, no doubt benefiting from the influx of tourism that the Exhibition itself attracted to London. A geographer and publisher of atlases, Wyld had the educational aim of offering a 'tour' of the physical world as visitors ascended its staircases, viewing the earth's spherical surface 'reversed' in concave. No doubt partly inspired by the success of the nearby Panorama (which had a rival on the Strand from 1802),[14] it may also have owed something to the growing popularity of moving panoramas which simulated journeys of exploration, and of ballooning, with its novel aerial perspective. A contemporary account of visiting Wyld's Globe reflected on the experience: 'All the World is before you; you have only to choose where to go to. With a patriotic rush your eyes run to England, and you are wonder-struck that a country which occupies so large a space in the thoughts of the world, should take up so little room on the surface of it. England, that has filled so many leaves in the world's history, is scarcely the size of a cabbage leaf; and London, which prides itself upon being the centre of civilisation, is not half so big as TOM THUMB'S nose'.[15]

Barker's Panorama, as well as its imitators after the original patent expired in 1802, would remain a cornerstone of London's spectacular entertainment until 1863, when the Leicester Square display closed.[16] But from the mid-1820s it faced competition from a newer attraction.

The Diorama was devised by Louis Daguerre, better known in media history as the official co-inventor of photography and of the Daguerrotype. Daguerre had previously worked on panoramas and was an accomplished painter of atmospheric landscapes and evocative buildings. His new entertainment, launched in Paris in 1822, provided the spectator with changing views of such scenes, achieved by painting on semi-translucent linen sheets, with the play of light on these carefully controlled by a number of coloured and opaque shutters.[17] In the elegant London building that Daguerre and his partner Charles-Marie Bouton opened in Regent's Park in 1823, 200 spectators could witness a gradual progression of lighting effects, from sunlight to cloud and twilight, on Trinity Chapel in Canterbury Cathedral, Holyrood Palace and the Rosslyn Chapel in Scotland, or even the emergence of Ruins in a Fog. By being able to rotate the entire viewing area, the audience could be transported magically from one such scene to another.

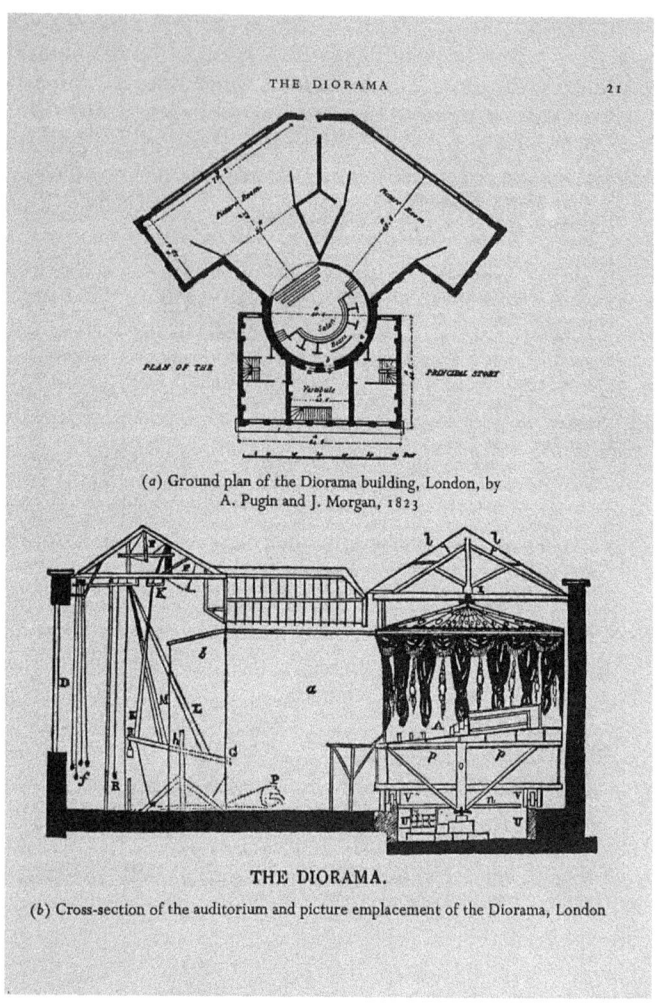

Plan of the London Diorama Building, Regent's Park, 1823.
Almanach des Spectacles.

The effects of the Diorama were considered highly artistic and answered to a growing taste for such scenes, encouraged by Romantic poetry and novels (Balzac was an early enthusiast in Paris, in an 1822 letter to his sister describing the Diorama as 'the marvel of the century'). Its technology also proved popular: London's first omnibus service, linking Paddington Railway Station with the City, ran through Regent's Park and its cars carried an advertisement for the Diorama, reinforcing the link between new forms of transport, especially the railway, and an appetite for landscape viewed in novel ways. Daguerre and Bouton's Diorama was quickly imitated by other operators, notably Thomas Hamlet, with his British Diorama, sited in the Royal Bazaar, which opened in 1828 on Oxford Street on the site of the former Pantheon assembly rooms.[18] The terms 'panoramic' and 'dioramic' began to be applied to large paintings, such as John Martin's apocalyptic scenes, not always to their advantage.[19] Meanwhile, Regent's Park consolidated its newfound association with visual spectacle when a majestic new panorama, the Colosseum, opened close to the Diorama in 1829. The Colosseum's main attraction was 'London from the Summit of St Paul's', a painting of some 3,660 sq. metres based on drawings that had been executed in a special cabin built precariously on top of the cathedral. But its appeal was boosted by a number of other features, including London's first hydraulic lift, to carry visitors up to the viewing platform, and a series of conservatories and smaller *trompe l'oeil* settings, such as a Swiss Cottage with simulated mountain views. Like the Royal and Queen's bazaars, with their shops and sideshows, the Colosseum was bidding to become a new kind of social space – and significantly, both would serve as backdrops for fashion plate advertisements.[20]

Alongside the new structures built specifically to house large-scale visual displays, 19th-century London saw a number of more traditional venues adapt to displaying screen entertainments. The facade of the Egyptian Hall in Piccadilly, commissioned in 1812 to house William Bullock's collection of stuffed animals and exotic curiosities, was influenced by the discovery of Egyptian antiquity that had been prompted by Napoleon's 1798 expedition. Ironically, one of Bullock's most successful presentations was of Napoleon's coach in 1816, bought after Waterloo. In the 1820s, it was rented for many temporary shows, especially of large paintings that benefited from the 'panoramic' vogue, such as Benjamin Hayden's *Christ's Entry into Jerusalem* (1820) and later in the same year, Géricault's *Raft of the Medusa*. In the 1850s, the Hall was particularly associated with the popular lecturer Albert Smith, whose account of climbing Mont Blanc, 'accompanying the exhibition of cleverly painted moving dioramic pictures and sublimities', would continue for six years.[21] Later it would be most famous for Maskelyne and Cooke's magic theatre presentations, under the by-line 'England's home of mystery', avidly attended by Georges Méliès when he lived in London during 1884-5.

Another distinctive London venue that established a reputation for its projected entertainment was the Royal Polytechnic Institution

Interior of the Pantheon, Oxford Street, London.
Prob. William Hodges, before 1790.

in Upper Regent Street. Originally launched in 1838, this offered a typical Victorian mixture of spectacle and educational display, but its 'dissolving views', projected by up to six powerful lanterns on a screen eight metres wide in the Great Hall and using special large-format slides, were considered outstanding. Accompanied by music, sound effects and narration, they became a major attraction, helping to keep the Polytechnic afloat until 1878.[22] Its success owed much to 'Professor' John Pepper, originally a chemist, who served as director from 1852-72, successfully combined scientific demonstration with the popular illusion known as 'Pepper's Ghost,' which created a spectral figure on stage, by means of an angled mirror. But while the Polytechnic offered what was perhaps the ultimate refinement of the lantern show, the last street performers of 'Chinese Shades' were also active around Leicester Square and Regent Street, as recorded by Henry Mayhew.[23] Using candles and a portable booth that also served for Punch and Judy shows by day, they would present popular tales such as 'Cobbler Jobson' and 'Billy Button's Ride to Brentford' to passers-by.

Projection was also the initial attraction of the Royal Panopticon, lavishly built in a Moorish style on the east side of Leicester Square in 1854. When the popular science programme proved uncommercial, the venue became the Alhambra Circus, trading on its imitation of the Moorish palace in Granada, and eventually a music hall in 1864. By this time, the music hall had become London's fastest growing form of entertainment, helped by a strict legal prohibition on conventional drama that allowed only three 'patent theatres' to operate in London until the mid-19th century. The mixture of often bawdy songs, dancing and variety acts that characterised the music hall proved immensely profitable. Starting with the Canterbury in Lambeth and the Middlesex in Drury Lane, ornate venues opened throughout the East and West End, eventually fanning out into the new residential areas. By the late 1880s, the largest of these variety theatres, especially the Alhambra and Empire in Leicester Square, and the Tivoli in the Strand, offered a range of spectacular entertainment which would start to incorporate 'animated photographs' in 1896.[24]

After near-simultaneous demonstrations in February 1896 of the Lumière Cinématographe at the Polytechnic and Robert Paul's Theatrograph at the Finsbury Technical College, the Empire and Alhambra respectively took these novelties into their programmes, where both continued for several years. Other music halls quickly followed suit, with a range of moving-picture presentations under various exotic titles. Many of these theatres would eventually become full-time cinemas, or would be demolished to make way for purpose-designed cinemas, such as the modernist Odeon Leicester Square, which replaced the Alhambra in 1937. Earlier, in 1909, the ornate Palace Theatre of Varieties on Shaftesbury Avenue launched Charles Urban and G. A. Smith's Kinemacolor process, and this continued until 1913 at the nearby Scala Theatre.

Many Londoners would first experience moving pictures, not in such historic or prestigious venues, but in mission and church halls, which were quick to see the potential of attracting young viewers, as they had previously with magic lantern shows; or in fairgrounds, where showmen were also traditionally alert to novelty. Full-time cinemas, which were likely to be known as 'bioscopes' or 'electric theatres', began to open around London in 1906, in locations near their likely audience of 'city clerks seeking cheap, quick entertainment', such as Bishopsgate, Brixton and Aldgate.[25] Jon Burrows revealed the existence of at least 160 'nickelodeon-style shows, mostly housed in converted shops' in London between 1906 and 1911,[26] while Luke McKernan has recorded the many unlicensed premises of 1907 giving way to a growing number of purpose-built cinemas after the passing of the 1909 Cinematograph Act. Entrepreneursm like Montague Pyke launched chains of cinemas around the city with seating capacity that soon rose from around 500 to as many as 2,000, in the case of the Grange Cinema, Kilburn, in 1914.[27]

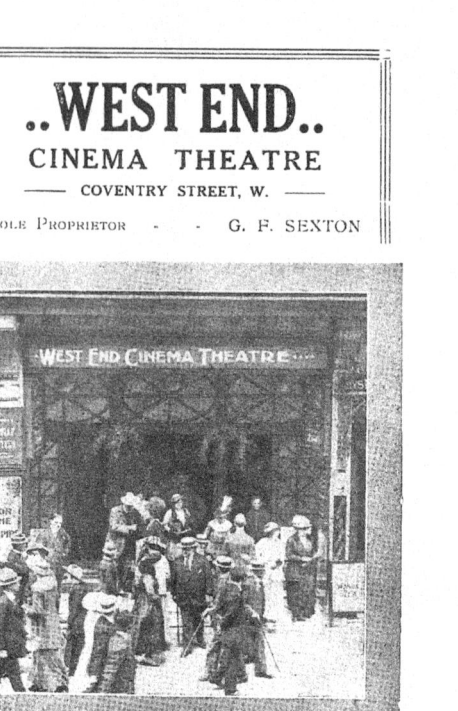

A poster for the West End Cinema Theatre, which opened in 1913 on Coventry Street. Architecturally ambitious and expensively decorated, it had one of the first neon signs in Britain..

By 1927, when Warner Bros.' venture into synchronised sound with *The Jazz Singer* launched the 'Talkies', London was exceptionally well provided with a range of different sizes and types of cinema, ranging from the 'supers', which showed new films first and exclusively, down to neighbourhood 'fleapits' that showed them later and more cheaply. Different strategies had been adopted to overcome the perceived vulgarity of cinema attendance. In 1913, the West End Cinema Theatre opened on Coventry Street, mid-way between Piccadilly Circus and Leicester Square, as the most architecturally ambitious purpose-built cinema, seating 700 spectators under a central dome.[28] Programming to match this ambition was supplied by *The Last Days of Pompeii* (1913), the most recent Italian iteration of this popular novel.[29] To boost the perceived status, the most expensive seats were an unheard-of 10s 6s or a half-guinea, with publicity stressing the quality of orchestral accompaniment and the film's educational value, and the basement housed a sophisticated Café Elysee restaurant, later to become the Café de Paris. Although the cinema was damaged by allegations of German ownership after the outbreak of the First World War in 1914, it had set a new benchmark, together with the New Gallery Kinema on Regent Street, also opened in 1913, with a restaurant, and a suitably 'literary' programme that included Forbes-Robertson in *Hamlet* (Hepworth, 1913) and the French Film d'Art production of *The Three Musketeers* (1912).[30] Alfred Hitchcock vividly recalled English attitudes to cinema in his interview with Truffaut: 'No well-bred English person would be seen going into a cinema; it simply wasn't done'. He then cited Paramount's creation of a block of very expensive seats in their art-deco Plaza super-cinema on Lower Regent Street in 1926, as a way of attracting more up-market English customers. Soon this became known known as 'Millionaires' Row'.[31]

Staged variety shows reappeared in cinemas in the 1920s and continued until after the Second World War. During the 1930s, two major cinema chains would transform the face of film exhibition in Britain. Gaumont and Odeon cinemas featured distinctive design, the latter often streamlined modernist, and luxurious interior fittings as the setting in which British film production would attract its largest domestic audience during the 1940s. London's suburbs benefited particularly from the two chains, with Odeons becoming the centrepiece of new shopping centres and remaining the backbone of the city's film exhibition base until the 1990s.

The climax of this phase of 'screening London' was reached in the mid-1930s with two spectacular new structures. Odeon's

Leicester Square flagship, on the site of the former Alhambra Music Hall and seating 2,116, was clad entirely in polished black granite, with a tower edged in neon to create an impressive effect of 'night architecture', a trend that had already appeared in Germany and the United States. In the same year, Gaumont Super Cinemas took over a project in Kilburn, which opened in December as the Gaumont State, described by Historic England as

> One of the largest and most impressive movie palaces ever constructed in Britain, the Gaumont State, Kilburn had the greatest audience capacity of any English cinema (4,004 seats). Both externally and internally, George Coles brilliantly orchestrated the decoration and space - the latter demonstrated by the subtle planning of the route between the main entrance and the auditorium achieved by placing a rotunda midway along the axis… The High Road facade is a building of monumental proportions, crowned by a soaring tower. The facade lies back from the street to align with the buildings to either side and is in the Moderne style, symmetrical and clad in cream-coloured faience.

Both of these palaces survive, largely due to their architectural status, although their capacity has long been redundant in the era of reduced cinema attendance. In the 1970s, Britain's decaying network of cinemas was shrinking, and suffering from ill-judged attempts to subdivide auditoria economically. However, the arrival of the American multiplex model in the mid-1980s led a revival of cinema building around Britain, which eventually reached London, with UCI's nine-screen complex part of the Whiteleys redeveloped department store in Bayswater in 1989.

Novelty, however, has also long played an important part in London's screen entertainment. Montagu Pyke was inspired to launch his cinema chain by seeing the success of a 'Hale's Tours of the World' show on Oxford Street in 1906. This international attraction placed spectators in a mock railway carriage, with specially shot films that reproduced the view through a moving window.[32] Some large cinemas of the 1920s, known as 'atmospherics', featured exotic foyer decoration that could extend into the main auditorium, with equally exotic lighting effects. An example that survives, albeit now used as a Pentecostal church, was the Finsbury Park Astoria, which opened in 1930, with decorative interior as a 'Hispano-Moresque fantasy'. The effect is worth describing in detail:

Above the proscenium arch and the canted bays and running back for the first four tiers of the gallery, is a detailed and romantic stage-set of a Spanish town; this extends along the side walls of the gallery in the form of a steeply raked arcade of barley-sugar columns and stepped parapet carrying urns, vases and exceedingly naturalistic foliage; at the rear of the gallery, flat-arched entrances with shouldered arches, and between them, an arcade of elliptical arches on squat columns supporting a frieze incorporating part of the lighting system. The ceiling, [was] originally blue and powdered with electric lights as stars.[33]

The Gaumont State cinema, also known as the Kilburn State. Opened 1937, with tiled Art Deco exterior, it remains Britain's and one of Europe's largest ever cinemas, originally seating 4004.

The Astoria would become the Rainbow Theatre for a decade after 1971, hosting many notable pop music acts, as did the Kilburn State. Before this, in the 1950s, as cinema audiences began to decline, various forms of 'wide screen' and large-format presentation were introduced with central London cinemas serving as flagship venues for these. The Odeon Leicester Square premiered *The Robe* in CinemaScope in 1953; the Prince Edward Theatre in Old Compton Street was adapted for the 'panoramic' three-strip Cinerama system in 1957; and in 1959 the Empire Leicester Square presented *Ben Hur* in 70mm for 76 weeks.

Giant IMAX 70mm projection, recalling the impact of the panorama, reached London in 1999, in the form of a dedicated IMAX rotunda built in partnership with the British Film Institute at Waterloo, currently offering the largest cinema screen in Britain.[34] Meanwhile, large video display panels at all London rail stations joined the traditional sites of illuminated advertising display, such as the historic Piccadilly Circus array, presenting programmes of news, information and advertising to commuters and passers-by. And for a short period (2008-10), Trafalgar Square hosted open-air screenings of classic silent films, and London archive material with live accompaniment, as part of the BFI London Film Festival.[35] All these, and many other occasional or 'pop-up' screenings, have been made possible by the advent of portable digital projection, enabling any space – from the domestic to any building or large outdoor venue – to display screen entertainment. Perhaps the most original and initially exciting use of this freedom has been the UK company Secret Cinema presenting a 'spatialised' experience of classic cinema by means of creating elaborate environments based on a range of films, in which audience members 'become part of the story', roaming amid recreations of settings and characters, and climaxing in a screening of the production's source film.[36]

Secret Cinema presentations may belong to a 'post-cinema' era, when the experience of watching a film continuously in a fixed venue forms only a small part of the global experience of 'film'. But they also evoke aspects of many historic phases of the cinema experience, from the elaborate scenography of 'atmospheric' cinemas and the prevalence of live performance accompanying films, back into the era of panoramas and pre-cinematic spectacle. If there is any thread or pattern to be discovered in the history of 'screening the city', it must surely be constant reinvention, or 'remediation',[37] driven by the twin dynamics of commerce and the seemingly perpetual desire to congregate socially before projected images – neither of which have any foreseeable end.

Screening the City 65

Secret Cinema in London, presenting a *Blade Runner* experience in 2018.

This essay originated in a lecture given at the 2008 Sorbonne Nouvelle-Paris 3 Summer School. A short version appeared in the collection *Extended Cinema: le cinema gagne du terrain*, eds. Philippe Dubois, Frederic Monvoisin, Elena Biserma (Campanotto Editore, 2010).

5.
The Anglo-Boer War in North London: A Micro-Study

Jonathan Lewis suggested in the book accompanying his 1991 television series *The Boer War* that this war 'has an uncanny way of pointing us to issues and emotions in our times – like a vaccination we have refused'.[1] One such issue, which certainly has a resonance in our contemporary reflexive culture, is the perception of the Anglo-Boer War as the 'first media war', which served as the subtitle of William Cran's valuable *Timewatch* programme in 1997.[2] Historians of early cinema have consolidated this reputation, with an exceptional quantity and quality of coverage, notably by John Barnes, Luke McKernan, Richard Brown and Barry Anthony, and in articles by Elizabeth Grottle-Strebel, Stephen Bottomore and Simon Popple.[3] A facsimile reissue of W. K. L. Dickson's pioneering contemporary account of his expedition to the Cape, and the surviving sales catalogues, further reinforce a sense of the Anglo-Boer conflict as widely and vividly mediated through the new medium.

Clearly there was an abundant supply of moving pictures from all the main producers of the period, so presumably there was demand, or at least acceptance. But how much do we know about the actual conditions of exhibition, let alone reception, of such material? Always in this field, there is a risk of privileging any evidence of film reception over an integrated understanding of how media interact and cohabit. Like Simon Popple, I am concerned with how film was inserted into existing cultural and social forms, and beyond this necessarily brief study I am interested in how such evidence might bear on the overview of communications technology and political economy first proposed by Harold Innis.[4] What might the new media ensemble of the Anglo-Boer War tell us about the troubles that increasingly afflicted the transcolonial empires in the 20th century? My focus here, however, is deliberately narrow, covering an area of London that lies north-east of the Holloway Road. During the 19th century, what had been a major thoroughfare out of London for over six centuries became the south-western base of the rapidly developing new residential suburbs, with a series of impressive department stores and music halls serving the dense grid of terrace housing that extended into the new borough of Hornsey, incorporated in 1903. At the northern boundary of this area, above the unsuccessful Alexandra Palace entertainment complex, a new 'aspirational' suburb emerged in the late 1890s. Muswell Hill was almost entirely built by two developers to an elegant and coherent plan, between 1897 and 1914, and in 1898 Robert Paul chose it as the greenfield site for his new studio and laboratory.[5]

Before looking at presentations related to the war, it is important to remember that Africa was already an established subject for magic lantern lecturers. Missionaries had long used lanterns as an attraction for their audiences at home; lantern displays of their fieldwork, in the style of lantern lecture 'travelogue', played an important part in helping to raise funds and ensure support for mission work among church congregations in Britain.[6] There was also an additional 'kith and kin' reason for continuing interest in Southern Africa; many Britons had been attracted by the development of diamond and gold mining in the 1970s and 1880s, thus helping create the tension between British and Boer settlers that first led to war in 1881, then to the major conflict that followed President Kruger's ultimatum of 9 October 1899. Another general consideration is the growth of new leisure facilities for the expanding middle-class population of boroughs such as Islington and Hornsey. The two significant venues that emerge from this study are the church and the music hall, both rising forces in the rapidly developing suburbs of North London at this time.

The two earliest war-related media events I have found, unsurprisingly both date from December 1899, and were as much traditional lantern 'travelogues' as war reports. Indeed, the first, a lecture entitled 'A Trip to the Transvaal', given at Muswell Hill Presbyterian Lecture Hall on 4 December by Mr D.S. Salmond and 'illustrated by cinematograph and oxy-hydrogen lantern', was actually an account of a pre-war group tour, which had now acquired topical interest.[7] The newspaper account of Salmond's lecture reveals that it began with a group of up to four films, showing the launch of the *Braemar Castle*, embarkation of passengers, departure and games onboard, followed by slides covering the voyage and arrival at Cape Town. Then followed two films of Cape Town, stressing the modernity of its electric trams, balanced by the more traditional image of a Cape Mounted Policeman 'cantering down the street [and] received with applause'. Finally came a sequence of slides ranging over Kimberley, Johannesburg, the Modder River, and various places 'where a battle has since been fought'.

All the films shown appear to be from the Warwick Trading Company's already extensive catalogue of pre-war and recent actualities from the Cape provinces,[8] but this was essentially a magic lantern lecture, incorporating two characteristic features of lantern practice. One was the forging of a personal link between the lecturer and his subject. In this case, Mr Salmond's second cousin was seen in Rietfontein, the scene of a recent battle, and a portrait was shown of King Khama, which the Ngwato chief from Bechuanaland had given to Salmond on the chief's widely reported visit to Britain in 1895.[9] Another report of Salmond's lecture (in the *Wood Green Weekly Herald*) mentions the inclusion of several songs in his performance, which fits well with the social culture of the period, in which musical performance was an integral part of almost every kind of social gathering. This kind of mixed format seems to have been common: Popple refers to Luscombe Searle's 'celebrated "chat"… illustrated with songs, the latest cinematograph and limelight views from the seat of the war',[10] and John Barnes reproduced the Tees' poster for their Animated Photographs taken at the Seat of War', a similarly mixed film and slide show given at the YMCA in Brighton in 1900.[11]

Another presentation in the same month shows what was happening in the music halls. The Stoll-Moss Holloway Empire had opened on Holloway Road just three months earlier, near the Nag's Head crossroads, and a regular item on its programme was 'Walter Gibbons' American Bio-Tableaux'. Gibbons was an important early supplier of moving picture shows to the halls and occasional filmmaker, who would later run the London Palladium and be knighted. Normally, no details of the Empire Bio-Tableaux programme were published, but for the week of 18 December 1899 'animated photographs of war scenes' had pride of place, just below Miss Lottie Collins 'of "Ta-ra-ra-boom-de-ay" fame'.[12] The twenty films listed form a travelogue-style narrative, 'a journey to South Africa', but although 'War Scenes, Episodes and Incidents' were promised, only three films appear to be actually war-related. Yet this was apparently enough to justify billing a topical show. As in the Presbyterian Hall lecture, most of the films appear to come from the Warwick catalogue, although the first two or three may have been from another distributor, Fuerst. *Coaling by Natives* is harder to identify. It corresponds to W. K. L. Dickson's Cape Town subject of November, except that Biograph films were still only on 70mm stock, so Salmond presumably could not have shown it on 35mm.

Despite the apparent difference of context, the two shows were strikingly similar. Both offer travelogue-style narratives that dwelt on picturesque aspects of South Africa, and, while 'war-motivated', touched only briefly on the war itself. Both were also attractions at newly opened venues. The Presbyterian Hall was only a year old, and the talk's proceeds went to the Church Enlargement Fund that would lead to an impressive building being erected on the corner of Duke's Avenue and the Broadway in 1902. Churches in general, and Nonconformist ones in particular, were a rising force in new suburbs such as Muswell Hill, and so the siting of this well-reported event was significant. Meanwhile, the Empire was one of a growing circuit of new music halls being opened outside the traditional inner-city places of entertainment, in this case by London District Empire Palaces, led by H. E. Moss and Oswald Stoll. Gibbons' 'Bio-tableaux' would remain the only fixed item on the programme for years to come, but rarely would its contents be specified at all, let alone in such detail. The outstanding question that remains is: was the Empire programme accompanied by a lecturer or by the hall's master of ceremonies? Presumably it was accompanied in some manner, otherwise audiences could scarcely have known what they were watching.

R.W. Paul's War Coverage
Robert Paul was already established as a leading producer by 1898 when he purchased open land on the outskirts of Muswell Hill and erected the first phase of a complex that would eventually include a stage, with scenery and costume facilities, a printing laboratory, and a factory for his main business of instrument making.[13] Although discussion of Anglo-Boer War films has often assumed that there were essentially two types – actuality and 'fake' – even a cursory examination of Paul's catalogues shows that he produced at least five distinct kinds of film, all responding to different opportunities and needs as the war developed. Paul's first instinct seems to have been to send cameras in order to capture actuality material, partly following established 'topical' practice and also perhaps stimulated by the fact that his two younger brothers had joined the City Imperial Volunteers.[14]

One of the cameras was entrusted to Colonel Walter Beevor, already a pioneer of using X-ray equipment in the field.[15] Paul later recalled that Beevor was 'able to get about a dozen good films', including one of the few actual scoops, of the Boer General Cronje in captivity.[16] But even before these appeared, dockside 'departures and arrivals' was an important genre that no doubt acquired extra appeal at this time of so many leaving for the distant Cape.[17] Something of the pathos of seeing distant friends and relatives on the screen is captured, albeit grotesquely, in Rudyard Kipling's 1904 story 'Mrs Bathurst'.[18] A third type of war film was the 'reproduction' of incidents, which Paul insisted on labelling clearly as such, and arranged to have supervised by an army officer. Altogether, there were six or seven of these, and although they generated some contemporary controversy, they were, along with Mitchell and Kenyon's, also innovative, as location-based dramatic narratives. Paul's reproductions were filmed several hundred yards from his studio, on Muswell Hill's newly located golf course, itself the first of London's new suburban courses.[19] From the evidence of the sole surviving film, *A Camp Smithy*, and some stills, these were generally more documentary in content and pictorial in composition than Mitchell and Kenyon's vigorous action subjects.[20]

Robert Paul foresaw the scale of likely interest in the Anglo-Boer War and produced a range of different kinds of films.

A fourth type of film was the precursor of later documentary. In 1900, Paul produced and apparently personally photographed a multi-part series entitled *Army Life*, covering almost every aspect of Army induction and training. With a running time of over forty-five minutes, this remained his single most ambitious film enterprise and was clearly prompted by the large recruitment drive and reserve call-up occasioned by the war. A central section portrayed 'a large body of reserves called up for service in South Africa [showing] the pleased expression on the faces of the men at the prospect of active service again'.[21] No doubt his early experience with series such as *A Tour in Spain and Portugal* (1896) contributed to the idea of this series, while his brothers being volunteers may also have had a bearing. It seems likely that the series was welcomed as recruiting propaganda, and may even have been commissioned as such, since Paul proudly proclaimed it to be 'under the patronage of the Commander-in-Chief' and produced a lavish booklet to accompany screenings.

Paul's fifth type of wartime production was a group of allegorical and sentimental pieces that offered opportunities for emotional engagement with the war and its consequences. In 1900, *Kruger's Dream of Empire* took the form of a vigorous live action political cartoon, while *His Mother's Portrait* and *Britain's Welcome to her Sons* both exploited framed flashback narratives to link the battlefield with the home front.[22] In the following year, amid a vogue for film and slide illustration of songs, which took him briefly into music publishing, Paul offered *Britain's Tribute to her* Sons, 'a patriotic song with Animated Illustrations'.

Films taken on or near the scenes of battles were rarely spectacular.

Lest We Forget![23]

As early as Christmas 1899, the early mood of curiosity and bravado that followed the outbreak of war had changed to apprehension, stiffened by patriotic fervour, as voiced by the *Hornsey Journal* editorial of 23 December: 'It is not with the usual feeling of quiet satisfaction that we approach the Christmas of 1899. There was no war cloud on the horizon twelve months ago, but we have now plunged into the hurly-burly and it is impossible to say when we shall emerge from it'. During the next two years, debate over the war continued throughout Hornsey, often in church meetings and in the local debating societies known as 'parliaments'. Local papers would regularly print letters from the Front, giving a personalised view of the war, and of special interest in family, friends and neighbours. The network of volunteer regiments ensured local involvement in despatching and welcoming home servicemen, and an interest in the continuing stream of films recording parades and embarkations. As the war entered its third year at the end of 1901, a novel item at the Holloway Empire involved a hundred local boys performing a stylised pageant of British-Boer fighting – a stage equivalent to the more elaborate films that Paul and others were producing by this time.

Kruger's Dream of Empire (1900) is Paul's only surviving allegorical tableau, at the Imperial War Museum.

After months of stalemate, the final peace was agreed upon on Saturday 31 May 1902, and was greeted with relief, controversy over the terms of the Boer surrender, and jubilation. When the news reached North London the following day, it was first announced in local churches. By Monday, Hornsey's main shopping streets were festooned with decorations, and 'flags and banners were hung out from nearly every window in Mount View Road', while in the evening a spontaneous public lantern show was staged. 'An enormous crowd assembled outside Hill's furniture store on Stroud Green Road on Monday night. A large screen was erected, and magic lantern pictures were shown from Taylor's drug stores opposite. The views consisted of scenes from the war and portraits of celebrities, which were loudly greeted or hissed at as the case might be. A portrait of ex-president Kruger met with a very 'warm' reception from the loyal crowd'.[24] The scene reminded many of Mafeking Night, as crowds set off from Hornsey to the City and West End for further celebrations, and Stroud Green Road's ad hoc lantern show might strike us as an anticipation of modern large public plasma screens.

But if we ask what distinctive part moving pictures played in the reception or perception of the Anglo-Boer War, the evidence is still inconclusive. There can be little doubt that, as John Barnes has claimed, the war gave 'cinema the fillip it needed', by prompting new genres and modes of relation to audiences. In the larger frame of reference proposed by Harold Innis, the technologies of the mass-reproducible image became essential in conveying the contemporary imperial concept to a home audience, as underlined when the films of the 1903 Delhi Durbar rapidly replaced those of the Transvaal War. But it was not film alone that achieved this: there is no evidence of purely moving picture shows related to the Anglo-Boer War. Instead, film appeared alongside the established lantern slide, as an extension or 'animation', while speech, music and conviviality were no less important to this major Victorian spectacle.

This first appeared in a collection edited by Laraine Porter and Bryony Dixon, *Picture Perfect: Landscape, Place and Travel in British Cinema before 1930* (Exeter Press, 2007). It is based on a presentation given at the 2003 British Silent Cinema Festival at Broadway, Nottingham.

6.
The Ghosts of Cinema Past: Screen Heritage in Australia

We are haunted by the ghosts of cinema everywhere today, and nowhere more so than in Australia. Walk down the main streets of Australian country towns, and you can recognise the half-disguised façades of one-time cinemas above the furniture stores and bars that now inhabit these spaces, once numerous and resonant with entertainment from half a world away. Some of the survivors and their ancestors in rural Victoria were the subjects of Sam Nightingale's evocative photographic documentation for *The Cinemas Project* in 2014.[1]

But this ghostly presence is even more pervasive. Australia's National Film and Sound Archive (NFSA) in Canberra holds a vast amount of material that records the nation's audiovisual history, and has made this accessible in a wide variety of ways.[2] There is a YouTube channel, with compilations and mashups of film recording life across the country and the century, and an online player that allows direct viewing access to many of its holdings. There are voices from the past in the archive's oral history collection. Like many archives around the world, the NFSA has found that its holdings of 'everyday' film are proving the most popular items. Documentaries, advertisements and amateur films preserve the textures of the past better than self-conscious fiction. What was once the debris cluttering up archives' feature film collections has become what lay consumers are most intrigued by.

Is this mere nostalgia? An accompaniment to the continuing passion for family history, bric-a-brac collections and eBay culture? Perhaps it is. But rather than see these as somehow inferior to 'real' history, we should perhaps pause and wonder why so many are avid for tangible, visible contact with the past. One of the first professional historians to explore the modern heritage boom was Raphael Samuel, an avowed socialist who nonetheless looked sympathetically at the widespread 1980s enthusiasm for cherishing the material culture of the Victorian and Edwardian past.[3] Against the 'heritage-baiters' who argued that this amounted to turning the past into sanitised tourist kitsch, Samuel cheerfully recorded the sheer scale of popular appetite for heritage artifacts and experiences, defending these against the sneers of a metropolitan elite and of academic critics who had espoused research practices that effectively insulated them from real-world experience. Since this defence of popular heritage culture, the internet has transformed the practices that Samuel observed in the 1980s and '90s, providing new ways of accessing and circulating a vast amount of evidence from the past, and allowing us to do new things with it. Media archaeology, as a new approach to mapping media technologies, proposes that we engage not just with surviving artifacts and images of the past but with the ways in which they were used, and crucially it rejects simplistic ideas of one-way progress. Instead of considering the technologies of early film as 'primitive', we can see them as innovative and experimental.

Evangelising by Limelight
This was certainly the case with the Australasian Salvation Army's pioneering limelight 'lecture' *Soldiers of the Cross*, produced in 1900 in a small wood-lined studio on top of the Salvos' headquarters in Melbourne, which can still be visited today. The story of the 'Limelight Brigade' has long been part of Australian cinema's master narrative, with *Soldiers* sometimes rashly claimed as the world's first feature-length film. It was in fact a magic lantern 'lecture' using some two hundred coloured slides and perhaps fifteen films, which aimed to draw recruits to the Army with its stirring account of the early Christian martyrs. 'Limelight' in the brigade's name referred to the high-intensity illumination produced by directing a flame fed by oxygen and hydrogen onto a block of quicklime. This had been used since the 1820s to light performances and power lanterns where maximum brightness was required.

We know that the premiere of *Soldiers of the Cross* in Melbourne Town Hall in September 1900 attracted an audience of over two thousand, and it would continue to be shown in different forms until at least 1909. But while a number of the slides survive, none of the original films do, so understanding the scale and impact of *Soldiers* involves an effort of imagination as well as varied kinds of research. Above all, to grasp it as an experience we actually need some first-hand contact with the magic or optical lantern – ideally accompanied by music and recitation, such as Martin Jolly offered in a magic lantern show in Canberra, as part of the ANU conference 'History, Cinema, Digital Archives'.[4]

Title slide for *Soldiers of the Cross*, Herbert Booth (1900).

The hybrid format of *Soldiers of the Cross*, combining slide and film projection with music and speech, was typical of the period from which the form we know as 'cinema' emerged approximately a decade later. And its rediscovery may have a valuable lesson to teach us today, as we contemplate the diversity of formats and devices involved in our contemporary experience of 'film'. Herbert Booth's Limelight Brigade harnessed the new technologies of the 1890s in the service of their gospel mission; and in doing so they helped create a mass audience for screen entertainment – which could be informative, even inspirational, as well as merely entertaining. Over a decade later, Charles Taze Russell, founder of the Bible Student movement in Pennsylvania, would deploy even greater audiovisual resources in his four-part *Photo-Drama of Creation*, which toured internationally from 1914 onwards. Whether or not Russell was inspired by the example of *Soldiers*, the launch of the *Photo-Drama* coincided with the emergence of spectacular ancient world dramas, such as *The Last Days of Pompeii*, *Quo Vadis?* and *Cabiria*, taking secular cinema to a new level of ambition.[5]

Before this, and also in Melbourne, the Tait brothers would benefit from an emerging audience which they helped to build by touring an English travelogue, *Living London*, in 1905, the proceeds from which would enable them to produce Australia's first acted narrative, *The Story of the Kelly Gang* in the following year. While this too has often been claimed as Australia's – and even the world's – 'first feature film', it belongs more to the tradition of representing notorious outlaws on stage and in broadsheets. Its hugely popular screenings across Victoria were very much performances, with live narration, music and sound effects, and in many cases the added attraction of a first experience of electrical power. As we contemplate the scattered traces and fragments of cinema's past, distinctive in every country, yet linked by common practices of production, distribution and exhibition, it is tempting to invoke Jacques Derrida's once fashionable concept of 'hauntology' – the spectral presence of the past in the present.[6]

But there are other ways of recognising how artworks can and almost always do encapsulate different temporalities, as art historian Keith Moxey has argued.[7] Time, as Moxey observes, runs at many different rates for different cultures and in different periods; and the concept of a universal 'standard' time is a recent one, closely linked to capitalism and colonialism. Art creates its own aesthetic time, which may bear no relation to the chronology of production, nor especially to that of art historians' linear periodisation. And for a visitor to Australia, starting to appreciate at first hand the country's ancient landscape and indigenous culture, the mysterious concept of the Dreamtime offers an irresistible metaphor for how the disparate elements that make up cinema's past, present and future might all belong to an anachronic whole.

The Return of Living London

'So what does this rediscovered film actually tell us about London?' This was an obvious question for a television journalist to ask, to conclude a report intended for a popular UK television news channel, but it was also one I was dreading. Confronted with some twelve minutes of actuality film dating from 1904, how to convey in a pithy couple of sentences the sense of 'time regained', the underpinning of the vibrant, bustling metropolis which this remarkable fragment revealed?

What had triggered this unusual level of media interest in an archival film was an imminent public screening in Trafalgar Square, London, in a programme of short films chronicling the city through the 20th century, as part of the British Film Institute's 2008 London Film Festival.[8] But the story that led to it had begun for me in 2000, when I proposed a strand in a research programme at Birkbeck College with the provisional title 'The London Project'. This was intended to study in detail the growth of the London-based film industry during the period 1895-1914, undertaking new empirical research into the explosion of entrepreneurs, companies and audiences that had combined to make London one of the key centres of the new moving-picture craze, a fact long obscured by an 'invention-centred' historiography of early cinema.

Much of the work for this project was undertaken by its research fellows, Luke McKernan and Simon Brown, who compiled a mass of information about moving-picture businesses and venues which was initially published in an online database.[9] Their studies of the rapid development of the film industry, initially clustering around Charing Cross Road, and of its diverse audiences, have also helped lay the basis for a new understanding of the relationship between the 'imperial metropolis' and its newest form of entertainment.[10]

But London is also a 'site of representation', with its population and topography providing the subject of many early films and a source of continuing fascination. It was my own work on both the early industry and on the cinematic mapping of the city that took me to Australia in November 2006, to speak about this at a conference in Melbourne.[11] Part of my visit was also to undertake new research in libraries in Melbourne, Sydney and Canberra on the early impact of moving pictures in Australia, revisiting the pioneering work by Chris Long in the 1990s.[12] As part of this, I visited the National Film and Sound Archive (NFSA) in Canberra, asking to view as much as possible of their early British, and especially London-related, material. And it was this request that led to me viewing footage that formed part of the Corrick Collection and was provisionally catalogued as 'London Scenes'.

The Corricks were a concert-party troupe who toured Australia, New Zealand and Southeast Asia at the turn of the century, adding film to their musical performance repertoire between 1901 and 1914.[13] So their having material that related to the old country to show audiences that would have included substantial numbers of expatriates made good sense. But it was one shot in particular that provided a clue to the identification of this material. Amid the scenes of London landmarks and street-life vignettes, there was a procession of sandwich-board men advertising 'Urbanora' and specifically 'A Voyage to New York'. This could only relate to Charles Urban, the dynamic and highly entrepreneurial American producer who had done so much to promote non-fiction film after arriving in London from the United States in 1897, initially to manage the company representing Edison's films.[14]

A woman with dust in her eye on Euston Road,
Living London, Charles Urban (1904-5).

An email to the leading Urban expert, Luke McKernan, elicited the suggestion that this could be part of the lost *Living London* of 1904-5, which featured a 'Brigade of Urbanora Sandwich Men' advertising Urban's forthcoming film.[15] Subsequent research by Bryony Dixon at the British Film Institute has suggested that the footage may actually belong to Urban's *Streets of London*, released in 1906, although it is not clear how much new material this included, or whether, as was common practice for Urban, it represented a re-edit of the original *Living London* footage.[16] Thanks to research by Sally Jackson at the NFSA, we know that *Living London* was very successfully shown around Victoria and New South Wales in 1906, and that its profits enabled the Tait family to produce *The Story of the Kelly Gang* in 1906.[17] We also know that the Corricks were showing what was announced as 'Living London' in Rangoon in 1908, although this may simply have become the most popular title for Urban's London material.[18]

While the NFSA undertook to include the newly identified fragment in their restoration programme for the Corrick Collection, I was able to spread awareness of the new discovery back in Britain, and used it to feed a growing interest in the nexus between London's early film industry and the representation of the city – an interest reflected in various ways in the first London Screen History Symposium at Birkbeck College in March 2008, and in a number of new publications. These included Charlotte Brunsdon's *London in the Cinema* (BFI, 2008) and Gail Cunningham and Stephen Barber's *London Eyes: Reflections in Text and Image* (Berghahn, 2007); the location-finding guides, Simon R. H. James, *London Film Location Guide* (Batsford, 2007) and Tony Reeves, *Movie London: Exploring the City Film-by-Film* (Titan, 2008), as well as movie maps and various interactive media.[19]

In what now seems a significant historical transfer, proceeds from the exhibition of *Living London* around Victoria funded the Taits' production of *The Story of the Kelly Gang* (1906), the first major treatment of an Australian subject and one of the longest dramatic films of the era.

One of these new explorations was a project by Patrick Keiller, already known for his feature *London* (1994). His *City of the Future* embedded early archival film from various British cities in an interactive display, together with period maps.[20] Part of this was included in the exhibition, *Moving Pictures Come to London*, which toured a number of London local history venues between 2006 and 2008. Keiller wrote that he had 'set out to explore contrasts between the familiarity of old city fabric, the strangeness of the past, and the newness of present-day experience'. In fact, the discovery of *Living London* took us back to a similar moment of intermediality a century earlier.

The title, and presumably the idea, came from an illustrated part-work by George Sims, a colourful character who had blazed an even more remarkable trail through late Victorian society than Urban was currently doing in the Edwardian era. Sims (1847-1922) began his career as a journalist and popular poet before making his mark as a dramatist with the melodramas *The Lights o' London* (1881) and

Romany Rye (1882), followed by many more, which toured widely. His ballads, including 'Christmas Day in the Workhouse', were widely sold and quoted. Having established himself as a specialist in London lore, he wrote about wretched living conditions in Southwark, joining the tradition of radical journalists calling for reform, which already included Henry Mayhew (*London Labour and London Poor*, 1851) and W. T. Stead (*The Maiden Tribute of Modern Babylon*, 1885). Sims' campaigning journalism appeared in book form as *Horrible London* (1889), before he embarked on chronicling the variety of metropolitan life in *Living London*, a series of volumes published between 1901 and 1903. The format of these handsomely illustrated books was to profile 'typical' London scenes and customs, using the new technology to reproduce photographs, making them the precursors of what would become known as photojournalism later in the century.

Charles Urban had developed an ambitious catalogue of non-fiction films, which would allow exhibitors either to add these to mixed programmes increasingly built around fictional attractions, or to construct thematic non-fiction programmes.[21] *Living London* represented a determined move towards offering a single film that would occupy a whole programme, albeit in four parts, but lending itself to focused promotion. Whether Sims was more closely involved than presumably approving the use of his title is not clear. The two men may well have recognised something of themselves in the other. Hhowever, the guiding eye behind *Living London* was clearly Urban's, giving the film not only a shrewd sense of what an audience would expect to see, but also a strong sense of focused composition and the brisk editing for which Urban would become noted. Amid the public buildings, familiar vistas and ceremonial scenes, the NFSA's surviving fragment included shots of an old woman huddled on a bench, children pushing a cart and bathing a dog in the Thames, and a striking image of a girl blinking, presumably due to dust in her eye from London's notoriously dirty air – all striking images of individuality amid the city's masses that testify to the new century's concern with the individual in the crowd.

So how should I have answered the journalist's question in 2008? By saying that *Living London* showed London as the most exciting city of the new century, especially for those with personal and, in the case of Australia and other parts of the British empire, political links. And how seeing *Living London*, with the added bonus of electrical illumination, must have seemed almost as good as visiting it. In fact, there were Australians who had visited London shortly before *Living London* appeared, as members of the Bushmen volunteer regiments raised to support Britain in the South African war of 1899-1903, Some of these reached the UK and wrote home about their impressions of the 'mother country'. Some were unimpressed... others recounted how much it matched their expectations, underlining how strongly the sense of 'belonging' was a part of early 20th-century Australian *mentalité*.

Is it too fanciful to imagine some of those 'Bushmen', now back in Australia, going to see *Living London*, no doubt with their families? Would they have been the ones calling out that they had 'been there and seen that'? In October 2008, there was a similar response among the crowd gathered in Trafalgar Square, as they identified the streets and buildings shown, many of them unchanged, including Trafalgar Square itself – a strange moment of seeming spatiotemporal synchronicity for the audience.[22] We cannot know what or how *Living London* communicated with its 1904-5 audiences, for whom the novelty of film was an important part of the experience, but we can perhaps learn something by analogy from how its re-mediated 'return' was witnessed, initially in a news bulletin on satellite television, and then digitally projected on a giant screen in the London of 2008.

This brings together two short pieces: a chapter in Bridget Crone's *The Cinemas Project: Exploring the Spectral Spaces of Cinema Book*, NETS Victoria, Melbourne, Australia, 2019; also 'The Girl with the Speck of Dust in Her Eye: *Living London* Returns', *Senses of Cinema*, February 2009.

Thanks due to Adrian Danks, Deb Verhoeven and Con Verevis, organisers of the XIII Biennial Conference of the Film and History Association of New Zealand, for their invitation to speak; also to Paolo Cherchi Usai, then director of the NFSA, and to his colleagues, Graham Shirley, Meg Labrum and, especially, Sally Jackson, for all their kindness to me while in Canberra, and for their subsequent help in making *Living London* available to screen at the LFF. Thanks also to Martin Jolly and to Lindsay Cox, Territorial Archivist for the Australian Southern Territory of the Salvation Army, for their contributions to informing this essay. In addition to the conference organisers in 2008 and 2014, I am grateful to the Ian Potter Foundation for supporting me as an RMIT Visiting International Fellow in Melbourne. And in 2014, I benefited from a Visiting Fellowship at the Australian National University in Canberra.

Revisions: Getting the Story Straight

7.
The Tarnished Myth of British Precedence: Friese-Greene, Paul and Will Day

The best known representation of cinema's 'primal scene', at least until Scorsese's *Hugo*, must be *The Magic Box*, a film made cooperatively by members of the British film industry as its contribution to the Festival of Britain in 1951. The story of William Friese-Greene, regarded as Britain's unjustly neglected pioneer, it includes a memorable sequence in which Robert Donat's excited inventor demonstrates his achievement to an initially sceptical policeman, played by no less than Laurence Olivier. Olivier acts out the tropes traditionally involved in a first encounter with film, looking behind the screen and wondering 'where' the figures he has seen have come from, before Donat explains and shows him a wide-gauge film strip with side-by-side images. The film is handsomely mounted and undeniably moving – even if we now know that it was based on a deeply flawed biography of Friese-Greene and grossly misrepresented what he did actually achieve, albeit with telling emotional impact.

So is it merely a period piece in a double sense, a nostalgic portrayal of the late Victorian and Edwardian era, and a monument to the collective belief that prevailed in Britain after 1921, that Friese-Green was the true 'inventor of kinematography', as his memorial in Highgate Cemetery proclaims? No historians of film or 19th-century visual media would support such a claim today. Indeed, most would reject the concept of a single 'inventor', pointing to an international network of experimenters who became increasingly active during the 1880s, with varying degrees of success – the 'workers of the eleventh hour', as Laurent Mannoni has described them.[1]

Yet for at least four decades, Friese-Greene was considered 'the inventor' by virtually all in Britain who took an interest in cinema history, with many texts and monuments testifying to this belief, as well as *The Magic Box*. The conviction seems to have persisted in the face of widespread disbelief in other countries, and a notable absence of empirical evidence. Part of its legacy, I suggest, has been an aversion to recognising the pioneering role of Friese-Greene's contemporary, Robert Paul – who did in fact demonstrate 'animated photography' to a police audience in 1895, among many more significant achievements. Arguably, Friese-Greene's reputation has also suffered from his posthumous canonisation, making it harder to discern his true stature and achievements behind the sentimental narrative of *The Magic Box*. Like its near-contemporary *Scott of the Antarctic*, these seem to bear witness to a recurrent pattern in national ideology geared to celebrating 'heroic failure', as identified by the (American) historian Stephanie Barczewski in her 2016 book.[2]

The circumstances of Friese-Greene's pitiful end fitted this template only too well. When he collapsed and died during a film industry meeting in 1921, he was a forgotten, near destitute figure. The immediate reaction to his death was a revival of claims that his 1889 patent for moving pictures had preceded, and potentially inspired, Edison's work that led to the Kinetoscope. The self-appointed historian of early cinema, Will Day, was quick to assert this, describing Friese-Greene just two days after his death as 'one of England's greatest if unrecognised inventors'.[3] In the same interview, Day provided what may be the first telling of the story of Friese-Greene becoming so excited by his achievement in 'throwing the first living picture on a screen' that he 'ran into the street, grabbed a policemen and dragged him into the house' to witness it. Another accessory to the canonisation was Muriel Forth, then a young journalist in London, who saw the funeral for Friese-Greene, arranged and paid for by an embarrassed film industry, and later wrote the undocumented biography on which *The Magic Box* was based.[4]

There were other consequences, which may have helped to secure Friese-Greene's foundational reputation. Soon after his death, a meeting of 'cinema veterans' was convened, which led to the establishment of an association that continues to the present. A 'veteran' was defined as having been 'actively involved in the Cinema Industry in (or before) 1903, and remained therein for a reasonable period'.[5] One hundred and one individuals who met this criterion apparently attended the first dinner, held in December 1924, and soon the association's treasurer was Robert Paul, long retired from the film industry, although active in the scientific instrument business.

The story of police attention being attracted by late-night success with moving pictures was indeed an anecdote by Paul, probably first told publicly in 1909, during an after-dinner speech at a fraught dinner being held in London to try to 'promote a more harmonious feeling between different branches' of the industry. This was in the aftermath of the recent Paris conference, at which producers from a number of countries had tried to create a combined front in the face of Pathé's price-cutting and exhibitors' increasing impatience. Robert Paul, widely known as 'Daddy Paul', and certainly the oldest producer in the room was chairing the dinner, no doubt seeking to create harmony, recalled 'the first film he had made': 'It was the time they had to punch sixteen holes in one impression. It was 3am in the morning when they had successfully finished their film, and they made such a cheering that the police came in to know what was the matter'.[6] Four years later, Frederick Talbot told the story in his book *Moving Pictures: How They Are Made and Worked*, although converting what could only have been a Kinetoscope demonstration into a primal scene of projection: 'They had just succeeded in throwing the first perfect animated pictures upon a screen. To compensate the police for their fruitless investigation, the film, which was 40 feet in length and produced a picture 7 feet square, was run through again'.[7]

Robert Donat as William Friese-Greene
and Laurence Olivier in *The Magic Box* (1952).

In 1937, the author of a popular history of cinema, Leslie Wood, told the 'policeman' story again, twice. First, following Will Day, he had Friese-Greene showing a '20 second movie he had taken in January 1889' to a 'passing policeman' dragged in to witness 'the cabs and passers by… on the makeshift screen' (sic). Twenty pages later, he told essentially the same story, now about Paul and set 'in the early hours of the morning' in Hatton Garden, with 'excited cries emanating from Robert W. Paul, aided and abetted by his assistants, roaring out war-whoops of joy... The constable was annoyed at this commotion and, to appease him, Paul showed him the marvel which he had just discovered'.[8] The improbability of this repetition is reconciled by invoking Talbot's 'perfect': 'A police constable saw Friese-Greene's world's premiere of the moving picture, and it was a police constable who saw the world's premiere of the first *perfect* movie [italics in original]'.

William Friese-Greene

Wood offered no dates for this supposed coincidence, but followed it with 'the strange case of Louis Le Prince', which, 'probably unknown to Friese-Greene, had in some measure anticipated his conception'. However, in a subsequent book, *Miracle of the Movies* (1947), he would repeat the Friese-Greene version, adding more colour to the story of the policeman, who 'blunders out into the night, mumbling through his beard: "It's a miracle. I've seen a miracle"'.[9] The substantial account of Paul's career in film that follows, allegedly based on an interview 'on the eve of World War II', and embellished with a number of vivid details, makes no mention of the policeman anecdote – which now belongs entirely to Friese-Greene.

Throughout the 1930s and '40s, Friese-Greene's reputation was in the ascendant, before climaxing with Allister's biography and its screen adaptation. Today, we may wonder what had sustained this support, in the absence of any tangible evidence. One important factor was the involvement of Friese-Greene in an American legal challenge to Edison's monopolistic Motion Pictures Patents Company in 1910. Invited to America by independents challenging the 'Edison Trust', Friese-Greene swore an affidavit in December 1910, which invoked his own patent of 1899 to cast doubt on Edison's claims.[10]

During the First World War, as Kristin Thompson demonstrated in her study of American films reaching national markets around the world, *Exporting Entertainment*, American studios had increased their domination of the world film market, putting European producers at a severe disadvantage.[11] Indeed, the London meeting during which Friese-Greene died had been called to address the challenge posed by American distributors. In this climate, the suggestion that a British pioneer lacked recognition due to America having monopolised credit for the origins of cinema had obvious appeal. Terry Ramsaye's major 1926 history, *One Million and One Nights*, for instance, omitted Friese-Greene completely, devoting instead a chapter to Robert Paul's unrealised 'time machine' project.[12]

After America's grip on world cinema tightened further with the arrival of synchronised sound, references to Friese-Greene increased. Discussing the 'boosting' of Friese-Greene in the interwar era, Geoff Brown has drawn attention to the frequency with which commentators such as the *Daily Express* critic G.A. Atkinson lauded Friese-Greene in 1928, at the cusp of the sound era. Brown notes that such references, and the appearance of portraits of Friese-Greene in popular histories during the 1930s, reflected a growing sense of inferiority over British cinema after the arrival of the Talkies.[13] Claiming a British 'true pioneer', ignored by the dominant Americanised view of cinema history, became a significant motif in the cultural politics of the interwar years.

By 1937, Friese-Greene's name had become a rallying banner among those contesting the 'Americanisation' of cinema. As Wood would write in his expanded popular history of 1947: 'to even the most obtuse it would appear that [Edison] did not seek to protect his 'invention' in Britain because he knew that William Friese-Greene had forestalled him'.[14] And the founder of Britain's National Film

Archive, Ernest Lindgren, wrote in a letter to the *Times* in 1939, correcting some minor statements in a feature about the history of cinema's invention: 'It is high time that Friese-Greene's priority in the field of cinematography should be recognised. I myself have never seen any satisfactory attempt to disprove the validity of the patent of June 21, 1889. The strength of the Edison claim lies, of course, in the fact that it was from his Kinetoscope that all the commercial developments in the cinematograph have sprung. Both R. W. Paul in England and the Lumière brothers in France worked from the Kinetoscope'.

Against this background, with Britain economically dependent on the United States after the war – and Hollywood demonstrating its strength in the American 'Bogart or bacon' film embargo of 1948[15] – the immediate post-war moves to boost Friese-Greene gain new meaning, as indeed does the rediscovery of Louis Le Prince.[16]

Celebrating the half-century of cinema was clearly an attractive post-war project, when the British Film Institute formed its History Research Committee in 1946, with a view to marking the fiftieth anniversary of 'cinema as a regular form of public entertainment'. Rachael Low was employed as its main researcher and must have quickly discovered that the origins of cinema were highly contested. A prefatory note to her first volume states that the BFI Committee's 'terms of reference did not include research into the invention of later history of cinematograph apparatus', for which 'the Science Museum is better fitted'.[17] It also offered an appendix, cautiously titled: 'some well-known claims and records of early demonstrations of screen projection', adding that the subject 'is extremely controversial and must ultimately receive separate treatment'. The first three entries in this Appendix summarise what was believed, and disbelieved, at this time.[18] Louis Le Prince of Leeds 'was said to have projected motion pictures on to the wall of his workshop'. Next 'Friese-Greene said to have demonstrated projection before members of the Bath Photographic Society', which has a footnote stating that 'Accounts in the *Amateur Photographer*, March 7, 1890, and the *Photographic News*, March 7, 1890, show that this was not in fact a true demonstration'. The third item reads: 'Feb 1895. R. W. Paul said to have succeeded in projecting motion pictures in his London workshop at Hatton Garden'.

But said by whom? Elsewhere in this volume, Low struck a similarly cautious note: 'whatever [Paul's] true place in the story of [film's] technical invention…', which also carries a footnote: 'The well-known story of the two Greeks, the kinetoscopes, etc', with a reference to Paul's British Kinematograph Society lecture given in

1936.[19] And above the paragraph on Paul, Low notes of Birt Acres that his 'early connections with R. W. Paul fall outside the scope of this work'. In the context of the late 1930s and '40s, attention was still firmly focused on projection, with the Kinetoscope period relegated to an obscure pre-history of cinema. Just as Talbot had recast Paul's 1895 anecdote in terms of a projected picture, so Wood and 'Allister' would assert Friese-Greene's priority with projection. The only known challenge to Talbot's account comes from Birt Acres' marginal annotation in his copy – 'No!' – but if this refers to the mistake of assuming projection was available in 1895, it does not cast doubt on the event having happened.[20]

By the late 1940s, especially after the standoff between the British government and Hollywood in 1948, there would be little chance of any doubts about Friese-Greene being voiced, and the policeman as first witness had become a firm part of the myth. Both Wood and Muriel Forth elaborated it in their popular histories, with *The Magic Box* bringing it to a wider audience. And even if the BFI History Committee might have had reservations about confirming the claims made on Friese-Greene's behalf, the institute's *Monthly Film Bulletin* accepted the film's premise: 'Friese-Greene at last succeeds, and shows the first moving pictures to a bewildered city policeman. He continues to develop his invention, increasingly frustrated by the knowledge that Edison and not himself is credited as the inventor of the motion picture camera'.[21]

Unsurprisingly, the American response was very different. Probably the most indulgent review was by Bosley Crowther in *The New York Times*: 'The subject of this unique production is a gentleman named William Friese-Greene, who has sometimes been advanced by the British as a movie pioneer to rival Edison. That claim is clearly unsupported by all the evidence there is at hand and, indeed, it is questionable whether Friese-Greene contributed more to the invention of pictures that move than a very crude camera-projector that apparently never proved practical. According to the dean of screen historians, Terry Ramsaye, his work was earnest but vain'.[22]

As Crowther noted, Ramsaye was regarded as America's most senior historian of cinema. He had taken strong exception to the credulous view of Friese-Greene's work presented in *The Magic Box*.[23] Others, notably Lindgren, preferred to ignore the film's historical basis, emphasising instead the 'human' aspects of this portrayal 'of a type of individual to whom we all unknowingly owe much: the obscure, unrecognised, patient, ever-hopeful dabbler in inventions who is prepared to sacrifice everything to his ruling passion'.²⁴ In retrospect, this elaborate characterisation might be judged to cover some unease about the presentation of Friese-Greene's achievements.²⁵

There had been earlier signs of doubt about the claims now widely accepted in Britain on behalf of Friese-Greene. In 1947, Howard Cricks, son of the pioneer film producer G. H. Cricks and a technical expert who would advise on *The Magic Box*, drew attention in a review of a French technical history of cinema to 'the scanty credit paid to William Friese-Greene'.²⁶ Tellingly, he asked what may, or may not, have been intended as a rhetorical question: 'Is our faith in the priority of the British inventor merely an illusion fostered by the film trade historian, the late Will Day?' Georges Sadoul, the leading French cinema historian, would express more candid reservations in the first volume of his *Histoire générale du cinéma*, published in 1946: if the claims made for Friese-Greene's early experiments could be substantiated, this would be important… but could they?²⁷

During the next fifteen years, this unease would turn to outright scepticism and finally rejection. Howard Cricks would admit his own reservations in a 1950 article in the *British Kinematography* journal.²⁸ In a 1955 article, framed by reference to the impact of *The Magic Box*, the technical historian Raymond Spottiswoode surveyed the evidence surrounding the 'Friese-Greene controversy'.²⁹ Having noted that Ramsaye had, in effect, dismissed all other contenders for recognition in favour of Edison, he proceeded to establish criteria for judging Friese-Greene, and indeed Le Prince, as the 'father' or inventor of cinema. On the evidence available, he concluded that 'Friese-Greene did not originate any of the major ideas of cinematography', or succeed in being the first to project film.³⁰

As a 3D specialist, who had overseen the Festival of Britain's programme of stereoscopic films shown at the South Bank Telekinema, Spottiswoode was also at pains to make clear that, while Friese-Greene had undoubtedly taken the earliest 3D moving pictures, he had no conception of how to project these. The article, by a British-born author appearing in an influential American journal, was measured and conciliatory in tone.

But it was undoubtedly a sustained campaign by the pioneer British photographic historian Brian Coe that toppled Friese-Greene from his pedestal.³¹ Between 1955 and 1969, Coe published a series of articles that systematically called into question any claim to have been the 'the inventor of kinematography'.³² This is not the occasion to interrogate Coe's case (which Peter Domankiewicz has been doing)³³, but importantly an increasing number of younger

Panels from the graphic novel by ILYA and Ian Christie, *Time Traveller: Robert Paul and the Invention of Cinema*, Derry: Nerve Centre, 2019, showing what may have really happened when Paul and Acres developed their first film.

film enthusiasts, who would become the first generation of 'film studies' teachers and scholars, initially became aware of Friese-Greene as a discredited figure. Since *The Magic Box* was largely inaccessible during the 1960s and 70s, this was hardly a relevant cause, but Coe's seemingly forensic demolition of Friese-Greene was. In a polemical study of post-war British cinema that would become a launchpad for new attitudes, *A Mirror for England*, Raymond Durgnat found *The Magic Box* 'deliciously symptomatic' of the effort to renovate and celebrate tradition in 1940s Britain. Bracketing it with *Scott of the Antarctic* ('a fine saga for boy scouts'), Durgnat identified these as both 'stories of gallant failure, as if, albeit unconsciously, the British could hardly respond to the idea of success without an aura of failure surrounding it'.[34]

Significantly, however, one of the first 'new generation' studies of early British film, Michael Chanan's *The Dream That Kicks*, published in 1980, took up the defence of Friese-Greene as a polemical project, making the crucial distinction between what he himself had claimed and left as evidence, as against what posthumous supporters and critics had claimed on his behalf.[35] Meanwhile, following a different rubric that might be characterised as an early form of 'media archaeology', based on the scrupulous examination of original documents and artefacts, John Barnes had published the first volume of his *Beginning of the Cinema in England* in 1976, which Chanan was able to draw upon. In this, and subsequent volumes, Barnes made clear his view that Paul had been the most important figure in early British cinema.[36]

We are unlikely to see a return of the 'populist hagiography' (in Deac Rossell's phrase) that surrounded William Friese-Greene during the interwar decades, although as Rossell noted in his admirably even-handed study of 'the origins of the movies', 'much of the Friese-Greene legend had already been embedded in the historical literature'.[37] And, indeed, it persists today outside of that professionalised literature in the form of unmoderated online sites, and appreciative comments on *The Magic Box*, as recorded in IMDb's 'user comments'.[38] It also reappears in Martin Scorsese's foreword to the book written by David Robinson and commissioned by the Library of Congress for the widely celebrated 'centenary of cinema' in 1995-96, where Scorsese vividly recalls seeing *The Magic Box* as one of his 'primal film experiences' at the age of ten.[39]

Having researched Paul over much of the last twenty years, I have been frequently reminded of the stubborn persistence of early conclusions, which can harden into dogmatic assertions and assumptions, even if they have been scrupulously challenged. It is also clear that 'having a good story' remains important in structuring historical evidence, which may indeed be why the 'policeman story' was first assigned to Friese-Greene by Will Day. So merely to label the policeman episode in *The Magic Box* as 'wrong', 'impossible' or an invention, is to ignore its narrative force and significance. Somewhat like Newton's apple, or Galileo's Tower of Pisa 'experiment', the inadvertent 'first viewer' represented by Olivier's policeman fulfils a function. It satisfies the desire for a myth or story of origin, and would indeed form part of the repertoire of early film subjects, as in Paul's *The Countryman and the Cinematograph* (1901) and its remake by Edison as *Uncle Josh's First Sight of the Moving Pictures* (1902) – and the fact that the story *is* substantially true, if not of Friese-Greene, underlines its value.

The desire to 'believe it' produced a strange, and so far unexplained footnote to *The Magic Box*. A full-page 1952 advertisement in *Punch* visualised the scene 'in the Hatton Garden workshop of a scientific instrument maker, in 1895, [where] strange new pictures were thrown on a magic lantern screen'. This was, the text explained, 'the first commercial practicable film projector to be made in this country – the Theatrograph', and 'its inventor, Robert Paul', is identified as 'one of the purposeful men who made the 1890s a period of promise unique in our history'.[40] What lay behind this advertisement for the Reed Paper Group, which was started by Albert E. Reed in that same year, is intriguing but far from clear. The artist, or advertising agency, must have based the concept on the theme of the Festival of Britain, and specifically on *The Magic Box*, which had been widely released five months earlier, but was also aware that its primal scene was mis-attributed to Friese-Greene, yet *not* aware (or preferring to ignore) that this had been a Kinetoscope viewing, and that the Theatrograph belonged to 1896.

As a pendant to the 1952 advertising image, we have produced a comic-strip 'corrective' sequence in the graphic novel *Time Traveller* (Ilya and Ian Christie, 2019), which sketches Paul's film career. Here the available evidence of the 'Clovelly Cottage' test film, showing Henry Short in cricket whites appearing in front of Birt Acres' house in Barnet, leads on to processing the film and running it on a Kinetoscope in Hatton Garden. We have assumed that both Paul and Acres were present, since they were certainly working together, and that Henry Short, who had introduced them, may also have been there to see himself on film. It is of course only a hypothesis, although something like it must have happened. But since the dispute between Acres and Paul has so overshadowed the period of their collaboration, it seems historiographically important to represent this. Likewise, in *Time Traveller*, we have shown the decision to buy land and build a studio in North London as one taken jointly by Robert and Ellen Paul in 1898. There is some documentary evidence supporting this, from a 1943 obituary of Paul, which stressed his wife's contribution to running the studio, on the basis of her previous theatrical experience.[41] But it too must be hypothetical, while intended to focus on the human issues that must have surrounded the Pauls moving from central London to a new suburb, and a new scale of commitment to film production.

While it may be impossible to identify the personnel responsible for the 1952 'Theatrograph' advertisement at this distance in time, it provides tantalising evidence of a level of knowledge about the endemic confusion surrounding the 'origins of cinema' in Britain not otherwise recorded.[42] After Coe's demolition of the hagiography surrounding Friese-Greene, and the emergence of a new paradigm of research into the emergence of moving-pictures amid late Victorian optical entertainments, there has been understandable reluctance to explore the idea of Britain as a major site of innovation in this field. Yet all the evidence of post-1970 research – on panoramas, stereoscopy, 'lantern culture' and dissolving views, as well as the intensive 'animated photography' experimentation of the 1880s, of which Friese-Greene was an active part (although by no means alone) – points to Britain, and specifically London, as the most vibrant capital of the new screen culture. There is good reason to be wary of claims that may be driven by anxiety about national status. But there are also substantial grounds for arguing that Britain, at least as much as France, Germany or the United States, was where cinema gained its first and largest popular audiences.

This is a modified version of an article for *Early Popular Visual Culture*, based on a presentation at the British Silent Film Festival in 2018.

8.
'Everyday Life' in Early Cinema

> People from 1896 in everyday motions, and here we are watching.
>
> One of 191 YouTube comments on Paul's *Blackfriars Bridge*[1]

I.
In autumn 1898, the English pioneer filmmaker Robert Paul announced that he was turning his back on subjects taken from everyday life – 'Trains, Trams and 'Buses', as he disparagingly described these – for a new phase of 'animated photography' production.[2] Henceforth he would exploit the new medium's 'capacity for producing BREATHLESS SENSATION, LAUGHTER AND TEARS', with a series of staged story-films. And through the combined efforts of a team of craftsmen and performers assembled at his new studio in North London, he was able to offer eighty of these, which he guaranteed would 'rivet the attention' of spectators.

What was Paul saying goodbye to in 1898? We might call it the 'demonstration' or 'novelty' phase of moving pictures, lasting from approximately 1895 to 1898, which has indeed appeared to offer 'slices of everyday life' to later spectators. The following account of the Lumière 'first film' is typical of an anachronistic view common today: 'What *La sortie de l'usine Lumière à Lyon* shows us is life, simple life, everyday life, without effect, without special effects, crying out "truth" despite the absence of color and above all of sound. The Lumière cinematograph thus heralds the triumph of realism in the future history of cinema. However, this natural simplicity does not exclude a certain form of "staging", that is to say here of preparation, which is an even more fundamental given for the development of cinema'.[3]

Here the original film has been conscripted into a powerful teleological narrative, which casts Lumière and Georges Méliès as the founding fathers of cinema, representing 'realism' and 'fantasy'. The fact that *La sortie* was carefully restaged over several months is reduced to conceding that it was 'prepared', and the issue of how the Lumière and other early films were actually presented – generally with an accompaniment of live music, or phonograph accompaniment, or spoken introduction and even sound-effects – is also elided, in order to cast it as preserving for us a vision of 'simple everyday life'.[4]

La sortie de l'usine Lumière à Lyon, Lumière cat. 91.1 (May 1895).

We can find a similar attitude in comments on an early Robert Paul film, *Blackfriars Bridge*, made a year later in mid-1896, and currently presented online by a London tourism organisation as 'a fascinating record of traffic on the bridge with pedestrians curious about the presence of the camera', when there is good reason to believe it was carefully staged.[5] But before considering these cases in more detail, it may be useful to review briefly the status and history of 'everyday life' as a frame of reference. This is very obviously a debatable concept, one that is likely to mean different things to different commentators, often without any need to specify further what is meant. As the sociologist Erving Goffmann observed: 'To speak… of "everyday life"… is merely to take a shot in the dark… a multitude of frameworks may be involved or none at all'.[6] But even if there is today considerable academic debate and controversy around the term, I want to suggest there are also two historical perspectives relevant to the creation and reception of the films of 1895-6.

One of these was the burgeoning of new literary genres in the mid-19th century, dramatising the life of the city in essentially non-fictional terms. Walter Benjamin coined the phrase 'panorama literature' in his study of Charles Baudelaire, evoking the rash of cheap publications designed to be sold in the streets of Paris, likening these to the 'plastic foreground of the panoramas and their anecdotal form'.[7] In France, the new fashionable form was the 'physiology', detailing 'types that might be encountered by a person taking a look at the marketplace'. Soon, Benjamin observes, 'the physiology of the city had its turn', and eventually the nation and all its inhabitants. Such 'physiologies' were intended to be innocuous, uncontroversial in an era of looming political censorship, and they gave birth to the better known concept of the *flâneur*, as celebrated by Baudelaire in his famous essay on Constantin Guys, 'The Painter of Modern Life' (1865). For such a 'passionate spectator', likened by Baudelaire to 'a mirror as vast as the crowd itself, or to a kaleidoscope gifted with consciousness, responding to each one of its movements and reproducing the multiplicity of life', it would be impossible to be bored in a crowd.[8]

Contemporary with the Paris of the arcades and the *feuilletons*, there were parallel developments in many European countries during the century. Edgar Allan Poe's 1840 story 'The Man of the Crowd', set in London, was quickly translated, and is now recognised as the prototype of the modern urban mystery (an 'X-ray of the detective story', in Benjamin's evocative phrase).[9] Even earlier, Charles Dickens had launched his career by contributing a series of anonymous 'Sketches by "Boz"' to a range of magazines in the early 1830s, which were subtitled as 'illustrative of Every-day life and Every-day people' when published as a collection in 1836. Benjamin cites Dickens' complaint that 'my figures seem disposed to stagnate without crowds about them'.[10] More systematically, the journalist Henry Mayhew profiled 'the London poor' in a series of articles for the *Morning Chronicle*, eventually published as four substantial volumes, illustrated with engravings in the 1860s. And in 1880, Anthony Trollope, already famous for his 'Barsetshire' novels about English provincial life, would enter this expanding market with his profiles of *London Tradesmen* for the *Pall Mall Gazette*.

Meanwhile, visual representation of everyday life had accompanied, and indeed often cross-fertilised, its literary and journalistic coverage (Dickens' Pickwick stories, which became his first novel, were originally commissioned as captions to illustrations). Constantin Guys, the subject of Baudelaire's essay, had worked extensively for the pioneering *Illustrated London News* before returning to Paris to portray its social variety. And from 1869, *The Graphic* competed with extensive illustration of its news and features, often employing notable artists, such as Luke Fildes and Hubert von Herkomer. As wood-block illustration was superseded by half-tone reproduction of photographs, the periodical reading public of the 1880s and '90s was thoroughly accustomed to seeing 'the very form and presence of events as they transpire, in all their substantial reality', as the *Illustrated London News* had promised as early as 1842.[11] And in addition to such abundant printed material, there were both projected photographic lantern slides and stereographic images widely available to offer even great immediacy.

Blackfriars Bridge. Robert Paul (1896).

None of this is to deny the impact of moving pictures from 1894 onward, as seen first on the Kinetoscope, or the enthusiastic response to pioneering projected shows during 1895. If anything, it is to underline that moving pictures reached audiences that were well prepared for a further degree of 'life-likeness', having witnessed rapid progress in recent decades. And, as we will see, the choice of early subjects made by both Lumière and Paul reflected this climate of expectations. But there is also another historical perspective to bear in mind: namely that of subsequent changing attitudes towards the first subjects shown. As cinema developed rapidly during the early 20th century, becoming mass entertainment after approximately

1910, neither the public nor the industry showed any interest in preserving early films. This resulted in the majority of all early films being lost – current estimates suggest an average of 20% surviving – with the Lumière catalogue very much an exception, due largely to the company having opted out of the commercial film industry and preserved its archive.

On the rare occasions when they were seen, or remembered, this was likely to be as objects of amusement or derision. The Studio des Ursulines in Paris, one of the first cinemas devoted to film as avant-garde art, ran a regular feature 'Ten minutes of pre-war cinema' during the 1920s, which apparently provoked mirth among its fashionable audience.[12] One of these, the young director René Clair, would later muse on such lack of respect for the recent past, reflecting on what it would mean for contemporary work seen in the future.[13] In Britain, with few if any opportunities to see early film, Virginia Woolf would write in 1926 about film seeming 'at first sight simple, even stupid', before listing typical newsreel subjects and reflecting on them 'having a quality which does not belong to the simple photograph of real life'.[14]

Later in this tantalising essay, she sets up a contrast between the clumsiness of literary adaptations and early filmmakers seeming 'dissatisfied with such obvious sources of interest as the passage of time and the suggestiveness of reality. They despise the flight of gulls, ships on the Thames, the Prince of Wales, the Mile End Road, Piccadilly Circus'. Almost alone among inter-war commentators, Woolf implied that early film portrayed an 'unexpected beauty… life as it is when we have no part in it', which was subsequently overlaid by 'enormous technical proficiency', while awaiting the discovery of 'some secret language which we feel and see, but never speak'.

The history of recovering film's earliest years has yet to be written, but it largely dates from the years after the Second World War, when film archives began to take stock of what materials had survived, and to make copies of these on the new non-flammable 'safety' film stock. Two circumstantial factors would leave their mark on this process. One was that most early prints were copied onto black-and-white stock, even if they had survived in coloured prints. The other was that early film's low frame-rate was routinely disregarded, leading to films being projected, and crucially transferred to video for use on television, at 'sound speed'. This would give rise to what came to be accepted as the inherent 'jerkiness' of early film – a mark of its primitiveness.

Apart from these material issues, the post-war period would see a succession of critical and theoretical paradigms adopted within the emerging field of Film Studies that prioritised 'progressive' aspects of early film practice: essentially those that anticipated the development of narrative editing. Not until the 1978 FIAF Brighton Congress, which assembled a large array of surviving pre-1906 films for viewing, were the conditions created for a non-teleological assessment of early film. There were also a number of other developments during the last decades of the 20th century that would affect attitudes towards early film. Growing interest and expertise in 19th-century photography, and in the history of pre-filmic 'optical devices', led to a more nuanced understanding of the work of film pioneers, including those 'workers of the eleventh hour' who had not previously been canonised.[15] And perhaps most important of all, the emergence of home video formats, and ultimately of sharing and streaming platforms, would lead to the wide diffusion of what had previously been a rare archival commodity. Much of the entire surviving corpus of early film is now freely available for all to view online, and continues to generate a constant stream of commentary, much of which is as nostalgic as it is historically uninformed.

II.

With these perspectives in mind, let us turn to the issue of early films portraying, or capturing 'movement caught live', as the Lumières would claim in their original Cinématographe patent.[16] There may be no question that the first cameras were *recording* the 'live' scene before them. But it seems doubtful that this was spontaneous or unrehearsed. More commonly, early 'test' subjects were intended to address some technical concerns. For instance, the first film taken by Birt Acres and Robert Paul in 1895, known as *Incident at Clovelly Cottage*, shows a woman in black and a man entirely in white outside the entrance to a house. We can surmise that this was designed to include extremes of tonal contract, to test what would be visible on viewing – in this case on a Kinetoscope.[17]

In the case of what has been commemorated as the 'first film' of the Lumières, *La sortie de l'usine Lumière a Lyons*, we now know that this was filmed at least three times, between March and July 1895.[18] The location was the Lumière photographic factory and the subjects its employees, making this already something of a commercial advertisement. The first version may have been, or was perhaps suggested by employees' normal 'departure', although given the bright sunlight this is unlikely to have been at the end of the working day. More likely it was prepared, with the mass of workers moving swiftly at a signal, to ensure that as much movement was captured on the short length of film used. Already, 'direction' is apparent: all the workers exit either to left or right, with only one woman coming diagonally towards the camera. This version was apparently shown at early demonstrations of the Cinématographe to professional audiences in spring and summer 1895. But its shortcomings must have been apparent to Louis Lumière, as an experienced photographer, even if he was facing the new challenge of composing in duration as well as within the pictorial frame. Hence the two reshoots, in which the workers appear in their Sunday best, apparently after attending Mass, presumably on their day off work, and again disperse to right and left, with one woman clearly steering her companion in the agreed direction. However, the third version not only has better contrast but includes significant temporal 'framing', with the factory gates seen to open and close, while some foreground 'business' involving a cyclist and the dog appears in all three versions.

The more we examine these three extant versions, helped by their repeatability online and our experience of 'reading' filmed scenes, the more apparent their purposeful organisation becomes. Similarly, we find the same attention to spatial and temporal parameters in other Lumière 'demonstration' films.[19] The blacksmith being handed a glass of wine after his labours and the naughty boy being punished by the gardener are both 'completed' events, while the two army clowning subjects, *La voltage* and *Le saut a la couverture* both present rounded performances, not unlike the vaudeville acts filmed for Edison in his Black Maria, subjects that would have been known to the Lumières. Photographic congress attenders disembark briskly from their cruise in a diagonal line, approaching the camera and exiting the frame both to right and left, with many doffing their hats to the operator. And in *La baignade*, a more informal sequence of boys advancing away from the camera along a platform to dive into the sea. The Lyons city street scene *Place des Cordeliers* may appear the least structured, open to the variety of city-centre traffic, yet this pivots around a passing horse-drawn tram as its main 'event'. Even *Le repas de bébé* turns out to be symmetrically structured by Auguste offering food to his infant daughter, while his wife pours herself a cup of coffee.

None of this attention to composition in developing a new form should be surprising. The Lumières were seasoned professionals in photography, and Louis would devote his later life to continued research, into developing a natural colour photographic process, and a means of transferring the already familiar stereoscopic illusion into film.[20] Yet the original corpus of films, made mostly by Louis Lumière in 1895-6, have now become a touchstone for the artless capture of 'everyday life', as noted earlier.

The Lumière *vues* would quickly become relics of an early approach to creating filmed subjects, as other producers entered the market. Moreover, that market had not been initially one for 'films', but rather for apparatus. The Cinematograph, Edison's Kinetoscope, and soon Paul's Theatrograph, were all expensive engineered machines, which were either luxury items for rich amateurs, or capable of being operated to enable the recoupment of investment. 'Subjects' to attract paying customers were therefore necessary, but were not initially the goal of the manufacturers. The Lumière organisation soon delegated their production to a number of travelling operators. And when a 'theatrical' market developed, somewhat unexpectedly, the showmen's *programme* became an essential organising structure for these brief 'slices' of contemporary life.

Among the 'inadvertent pioneers', Robert Paul was an electrical instrument maker when he embarked on a moving picture sideline to his main business in 1894. Initially commissioned to produce replicas of Edison's Kinetoscope – the device which had also sparked Antoine Lumière's interest – Paul became first a manufacturer of these viewing machines, then a producer of subjects to support their exhibition.[21] In partnership with a photographer, Birt Acres, during the early months of 1895, they produced at least fourteen films to supplement the stock of Edison titles. In some respects, these cover a similar range of subjects to the Lumières' early production, with a greater emphasis on 'national' events such as the Derby horserace and Oxford and Cambridge boatrace. Four are 'performances', by dancing girls, a 'Lightning cartoonist', boxing kangaroos and dancing bears, and two are 'genre pieces': a comic shoeblack working in the street, and a carpenter's shop – this last no doubt inspired by Edison's blacksmith scene, like the Lumières' *Les Forgerons*. Significantly, all three of these would show the workers enjoying a drink after their labours.

Two of the Paul-Acres Kinetoscope subjects are exceptional, with one enjoying an unusually long career. *Arrest of a Pickpocket* (April 1895) shows a skirmish, as two men catch and hold a struggling pickpocket, and is by far the most violent of all early scenes staged for the moving picture camera.[22] Two months later, waves breaking over a pier at Dover would make a striking sea picture that remained in Paul's catalogue well into 1896 and was acclaimed as the highlight of Edison's first projected show in New York in April of that year.[23]

Unlike many of the Lumière exhibitions, we have no details of Paul's programmes for the early part of 1896 and comparatively few of his films from this period have survived. But one that repays close study, *Traffic on Blackfriars Bridge* (June 1896), was commended in Paul's early lists for showing 'beautiful detail'. And thanks to its survival, we can still appreciate the detail of the vehicles and passers-by that populate it.

In this context, the first question that arises must be whether it presents a spontaneous, unrehearsed view of pedestrian traffic on the bridge. Here again, we find the assumption that an early street film will offer a spontaneous 'record', when to a more sceptical eye the sheer number and rhythm of pedestrians that follow the film's early wagons and omnibuses suggests a more carefully organised scene. No fewer than eleven pedestrians are seen to pass on the near pavement in just 36 seconds, with five looking very deliberately 'to camera', and the other six pointedly looking away.[24] The passers-by also seem to represent a sample of Londoners 'balanced' by age, gender and class. Of the two young boys, one looks confidently to camera, while the second, near the end, is completely immersed in reading an illustrated paper as he walks. A confident woman in dark formal dress walks alone, ignoring the camera, followed by a fashionably dressed couple, of whom the man looks to camera, while his companion ignores it. Next, two 'city types' intersect as they walk in different directions, while an older man appears between them, and is the only figure in the film to stare intently at the camera, looking back over his shoulder.

Looking at the camera is indeed a familiar trope of almost all early films taken in public places, so what is immediately striking about *Blackfriars Bridge* is that so few of its subjects do so – suggesting that they may have been briefed, or 'directed' accordingly. Equally striking is the brisk pace at which all move, apart from the elderly man looking back, and the seeming choreography of entrances and exits. Like the Lumière's *Sortie*, this packs a considerable amount of varied and almost rhythmic bodily movement into a short duration, making it a suitably modernised procession of London 'types' in the tradition dating back to Dickens' *Sketches by 'Boz'*. Unfortunately, we have none of Paul's other street films of this period, except part of *On Westminster Bridge*, which has been reanimated from a Filoscope copy and is now believed to include the figure of Paul himself, wearing a straw boater and looking back over his shoulder towards the camera.[25] If this is correct, it may connect with a 'silent', self-referential dimension of *Blackfriars Bridge*. The camera points north, showing in the background on Victoria Embankment a building with a steeply pitched roof and small spire. This was the then new City of London school, which Paul had attended as part of the first cohort of pupils to use this new building in the 1880s. We might therefore see in the film a discreet homage, through London's dense haze, to his alma mater.

Just as Louis Lumière was discovering the parameters of his new medium in 1895, so Paul was pioneering a new way of representing a traditional subject in *Blackfriars Bridge*. 'London bridge scenes' were already a well-established pictorial genre, invariably emphasising their typical density of traffic, as in Gustav Doré's 1872 image of London Bridge and similar graphic works.[26] A photograph from the 1890s follows this convention, showing London Bridge densely packed with horsedrawn vehicles.[27] Yet Paul's *Blackfriars* favours pedestrians over traffic, and in this it bears some similarity to Gustave Caillebotte's famous *Le Pont de l'Europe* (1878), although without the painting's distinctive exaggerated perspective. What filming brings to the scene is a sharp sense of serial individuation, which is rarely present in paintings or in early street photographs, where a small number of figures give scale to the urban spaces. Here, the procession of passers-by *is* the subject: the old man who looks quizzically towards the camera, the boy lost in his reading, the prosperous couple who cruise past, exuding a sense of entitlement. And this focus on individuals among the urban crowd also occurs in the few other street films we have from 1896, including the Lumière *Street Dance in Drury Lane*, taken in February 1896, when their show opened at the Empire Theatre of Varieties in Leicester Square.[28] Although the girls dancing on a street corner are the ostensible focus, the gathering group of onlookers becomes as much a part of the scene, serving to animate it further. And thanks to recent scholarship, we can identify at least one of these as Félicien Trewey, the impresario responsible for overseeing Lumière presentations in London.

Clearly the first cinematographers understood from established photographic practice that their subjects were more striking when filmed at close range, with relatively few figures in frame. And as stereograph photographers had learned to compose their images 'in depth', with separation between near and distant planes to enhance the stereoscopic effect, so the first film cameramen knew, or quickly learned, that figures needed to be separated from backgrounds, and that diagonal movement across the field enhanced the quasi-stereoscopic effect of animated photography.[29]

We can also see how these lessons soon carried over into filming in more exotic situations, as in a surviving film from the Egyptian series that Paul commissioned in early 1897, *Women Fetching Water from the Nile*, in which a line of women with pitchers on their heads file past.[30] Although we know all too little about how programmes were made up and seen in 1896-7, a rare exception is the printed programme from Paul's nightly show at the Alhambra Music Hall in Leicester Square, dating from August 1896.[31] If this is indeed the sequence of titles, we can make some deductions about what was proving popular among these very short subjects, compiled into a c.20-minute programme. Streets, boating, children, sports events – and the tentative beginning of fiction filmmaking, pioneered in Paul's *The Soldier's Courtship* as early as April 1896, at the suggestion of the Alhambra manager.[32] But although Paul made a decisive shift into fictional, dramatic production from 1898, he did not abandon 'scenes of everyday life', and his catalogues would swell with street scenes from most major cities in Europe, as well as a new hybrid genre of fictionalised films built around incidents staged in the suburban streets around his studio. In the stop-action 'trick film' *An Extraordinary Cab Accident* (1903), a man is apparently knocked down and killed by a cab in a Muswell Hill suburban street.[33] But when passers-by intervene and he is declared dead, the man suddenly 'revives' and runs off with the lady he was originally talking to. Paul's 1903 Christmas catalogue declared this to be 'realistic, exciting, and containing nothing of an objectionable nature'.

III.
We wonder, inevitably and perhaps increasingly amid contemporary digital media developments, what contemporaries made of this new arrival, which has led to several texts from 1896 becoming standard references. One in particular, by the Russian Maxim Gorky, then a journalist and emerging short story writer, has become canonical, widely reprinted.[34] Shorn of its circumstantial and cultural context, this is no less difficult to interpret than Woolf's essay of thirty years later.

Gorky framed his report on witnessing a film show at the annual Nizhni-Novgorod fair with an elaborate comparison between the monochrome images shown in silence and contemporary Symbolist painting, like a 'visit to the kingdom of shadows'. The Paris street scene that Gorky describes must be the Lumière view of the *Champs-Elysees*, dating from April 1896, which has children playing in the foreground, and pedestrians threading through the carriages.[35] But what has attracted most attention over the years is his vivid description of a train that 'speeds straight at you… [likely to] turn you into a ripped sack of lacerated flesh and splintered bones'. Even though Gorky admits that this is but a 'train of shadows', which stops and discharges its convivial passengers, his melodramatic imagining of a train crashing into the auditorium has served to feed the myth that early spectators were alarmed by *Train Entering the Station at La Ciotat*.[36]

Almost certainly the film Gorky described seeing in Nizhny-Novgorod: *Champs-Élysées*. Lumière cat. 151 (1896).

Gorky's highly fictionalised account of a 'first encounter' ended with a lurid evocation of likely pornographic subjects to come, inspired by the show's setting in a reproduction of a Parisian café concert known to operate as a brothel. It may be the least authentic of all early responses to film, despite satisfying later expectations of a dramatic epiphany. More typical were the two Paris newspaper notices of 30 December 1895, which hailed 'the illusion of real life' (*Le Radical*) and 'life itself, movement taken from life' (*La Poste*), the latter adopting a phrase commonly used of artists 'working from life'.[37] However, an early 1896 response by the Paris theatre director Jules Claretie made an interesting distinction.[38] 'When the scene is staged [*composé*], for example when two friends quarrel over a newspaper article, the sense of absolute truthfulness, of reality, disappears'. The conclusion he drew is that 'animated photography must be taken from life without posing' [*pris sur la vie sans pose*]. 'With any sign of preparation, goodbye to the illusion'.

This issue of creating an illusion of everyday life would continue to resonate through both early responses to animated photography and the beginnings of explicitly 'staged' prod-uction. An essay, published in Britain only weeks after moving pictures made their public debut in London in February 1896, predicted the prospects for animated photography, describing it as showing 'life moving without purpose, without beauty, with no better impulse than a foolish curiosity... it proves the complete despair of modern realism'.[39] But this still-unidentified critic was proved wrong. Film would not join forces with the naturalism that 'O. Winter' despised in art: it would quickly develop a narrative grammar and generic structure of its own, cross-fertilised by the contemporary popular arts of photography, cartooning and stage performance. 'Everyday life' would continue to be a staple element, but 'with a different reality from that which we perceive in daily life', as Woolf put it. What might be called a heightened, intensified, or more broadly, stylised reality. And the difference between lived and screen realities would quickly become a comic subject for Robert Paul in his *The Countryman and the Cinematograph* (1901), with its smock-clad yokel cavorting before a screen, attempting to interact with a succession of filmed scenes before the screen collapses and reveals a projector and projectionist.[40]

I have suggested that that the 'reality' or 'everyday life' long admired in early films from the 'demonstration phase' of cinema was selected and constructed, or staged, according to prevailing models in photography and social reportage. 'Everyday life' was already a popular genre in the literary and pictorial arts of the *fin de siècle*; and moving pictures were able to *remediate* its appeal in a technologically novel fashion. Jay Bolter and Richard Grusin proposed the concept of remediation to explain how a recurrent pattern in modern culture has been new media 'reforming or improving' their predecessors.[41] Instead of 'fixing stillness', *La Poste* was quick to note, photography could now 'perpetuate the image of movement'. The discourse that greeted animated or moving photography in 1895-6 is replete with references to images that 'come to life' (Gorky), encouraged by the Lumière presentation trope of starting each film as a still image which then begins to move. But all early moving picture media served to create what Bolter and Grusin term 'transparent immediacy', or the capacity to make viewers 'forget the presence of the medium... and believe [they are] in the presence of the objects of representation'.[42]

While the testimonies of 'first viewers' remain valuable, they also need to be understood in the fuller contexts in which they appeared. To abstract them as fragments of 'evidence' is to ignore what in a different context the art historian Michael Baxendall called 'the period eye', referring to the visual skills and shared culture that shaped contemporary responses in 15th-century Italian painting.[43] We may see in a gallery today the 'same' Botticelli or Bellini painting that its original viewers saw, but Baxendall's point is that there is much cultural context we lack – however much we may feel the images 'take us back' to the Florentine or Venetian Quattrocento. The Lumière workers leaving the Lyons factory and the pedestrians crossing Blackfriars

Bridge do indeed give us a vivid sense of connection with particulars of the world of the 1890s, all the more so due to the considerable interval that now separates us from that time. But they were never naïve 'slices of everyday life'; and the expectations we bring to our viewing, on very different apparatus from that of 1896 and in very different worlds, are inevitably far removed from those of their original creators and audiences. Crucially, these films were once new and exciting – as demonstrations of virtual reality may appear today – while for us they are now quaint and nostalgic, subsumed in categories such as the 'Belle Epoque' and 'Victorian London', as evidenced by the quantity of online commentary and reaction that accompanies them.

Perhaps Benjamin's distinctive technique for dealing with the evidence of the past, in assembling the materials for his never to be completed Arcades project, or in the memory images assembled for his *Berlin Childhood circa 1900*, may point towards ways of better understanding 'early film in the digital era'.[44] In his chapter on the Kaiserpanorama in the latter work, Benjamin made clear that this automated stereo-viewing attraction was already an anachronism when he encountered it as a child and immersed himself in its images of distant places. He evokes the fantasy of believing he might have visited the Cours Mirabeau in Aix, and also the vain hope that one could exhaust the splendours of each stereograph before the machinery cut it short. His delicate dialectic of mediation and memory seems highly relevant. We have the luxury of being able to 'visit' Lyons and London repeatedly, for just 40 seconds. But we also need to bear in mind the strictures of both Benjamin and Baxandall on believing that this offers any simple *vademecum* or time travel.

Based on a chapter in Francois Penz, Janina Schupp, eds., *The Everyday in Visual Culture: Slices of Lives* (Routledge, 2022).

9.
'Something to Look At': On the Disappearing History of Lantern Slides

This collection of essays began life with a three-day con-ference held at the elegant Bloomsbury Square premises of the German Historical Institute London,[1] a short distance from the British Museum and the Warburg Institute. For me, it proved to be a location conducive to thinking about the origins of 'public enlightenment', many of which have their roots in this area of London. First developed in the late 17th century, when the modern city's topography and institutions were taking shape, Bloomsbury Square would later house a generation of enlightened patrons, who included John Radcliffe, benefactor of Oxford's Radcliffe Library, and Hans Sloane, whose collection became the basis of the British Museum when this was launched just round the corner at Montagu House in 1759.

The current British Museum is one of London's – indeed the world's – great educational institutions, but how many of its millions of visitors realise that long before the internet, much of its outreach work was carried on through loaning lantern slides for lectures?[2] In the case of the Warburg Institute, which came to London in 1933 to escape the Nazi regime that would have destroyed Aby Warburg's great collection, this included 'thousands of slides' along with the books that are often regarded as its main resource.[3] How many today realise the revolutionary role played by photography and lantern slides in Warburg's work on 'illustrating the processes by which the memory of the past affects a culture'?[4]

Is it fanciful to think of Bloomsbury, with its modern concentration of universities, museums and specialist institutes, as haunted by the ghosts of lanterns and slides that once were the principal means of disseminating visual infor-mation to audiences? Throughout the later 19th and early 20th centuries, these slides were 3¼ inch square glass, and projected by lanterns once called 'magi' and later 'optical', as the new educators and propagandists sought to throw off associations with the childish (or occult) history of the lantern. For a century, such lanterns and their associated slides held sway, until the rise of reversal film after the Second World War, and the adoption of 35mm slides during the 1950s, pushed lantern slides into obsolescence. As a timeline on the history of visual resources in academia notes:

> 1952. All camera film is now triacetate based, paving the way for widespread adoption of 35mm film in both amateur and academic markets.
> 1952+. American faculty widely divided in their allegiances to lantern slides for their clarity or to 35mm slides for their ease of production and transport to class.
> Huge debates begin about whether 35mm colour film is stable enough for adoption and whether the loss of clarity will ruin the teaching of art history. Younger faculty adopt 35mm film, while older faculty prefer lantern slides.[5]

'Thousands of slides' accompanied 60,000 books to the library of the Warburg Institute, as refounded after its evacuation from Hamburg to London, and now part of the University of London.

The rise of 35mm slides, combined with the pre-programming and speed of transition offered by the Kodak Carousel after 1964, quickly consigned not only the older large-format lantern but even straight-tray 35mm projectors to obsolescence. For another 40 years the 35mm slideshow, with its increasingly sophisticated transitions and capacity to be automated, held sway, until displaced by data projectors and digital 'slides' in the early years of the new millennium.

Part of Aby Warburg's unfinished 'Mnemosyne Atlas', attempting to map the 'afterlife of antiquity' with photographs, and which has itself only survived in photographic form.

This progression is a familiar story for older teachers and lantern scholars, ever keen to stress the continuity of projection practices, although I suspect it remains less widely recognised, or even known, in academic circles that continue such practices. This may be due mainly to neither projection nor the slideshow being considered 'media'.[6] But I would suggest it also reflects an entrenched suspicion of technology in education, which persisted through much of the 20th century, in spite of mounting evidence of benefits from psychologists and progressive educationists. 'Visual aids' were 'often looked down upon by traditionalists as benefiting only the less able', or in some ill-defined way 'coming between' teacher and pupil. A report from Britain's National Education Association in 1909 which cast doubt on 'the value of bioscope pictures in education' based its argument on describing how 'a good teacher [...] regulates his pace and the fullness with which he treats his subject', adding that 'this is possible when using pictures, diagrams or even lantern slides'.[7] That 'even' hints as a residual unease with the lantern, already widely used in education, which may stem from a still older iconoclastic tradition of doubting the image against the word.

A lantern slide from a *Pilgrim's Progress* set.

Despite this, however, progressive thought about both evangelism and education had long recognised the power of images. As Annemarie McAllister has noted, John Bunyan's view of the evangelistic advantage of 'Eyegate' over 'Eargate' was well known to Band of Hope activists.[8] The same recognition is present in John Locke's 1693 essay *Some Thoughts Concerning Education*, a cornerstone of subsequent educational theory and prescription. Discussing how to encourage children's early reading, Locke recommended Aesop's fables, noting that 'if his Aesop has pictures in it, it will entertain him much the better'.[9] Two centuries later, in the heyday of the lantern, the critic and art historian John Ruskin would preach the doctrine of visual education in his own teaching and voluminous writings. Ruskin wanted to make art the core of a new regime of education and of morality. While his emphasis was on drawing as a tutelary discipline, supported by studying reproductions of great artworks, he also mentions the most important optical instruments of the mid-century, the microscope and the lantern, in this typically rhetorical passage: 'The vast extent of the advertising frescos of London, duly refreshed into brighter and larger fresco by its billstickers, cannot somehow sufficiently entertain the popular eyes [...] and I find my charitable friends inviting the children, whom the streets educate into vicious misery, to entertainments of scientific vision, in microscope or magic lantern, thus giving them something to look at, such as it is – fleas mostly; and the stomachs of various vermin; and people with their heads cut off and set on again; – still, *something* to look at'.[10]

For Ruskin, even the knockabout imagery of the popular lantern show was preferable to the 'corrupted modernity of the streets'.[11] Clearly familiar with the magic lantern from childhood, he invokes it as a common experience in one of his stories for children, in which the moon is compared to 'the biggest disc of light ever thrown by a magic lantern'.[12]

Lanterns and slides were omnipresent at the time Ruskin was writing; and they would remain so until the rise of 35mm equipment pushed them first into basements, before finally making an inglorious exit to junk shops and dustbins. Their disappearance, and later resurrection as exotic objects of wonder, has perhaps created something of a mystique. The issue, however, is surely not the lantern apparatus so much as the many and varied uses to which it was put in what Charles Musser has identified as 'screen practice'. As I have argued elsewhere, the 'hardware' of optical instruments certainly matters, and may tell us much about how various devices were conceived and perceived, but recognition of this runs the risk of fetishising the apparatus and endowing it with mysterious properties held to constitute 'the medium', which can only be properly understood as a set of practices which make use of technologies, but are not necessarily defined by them.[13] These essays make a real contribution to shifting attention away from the apparatus *per se*, towards evoking a range of practices that reflected the moral and political concerns of the 'long *fin de siècle*'. These ranged from traditional children's entertainments and Christmas shows which – as Eifler and Henkes show – moved from slides to film during this period, to the popular balladry of George Sims revealed by Joss Marsh and David Francis, and the surprisingly extensive political uses of both slides and film by Britain's Conservative Party, as demonstrated by Stephen Bottomore.[14] All these are essentially *social* practices, which made use of available, as well as novel, presentation technologies.

Does this sound like heresy to anyone brought up on Marshall McLuhan's motto 'the medium is the message', or on 'apparatus theory' and the passionate debates about filmic specificity that first erupted in the 1920s and resurfaced in the 1960s and '70s?[15] Only if we regard the medium or the apparatus in either a reductively literal or an extravagantly analogical sense. Certainly there were affective and material qualities associated with large-scale lantern shows, just as there must have been with the mixed lantern and kinematograph shows that took place for at least twenty years from 1895 until the late 1910s, and with various stages of the evolution of 'all film' presentation. But rather than isolate some few characteristics of these as 'defining the medium', which was a preoccupation of some phases in film and media theory, it would be more productive to locate what we know about such practices in the much larger 'hidden history' of non-theatrical exhibition, which film scholars such as Gorham Kindem, Dan Streible and Greg Waller have been exploring for some time.[16] And what can be traced across many of these essays is evidence of a welcome turn towards the de-centring of apparatus in media history, accompanied by a corresponding social or ethnographic turn.

In short, what matters is the overall communication context, whether this is the pre-1900 campaigning lantern shows of William Palmer in England or Jacob Riis in America, as discussed by Bottomore and Yochelson, or the large children's film shows staged by the Salvation Army, or pioneering uses of film for health education as documented by Dalquist. Context, I would argue, is crucial, which involves trying to understand the expectations of presenters and audiences, as well as the material framing of the presentation. What was shown, in terms of identifiable slides or films, turns out to be less significant than traditional 'title-oriented' history would assume.

It has been claimed, with some justice, that the intensive study of early film that began in the 1980s helped bring about a major shift in the focus of film studies, challenging the dominance of an often ahistorical 'theory' and reinstating interest in material and contextual factors within a wider historical framework. From the evidence of lantern history, as it is emerging, the direction of influence may have reversed. Scholarship trying to deal with the fast-changing profusion of multi-platform and mobile media focuses on convergence rather than difference, while calling into question any clear distinction between media based on their technology, and is above all concerned with the user experience. What we *do* with contemporary media has made McLuhan's other famous claim about 'media as extensions of ourselves' an obvious field of exploration – to text, to Google, to satnav is literally to extend our capability.

So the challenge to historians of the seismic media-accompanied revolution of c.1880-1914 should be to investi-gate more fully media *experience* rather than its technology, in the spirit of media ethnography, which aims to study how media are used and navigated, whether historically or contemporaneously.¹⁷ But at the same time, we need to challenge the imminent erasure from history of 150 years of modern analogue recording and projection systems, and rescue their surviving artefacts. It is surely ironic that the British Museum proudly displays the fragments of early inscriptions which are our link with antiquity. If the mighty CERN subatomic particle research centre in Switzerland can commemorate how one of its staff, Tim Berners-Lee, created the World Wide Web in 1989, should not the British Museum display at least an Optical Lantern and early Theatrograph projector, to remind its visitors of the continuity between this 'intermediate' technology and the electronic media of today? And if the Museum had accepted Robert Paul's offer of his early 'animated photographs' in 1896, Britain would have had the world's first film archive.¹⁸

A version of this formed the Afterword to Ludwig Vogl-Bienek, Richard Crangle eds., *Screen Culture and the Social Question 1880-1914* (KINtop Studies in Early Cinema/John Libbey, 2014).

10.
A 'Stagey Marvel':
The Genealogy of an Early Trick Film

It is hardly surprising that much of the existing literature on trick films relates to Georges Méliès, considering his pre-eminence in this genre. Yet Méliès was by no means the only producer of trick-based subjects around 1900, and even if he created the market for such entertainments and effectively set the standard for others, differences of style and technique soon emerged. The recent discovery that two fragmentary versions of a 1901 Robert Paul film, *The Magic Sword*, allow the complete film to be reconstituted has prompted further consideration of the 'trick' genre, in terms of its genealogy and national variations.[1] Why, after all, should we care that the final scene is now restored unless the film's text has some cultural, as distinct from merely technical, significance?

Paul Hammond was probably the first to explore such issues, albeit within the French tradition, in his pioneering article 'Georges, this is Charles,' which compared in some detail Méliès' *The Bewitched Trunk* (*Le Coffre enchanté*, 1904) and a Pathé trick film directed by Gaston Velle, *Japonaiserie*, dating from the same year.[2] While these two films both feature conjurors as hosts, performing elaborate variations on what is in essence stage magic, Hammond detected significant differences of approach. 'Méliès: hand over eye. Pathé/Velle: eye over hand. Méliès: the eye in the service of the hand; the eye does not see one thing changed into another, it is fooled by the substitution trick. Pathé/Velle: the hand in the service of the eye; the hand is seen to cause the disappearance and reappearance of the image, it knocks the brick wall/screen over'.

More generally, Hammond saw the trick film as 'a genre ill-equipped to push film language on... an involuted form'. Admittedly, he was writing before the 'cinema of attractions' paradigm shift, which put an end to loose talk of 'primitive' cinema. But he was also writing as an early Méliès connoisseur and champion of non-narrative aspects of film. Six years later, one of the authors of the 'attractions' concept, André Gaudreault, argued against a simplistic dichotomy between 'theatricality and 'narrativity' in early film, insisting that Méliès was committed to a concept which he termed 'trickality', in which narrative is present, but secondary to the conjugation of tricks.[3] More recently, on the other side of this divide, Elizabeth Ezra sought to rehabilitate Méliès further as a true filmmaker by refuting the 'myths' that his work consisted largely of fairy tales and fantasies, presented in a theatrical style with little or no narrative structure.[4] My concern here is not with interpretations of Méliès but with the historical category of the trick film, and with extracting this from debates about its most famous practitioner in order to shed fresh light on its other exponent, Robert Paul.

Paul is of course closely linked with Méliès in a kind of zigzag pattern which must have been at least partly competitive. In April 1896, after the Lumières refused to sell him their Cinématographe, Paul supplied the Frenchman with his first projector, which Méliès then used as the basis of his first camera.[5] Paul and Méliès launched their catalogues of films for sale at roughly the same time later that year; and in 1897 Méliès built his first glasshouse studio outside central Paris in Montreuil – a step which Paul would emulate in 1899, when he built a studio and factory in the London suburb of Muswell Hill, at which point Méliès enlarged his studio to approximately the same scale.

By 1901, both Paul and Méliès had reached their highest level of output, with the former releasing some 58 titles, of which fourteen might be considered trick-based, while all but a few of the latter's 27 productions exploited his established reputation in this genre. For Paul, trick effects were clearly both a proven attraction in their own right and a means of enhancing different kinds of film. In Paul's 1901 catalogue, trick techniques contribute to temperance tracts, to his new line of 'song films', to conjuring displays, physical comedies, and to a number of more ambitious 'trick' and effects-based subjects, including *The Haunted Curiosity Shop* and *The Magic Sword*, which latter was Paul's longest film to date, at 180 feet.

Clearly seen as an achievement, this was given two full pages in Paul's 1901 catalogue and described as 'a sumptuously produced extravaganza in three dissolving scenes, with many novel and beautiful trick effects'. The catalogue went on to claim that 'the facts of the actors and costumes being Old English, together with the original nature of the plot, cannot fail to please English-speaking audiences, who have become weary of foreign pictures of this kind'. The only obvious 'foreign' competitor in this genre would have been Méliès, so Paul was apparently playing a patriotic card by offering indigenous fantasy. But how exactly is *The Magic Sword* English?

TRICK CINEMATOGRAPHY: THE MYSTERY OF "THE MAGIC SWORD" EXPLAINED.
Scene A was photographed first on one film. The second film B carried the pictures of the ogre, photographed against a neutral background, the camera being brought very close to the figure. When the two negatives were superimposed the startling effect, C, was printed on the positive.

Illustrations explaining the trick-work in *The Magic Sword*, from Frederick Talbot's *Moving Pictures: How They Are Made and Worked*, London: Heinemann, 1912.

Subtitled 'a Mediaeval Mystery', the film's narrative is surprisingly complex, if not downright cryptic. With the help of the detailed catalogue synopsis, it can be outlined as follows. The first scene is set on a moonlit castle battlement, where a knight has a romantic tryst with his beloved. As they are about to embrace, a ghost appears (described rather obscurely in the catalogue as 'a ghost of the knight') and distracts the knight, while a witch also appears and tries to capture the lady. The knight fights off the witch, who flies away on her broomstick, but the ghost appears again and draws the knight away, which allows a giant ogre to reach over the battlement and seize the lady, carrying her off 'through the darkening clouds'. As the knight despairs, a good fairy appears and gives him a flaming sword to help him in his search.

This scene dissolves to a rocky cave entrance, with a steaming cauldron in the centre foreground. The witch appears with her captive, but before the knight arrives, manages to turn her into a second witch. To prevent the knight realising what has happened, the witch creates a series of spectacular effects. A winged cherub emerges from the cauldron, followed by a large head blowing smoke, and when the knight strikes this with his magic sword, it become a skull, which then transforms into two ghostly forms, which rise and float towards the spectator 'until they fill the entire picture'. The knight wields his sword, but the witch apparently turns herself into a beautiful girl, while the second witch (actually his lady love) tries to make him realise who she is. The sword allows her to change back to her original state, but when the knight drops it to embrace her, the witch seizes it and is about to attack the pair, at which point the good fairy suddenly reappears and, disarming her, turns her into a roll of carpet – which becomes the vehicle for the lovers to 'float upwards and out of sight'. The cave is then shattered and blown up by an enormous explosion, after which the third scene appears. This shows a group banqueting in front of a castle which the catalogue identifies as the father and mother of the lost girl with their guests. Abruptly the carpet and its passengers 'drop from the clouds among them', and 'a scene of general rejoicing ensues, finishing with a striking and artistic tableau, over which the good fairy is seen hovering'.

An immediate response is to wonder how easy this would this have been for contemporary viewers to follow. However, perhaps a more useful question to ask is what kind of attention or comprehension it might have invited. Eleven years after its appearance, Frederick Talbot described it as 'one of the best and most successful trick films Paul ever produced,' suggesting that it appealed to the grown-ups because of the astonishing effects produced, and to the children 'for the reason that it provided an intimate glimpse of fairyland with its giants, witches, good and bad fairies'.[6] The fact that Talbot goes on to paraphrase the original catalogue account, and acknowledges Paul's help with his book, including illustrations showing separate elements involved in the 'ogre shot', might not inspire confidence in his impartiality. But, correspondingly, it does indicate that Paul still regarded *The Magic Sword* as a landmark, even shortly after he had left the film business. A quarter of a century later, Paul would himself evoke 'this fairy story, lasting three minutes on screen, as an example of what was done at the beginning of this century to pack the maximum of movement into 180 feet of film'; and as 'an example of the position of the art as regards trick photography'.[7]

The trick effects were indeed at the forefront of film technique in 1901, and two specific effects may well have been introduced for the first time.[8] The giant ogre, described as 'no less than fifteen feet tall', is of course a separate image of an actor 'photographed with a short-focus lens from a point nearer the object than the [other] characters in the scene' and against a black background, who reaches over the wall covered with black cloth, later combined with the primary image of the knight and lady on the battlement. But this effect had not yet been widely, if at all, used for such purposes. Early in the following year, Méliès would develop a variation in which an inset image, combined with one of normal scale, is seen becoming larger, and use this in no less than four films, ranging from *La bataillon élastique* to *Nain et géant*.⁹ This is referred to as a new effect [*un effet inédit*] in his American catalogue, but he does not seem to have used it in 1901. The second effect claimed as original by Paul was used to simulate the witch's ride. According to Talbot, this involved the camera lens being raised and lowered 'independently of the film itself', with the actor merely moving across the black-covered floor of the stage' in order to simulate 'the action of riding through space in the traditional manner'.¹⁰ In addition to these, the film uses a full complement of stop-action and superimposition effects for the fairy, witches and assorted supernatural apparitions. A further novel effect in *The Magic Sword* is not strictly the result of stop-action or double printing, but perhaps deserves to be considered as innovative as was the linking of two disjunct spaces in Paul's *Come Along, Do!* of 1898. The transition from the witch's cave to the castle grounds is narrativised as an explosion, and is figured on screen by means of a brief close-up, dissolved into and out of smouldering rocks.

The Magic Sword certainly packs movement and spectacle into its short compass. But what of the much-vaunted 'English' character? Paul's catalogue places it in a category of Novel Trick and Effect Films', which also included *Chinese Magic Extraordinary*, *The Countryman's First Sight of the Animated Pictures*, *Artistic Creation* and *The Cheese Mites*. Of these, *Chinese Magic* and *Artistic Creation* both centred on magician figures who perform a series of stop-action tricks; while the other films use inset double-exposure 'matte' effects which play off an innocent protagonist's bewilderment. *The Magic Sword*, however, aspires to a more complete entertainment, almost like a compressed pantomime, and it was released in the run-up to the Christmas season, with the magician Nevil Maskelyne's praise of it as 'the finest trick subject he had yet seen' featured in Paul's Era advertisement.¹¹

Maskelyne was well known as the proprietor and main attraction of 'England's home of mystery', The Egyptian Hall on Piccadilly, where since 1873 he had presented an eclectic programme of conjuring. mechanical novelties, and dramatic sketches which involved illusion in the representation – and debunking – of the supernatural. 'Living' or 'Animated' photographs formed part of the Egyptian Hall's programme from March 1896, when Paul's Theatrograph was introduced by one of Maskelyne's collaborators, the magician David Devant. Although Maskelyne's distinctive form of entertainment would famously inspire Méliès when he took over the Théâtre Robert-Houdin in Paris in 1888, the latter would go much further with film. While Maskelyne presented mainly actualities up to the end of his career at the Egyptian Hall in 1904, Méliès began producing filmed versions of his stage magic acts and tableaux, and using these to replace live performance in the evenings from September 1897.

The more direct influence of Maskelyne's 'magical comediettas' on Paul can be seen in such titles as *Upside Down; or, The Human Flies*, *The Waif and the Wizard* and even as late as *The Medium Exposed* (1907).[12] But *The Magic Sword* seems to draw on other sources. Katherine Singer Kovacs has shown how the French popular theatre tradition of the *féerie* provided Méliès with many of his 'techniques, plots and themes'.[13] As the century progressed, the *féerie* developed from its poetic beginnings as *melodrame-féerie* towards *vaudeville-féerie*, with interpolated humour and song, and a growing reliance on elaborate stage tricks and spectacle. All of this fed into Méliès' cine-dramaturgy, so that allegorical figures, chorus girls and acrobats quite naturally mingle in his films, whatever their ostensible subject.

But what were the distinctively English traditions, other than Maskelyne's magic theatre, that nourished Paul's excursion into fantasy narratives? To unearth these requires some archaeology of what have long been despised or little-known genres within Victorian entertainment. If we start from the premise that *The Magic Sword* most closely resembles a *féerie*, then its English ancestry would lie in the series of 'fairy extravaganzas' devised by James Robinson Planché between 1836-40 for Eliza Vestris, a gifted singer and actor who was also licensee of the Olympic Theatre in London. Faced with competition from other companies offering classical burlesques, Vestris asked her regular author for something different, which led Planché to adapt his own translation of a *mélo-féerie* he had previously seen in Paris in 1820. The success of *Riquet with the Tuft*, originally based on a fairytale by Charles Perrault, led to a series of such pieces, moving to the Theatre Royal Haymarket in the 1840s, and eventually feeding into the Christmas pantomimes at Covent Garden by the following decade. Planché had started from a scholarly interest in the French fairy tale, but as a practical (and impecunious) man of the theatre, he grafted on features needed to appeal to the emerging middle-class theatre audience of the early Victorian era. 'His extravaganzas featured gorgeous special effects, excellent singing and dancing, and eye-catching costumes [as well as] abundant topical references and puns'.[14]

Despite the wide success of these – Queen Victoria was an admirer, and W. S. Gilbert an imitator – Planché's work was long dismissed by British theatre historians for its literary shortcomings and remains difficult to visualise or evoke. However, a trace of his extravaganzas has been preserved in the toy theatre tradition which is kept alive today by Pollock's Toy Theatres.[15] One title in the Green's Juvenile Drama series is *The Castle of Otranto, or Harlequin and the Giant Helmet*, which is dated 1841 and undoubtedly based on Planché's otherwise unpublished opening segment for the 1840 Theatre Royal Covent Garden pantomime.[16] Thanks to this edition, with its cut-out characters and settings, we can get some idea of the heterogeneous world of what was billed as 'a new romantic comic pantomime'. The starting point may have been Horace Walpole's original 'Gothic story' *The Castle of Otranto*,[17] but after its opening scenes the piece bears little resemblance to its alleged source, offering instead a series of set pieces, including a Ruined Monastery, where the Spirit of Romance holds court; a courtyard where the juvenile lead is imprisoned under the giant helmet; a Gothic Hall with speaking portraits; a Hall of Chivalry, with the Spirit of Pantomime; then a series of London scenes, set in Trafalgar Square, Furnished Lodgings and a China Warehouse and Grocer's Shop; ending with a grand finale in the Palace of Neptune. Essentially, it is a pantomime, with the traditional *commedia dell'arte* characters supplemented by Gothic figures, spirits and some comic contemporaries, where speed, spectacle and a number of 'tricks' substitute for any coherent narrative.

Characters for *Jack the Giant Killer*, Pollocks Toy Theatres.

Tricks were plentiful in both *féeries* and fairy extravaganzas, where they evolved from being a means to represent the supernatural to becoming an end in themselves. The French architect and theatre historian Georges Moynet, writing in 1893, already sounded nostalgic for the days when mechanical ingenuity was paramount: 'Included under the general heading of trick-work are all changes in the appearance of objects which take place before the eyes of the audience. The more unexpected the change is, the more successful the trick... A whole setting could be a trick one [if] its appearance is able to be changed instantly without the audience seeing how... A costume might also be a trick one, it can disappear in full view of the audience, leaving the actor quite differently dressed'.[18]

Interestingly, the sprung trapdoor used in such tricks was known in France as a *trappe anglaise* and the most famous practitioners of such acrobatic trick theatre were an English troupe, the Hanlon-Lees. Moynet characterised the national differences: 'Such trick-work is traditional in English pantomime. If our own spectacular theatre does not use these effects quite so much, it is because we do not have the actor-tumblers who seem to be a British speciality... An actor who can sing, play the fiddle, perform death-defying leaps and falls, who is in fact good at every-thing, except perhaps acting!'

As early as the 1830s, pantomime had become a staple of the English theatre during the post-Christmas period. Until around 1850, Harlequin remained at least the nominal protagonist, although usually joined to an historical or fairy tale, as in Harlequin and Good Queen Bess or Harlequin and Cinderella.[19] Originally, the transformation was the moment in traditional pantomime when the actors took off their disguises to reveal themselves as the familiar commedia dell'arte characters. But as Victorian pantomime became increasingly lavish, transformations of scene rather than character became an acknowledged feature of the entertainment in their own right, with the scenery painter William Beverley emerging as their leading exponent between the 1850s and 1880s.[20] This trend was accelerated by Augustus Harris, as manager of Drury Lane from the mid-1880s, who added to Beverley's visual spectacle lavish costuming and growing numbers of performers, reaching over five hundred in his *Forty Thieves* of 1886.

Such massive shows combining traditional pantomime with music hall elements would remain popular well into the 20th century, but Harris also had a shrewd understanding of the voracious appetite for novelty that he had helped create. Paul recounts in his 1936 memoir how, on the morning after his first Theatrograph demonstration at the Royal Institution, in February 1896, Harris 'telegraphed me to meet him at breakfast, and proposed to me the installation of a projector at Olympia on sharing terms'. Harris had recently seen animated photographs in Paris and, 'despite believing their appeal would be short-lived, was keen to secure them for the spectacle he also managed at Olympia in West London'. The image of Olympia's various entertainments, ranging from tightrope walkers to a ladies orchestra, was more middle class than the music hall, and well suited to presenting Paul's Theatrograph as 'the most wonderful scientific marvel of the age'.

A giant helmet falls from the sky into a castle in Horace Walpole's early Gothic novel, *The Castle of Otranto* (1764).

Combining spectacle, novelty and 'improvement' had become an important aim in Victorian society, following in the vein sanctioned by the Queen's consort, Prince Albert. So another distinctive strand of the genealogy of Paul's trick films lay in the history of the Royal Polytechnic Institution and its celebrated Magic Lantern shows.

Like the Egyptian Hall, the Polytechnic was a unique London venue which came to define a genre of entertainment. Launched in 1838, in Regent Street, the institution quickly gained royal assent and was visited by the Prince Consort and Queen Victoria during the early years, when it hosted photographic and scientific displays. From the 1840s onwards, and especially after John Henry Pepper became lessee in 1854, the Polytechnic became famous for its elaborate lantern shows, using up to six lanterns, together with sound effects and live speech and music. The Polytechnic's large format lantern slides were specially painted by the leading specialists of the time;

and its 'dissolving views', as slides were cross-faded, achieved a visual impact unmatched until the later development of moving pictures.[21] However, despite the success of its annual Christmas show, the Polytechnic's economy was always precarious, and it closed around 1830, before becoming the site of a new philanthropic institution in 1882, and soon after, as the Regent Street Polytechnic, the site of the first Lumière Cinématographe presentation in London.

'The Spectre Drama at the Polytechnic Institution', *Illustrated London News*, 1 May 1863.

At the height of its fame in the 1860s, the Polytechnic's most popular show demonstrated a stage illusion known as 'Pepper's Ghost,' in which a spectral figure appears on stage amid real actors and setting, having been reflected from below by an invisible angled glass sheet. For some contemporary spectators of *The Magic Sword*, its ghostly figures and demonic imagery would have seemed close to the tradition of the early magic lantern Phantasmagoria, while the scenic transformations would have recalled the Royal Polytechnic's dissolving views, as well as the elaborate transformations of the contemporary pantomime. When, after a spectacular (in filmic terms) explosion, the Good Fairy transports the rescued knight and lady to the banquet before her parents' castle, and all dance, this achieves in miniature the effect of a pantomime finale. The idiom, in short, would have been thoroughly familiar, even if the medium was new.

But what did contemporary spectators think of such work? One kind of explanation no doubt lies in the concept of 'remediation', proposed by Grusin and Boulter, whereby new media gain acceptance by re-mediating their forerunners, showing how something familiar can be done 'better' by novel means.[22] Another form of explanation, not incompatible, would point towards the 'juvenile' or nostalgic quality of early films such as *The Magic Sword*. In the absence of any truly evocative recorded responses to early films, the toy theatre may serve as a useful intertext. A memoir by the pioneer English filmmaker George Pearson makes this linkage, when he recalls his childhood discovery of 'the pantomime's transformation scene [as] a miracle of magic', leading to the cherished present of a Pollock's Toy Theatre.[23] Later, going to buy a new sheet of characters for the theatre takes him to Lambeth Walk, and to his first revelatory encounter with 'living pictures' in a 'derelict greengrocer's shop serving as a penny gaff.' The best account of the toy theatre's peculiar appeal, however, is Robert Louis Stevenson's famous essay 'A Penny Plain, Twopence Coloured', with its loving inventory of titles once owned – and frank acknowledgement of their brief, poignant appeal: 'The purchase and the first half-hour at home was the summit. Thenceforth the interest declined by little and little. The fable, as set forth in the playbook, proved to be not worthy of the scenes and characters: what fable would not?'[24]

Stevenson admitted that 'as literature these dramas did not much appeal to me', and he wrote candidly of the 'long-drawn disenchantment of an actual performance' with the cut-out figures. But the appeal of the toy theatre lay deeper: 'The stagey is its generic name; but it is an old, insular, home-bred staginess; not French, domestically British; not of today, but smacking of O. Smith, Fitzball, and the great age of melodrama; a peculiar fragrance haunting it; uttering its unimportant message in a tone of voice that has the charm of fresh antiquity'.[25] Here, perhaps, is a better evocation of the kind of pleasure that *The Magic Sword* might have offered in 1901 than any we have from the literature of cinema, capturing early film's 'remedial' fascination with a culture that was already slipping into the past.

Three years later, J. M. Barrie's *Peter Pan* would decisively renovate this tradition in the English theatre, while Paul would continue to make a wide variety of trick-based films through the remaining eight years of his career as a producer, oscillating between nostalgic magic theatre and pantomime subjects, and a knowing engagement with the modern world – like cinema itself.

First appeared as '*The Magic Sword*: Genealogy of an English Trick Film', *Film History*, 16.2, 2004.

11.
Now You See It...
From 'Tricks' to 'Effects'

The replacement of a cinema that showcased, and to a large extent depended on 'tricks' by one which privileged spectacle and narrative, has long been the master-narrative of early cinema history. It is closely bound up with claims about the growing sophistication of films and their audiences between about 1907 and 1913, and the corresponding growth of 'feature films'. An early theorisation of this process was provided by Tom Gunning's much-quoted 1986 article on 'the cinema of attractions'.[1] Here Gunning defined attractions as 'directly solicit[ing] spectator attention, inciting visual curiosity, and supplying pleasure through an exciting spectacle'. Although the term 'attraction' was borrowed from Sergei Eisenstein's use of it in his famous formula 'the montage of attractions' (dating from 1924), Gunning explained that in the context of early film entertainment it could refer to a unique event 'of interest in itself' when filmed, or to a range of 'cinematic manipulations' involving trick effects.

But even if such 'attractions' would reappear in avant-garde film of the 1920s, especially in France and the Soviet Union, Gunning maintains that they largely disappeared in the period 1907-13, which 'represents the true *narrativisation* of the cinema, culminating in the appearance of feature films which radically revised the variety format' – a format where film-attractions had functioned like variety acts. 'Playful "tricks"', he suggests, become 'elements of dramatic expression', ceasing to draw attention to their trickery. Nonetheless, Gunning insisted in this early and highly influential article that we should not simply create an opposition between 'attractions' and narrative, but remember that 'effects are tamed attractions'. I want to consider in more detail how this process actually happened in the era of transition, and beyond.

Let me bring on-stage a concept that is actually more historically grounded than 'attraction': that of 'sensation'. Annemone Ligensa has shown how widespread the culture of sensationalism was in the 19th century, with Dickens claiming that 'the dramatic "sensation," more or less modified, will always be in favour';[2] and Walter

Benjamin powerfully evoking the poster that launched Wilkie Collins' 'sensation novel' *The Woman in White* in the London of 1860.[3] Sensationalism may have been deplored by guardians of public taste and morals, but it was a well-established current within entertainment for over half a century before moving pictures made their debut, addressed to these audience members seeking 'strong effects' amid the distractions of modern life, Ligensa quotes from an early Swedish encyclopedia definition: '*Sensational:* highly arousing of attention, suspenseful [...] *Sensational article... narrative... news... novel:* essay...narrative etc that intends to create a strong impression or succeeds in doing so... intends to create strong effects'.[4]

There is ample evidence to indicate that film quickly demonstrated its ability to convey such sensation in a novel and efficient way, especially by reviving and modernising a range of effects that had first appeared as part of the gothic culture of the late 18th/early-19th centuries – supernatural, spectral, perverse: ghosts, dungeons etc. Consider how early film gravitates towards such scenarios, and how tricks make possible a lively neo-gothic, in Méliès certainly, but also in films such as Robert Paul's *The Haunted Curiosity Shop* and *The Magic Sword*.[5] Here the basic techniques of stop-action and superimposition were combined, as they would often be in Méliès' and others' films.

According to received opinion, the frequency of such devices being displayed for their own sake peaked before 1906 and thereafter diminished rapidly. Barry Salt maintained as early as 1983 that 'excessive attention has been devoted to early trick films... especially in view of the fact that they proved a dead-end as far as the development of the cinema is concerned'.[6] Salt's study is particularly valuable, since it was based on a wide range of viewing and animated by a willingness to challenge received opinion. We can accept, therefore, that the incidence of *obvious* trick effects did reduce; and it seems plausible that this was linked to the narrativisation process described by Gunning. Excessive trickery would destabilise the illusionism required by narrative absorption. There are however several objections to this diagnosis. Two genres which became immensely popular from around 1911 onwards, the crime thriller and the ancient world spectacle, both made extensive use of 'tricks', although in rather different ways from the early trick-centred fantasies of Méliès and his competitors.

The Éclair company pioneered a new kind of crime-based narrative with its first adaptation of a popular novel by Léon Sazie, *Zigomar King of Thieves*, directed by Victorin Jasset in 1911.

Éclair's publicity described its aim as to 'explore the strange and the fantastic within the very real fabric of modern life'.[7] And within its use of authentic settings, there were elaborate disguises assumed at improbable speed, together with an evocation of the master criminal Zigomar's eerie powers. In Richard Abel's vivid account:

> Through stop-motion filming the gambling casino is transformed into a recital hall, complete with a small ensemble of musicians. At the hotel [Zigomar's] double performs as a magician – producing a table and matching candelabra, servants, and a greyhound, all out of thin air – while Zigomar himself, at the end of the heist, plays the acrobat, pushing away from the mansion on an upright ladder and dropping into a passing getaway car. Finally, in the opium den, a man lying full length on the floor, dreams of geishas who dance above him in superimposition and eventually close in around him. But this turns out to be a ruse, for the spectator as well as [the detective] Nick Carter, when the detective creeps in to attack – for behind the back wall tapestry lurks Zigomar, poised to seize his prey.

Zigomar would continue in two sequels, with a rival in the shape of Léonce Perret's *Main de fer* series, and in 1913 the first of Gaumont's *Fantômas* adaptations. Possibly due to the political and moral outrage stirred by these unashamed celebrations of ruthless law-breaking, Fantômas appears less fantastic in the exercise of his powers, although these are no less magical.

Feuillade's relatively sober *Fantômas* films appear almost primitive compared with many of their contemporaries, avoiding the cut-ins and close-ups that were becoming a mark of narrative sophistication in other genres. What animates them and made them immensely popular and influential across the world, are sudden eruptions of the uncanny – as when Fantômas escapes capture by shedding a false hand made of a dead man's skin, or the capture of Philippe Guérande in the *Fantômas* sequel *Les Vampires* by means of a noose that seems to drag him down towards his captors. This latter sequence has been well described by Vicki Callahan: 'The cuts back and forth from medium to long to medium shots facilitate the trick and the substitution of a dummy for part of the fall does not hamper the sheer facticity of the event we have witnessed. The cinema has shown us something that is, in effect, impossible to see. And our faith in cinema's record of the real, and the very relationship between vision and knowledge, are thereby questioned'.[8]

A tight spot in *Zigomar Contre Nick Carter*, Éclair (1912).

Here is a perfect example of sensationalism modernised by means of a filmic structure that may have been archaic in terms of 'narrative integration' but was highly effective in stimulating the jaded appetites of viewers – which no doubt explains the worldwide appeal of *Fantômas* and its successors and their many local imitations.[9]

The other new genre that began to have a dramatic impact in 1913 was the ancient world drama, headed by ever more spectacular adaptations of bestselling novels from the previous century, *The Last Days of Pompeii* and *Quo Vadis?*[10] Italian versions of these two appeared in 1913 and became standard-bearers in cinema's search for a new respectability, countering the highly suspect success of the crime serials. With their overt Christian morality and 'educational' portrayal of the Roman world, these led a new drive to bring middle-class audiences into the rapidly spreading super-cinemas and suburban halls.[11] But they also called upon the skills of filmmakers who had already mastered the techniques that made possible the realistic portrayal of catastrophe and use of models for large sets.

While little is known about who exactly worked on the spectacle of Ambrosio's *Last Days of Pompeii* or Cines' *Quo Vadis?*, the film that formed the climax of this genre, *Cabiria* (1914), made use of the talents of cinema's earliest 'special effects' virtuoso. The Spaniard Segundo de Chomón (1871-1929) is mostly noted in cinema history for his work on a series of Pathé shorts between 1906 and 1910 which emulated and in some cases surpassed those of Méliès in France and James Stuart Blackton in the United States.[12] But he worked in Italy between 1912 and 1917, largely as a director of photography, collaborating with Giovanni Pastrone. The impact of *Cabiria* has been widely documented, although is perhaps worth recalling in the terms of contemporary responses. The *Times* judged that 'merely as a spectacle the film would be an assured success – some of the scenes of the siege of Carthage are very effective – but it has the added advantage of a well-defined plot, the interest of which is sustained for a full two hours,'[13] and commented in subsequent notices on 'fire effects, a volcanic eruption, battles, thrilling adventures on land and water, crowds of actors… almost unbelievable visions of Etna in eruption, destroying palaces and villas, of Hannibal crossing the Alps, of living sacrifices to a nightmare of a Moloch, of the court of the courts of Hasdrubal'. The future playwright Eugene O'Neill, then a Harvard undergraduate, was equally impressed by the set-pieces of 'the destruction of the Roman fleet at Syracuse by the reflecting mirrors of Archimedes', Cabiria's rescue from the temple of Moloch, and the siege of Carthage by Scipio, all 'done with the grimmest realism and… bloodstirring in their gripping action'.[14]

Poster for *Zigomar the Eelskin*, an Éclair serial of 1913.

Autochrome photograph of a Paris cinema reviving *Zigomar Contre Nick Carter* in 1918.

In 1913, Cines' *Quo Vadis?* became a standard-bearer in cinema's search for a new respectability.

What newspapers and viewers found remarkable and impressive in *Cabiria* seems to have owed much to de Chomón, who was responsible for integrating miniatures with live action – as in the sequence of Aristotle burning the Roman fleet by means of giant mirrors – and for the moving camera that made the studio-built Carthaginian setting even more spacious and spectacular. Sadly, when the film was comprehensively restored and presented in Turin and Berlin in 2007, most of the praise was reserved for Pastrone, with only a single reference by Alberto Barbera, to 'his ingenious collaborator Segundo de Chomón'.

We will probably never know exactly what de Chomón contributed to *Cabiria*, although there is evidence of a continuing relationship with Pastrone in the 1917 film that de Chomón directed, *Il Sogno di Momi* [*The Dream of Momi*], a pacifist fantasy in which a boy whose father is away fighting falls asleep and dreams of life at the front with his toy guns and soldiers. Here de Chomón's experience of model work and stop-frame animation served to create an unusual hybrid, made at the height of the first decade of narrative feature films. He would go on to work on two further films with Pastrone before moving to France, where his final credit was for (unspecified) special effects on Abel Gance's *Napoleon* (1927). Special effects had indeed become a standard ingredient in large-scale production on both sides of the Atlantic by the 1920s, with further subdivisions between 'mechanical' and 'visual effects', and de Chomón's career from the early 1900s to the climax of silent-era spectacle spans that development.

But it also underlines the diminishing valuation that attached to such work, even if it played a large part in the impact or reputation of major films. Whereas de Chomón is still normally credited as the main author, or director, of trick-based films up to around 1909, thereafter he becomes a 'collaborator' or merely a technician. The specialists in various categories of 'effects', such as Coy Watson, one of the pioneers of mechanical effects in Hollywood, who executed many of the flying effects in Fairbanks' *Thief of Bagdad* (1924),[15] or the matte painter Percy Day, whose career ran from 1923 until 1950, have largely remained shadowy figures, occasionally celebrated for their illusionistic skills, but never given the same artistic or authorial credit as directors.[16] Michael Powell paid tribute to Day at several points in his memoir *A Life in Movies*, describing him as 'the greatest trick-man and film wizard' that he'd ever known.[17] Powell's last and longest reference to Day deals with his work on the whirlpool sequence of *I Know Where I'm Going* (1945), where he compares the mechanics of creating a water spectacle in the studio in 1945 with the legendary divine 'parting of the Red Sea' effect in Cecil B. DeMille's *The Ten Commandments* (1923). For Powell, the triumph of this effect in his Hebridean film is that a frame from the film was reproduced in a book as 'the only authentic picture of Corryvreckan in action'.[18]

Segundo de Chomón worked on the special effects for Pastrone's *Cabiria* (1914), judged by *The Times* as 'an assured success for its spectacle'.

As 'realism', however stylised, came to be the most prized quality of cinema in the sound era, so the artifice that made possible spectacular scenes had to be hidden, or at least not foregrounded by the kind of special explanation that Powell recalled from 'popular magazines like *The Strand*' at the time of *The Ten Commandments*.[19] When Merian C. Cooper and Ernest Schoedsack followed the success of their *King Kong* (1933) with a remake of *The Last Days of Pompeii* (1935), the contribution of their model maker Marcel Delgado and special effects artists, Harry Redmond and his son Jack, was not advertised. Whereas the creation of a convincing giant ape for *Kong* by means of an animated model had been widely explained and celebrated, the destruction of Pompeii was intended to appear 'real'. However, the need to give credit for what was clearly both central to the impact of *King Kong* and at the same time impressively illusionistic led to Willis O'Brien being openly feted as the main creator of the giant ape in *Kong*.

The case of O'Brien is surely paradigmatic of the new status of 'visible' effects. Originally a model maker for small-scale educational films in the 1910s, he worked on an abandoned feature *Creation* (1931) immediately before *King Kong*, having previously done model work (uncredited) for *The Lost World* (1925), based on Arthur Conan Doyle's Professor Challenger story about a realm where prehistoric life survives. Hall would remain a noted figure, followed by other 'creature' animators such as Ray Harryhausen, who were responsible for giving life to the fantastic. Yet the army of painters and mechanics who would create the complex worlds of studio films of the 1940s and '50s would remain essentially anonymous and invisible – forerunners of the vast numbers of digital technicians who are employed in today's fantasy cinema.

First published in *Early Popular Visual Culture*, vol. 13.3, 2015.

Structuring a New Industry

12.
Staffing an Early Film Studio

Dedicated to the memory of Richard Brown

Almost everything we know about the organisation of early film studios has traditionally come from anecdotal memoirs, all dating from long after the period in question, and mostly affected by what Richard Brown and Barry Anthony called, as long ago as 1999, 'the myth. depressingly similar formulaic pattern of myth creation'.[1]

When pioneers came to write their memoirs, usually in the mid-20th century, they usually 'cultivated the impression that the early days were rudimentary and disorganised', to quote Brown and Anthony again. A good example of this pattern is Albert Smith's *Two Reels and a Crank*, covering the early years of Vitagraph, which moves from early escapades of filming on New York rooftops and on location in Cuba, to the building of studios on Long Island.[2] There are occasional references to employees – cameramen and bookkeepers – but attention is focused on the three partners who created the company: Smith, James Stuart Blackton and William 'Pop' Rock. Typically, Smith recreates scenes with full dialogue in this book, published over fifty years after the earliest events it covers. In Britain, the fullest such memoir we have is Cecil Hepworth's *Came the Dawn*, published in 1951, which, as Simon Brown observed in his study of Hepworth's company, conforms assiduously to the pattern of the 'pioneer myth'.[3]

Two recurrent features of this pioneer myth were its insistence on a small number of people involved in early production – one or two individuals 'are' the company – and its reliance on anecdotal recollection of the unexpected, and especially the accidental, in this new activity. What is missing from such accounts is any acknowledgement that film production was a business from the outset, however small-scale. And that it was usually undertaken by people who were already established in a related business. If we think of Britain alone, Paul was a precision instrument maker when he embarked on Kinetoscope manufacture in 1894. G. A. Smith in Brighton was a lanternist and entertainer before becoming active in film from 1897 and creating what he described as a 'Film Factory' in the St Ann's Well pleasure garden in Hove. And Hepworth, the son of a noted magic lantern lecturer, was a photographic journalist before undertaking varied roles in the early moving picture business.

A FULLY EQUIPPED STUDIO, with Scenery and Accessories, for the production of set Scenes, is available at my Muswell Hill Works for the use of Customers by special arrangement.

The temporary stage that Robert and Ellen Paul built on the outskirts of London in 1898.

British Mutoscope and Biograph, as a branch of the parent American company, established a short-lived central London studio in 1899 and may have been highly organised, like its French equivalent, as Brown and Anthony surmised.[4] However, this was apparently no more than a rooftop filming studio, with processing and sales carried out elsewhere. Hepworth was already active in selling equipment and processing film from 1897, before establishing his own studio at Walton-on-Thames in 1904. And the Warwick Trading Company, headed by Charles Urban, which would act as distributor/agent for Smith and many others, was initially a sales and distribution organisation, based off High Holborn in Central London. Among these, Paul's Animatograph Works, established in the developing London suburb of Muswell Hill in mid-1898, is the earliest example of a stand-alone 'full-service' studio. His original electrical instrument business, located in central London, in Hatton Garden and Holborn, had apparently served adequately as a base for what was predominantly actuality and topical production. But by 1898, when 'the public interest in animated pictures seemed to be on the wane', Paul saw the need 'to secure space for taking subjects on a more ambitious scale'.[5]

In making this move to a newly developed residential suburb on the outskirts of the city, where he could buy a four-acre greenfield site, I have argued that Paul must have been supported, perhaps even encouraged by, his wife, Ellen, who had had a stage career at the Alhambra Music Hall before their marriage in 1897. An obituary for Paul, written by a professional colleague who seems also to have been a family friend, noted that Ellen had played a major part in running the studio, as 'producer, stage manager or principal lady in many a playlet for which her expert knowledge eminently fitted her'.[6] The same obituary described Paul 'painting scenery at night after the day's work is done' – although given his prior responsibilities in the instrument business, this may well only have been in the early phase of establishing the new studio.

Two other sources imply that Ellen Paul continued to have an active role in running the studio, as well as appearing in a number of its productions from 1898 onward.[7] But most tellingly, as evidence of growing professionalisation, Paul's 1898 advertisement for a large release of fictional subjects boasted of 'a staff of Artists and Photographers [who] have been at work in North London' in the new studio.[8] Just consider the range of activities that were already required by a film production business in the late 1890s:

1. Shooting films – now in the studio, as well as externally
2. Processing and duplicating films
3. Sales and despatch of prints
4. Equipment sales
5. Accounting
6. Publicity, including catalogue production

Very soon there would need to be added: studio management, dealing with contacting and contracting performers; production of scenery and props; and the planning of repertoire.

Granting that all early studios undoubtedly differed in character and organisation, depending on their founders and what other services they were connected to, can we identify more precisely how a studio like Paul's was staffed? A starting point might be the record of Paul's electrical business in Hatton Garden, launched before he embarked on substantial film work. In 1896, his accreditation with the Institute of Electrical Engineers recorded him employing 'about 30 hands'.[9] This may seem a considerable number, especially in what appears to have been a cramped corner building, shared with other businesses, even if many of the employees may have worked off-side under the 'putting-out' system.[10] Staffing may seem generous by modern standards, yet wages were low and the apprenticeship system, which Paul certainly used in his electrical business, meant that no wages were paid for the first six months of employment. Some information about typical wages in this period can be found in a cashbook kept by another of the English pioneers, G. A. Smith in Brighton. Here Smith recorded employing a carpenter in 1897 at 8d per hour, for 44 hrs, at a total cost of £1. 9s 4d.[11]

Staff at work in the finishing room of
Paul's Animatograph Works, from the 1901 catalogue.

When Paul established his studio in Muswell Hill, early in 1898, it is unclear if this was solely devoted to film work or whether he might have transferred some of the staff formerly employed on electrical work in Hatton Garden. The first real evidence of the scale of operations in Muswell Hill, or New Southgate as it was then known, comes with his 1901 catalogue, which included photographs of the Drum Room (for developing), Drying Room, Three Large Dark Rooms, an Examination Room, and an Experimental Department.[12] This catalogue also lists the Stock and Show Rooms at High Holborn and a Hire and Exchange Department, likely also have been at the same premises in Central London.

Estimating the scale of employment at Paul's Animatograph Works in 1900 must be speculative. In the 1901 promotional catalogue, just three men are pictured in each of the photos of the Works, evidently posed to convey an air of diligent application in this impressively modern setting. The studio is described as having 'a capacity to process 8,000 feet or 1½ miles of film per day', although we obviously don't know if that was regularly achieved.[13] Most of the films Paul was producing at this time averaged 100ft, which would allow for 80 copies a day, and his production for 1901 amounted to 57 titles, together with potential orders from the back catalogue and any commissioned films. There are no financial or other company records for Paul after his unsuccessful 1897 flotation, since the company remained private. But making some broad assumptions, perhaps the best estimate is a minimum of twenty staff on the 'laboratory' side and perhaps initially ten in production.[14]

This seems to match what has been surmised of Hepworth's studio, located in an equivalent suburban district of South London, and comparable to Paul's in terms of its output, with roughly the same balance between fiction films made in the studio and actualities filmed in the field. Simon Brown has calculated that Hepworth employed a total of thirty by 1907, while his sales and distribution were initially handled by Charles Urban's Warwick Trading Company.[15] If Paul's studio may have required thirty staff, his showroom and distribution might have needed another ten, with no doubt a number of part-time or freelance operators. Perhaps, then, a minimum of forty, with a substantial number of 'casuals'.

From around 1899, we know the names of some of his key staff: Jack Smith, who Paul says became 'sales manager in 1900', and would later become responsible for actualities, with accounts of him travelling overnight to Scotland to oversee filming and processing on location.[16] J. H. Martin, a future director, seems to have been an early employee, initially involved in processing, as was Frank Mottershaw, who would later launch his own company in Sheffield, making the influential *A Daring Daylight Burglary* in 1903.[17] The conjuror Walter Booth started to appear in Paul's films from 1899, especially those associated with magic and trick-work, such as *Upside Down; or, The Human Flies* (1899). And thanks to correspondence recently discovered with the actor and later director Alf Collins, we also know more about how performers were contracted to appear in early productions. A surviving telegram, preserved by Collins' descendants, records him being summoned by telegram to the studio to appear in what was probably the trick-based comedy *Pocket Boxers* (1903).[18]

Women 'joiners', or editors, at work in
the Hepworth Studio at Walton-on-Thames.

There were clearly opportunities for progression in this new industry. Everyone who joined was learning new skills on the job, whether technically as camera operator, film perforator, developer, 'joiner' (in modern terms, editor), or as a performer. Hepworth's memoir, *Came the Dawn*, recalled how 'all and any of these young people were liable to be called upon, the girls specially, to take on various jobs… drying, sorting, labelling, boxing, or even running errands'.[19] Simon Brown cites a memoir by Chrissie White, soon to become a major star in Hepworth's productions, in which she 'remembered that on rainy days when no filming was possible we used to help in the processing rooms, joining up the lengths of film. There was never any 'star system' at Heppy's studios.[20] Brown cautions, however, against reading this testimony as evidence of the 'pitch-in-and-help' ethos proclaimed by the 'pioneer myth'. If it was how the Walton studio operated in the early days, 'by 1909 Hepworth was running a studio with a detailed division of labour'.[21]

Equal caution is needed, I suggest, in applying modern job titles, especially that of 'director'. Largely due to the institutionalisation of filmographic information, assigning a director to all films has become routine. Yet we know that this does not correspond either to working practices or professional categories in early cinema. To describe Louis Lumière or Robert Paul as 'producer' or 'director' is plainly anachronistic. Similarly, to claim Walter Booth as the 'director' of all of Paul's trick-based films from 1889 to 1906 is to make both an anachronistic and presumptive claim. Merely because we can now recognise Booth performing on-screen in some highly inventive trick films released by Paul does not make him their director.[22] Much more likely is that Booth, already skilled in the mechanics of performing 'magic' on stage, would have learned or developed many of the techniques to be seen in his later independent prod-uctions during the years working with Paul, between 1900 and 1906. Thirty years later, Paul would acknowledge his contribution in his 1936 paper for the BKS, but in this he also described in detail how the special effects of *The Magic Sword* were executed in 1901, which strongly suggests that he was closely involved in its making.[23]

It appears that the identification of Booth as a director was begun by Denis Gifford, who managed to interview some of the surviving pioneer generation and their descendants.[24] There is perhaps an inevitable tendency for the often partisan historians of early cinema to promote their discoveries, and for crowd-sourced listings such as IMDb to accept such claims. But it is also important to contextualise the newly researched biographies that have emerged alongside long-familiar pioneer names, especially in relation to the profound changes in production practice under way in the early 1900s. After ceasing to work for Paul, Booth appears to have established his own small specialist studio in the West London suburb of Isleworth.[25] Here he dramatically increased the output achieved working with Paul, employing a dedicated cameraman and producing 23 titles in 1907 alone.

Nor was this an isolated case. American film scholars were the first to identify a major shift in production practice that can be dated to 1908-9, now known as 'the director system'. 'In this system of production, one individual staged the action and another person photographed it… The director managed a set of workers including the craftsman cameraman'.[26] Laurent Le Forestier has suggested that this shift may have happened earlier in Europe, specifically at Pathé.[27] He draws a striking contrast between the terms in which Georges Méliès recalled his experience in 1907, and how Pathé was promoting itself in that same year. Méliès was clearly describing his own earlier practice when he claimed that: 'The author must know how to work out everything by himself on paper… and so he must be the author [writer], director, set designer and often an actor if he wants to obtain a unified whole'.[28]

In contrast, Pathé's 1907 catalogue included a short 'history of cinematography' which described how the company had 'resolved to industrialise this invention': 'Driven by the sort of faith that is necessary for any enterprise, the Pathé brothers trained personnel, created a physical plant, and brought together every skill in this special line of business'.[29] Le Forestier describes the director as like 'the foreman in a factory... generally under the supervision of a manager or *directeur*' – in its administrative rather than filmic sense. Confusingly, in Pathé's case this figure was Ferdinand Zecca, sometimes referred to as the company's 'head of production', in addition to being identified as director of many of its films.

There is clearly scope for misinterpretation here, mainly through applying terminology in its later senses to a period of transition, when figures such as Booth and Zecca – originally a 'drawing-room conjuror' and 'café concert entertainer', respectively – were rapidly progressing in a fast-developing industry. In Booth's case, this meant becoming an independent producer-director, and allying himself with Charles Urban's expanding distribution and exhibition network. Urban would handle the output of a range of such independents, including the naturalists Francis Martin Duncan, and later Percy Smith, both pioneers of popular science films. As his ambition grew, Urban would also promote the work of a number of expeditionary cameramen, of whom the most notable was Joseph Rosenthal, who filmed in Canada and in Port Arthur during the Russo-Japanese War of 1904-1905.

Essentially, this vast portfolio of non-fiction material 'ran counter to what the market was starting to dictate', as Luke McKernan observed in the study of Urban's career.[30] Booth's satirical comedies and fantastic dramas formed an exception in his catalogue, yet the strategy of combining a number of distinctive filmmakers within an overall catalogue served both Urban and his suppliers well for the remainder of the decade, boosted by the success of his venture in colour cinematography with G. A. Smith, Kinemacolor. In some ways, it paralleled what was happening in fictional production, with American companies such as Selig and Biograph operating a number of separate director-producer units by 1911, to maintain supply to exhibitors who needed between 20 and 30 new films per week.[31] In contrast, the business strategy of Pathé was increasingly to centralise and concentrate the bulk of fiction production at their Vincennes studio, seeking economies of scale, with Zecca serving as overall head of production, in addition to directing films personally. However, Pathé would also maintain a range of other kinds of production outside their main studios, as well as managing a network of international affiliates with varying degrees of autonomy.

Pathé's Vincennes studio, c.1905.

Specialist roles were already emerging within the artisanal structure evoked by Méliès, although it would be some years before these were formalised. The main point of the 2020 Domitor conference was to foster a wider appreciation of the growing range of skills needed in early production, and in its commercial exploitation. Skills that were for the most part not creative or artistic, or even especially technical in modern terms. Yet, by the standards of the era, early film studios were far from quaint cottage industries. They employed a considerable staff, with a wide range of skills, some drawing on traditional business practices and stagecraft, and others newly acquired and developing. They were proto-'new media' businesses – more like, for instance, the contemporary sound recording companies than lantern slide makers and photographic studios of the 19th century.

It was indeed in the phonograph business that Charles Pathé had started, before he followed the same route as Paul, through Kinetoscopes to film production, equipment sales, and studio operation. In fact, both of the established media industries of slide-publishing and photography were also changing, with new techniques of mass production and assembly-line working, which would be introduced in film production in both Gaumont's and Pathé's studio-factories, on a much larger scale than in the earlier

Paul and Hepworth studios. As Brown and Anthony warned, it is important not to fall victim to the nostalgic pioneer myths of memoirs, and thus underestimate the new complexity of industrial organisation already needed in the first studios. Nor should we retrofit modern concepts of 'auteurism' onto this transitional phase in modern media production, where new skills were being learned, and opportunities seized. Perhaps the main lesson to learn from attempting to chart employment practices in the first industrially organised studios is that early film history still lacks accepted paradigms to describe this crucial phase in cinema's evolution.

An earlier version of this, given as a paper at the 16th Domitor Conference in 2020, subsequently appeared in the proceedings: *Crafts, Trades, and Techniques of Early Cinema*, edited by Ian Christie, Priska Morrissey, Louis Pelletier, Valentine Robert, Jean-Pierre Sirois-Trahan and Tami Williams (Michigan Publishing, 2024).

13.
The Lost World of Early North London Filmmaking

Travelling north of London today, it's hard to miss signs to two major film studio complexes, Elstree and Leavesden, which happen to be respectively the oldest and the newest of British production facilities. Yet how many realise that during nearly 130 years of filmmaking in Britain, there have been as many as fifty studios in the London region, most now defunct and largely forgotten? And perhaps unexpectedly, three other North London locations played an important part in the pioneer years: Muswell Hill, Walthamstow and Alexandra Palace. Reviving awareness of these certainly adds to local history knowledge, especially when so little early cinema fabric survives, but thanks to digital access it can also play a part in bringing to life unknown parts of Britain's patchy film history.

There is in fact a substantial gap in the early history of British film still waiting to be filled. One that stretches across the first two decades of the last century, when the national film industries that would shape the century's imagination were developing. How many, even among ardent cinephiles, could name more than a handful of British films made between Paul's and Acres' productions of the 1890s and the early silents of Alfred Hitchcock in the mid-1920s? This is largely because Britain suffers from both a massive material loss of its earliest films and – no doubt closely connected – an equally massive lack of confidence, pride or even simple awareness of its early film industry.

London as the Birthplace of Cinema
That industry actually began in London before any other city, towards the end of 1894. Robert Paul was a young electrical engineer based in Hatton Garden when he was approached by two Greek entrepreneurs, Demetrius Georgiades and George Trajidis, who wanted to commission the local manuf-acture of Edison's Kinetoscope viewing machine, unpatented outside the United States.[1] We now know that Georgiades and Trajidis had already been active in Paris, where the Kinetoscopes they had brought from America

inspired the Lyon photographic manufacturer Antoine Lumière to start his sons Auguste and Louis working on what would emerge as the Cinématographe camera-cum-projector. Meanwhile, Paul was soon busy manufacturing Kinetoscopes, at his Hatton Garden premises and in nearby Saffron Hill. During 1895, he also became an exhibitor, running a successful Kinetoscope salon from May to October as part of the Empire of India exhibition at Olympia.

The next step was to move from peep show to projection, using the well-established technology of the Magic Lantern to project moving images on a screen, as the Lumières were already doing in France. There was also a supply problem with film subjects to show, after Edison rebuffed Paul's suggestion that they might cooperate, no doubt hoping to put his British competitor out of business. Paul now urgently needed a camera to supply his Kinetoscope customers with new material, and was introduced to the Barnet-based photographer Birt Acres in early 1895.

Almost every aspect of their short-lived partnership would later be contested by Acres and Paul. But they did succeed in building a camera and shooting up to twenty varied films in the early months of that year, before the agreement was acrimoniously ended. One of these, now known by archivists as *Incident at Clovelly Cottage*, was taken outside Acres' house in Park Road, Chipping Barnet. This seemingly unremarkable view of a woman pushing a pram and a man in cricketing whites can probably be considered the first successful film shot in Britain, and appears to have been among several sent by Paul to Edison, to back up the proposal that they might collaborate. One of their other productions, the more spectacular *Rough Sea at Dover*, would provide the hit of Edison's own Broadway debut in April 1896, with its source unacknowledged.

Both Paul and Acres continued to use the camera design and films they had created, although separately. Acres established his own company, the Northern Photographic Works, on Salisbury Road in Barnet, and showed his productions to the local Lyonsdown Photographic Society in January of the following year. Meanwhile Paul unveiled his Theatrograph projector on 20 February 1896, at his old alma mater, the Finsbury Technical College, on the same day that the multitalented juggler and 'shadowgraphist' Félicien Trewey introduced the Cinématographe at the Polytechnic in Regent Street.

Enter the Animatographe
Thanks to a diligent reviewer in the electrical journal *Lightning*, we know that both of these premieres had teething problems. Some of the Lumières' fast-moving figures were jerky, and Paul's picture

'joggled up and down on the screen', due to poor mounting of the machine. But the writer was confident that both apparatuses had a bright future. And before long, they would be competing head-to-head in London's entertainment hub, Leicester Square. After the Cinématographe opened at the Empire Theatre in March, its neighbour, the Alhambra Music Hall, moved quickly to sign up Paul, renaming his projector the 'Animatographe'.

In May 1896, the Alhambra's manager, Alfred Moul, realised that the Animatographe programme needed some-thing fresh and more in keeping with the style of the theatre. He proposed to Paul that they 'add interest to wonder', as Paul later recalled, and make use of the theatre's resources to stage a comic scene on the roof. The result was *The Soldier's Courtship*, starring the Alhambra's leading dancers, Fred Storey and Julie Seale, as lovebirds whose passionate tryst is disturbed by a large matron installing herself on their park bench. When they fail to dislodge her, the soldier tips over the bench and she retreats furiously, leaving him and his girl to return to their lovemaking.

By all accounts, *The Soldier's Courtship* was immediately popular, hailed by the showman's paper *The Era* as adding 'humour' to the animated pictures by means of 'clever invention'. A relatively recent restoration of this pioneering film, co-ordinated by the Cineteca Nazionale in Rome and using elements from various archives, shows how successful this was.[2] Compared with Edison's contemporary *The Kiss*, a rather tame and lugubrious moment from a play filmed in close-up, Paul's three performers throw themselves into the action with style and commitment. And the production would have a lasting significance for Robert Paul, when eighteen months later he married the dancer who had played the 'lady of mature years' described by *The Era* – Ellen Daws, padded up in her costume and just 29 at the time.

There would be more 'adult humour' in another film made by Paul in August that year. *2 a.m.; or, The Husband's Return* was, like Edison's *The Kiss*, taken from a popular stage work of the day. In this case, it is the Parisian actor Paul Clerget, rolling drunk after a night out, who is coaxed into bed by his exasperated wife. But it would be a mistake to judge the few brief extant films of this period solely on what we see. Contemporary audiences were capable of reading much more into them, especially in the novel conditions of darkened theatres which early film projection required, unlike then normal levels of theatre lighting. A striking example of this comes in an 1897 story by the multitalented George Sims, described in his *Times* obituary as 'a highly successful playwright... a zealous social reformer, an expert criminologist, a connoisseur in good eating and drinking, in racing, in dogs, in boxing, and in all sorts of curious and out-of-the-way people and things'.[3]

Sims' 'Our Detective Story', published in *The Referee*, is narrated by a private detective who recalls a visit to the Alhambra – which is showing Paul's series *A Tour in Spain and Portugal* – where he sees a former client and his wife. The detective's brief had been to shadow the wife, suspected of adultery, in Madrid; and as they talk, the lights go down and the pictures begin. When they reach a scene in a Madrid park, both the husband and detective recognise the wife with another man. 'Stay madam,' the husband hisses, 'I will see the end of this'. The story ends with a coda, 'In Court', where the divorce case is being heard, with the film as evidence of adultery. The idea that films could provide evidence of wrongdoing would often be exploited in the years to come, but this remarkable early example reveals a shrewd understanding of what Victorian imagination could bring to early film shows. Whether this scene from the *Tour in Spain* does include a kissing couple must remain a mystery, since most of the film is lost.

Moving to Muswell Hill

Early in 1898, after the temporary boost that Queen Victoria's 1897 Diamond Jubilee had given the emerging film business, attracting camera crews from around the world, Robert and Ellen Paul made an important decision that would launch production in London's northern suburbs. Buying a field in what was then known as New Southgate, they built a studio, with provision to fly scenery around an open-air stage, and room for a nearby processing laboratory. What attracted the Pauls to Muswell Hill? Possibly it was the proximity of Alexandra Palace, as well as relatively cheap land on which to build an open-air stage and laboratory facilities. Over the next ten years, Paul would film a range of events in the Palace grounds, including several airship ascents, although only the Switchback Railway film is extant.[4] We know that they rented various houses on Colney Hatch Lane, near the end of Sydney Road, which was still under construction.[5] Later that year, Paul was able to announce that his staff of 'Artists and Photographers' had produced no less than eighty films, 'each of which tells a tale, whether Comic, Pathetic or Dramatic… with such clearness, brilliancy and telling effect that the attention of beholders should be riveted'.

Paul's boast of a studio staff is significant, and probably the earliest acknowledgement that filmmaking was a team effort from the start.[6] Over the next five years, Paul became the recognised leader of the British film industry, ably supported by Ellen, putting her theatrical experience to good use as studio manager and occasional actor. Although fewer than a tenth of the 800 films they made survive, many of these demonstrate the ways in which Paul laid the foundations for future cinema, starting with the production of multi-scene narratives, such as *Come Along, Do!* (1898), adding printed titles, and developing a range of ingenious special effects, as in *The Magic Sword* (1901). The great French film historian Georges Sadoul believed that Paul's films were closely studied by Méliès and especially by Pathé's emerging filmmakers, shaping the directions they would follow.[7]

Paul's studio would produce a wide range of film types, pioneering many genres, such as the knockabout 'chase', adaptations of familiar literary works like Dickens' *Christmas Carol*, and a number of highly original fantasies, ranging from *Upside Down; or, The Human Flies* (1899) to *The '?' Motorist* (1906). Although little information about the studio's operation has so far emerged, a family friend fondly recalled 'the little company [and] the shed with the glass roof and Mrs Paul with her sewing machine'.[8] She also described how local schoolchildren would turn out to see exteriors being filmed in the streets of Muswell Hill, indicating that the activity of the studio was not confined to the site off Sydney Road.[9]

When Paul closed his film business in 1909, this might have marked the end of North London's pioneer role in film production, although his electrical instrument business continued on the site for some decades. The reason he gave nearly thirty years later for leaving the industry was that film production had become 'too speculative', and indeed the scale and variety of films on offer to exhibitors by this time was far greater than the modest Sydney Road studio could have produced. Italian companies in particular were producing increasingly spectacular versions of subjects which had first been attempted a decade earlier.

Paul made a single-shot tableau of the popular Victorian subject *The Last Days of Pompeii* in 1900, very likely inspired by the Palace's popular 'pyrodrama', in which the climactic eruption of Vesuvius was a spectacle presented by James Pain's fireworks company. In Paul's original film, the destruction of Pompeii was represented by a miniature view of the volcano, as if seen through a window, and some collapsing pillars (only a still from Paul's catalogue survives). But by 1908 there was a 15-minute Italian version, with considerably enhanced spectacle, and in 1913 two full-scale versions with enormous casts and impressive special effects were competing for attention.

By 1905, Paul's Animatograph Works was producing elaborate dramas, such as *Goaded to Anarchy*, inspired by the recent failed Russian revolution.

Crime Conquers All

However, ancient world spectacle was not necessarily what most attracted audiences around 1910. Two related new genres had emerged that would dominate future film production: stories of detective heroes and criminal gangs. Traditionally, this trend in popular filmmaking has been firmly identified with French cinema. Thus, 'Nick Carter, King of Detectives' was the protagonist of three French series during 1908-9, directed by Victorin Jasset for the Éclair company. Jasset followed this with the saga of 'Zigomar', an elusive master criminal locked in perpetual combat with an intrepid detective which would take them to many colourful locations. The larger Gaumont company responded with *Fantômas* (1913) directed by Louis Feuillade, also based on an already popular series of books, which has come to be regarded as the quintessential crime syndicate serial.

Fantômas was admired by such varied figures as the Surrealist painter René Magritte and members of the early Soviet avant-garde, but its genre was replicated in many countries, including Britain. The British & Colonial company, usually known as B&C, had opened its first studio at Newstead House in East Finchley in 1908, and soon delivered a success with *Her Lover's Honour* in the following year. Like most films from this era, no copy survives, but we know from reviews that it was a tale set during the era of Alexandre Dumas'

Three Musketeers, with a plucky girl saving a king's messenger from the clutches of Cardinal Richelieu.

Ivy Martinek, best known as Three-Fingered Kate, played fearless heroines in many lost B&C action adventures, although *The Mountaineer's Romance* (1912) survives.

The lead actors were Austrian-born Ivy Martinek and her husband Henry Oscar Martinek, also the film's director. Both had been acrobatic circus performers, including a stint with Barnum and Bailey in America, and began in cinema with Pathé in France before coming to Britain. Together, they formed the team leading B&C's expansion over the next five years. Their first popular success was the seven-episode 'Three-Fingered Kate' series made between 1909-12, with Ivy as Kate, a master criminal who consistently eludes the cheekily named detective Sheerluck, and all filmed around B&C's East Finchley base. Next, Ivy and her husband appeared in various of the Lieutenant Daring adventures produced by B&C. Within a few years, the plucky American heroines of *The Exploits of Elaine* and *The Perils of Pauline*, cliffhanger serials produced by Pathé's American branch, would be internationally famous, and are now generally considered the original 'serial queens'. So why has Kate been forgotten?

Apart from the fact that very little of the 'Three-Fingered Kate' films has survived, one contributing reason must be Britain's enduring cultural condescension towards popular cinema, and especially towards native versions. Another would be the shrinking and eventual disappearance of British producers' export markets, as other nations started to dominate world film trade after 1907. The Martineks' work for B&C, although apparently very popular in Britain, would have faced stiff competition in foreign markets.

Walthamstow to Alexandra Palace
With demand for new 'product' rising, stimulated by a boom in cinema building, the suburb of Walthamstow now became a temporary hub for production in the early 'teens. A first studio was opened on Wood Street in Whipps Cross by the Precision Film Company in 1910. Precision had scored an earlier success with an opportunistic reconstruction of the 'Tottenham Outrage', entitled *Anarchy in England*, in 1909. Their new glass-roofed studio would set a trend, and housed the first of many productions of the melodrama East Lynne in 1910. Meanwhile, B&C, now under new management and needing more space, moved into a former roller-skating rink on Walthamstow's Hoe Street in 1913. As the second largest studio in Britain at the time, this had room for up to twenty sets, enabling simultaneous filming of different titles under the same roof. And in that year, the company produced the first British film to equal imported spectaculars, *The Battle of Waterloo*. Running for 60 minutes, with a large cast that including borrowed dragoons shown in cavalry action, it commanded the unheard-of price of £5,000 from its distributor. Maurice Elvey, a prolific pioneer director who would be still working into the late 1950s, started his career at B&C with an ambitious series of dramas, promoting his protégée Elizabeth Risdon as one of Britain's first screen stars.

Two future stars would emerge from other developments in Walthamstow. A studio at 245 Wood Street first housed Cunard Films in 1914-15, then Broadwest, which survived into the 1920s, and specialised in the adaptation of novels and plays. One of Walter West's actors at Broadwest was Ronald Colman, who left for America in 1920, to became a leading Hollywood figure in the 1930s. On the boundary of Walthamstow and Leyton, a former tramshed on Lea Bridge Road became the studio of I. B. Davidson, a company specialising in 'spy stories, sentimental films and boxing yarns'.[10] Two of Davidson's boxers would achieve fame in their later careers. 'Bombardier' Billy Wells was the man ringing a gong in J. Arthur Rank's famous logo; and Victor McLaglen would become a mainstay of John Ford's stock company in Hollywood, winning an Oscar for *The Informer* in 1935 after making his debut in boxing roles with Davidson in 1920.

The Lost World of Early North London Filmmaking   163

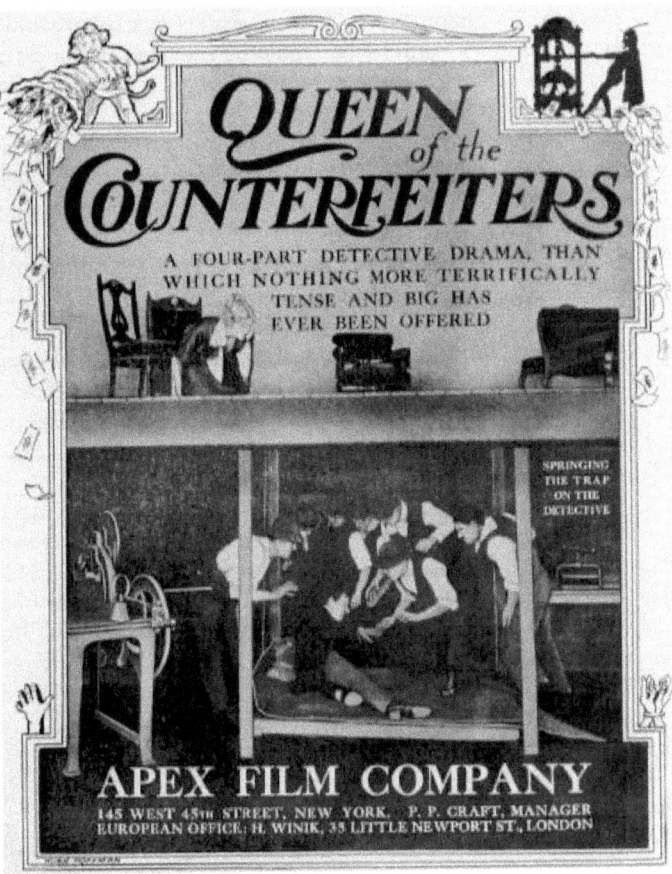

Queen of the London Counterfeiters, a 1914 B&C thriller by American director James Young Deer, was successfully sold for US exhibition.

By 1913 the demand for more studio space saw one of the Pathé UK subsidiaries, Union Films, abandon their Portland Place studio in Central London for larger premises at Alexandra Palace. This seems to have involved taking over the Palace's roller-skating rink as a studio, and making some thirty films that would be released under the 'Big Ben' brand over the next three years. Many of these were directed by Henry Martinek, often starring his wife Ivy as during the B&C period, but even without any known to survive, the titles and synopses speak for themselves: *The Power to Kill*, *In the Grip of Spies*, *Black Roderick the Poacher*, *The Hidden Witness*, *The Octopus Gang* and *The Rajah's Tiara*, in which 'the Gang of the Pointing Finger steal gems by using an X-ray device to see through walls'.

The Big Ben-Union period at Alexandra Palace also saw some auspicious debuts by figures who would play a larger part in later British cinema. George Pearson was a school-master who turned to filmmaking in 1913, and directed Godfrey Tearle in a film inspired by Rudyard Kipling's poem *A Fool There Was*, and a drama of industrial conflict, *Heroes of the Mine*, both for Big Ben. Tearle, coming from a distinguished theatrical family, would appear on screen over the next three decades, before his major role in Michael Powell and Emeric Pressburger's *One of Our Aircraft Is Missing* in 1942. Pearson would direct the earliest version of Conan Doyle's *A Study in Scarlet* and later create an authentic homegrown star in Betty Balfour during the 1920s. But during the war, he was also responsible for what was probably Britain's major contribution to the crime mystery genre, with the *Ultus* series of 1915-17. These starred a ruggedly handsome Australian-born actor, Aurelio Sidney, as 'the man from the dead.' Miraculously, one episode has largely survived.[11]

Alongside the market for sensational drama, there was also a constant demand for comedy, soon to be dominated by American slapstick, headed by Mack Sennett and former English music hall star Charlie Chaplin. Among music hall comedians who ventured into film at home, the 'eccentric' Will Evans filmed several of his famous sketches at Alexandra Palace, including *Whitewashing the Ceiling* and *Harnessing a Horse*. Meanwhile, his nephew Fred Evans created the character of 'Pimple' to satirise many of the era's film dramas.

Two other pre-First World War studios in North London deserve commemoration. One was Woodlands, an all-glass stage in the grounds of a country house in Whetstone, which housed Zenith productions and later British Empire Films. Zenith specialised in making screen versions of stage successes, and its studio could accommodate large scenery, brought from His Majesty's Theatre. Its greatest success was a film of the Lyceum production of *Ivanhoe* in 1913, starring King Baggot and directed by Herbert Brenon, boasting in its publicity of a large cast of fully costumed extras.

Elsewhere, beyond the outskirts of North London in Bushey, the distinguished Victorian painter Sir Hubert von Herkomer turned a theatre in the grounds of his large house into a film studio in 1913. Having created some of the most memorable social images of the era in engravings for *The Graphic*, and paintings such as *Hard Times* and *On Strike*, Herkomer developed an interest in the new medium and proclaimed in 1912 that he was abandoning traditional art to take up film. With his son Siegfried, Herkomer produced and appeared in a series of dramas in 1913-14 which attracted wide attention, especially within the film industry, due to his fame as an artist. From synopses (none of the films survive), it seems that the Herkomers recognised prevailing popular genres, with a film like *The Grit of a Dandy* (1914), in which a rejected dandy saves a doctor's daughter from abduction by menacing burglars, while also aspiring towards more 'artistic' subjects, with *The Old Wood Carver* (1913), featuring Sir Hubert himself.[12]

A short-lived Big Ben studio in Alexandra Palace, North London.

Evidence from What's Survived
Unfortunately, the venture proved short-lived, as the 65-year-old Herkomer died early in 1914. However, the studio he had created in the grounds of Lululand was taken over by the actor A. E Matthews, who attracted others from his profession to create the British Actors Film Company. As usual, nothing survives of this studio's productions, although one production in particular remains intriguing. *The Real Thing At Last* (1916) was a comic satire on styles of production, contrasting a British 'drawing room' version of *Macbeth* with a tough American one, written and probably co-directed by the playwright James Barrie, an enthusiastic amateur filmmaker.[13] Although appreciative newspaper reviews of many films of this period survive, Britain's pioneer film historian, Rachael Low, relentlessly complained of their 'theatricality'.[14] Low, like the founders of the National Film Archive, regarded the theatrical roots of much early British cinema as contrary to their concept of the

'cinematic', influenced by Soviet montage cinema. This, together with a strong sense of Britain's inferiority in cinema, must help to explain why so little trouble was taken to preserve films from the early decades of the century.

If Ideal's *The Life Story of David Lloyd-George* had been released, rather than suppressed, in 1919, might the reputation of British post-First World War production have been very different?

Yet when one of the rare survivors from this period is available to assess, such as Fred Paul's version of the Oscar Wilde play, *Lady Windermere's Fan* (Ideal, 1916), the result can be an agreeable surprise. Not only is this an ingenious adaptation of the stage original, inserting lively filmic interest, but it can clearly be seen as paving the way for the celebrated Ernst Lubitsch 1925 version, made for Warner Bros. in Hollywood in 1925. Ironically, the British film only survives because it was bought for US distribution, where it may well have influenced the scripting of Lubitsch's version.[15]

This is one case where the evidence we have points towards genuine British achievement. But another unex-pected discovery makes the point even more dramatically. The Ideal company, responsible for *Lady Windermere's Fan*, was committed to a policy of filming classic British subjects, although nothing else from its wartime output appears to have survived. However, at the end of

1918 Ideal undertook a major production on the life of the wartime Prime Minister, which was abruptly suppressed on the brink of release, apparently for political reasons. In 1994, a copy of *The Life Story of David Lloyd George* was unexpectedly found in the attic of its subject's grandson.[16] Now restored and tinted in the style of the era, *Lloyd George* rightly prompted speculation that, if it had been released in 1919, instead of mysteriously disappearing, the perception of British post-First World War production might have been very different.

Ideal's *Lady Windermere's Fan*: an ingenious adaptation of Wilde's play.

The lesson of continuing film discovery and restoration is that no film can now be considered definitively lost. And after the discovery of *Lloyd George* and the tantalising fragment of Pearson's *Ultus* serial, more of the output of London's early studios may yet appear. Further evidence of production around London's many studios undoubtedly also exists.[17] Future discoveries may be encouraged by a wider awareness of how rich the region was in filmmaking activity, long before the arrival of Harry Potter at Leavesden.[18]

An earlier version appeared in Hornsey Historical Society *Bulletin* 64, 2023.

14.
'Fumbling Towards Some New Art': The Structure of Cinema Programmes c.1909-13

Ian Christie and John Sedgwick

> Young industries are often strangers to the established economic system. They require new kinds or qualities of materials and hence make their own; they must overcome technical problems in the use of their products and cannot wait for potential users to overcome them; they must persuade customers to abandon other commodities and find no specialised merchants to undertake this task. These young industries must design their specialist equipment and often manufacture it.
>
> George Stigler [1]

In film history, the period between 1907 and 1914 has been described as one of 'transition' and 'transformation'.[2] It is the period in which film, as a commodity type, reached a mass audience. To do this required the application of modern business throughput systems and an industry structure that allowed for the necessary division of labour. In the United States, daily changes of programme for first-run cinemas and twice-weekly changes for most of the rest became the exhibition norm during this period. Considering that there were some 8,000 motion picture theatres in the US in 1909, increasing to 14,000 by 1914, the logistics of this operation must have been formidable.[3] For both Eileen Bowser and Charlie Keil, 1907 marked the divide between film as essentially a handicraft industry and one built along big business lines.

This was also the year in which innovation in film-making technique allowed producers to build audiences through product development. We contend that film length provides an important indicator of the relationship between filmmaker and audience. The ambition to make longer films no doubt had aesthetic as well as economic components, but above all it required willing audiences. In effect the process was one of experimentation, as filmmakers discovered how to deliver longer narratives that audience were able to follow and appreciate.[4] Following the conventional 'film grammar' understanding of this period, Bowser identified innovations in 'connecting shots' which enabled filmmakers to produce a more 'complex narrative' while enlisting the spectator's emotion in the film';[5] while Janet Staiger has argued for a more fundamental interpretation of the linkage between changing forms and the market: 'We need to understand that the production of meaning is not separate from its economic mode of production nor from the instruments and techniques which initials use to form materials so that meaning results'.[6]

To a large extent, this is the underpinning of David Bordwell's 'basic' story of film history: filmmakers and audiences learn how to make and follow more complex – which also means longer – films, and so the modern 'feature' is born.[7] But a closer examination of data from this period, and especially of the discourse of trade magazines and their advertisers, shows that this was far from a smooth transition. Nor was it necessarily led by 'meaning', the shared desire of makers and viewers to develop film's dramatic potential so often assumed by teleological film history. There were strong economic reasons for the shift towards long films becoming the staple of cinema programmes, and the implications of this shift were momentous for many producers and producing nations.

This study focuses on five key aspects of film during the 'transitional' period: programme composition, film length, genre balance, market share, and the shift from a footage sales business model to an 'exclusive' rental model. Based on empirical evidence from the British market, it aims to add to the growing body of knowledge about how film became the distinctive transnational industry that it did in the years before the outbreak of the First World War in Europe.

Context
In 1907 the London-based American film producer and entrepreneur Charles Urban declared that: 'the entertainment side of the business has now reached its maximum and… and future development will be upon the educational side'.[8] Urban, like so many leading figures in the industry, was desperate to improve the social status of filmgoing in order to attract the middle class. Indeed, it is clear from his film catalogues and writings that he expected the

instructional role of film to become much more prevalent, with schools, technical colleges, medical schools and industrial training centres becoming future exhibition venues. His instincts were correct insofar as the middle classes were, at the time of his writing, showing a nascent interest in going to the 'pictures', but he was hopelessly wrong about their taste in films. Like the working-class audience, they wanted to be enthralled and entertained by films that were comic and/or dramatic, and able to convey meaning through a narrative structure that was both coherent and succinct.

As filmmakers became better able to tell such stories, adapting their methods from the existing narrative forms, so the length of films increased, and with this the degree to which films differed from each other also increased. Another factor in attracting middle-class audiences was the emergence of purpose-built cinemas that were not only attractive buildings architecturally but comfortable and safe to be in. These two factors combined to secure a committed and growing audience for moving pictures before 1914, an audience that had learned to discriminate between films, being attracted to the cinema increasingly by particular producer 'brands', subjects, and the actors who appeared in them.

The development of film as a commodity and the 'system of provision' built around it took essentially the same path in the three leading markets of France, Great Britain and the United States, reflecting the international scope of the industry from the very beginning. Robert Allen has underlined the importance of vaudeville in securing an audience for films in the US during the first ten years: 'Until the advent of the nickelodeon around 1906, American vaudeville provided the embryonic picture industry with hundreds of exhibition outlets across the country and an audience of millions'.[9]

Whilst the timing and diffusion of the various modes of exhibition may have differed marginally, the British and French filmgoing experiences were essentially identical. In cities and towns, 'vaudeville' meant 'music hall' or 'variétés'/'cafe concert'/'fête foraine', and 'nickelodeon' were known as 'penny gaffs' or 'cinématographes' (by 1907 'cinéma', the abbreviated name of the Lumière apparatus, had become the enduring designation of the premises) in Great Britain and France respectively. Rural communities in all three countries were served right up to the end of this period by 'travelling showmen/women' playing a variety of fairgrounds and community halls.[10] By 1910, however, audiences in each of the three countries were increasingly watching films in fine 'theatrical' settings. Each of the national audiences also saw the same films, at least until the formation of the Motion Picture Patents Company (MPPC), the Edison-led cartel incorporated in 1908, which restricted the exhibition opportunities in the American market of non-cartel US and all foreign film producers except Pathé Frères and Gaston (brother of Georges) Méliès.[11] The absence of language barriers and the fact that both European and North American audiences – many of whom had of course recently arrived from Europe – were able to appreciate films from producers based in various countries, encouraged an international market for film subjects.

Programme Composition

Multi-film programmes had of course been the norm since the beginning of cinema shows, dictated by the brevity of the earliest subjects. The first demonstration programmes of early 1896 in Paris, London and New York consisted of around ten films, each lasting about 50 seconds, but by the autumn of that year, Robert Paul was showing at least 20 films in his segment of the Alhambra Music Hall programme.[12] With films issued at between 50 and 100 feet in length (60 feet = 1 minute at 16 frames per second), many were clearly required to make up a commercially viable show. And even when film length had increased by 1907 to include subjects of typically between 300-600 ft (5-10 minutes), at least 4-6 titles were needed.

There was in fact no commercial incentive for producers to make longer films, so long as films were sold outright by the foot, especially if the cost of elaborating a longer film was likely to be greater than making an equivalent footage of short ones. Whatever pressures there were to increase length presumably came from the exhibitors, based on their experience of audience preferences.[13] Discovering the exact composition of a typical film programme of c.1907-1910 is difficult, but from reports in a British trade journal the following is likely to be typical of 1909 (Table 1).

The most obvious features of this programme are the two longer films, both identifiably from French producers, one of which is already acting as the main attraction, or 'headliner', as it would become known, and the other an episode of a serial intended to encourage the audience to follow this weekly. Of the remaining seven subjects, two appear to be non-fiction, while four read like comedies from their titles. The headliner could equally have been a Vitagraph 'quality' film from the US, but is unlikely to have been a domestic production. Only four 1,000 feet subjects had been released by British producers before 1909 (Table 2).[14]

Table 1. Typical programme screened at the Prudential Hall, South Shields[15].

Film Titles	Length in feet	Length in minutes
The Fear (Pathé Art series)	900	15
Morgan the Pirate: pt 2 (Éclair)*	785	13
*Sailor's Adopted Children**	500	8.33
*Shark Fishing in the North Sea**	500	8.33
*Trollhatten Falls in Winter**	500	8.33
*Mr Absentminded**	300	5
*A Disastrous Oversight**	300	5
*Bridget's Evening Out**	300	5
*The Donkey That Was Not an Ass**	300	5
Film programme total	2,700	73

Source: *Kinematograph and Lantern Weekly*, 15 April 1909.

Note: The programme was accompanied by Cinephone; one of a number of mechanical synchronisation systems in wide use during the 1900s, providing the experience of recorded music accompanying film as a special feature, before this became routine with sound-on-film systems after 1927.

British exhibitors were already moving towards greater differentiation in their programmes, with longer and more spectacular films becoming an important attraction. But British producers, who had been important international suppliers until the early 1900s, did not succeed in meeting this demand and so lost market share. How had this happened?

Film Length and Genre Balance in British Fiction Films

A good idea of the growth of British film production of 'entertainment' films in the period before the First World War can be obtained from Denis Gifford's catalogue.[16] Although counting films is a crude measure of industry vitality, failing as it does to capture qualitative differences between films and audience preferences, as reflected in the number of prints made, it is at least a place to start.[17] Table 2 shows a dramatic annual growth over the first 20 years of moving pictures in the number of films made by British producers, their aggregate footage and their average length and running time.

Taking the early years first, it was not until 1906 that the average length of films exceeded five minutes. A genre breakdown of the years before 1908 based on Gifford's catalogue reveals that British producers concentrated on comic films. Between 1904 and

Table 2. Annual Statistics of British 'Entertainment' film production.

Year	Number of films	Aggregate length (feet)	Number of films ≥ 1,000 feet	Number of films ≥ 2,000 feet	Longest film (feet)	Mean length (feet)	Mean running time (mins)
	(1)	(2)	(3)	(4)	(5)	(6)	(7)
1895	3	80				27	0.44
1896	31	1,343				43	0.72
1897	44	2,171				49	0.82
1898	89	6,398				72	1.2
1899	104	6,933				67	1.11
1900	121	9,877				82	1.36
1901	94	10,021				107	1.78
1902	135	16,444				122	2.03
1903	128	20,879				163	2.72
1904	224	42,664				190	3.17
1905	246	60,734				247	4.11
1906	277	83,757	1			302	5.04
1907	314	97,294	1			310	5.16
1908	341	131,754	2			386	6.44
1909	369	150,485	5		1,630	419	6.98
1910	362	191,302	5		1,500	528	8.80
1911	409	231,687	15	2	2,500	571	9.52
1912	583	440,675	128	15	4,300	770	12.83
1913	666	675,244	216	79	7,500	1,050	17.50
1914	831	1,033,380	360	190	5,749	1,260	21.00

Note: A number of films are not given a length by Gifford and do not contribute to the estimates found in columns 6 and 7. A reel of film – 1,000 feet in length – was screened at 60 feet per minute and hence lasted for 16.67 minutes. *Source*: Gifford (1973).

Figure 1. The Growth in the Mean Length of British 'Entertainment' Films, 1895 to 1908.

1908, of the 1,402 films released just fewer than 60 per cent (808) were comedies while Gifford classified less than 25 per cent (333) as dramas. However, as Figure 1 shows, the genre that served as the driver to greater lengths was the drama. By 1908 the mean length of films in this genre had risen to 522 feet, some 122 feet longer than the mean length of all films and 160 feet longer than the average comic film. 1908 also saw a noticeable annual rise in the number of British dramatic films increasing from 63 to 108 over the year, with their aggregate lengths doubling to 54,00 feet, comprising 40 per cent of all output.

Between 1907 and 1914 the number of British films marketed grew on average by 13 per cent per annum while aggregate film length grew at the annual rate of 34 per cent, with the number of 1,000 feet or more films increasing from 1 to 360 and the average film length quadrupling over these eight years. However, it is clear the real impetus for growth of both aggregate output and average running times occurred during the last four years of the period, from 1911 onwards, with the emergence of films of 2,000 feet or more of particular interest.

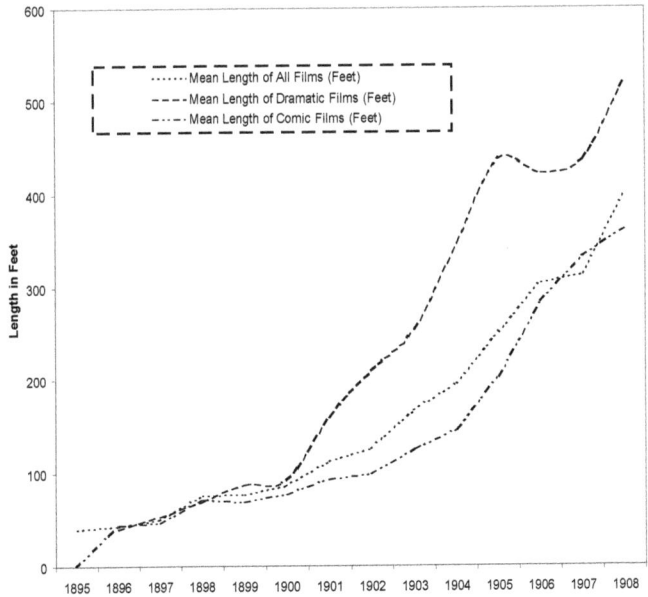

Source: Gifford, 1973

The Wider Film Market in Britain

British exhibitors had never shown British fiction films as a matter of principle, despite occasional patriotic appeals in the trade papers. Yet there are a number of dramatic shifts apparent if we compare the situation in 1907-08 with 1912-13 in respect of the proportion of British films on the British distribution market, the average lengths of these and the genre composition. Two datasets have been created, consisting of all known films exhibited in Britain over two twelve-month periods – June 1907 to May 1908 and May 1912 to April 1913. The earliest of the datasets was obtained from the 'recent publications' entries in the trade journal *Kinematograph and Lantern Weekly*, while the later one was derived from the *Kinematograph Film Monthly Record* listing of new films released in Britain.

Table 3. Films marketed in Britain and their genre composition, June 1907 to May 1908.

	Drama	Comic	Trick	Musical	Interest	News	Other	Total
British-made films	71	157	17	68	120	100	3	536
Foreign-made films	237	235	51	0	43	5	0	571
Total Films	308	392	68	68	163	105	3	1107
Import penetration (%)	76.9	59.9	75.0	0	26.4	4.8	0	51.6

Source: *Kinematograph and Lantern Weekly*.

Table 3 shows that over half of the films released in Britain during 1907-1908 were of foreign origin. While bulk of interest and news films were made by British producers, reflecting the culturally specific nature of such films, the same is not true of the entertainment genres of drama, comedy and trick. Given the importance of drama in the development of storytelling techniques and marketing strategies, the extent of import penetration here is of special interest and suggests that already by this stage in the history of film, British producers lagged behind some of their European and American counterparts.[18]

The market shares of the major players in the British market are to be found in Table 4. Between them, the seven largest producers in 1907-8, counting separately the British and France wings of Gaumont, supplied two thirds of all films, with Pathé Frères, as in the US, the market leader.[19]

The contrast in the scale of the industry between 1907-8 and 1912-13 is dramatic. Between May 1912 and April 1913 approximately 4,800 films were marketed in Great Britain, four and half times the number released in 1907-1908. Of these, the *Kinematograph Film Monthly Record* listed the lengths of 4,446 films, whose combined length of just over 4 million feet represented something like a tenfold increase on the estimate of film lengths over the 1907-8 season. (Remember the films in the two datasets, 1907-8 and 1912-13, consist of all films marketed in Britain, compared to the 'entertainment' films produced by British producers, listed by Gifford and recorded in Table 2[20].)

Table 4. Market shares in the British market, June 1907 to May 1908.

Producers	Films marketed	Percentage of the entertainment market	Percentage of the news and interest market	Percentage of the overall market
Pathé Frères	164	15.9	11.6	14.8
Urban Trading	111	2.3	34.0	10.0
Gaumont (U.K)	101	4.4	14.2	9.2
Gaumont (France)	99	11.8	0	8.9
Hepworth	95	7.3	12.7	8.6
Vitagraph (U.S.)	94	11.2	0	8.5
Walturdaw	75	5.9	9.7	6.7
Total	739	58.8	82.2	66.7

Source: *Kinematograph and Lantern Weekly*.

The statistical distribution of film lengths for the 1912-13 season is captured in Figure 2, showing that the bulk of releases (77 per cent) were still 1,000 feet or less in length, although something of an industrial standard prevailed, in that the most frequent class interval of film length were films between 901 and 1,000 feet, most of which were 1,000 feet in length, and many of which were produced by the Edison-led trust, the MPPC.

The genre composition of this distribution indicates that 'long films' were almost exclusively dramatic in form and that the proportion of dramas declines as film length falls, with the crossover point with the comedy genre occurring in the class interval 700-799 feet. The comedy genre dominates in the subsequent four lower class intervals while dramas fall to zero. Among the shorter films, travel and interest co-exist with comedy; and an interesting feature of the evolution of film length on the UK market between 1909 and1912 is that shorter films do not immediately decrease in number or proportion of the whole, even as 1,000 feet films make their appearance (see Figure 3). The doubling in number of films between 400-600 feet in 1911 has no obvious explanation, except to show that the rise of the long film did not lead to any immediate suppression of shorter subjects. Indeed, the continued presence of films lasting between 6-10 minutes testifies to a persistent belief among some exhibitors that audiences preferred 'variety' to the tyranny of the long film.

Figure 2. The frequency distribution of film lengths by genre of new films released into the British market, May 1912 to April 1913.

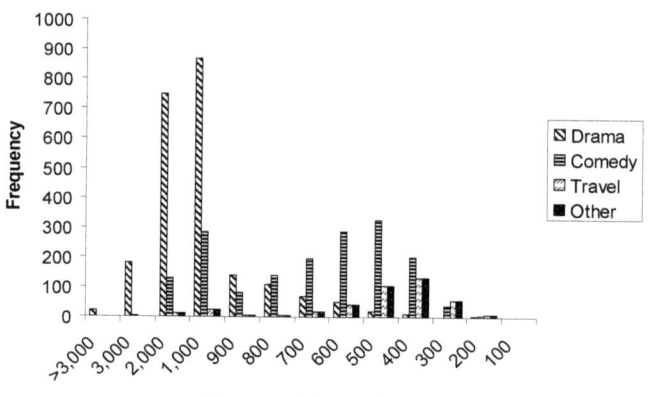

The statistical distribution of film lengths for the 1912-13 season is captured in Figure 2, showing that the bulk of releases (77 per cent) were still 1,000 feet or less in length, although something of an industrial standard prevailed in that the most frequent class Source: *Kinematograph and Lantern Weekly*.

Enter the 'Exclusives'
Rachael Low drew attention to the impact of the 'exclusive' system of renting as long ago as 1948, and we want to build on this pioneering account, while also integrating it with our study of film length.[21] We have seen that by 1909, a typical programme already included 'headliners' and shorter supporting items. In the market situation of 1909, exhibitors were experiencing difficulty in identifying what they should be booking, and wondering whether their nearest rivals might be offering the same films. One of the services that began to be advertised was agents offering complete programme packages at fixed prices, together with the security of knowing that this package was 'exclusive' to a particular area – for which guarantee exhibitors would pay more.[22]

Figure 3. Comparison of lengths of all films released on British market: March 1909, January 1911, and March 1912.

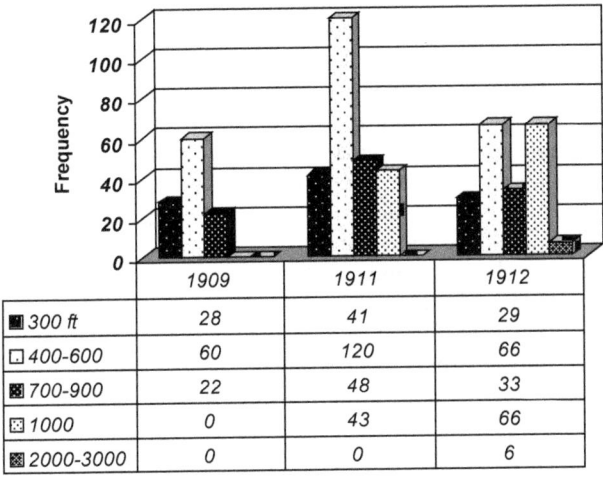

	1909	1911	1912
300 ft	28	41	29
400-600	60	120	66
700-900	22	48	33
1000	0	43	66
2000-3000	0	0	6

Source: *The Bioscope* Film Releases Supplements, 1909, 1911, 1912.

Low cites Nordisk's *In the Hands of Imposters*, released by New Century Film Services in 1911, as the 'first film in this country specifically handled as an exclusive'.[23] The trend had actually begun earlier, with Clarendon announcing *The Invaders* on an exclusive basis in 1909, but by April 1911, the system appears to have been in full swing. The Cinematograph Film Hiring Company was offering *Temptations of a Great City* as 'the big boom for your show', with all bookings for London and the suburbs for the first two weeks already taken, but 'some vacancies' for subsequent weeks.

As Low noted, the concept of incentivising bookings probably owed something to the extraordinary publicity stunt perpetrated by Will Barker earlier in the same year. Barker announced that his film of Sir Herbert Tree's production of *Henry VIII* would only be distributed for six weeks, after which all twenty copies would be burned.[24] Renters' advertisements in 1911-12 repeatedly stress large potential returns from the latest sensation, and the need to act quickly to secure an exclusive booking.

The effects of the 'exclusive' boom were threefold. First, to drive up the prices paid by renters to secure these desirable films, which led to higher charges to exhibitors, organised on a sliding scale according to how close the booking was to the original release. The highest prices asked – 12 guineas for Fox's *A Fool There Was*, starring Theda Bara in 1915 – were only affordable by the biggest city-centre cinemas, which encouraged stratification of types of venue. Second, the films deemed suitable for such promotion were almost invariably imported: initially, Italian, Danish or French, then mainly American, which accelerated the down-grading of British films, despite efforts by local producers to enter this lucrative new field.[25] Third, the currency of exclusives, which were all long films and became longer within a few years, consolidated the 'feature' as the centrepiece of the cinema programme. However, there is also some incidental evidence from trade papers and advertisements that programmes became longer to accommodate these features, retaining numerous short films until well into the 'teens.[26]

Table 5 shows the impact of these trends on the upper end of the rental market by 1912-13. The 28 films with running times of 50 minutes or more (3,000 feet, and above) are all dramas and were mostly made in Europe although, interestingly, the list is not dominated by any single producer or by producers from any one country.

Conclusion

What can we learn from this admittedly imperfect compilation of data? Whatever its various origins and motivations, the 'long film' emerged around 1909 as an innovative product which soon acquired premium value in the changing business structures of the young industry. It favoured – or perhaps required – drama, rather than comedy or topographical interest, which had been the specialisms of British producers. Its use by renters to engineer new terms, whereby they would encourage competition among exhibitors and so drive up the potential value of certain films, would create the tripartite structure of production, distribution and exhibition which has remained in place for nearly a century. Italian ancient

Table 5. Films of 3,000 feet or more released onto the British market, May 1912 to April 1913.

Title	Date rel.	Producer or Distributor	Length in feet	Minutes
Quo Vadis?	Mar-13	Jury	8,000	133.33
Ironmaster, The	Mar-13	Ruffell's	3,800	63.33
Oliver Twist*	Oct-12	Hepworth	3,700	61.67
Tigris	Mar-13	Itala	3,600	60.00
In the Springtime of Life	Feb-13	Pathe	3,425	57.08
Nihilist, The	Nov-12	Skandinavia	3,377	56.28
On the Steps of the Throne	Feb-13	Pasquali	3,350	55.83
An Evil Fascination	Jun-12	Brockliss	3,335	55.58
Woman's Ambition, A	Sep-12	Pathe	3,270	54.50
Zigomar	Mar-13	Éclair	3,265	54.42
Mathilde	Feb-13	Éclair	3,250	54.17
Chancellor Called the Black Panther, The	Aug-12	Kinografen	3,240	54.00
Stolen Treaty	Feb-13	Nordisk	3,165	52.75
For Love Is Life	Feb-13	Pathe	3,156	52.60
Greed of Gold, The	Oct-12	Pathe	3,145	52.42
As You Like It**	Feb-13	Vitagraph	3,115	51.92
Witchcraft	Nov-12	Cines	3,100	51.67
Shaughraun**	Mar-13	Kalem	3,075	51.25
Devil's Daughter	Feb-13	Nordisk	3,008	50.13
Dice of Life	Jul-12	AFR	3,000	50.00
Lady Detective, The	Aug-12	Cosmo	3,000	50.00
Outcast, The	Aug-12	Walturdaw	3,000	50.00
Word Of Honour	Sep-12	Hubsch	3,000	50.00
Twixt War and the Girl	Sep-12	Walturdaw	3,000	50.00
Fatal Ring, The	Oct-12	Gaumont	3,000	50.00
Lucile**	Nov-12	Thanhouser	3,000	50.00
Theodora	Mar-13	Gaumont	3,000	50.00
Woman's Crime	Mar-13	Ruffell's	3,000	50.00

Source: *Kinematograph Film Monthly Record.*
Notes: *British **American. All 28 films listed were dramas.

world spectaculars and Danish thrillers were the distinctive new genres that pioneered the long film between 1909-13, but once its value was recognised, American producers became the most successful and reliable providers of its most popular genres in the 'teens: the western, the social problem film, and the historical epic.

Meanwhile, in London in 1913, *The Times* carried a sustained reflection on the potential significance of this new phenomenon that was monopolising the attention of so many:

> It is not life, it is not art, it is not music, it is not literature. Whether, all the same, we are fumbling towards some new form of art which is to have movement and shape, to be like life and yet to be selected and arranged as a work of art, who can say?[27]

The previous twenty years of 'fumbling' had seen Britain move from pioneer status to the position of becoming a major consumer of the developing long film, while dramatically losing market share in their production. Ironically, the short film comedy would see an exuberant, if temporary, revival in 1914, largely due to the early work of an expatriate British comedian: Charlie Chaplin.

Following a conference presentation at Siegen, this first appeared in Annemone Ligensa and Klaus Kremeier, eds., *Film 1900: Technology, Culture* (John Libbey, 2009).

15.
'What is a Film?' Legal Controversy and Cases Before 1910

> The film was neither a print nor a book, nor – in fact, everybody could say what it was not, but nobody could say what it was. The scheme was not exactly pigeonholed. The real trouble was that nobody could say to which particular pigeonhole it belonged.[1]

This wry comment appeared in the British showmen's newspaper *The Era*, in October 1896, referring to a widely reported proposal by Robert Paul to deposit samples of his Animatograph films at the British Museum, as a record of contemporary history. The affair was reported in an article by Stephen Bottomore as long ago as 1995, incorporating research by Richard Brown.[2] Whatever Paul's motives for making this proposal and for publicising the Museum's delay and confusion over its response, it is clear that he was *not* trying to register the film's copyright. To do this in Britain in 1896 would have required a deposit and or registration of the films at Stationers' Hall. And indeed a number of early British filmmakers did deposit copies of single frames from their films at Stationers Hall, apparently believing this to be the best – or only – way to register copyright in the new medium.[3] We know that other manufacturers were doing likewise in other countries, according to the requirements of their national copyright legislation: Edison had started sending films to the Library of Congress as early as 1893, while the Lumières in France were also depositing copies in order to establish *droit d'auteur* on their films as publications.[4]

But *was* a film a publication? To what 'pigeonhole' did these anomalous new objects belong? One of the legal cases from this early period that offers some insight is the prosecution of Walter Gibbons by Charles Urban in 1901, for duplicating or 'pirating' films owned by Urban's Warwick Trading Company. Urban recounts in his memoirs that he had suspected Gibbons of making unauthorised copies, especially since the latter's print order had gone down, even though Gibbons' exhibition business around the London music halls was increasing in scale. But Urban needed evidence, which he eventually managed to get in a suitably melodramatic way – forcing one of Gibbons' employees to take him to the scene of the crime, where, by candlelight, he found 'three short duplicated films, even bearing the Warwick trade mark at each beginning'.[5]

Finding the trademark was important, since Urban intended to accuse Gibbons of 'forging the company's trade mark by photography', which he threatened to do at the end of 1901.[6] Trademark protection was certainly a clearer legal issue than the status of films around 1900.[7] In the course of recounting the Gibbons affair, Urban stated: 'The copyright of a picture according to English law belongs to the man who operated the camera' – followed by: 'Our camera men however understood that all films they took while in our employ were the copyright of the company'.[8] Here is indeed one of the first problems in arriving at a legal definition of film – a problem that went back to the difficulty originally raised by photography. The legal status of photographs was first defined in English law by the Fine Arts Copyright Act of 1862, which stated that the author of a photograph has 'sole and exclusive right of copying, reproducing and multiplying' a photograph; but also that this right may be assigned to another, and that neither copyright nor assignment is valid unless registered at the Hall of the Stationers' Company.

In fact, Robert Paul seems to have been the first British filmmaker to register copyright in this manner in March 1897, as shown by a registration form for the most popular item in his Spanish and Portuguese series *A Tour in Spain and Portugal* (and here I must pay tribute to Richard Brown for his pioneering work on copyright and for providing me with copies of Paul's copyright claim forms).[9] In the case of *A Sea Cave near Lisbon*, Paul records the 'date of assignment' from his cameraman Henry Short to himself as January 1897. Six years later, in July 1902, Paul was again registering copyright on a film of the Prince and Princess of Wales and their children, filmed by 'G. Francis'; but there had been a dispute, as Paul's accompanying note reveals: 'I am quite unable to give his full name, legal proceedings being pending between us [however] the assignment to us has been signed and such assignment has been legally approved of'.

At this point we might wonder how much of a problem protecting the copyright of early films was. According to André Gaudreault, writing in 1985: 'A practice that was extremely common in the film world between 1900 and 1906, and one in which all the major production companies partook in England, France and the United States: film piracy... All producers at the time [1900-06] enthusiastically pirated (by duping a print) the films of competitors who had not taken the precaution of copyrighting them at the Library of Congress'.[10]

A Sea Cave Near Lisbon. Shot by Henry Short for Robert Paul, and the first British film to be copyrighted, in 1896.

Richard Brown subsequently challenged Gaudreault's 'sweeping statement', noting that he offered no evidence, and suggesting instead that 'whilst film "duping" probably existed in England before 1912, it was certainly not the high-profile activity it was in the United States'.[11]

This is probably correct, due in part to the British film trade being relatively collegial and highly concentrated around a London West End centre, with similarly concentrated regional distribution centres. Certainly there had been extensive unauthorised copying of films in the earliest period: Edison copied Acres' and Paul's first films, notably their *Rough Sea at Dover*, which was the hit of his 1896 Broadway screening;[12] and Paul may have copied Edison's films, or at least the purchasers of his replica Kinetoscopes could have done so. But by the early 1900s, systematic piracy would almost certainly have been detected – as it was by Charles Urban's threatened prosecution of Gibbons, and in the United States in 1903 a case brought by Edison against Siegmund Lubin for copying his subjects suggests that early producers were increasingly concerned to protect their investment. Further evidence of this concern came in a four-part series of articles that appeared in the UK *Kinematograph and Lantern Weekly* in November 1907, which do not seem to have had the attention they deserve, as the most substantial attempt to clarify the copyright position of film outside an actual case at trial.

The articles were based on a paper read to the Kinematograph Manufacturers Association by a barrister, William Jago, and it seems likely that Jago had been commissioned by the newly formed association's first president, Robert Paul, as part of efforts to develop the infrastructure of the new industry (these included setting up a certificate course for projectionists in partnership with the Northampton Polytechnic Institute). The journal was itself new, having been launched in May 1907, as successor to the *Optical Lantern and Cinematograph Journal*, which had collapsed in bankruptcy. So we can see this extended survey of 'The Law of Copyright in Kinematograph Pictures' as something of a platform statement, both for the new association and its would-be trade journal.

Jago starts by distinguishing two senses of copyright. The first is 'the right which a man has to control, and if he wishes, to prevent the publication of his literary publications'. The second sense is 'the exclusive right of multiplying the copies of such production after publication'. Once published, a work was protected by the Copyright Act of 1842, although as Jago admits 'there is nothing legally literary about a kinematograph picture'. There would, however, be redress under common law if someone was shown to be 'passing off' their work as that of another. But what protection might there be for the subject or performance embodied in a film?

Jago cites an important historical case, that of Turner vs. Robinson, dating from 1860, and heard at the Rolls Court in Dublin, Ireland (then part of Great Britain).[13] The Turner in question was not the famous painter J. M. W. Turner, but Robert Turner, a print-seller in Newcastle, who had bought the engraving rights to Henry Wallis' hugely popular painting *The Death of Chatterton* (1856). James Robinson, of the Polytechnic Museum and Photographic Galleries in Dublin, one of the first generation of stereographic publishers cashing in on the new fashion for stereoscopic views, had published a stereograph of 'The Death of Chatterton' in 1859, which Turner claimed was a 'piratical imitation' of the Wallis painting.[14] We learn from a contemporary account of the case that this had come about when Turner shipped the painting to Dublin in order to attract subscriptions for his engraving, whereupon Robinson had announced that he would soon offer 'the beautiful stereoscopic figure of the last moments of Chatterton'.[15]

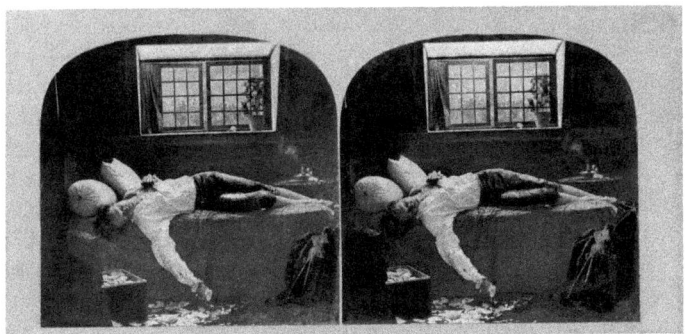

Stereograph of *The Death of Chatterton*,
subject of an important legal case over copyright of an image in 1859.

When Turner applied for an injunction, Robinson's defence was that 'his stereograph was not copied from Mr. Wallis' picture, but was an independent study from the biography of Chatterton' and that he had 'from recollection built up the subject in his studio and made a stereoscopic photograph of it'. At a second hearing, he further argued that 'it is impossible to take pictures for stereoscopic slides from a plain surface such as a picture'.[16] Despite this, Turner succeeded in getting an injunction against Robinson on the grounds that, although 'the stereographic slides are not photographs taken directly from the picture, in the ordinary sense of copying, they are photographic pictures of a model, itself copied from and accurately imitating in its design and outline the petitioner's painting'.[17]

Jago pursues at length the two – let us say 'ontological'- issues that continued to perplex those seeking to apply statutes introduced before moving pictures appeared: whether sequences of photographs could be regarded as '*a* picture'; and whether the representation of a performance can be treated *as* a performance. On the first, he argues that although the negative of a film consists of a series of pictures, 'their sole use is for the purpose of producing when exhibited one picture only'. And on the latter, he suggests that 'no one who has heard the roars of laughter caused by a comic moving picture can doubt that a Kinematograph exhibition may certainly cause the same emotions as those produced by a representation by actors of the same scene or event'.

Jago does not mention, but may well have been aware of, the landmark U.S. Federal Court ruling in Edison vs. Lubin in 1903. This has often been characterised as one pirate taking another to court, although in truth American copyright law at this time was radically unclear about the status of film. Lubin's defence against the Edison charge of piracy was that Edison should have registered each frame of his films individually to secure protection under the 1870 U.S. Copyright Act. This was upheld in the lower court, before being reversed in the Federal court of appeals, which held that 'while the advance in the art of photography has resulted in a different type of photograph, yet it is none the less a photograph'.[18]

Citing judgements in which 'scenic entertainments' and 'producing emotions' had been regarded as criteria for something being considered a 'dramatic representation', Jago concludes that 'a kinematograph representation can claim the protection afforded by the Dramatic Copyright Act of 1833, while the Fine Arts Act protects the film itself 'from all trafficking, whether by copying, multiplying or exhibiting'. But whatever satisfaction the Kinematograph Manufacturers might have felt after this learned analysis of their situation was about to be rudely disturbed in April of the following year, 1908.

The landmark case of Karno vs. Pathé Frères has been shrewdly analysed by Richard Brown.[19] This turned on the impresario Fred Karno's claim that the Pathé film *At the Music Hall* infringed his copyright on the music hall sketch 'The Mumming Bird', which he had registered in 1906. After the court visited the Oxford music hall to see the sketch performed, and viewed the film, the judge found that the film was indeed 'a representation of the plaintiff's sketch', but that this sketch did not qualify as a 'dramatic or musical performance'!

Although the judgement disappointed Karno and left open the question of who might be liable if such a case *were* proved (the producer or the exhibitor of the film?), it established that no 'legitimate' dramatic work could be filmed without the author's permission. A parallel case in the United States, Harper Brothers vs. Kalem Company and Kleine Optical (1908), which arose from Kalem's unauthorised filming of Lew Wallace's *Ben-Hur*, already a popular stage and arena entertainment, turned on whether Kalen's dialogue-free adaptation of a literary work could be considered a 'dramatisation'. In an eventual Supreme Court ruling delivered by Justice Holmes, Kalem's screen version was judged to have infringed upon Harpers' copyright, thus establishing the rights of the owners of the source-work of a film.[20]

Later in the same year, an international copyright conference in Berlin revised the original Berne Convention of 1886 and its 1896 Paris revision, including for the first time an article that referred to film. In Britain, a new Copyright Act followed in 1911, which incorporated the Berlin provisions, thus giving film formal copyright status for the first time.[21] America, meanwhile, continued to reject the principles underlying the Berne Convention until nearly the end of the 20th century.[22]

Kalem's unauthorised film of Lew Wallace's *Ben-Hur* in 1908 led to a landmark US ruling on copyright infringement of a source-work.

So much was changing within both the business and the art of film in 1908-9 – from the launch of the *film d'art* in France, which would eventually transform production everywhere, to Edison's formation of the Motion Picture Patents Company – that it is hardly surprising that clarifying copyright should have become an urgent priority. Films were getting longer, more expensive to produce and distribute, and increasingly worth protecting – or pirating.[23] For producers prepared to stay in the business – unlike Paul, who was among the pioneers that soon bowed out – and for the authors who would start to reap major rewards from this increasingly dramatic medium, stabilising and harmonising copyright would indeed prove crucial to the building of the new industry.

A version of this appeared in the proceedings of the 2010 Domitor Conference, *Beyond the Screen: Institutions, Networks and Publics of Early Cinema*, eds. Marta Braun, Charlie Keil, Rob King, Paul Moore and Louil Pelletier (John Libbey, 2012).

16.
Measuring Early Screen Stardom in Europe

Is it heretical to suggest that perhaps the major obstacle to understanding what I will call, provisionally, 'film fame' is the popular field of 'star studies'?

Historically, this phenomenon was one of the first topics within film to attract scholarly study, with several generations of sociologists, anthropologists and early film scholars all fascinated by the star phenomenon, beginning with Hortense Powdermaker and Edgar Morin in the 1950s, and continuing with Alexander Walker in the 1960s and Richard Dyer in the 1970s.[1] Much of this early work focused inevitably on the post-1920s star system operated by the major studios, and therefore naturally has a strong Hollywood bias. We hear routinely about Florence Lawrence and Mary Pickford becoming the 'first' film stars, but this results from projecting *back* a later and overwhelmingly American conception of studio-based 'stardom'. It is therefore unlikely to shed much light on the Asta Nielsen phenomenon, or early screen fame more generally, and may indeed be actively unhelpful in creating a teleological pull towards the studio era as paradigmatic.

So, clearly we have to begin by rejecting the routine claims in star studies that there were 'no stars' before around 1908-10.[2] A 'star system' manifestly existed in 19th-century performing arts, and established stage and entertainment personalities were prominent in the very first film programmes presented in Britain and the United States by Robert Paul and Thomas Edison. Edison had already filmed such vaudeville stars as the strongman Eugene Sandow and sharpshooter Annie Oakley for the Kinetoscope as early as 1894, before these subjects were projected during 1896; while Paul offered a range of music hall performers, such as the eccentric comedian Chirgwin, the magicians Nevil Maskelyne and David Devant, and the dancing Sisters Hengler. The reasons for filming these are obvious: they were established performers and their presence lent distinction to early animated photography and Vitascope shows. Although they had all begun on stage, their fame was enhanced by the explosion of new media: lantern shows, postcards, cigarette cards, pictures in newspapers and magazines, and now appearances on screen. And with the appearance of sound synchronisation systems in the early 1900s, some of these musical stage stars could extend their existing fame, as with the *Tonbilder* launched by Oskar Messter in 1903, which eventually comprised a repertoire of 500 subjects,[3] or the series of Harry Lauder synchronised films offered by Gaumont through their Chronophone in 1907.[4]

Among the pioneers, Lumière were unique in not offering established entertainers in their earliest films. The first named figures to appear in Lumière films were heads of state – Tsar Nicholas of Russia, the King and Queen of Italy, President Porfirio Diaz of Mexico, Kaiser Wilhelm II, Queen Victoria, all in 1896 and 1897 – who thereby acquired a new kind of celebrity through their frequent appearances on screen. Martin Loiperdinger has shown how the Kaiser's 'star' status in early German cinema derived from and helped reinforce a pre-existing fascination with the Hohenzollern court.[5]

The British Mutoscope and Biograph also filmed statesmen and, famously, Pope Leo XIII in 1898. British Biograph had a policy of featuring well-known actors, starting with Beerbohm Tree in a scene from his production of Shakespeare's *King John* (1899). Here, as in later films starring Herbert Campbell and Dan Leno, the performers' names were an essential part of the films' appeal.[6] However, apart from these 'pre-existing' celebrities it is true that performers in the majority of comic and dramatic films made before 1908 – and many made up to the late 1910s – were effectively anonymous; while by 1920, stars had indeed become desirable, if not essential, for the marketing of films.

Argument over how and why this happened is almost as old as writing about the history of cinema, with early accounts provided by Terry Ramsaye and Benjamin Hampton,[7] and these have been analysed, along with additional factors, by Richard deCordova, David P. Marshall and many others.[8] It is not my purpose here to add to this debate about causes and motivations, much of which remains heavily biased towards American companies and their domestic market (again, projecting back from the undeniable importance of American producers and stars after the mid-1910s). My perspective is essentially European, and in this context the obvious starting point is not the celebrated defection of Florence Lawrence from her anonymity at Biograph to being heavily promoted in her own name by Carl Laemmle at IMP in 1909. It is, rather, the trend that began in the previous year towards harnessing theatrical reputations to a new kind of production: the *film d'art*.

The extravagantly costumed Hengler Sisters were already subjects of postcards before Robert Paul filmed them in 1896, among a number of other theatre and variety subjects.

The Societé Films d'Art was launched in 1907 with the aim of 'making [films] based on scenarios written by contemporary authors, involving recognised artists'.⁹ Among its leading figures were two actors, Charles Le Bargy of the Comédie Française and André Calmettes, and although the company was not commercially successful, its example was widely noted and continued, both by Pathé (which took it over) and by Pathé's international branches and other companies. 'Film d'art', variously translated, became a recognised genre over the next five years, signifying a level of production values in acting, costume and décor, usually with an historical setting. In Italy and Russia, the genre's impact was decisive: production in both countries began to exploit national-historical traditions, attracting domestic audiences, and producing exportable films. It also brought 'recognised artists' into film more regularly, and an example of this is British Gaumont's announcement in 1908 of 'over 40 of London's foremost artistes' appearing in a film based on the Lyceum production of *Romeo and Juliet*.[10] From this point, Jon Burrows has traced a steady progression of what Gaumont called 'celebrity films', with featured actors; and as so-called 'art series' proliferated in France, Italy and Britain, the marketing of these seems to have automatically included the names of their cast. So we can be fairly clear that named actors were a major part of the appeal of the more ambitious new European productions by 1909 – which is of course the tumultuous year when Florence Laurence exchanged her anonymity at Biograph for fame at IMP.

If we look in more detail at the British market, by 1910 and 1911 the names of actors were being noted in trade advertising and reviewing, while famous actor-managers, such as Beerbohm Tree – and soon living legends like Sarah Bernhardt – were also being widely featured in consumer publicity. This, then, is the context in which Asta Nielsen's first films appeared in 1911 and quickly became a major attraction for trade and public alike. By July 1912, perhaps uniquely, her films were being offered to British exhibitors as a 'brand': 'Great Asta Nielsen Dramas'.[11] In Britain, Florence Lawrence and Mary Pickford were the only other actresses regularly recognised by name, although a series of the male film comedians, Max Linder, André Deed and 'Prince', were already established and prolific brands, anticipating the cult of Chaplin that would begin in 1914.[12] But how are we to interpret the fascination that developed around early non-comic and almost exclusively female stars? Before moving on to the anthropological and sociological diagnosis that would become commonplace, we should perhaps try to see it in contemporary terms, since there were observers outside the film industry who noted the emergence of this new form of fascination from contrasting, yet informed, standpoints. Two of these, Hugo Münsterberg and Luigi Pirandello, were both widely known and respected for very different reasons than their interest in film when they published on the subject within the same year, 1916. And in both cases, their positions on the cinema have been subject to dispute.

Asta Nielsen

Asta Nielsen would become a global star in the years before the First World War, with a corresponding volume of postcards recording her many contrasting roles.

Münsterberg was a Harvard professor when he published his 'psychological study', *The Photoplay*, in 1916.[13] A distinguished practitioner of experimental psychology in Germany, Münsterberg moved to Harvard in 1897, where he worked in different fields, including forensic and industrial psychology. It was only near the end of his life that he 'discovered' cinema, to which he brought the same enthusiasm that had marked his other work, apparently watching films voraciously for the first time in his life and writing about his reactions for popular magazines as well as preparing a monograph. His fundamental and still controversial insight in *The Photoplay* is that the spectator's mind 'moulds' or interprets the scenes in a film 'until they appear the embodiment of our feelings',[14] in a kind of projective fantasy relationship. Combining aesthetic and psychological analysis, Münsterberg arrived at 'a unified principle': 'The photoplay tells us the human story by overcoming the forms of the outer world, namely, space, time, and causality, and by adjusting the events to the forms of the inner world, namely, attention, memory, imagination, and emotion'. Later, he would express this even more euphorically: 'The massive outer world has lost its weight, it has been freed from space, time, and causality, and it has been clothed in the forms of our own consciousness. The mind has triumphed over matter and the pictures roll on with the ease of musical tones. It is a superb enjoyment which no other art can furnish us'.

Immersion in films can produce strange psychological reac-tions in the audience – neurasthenic symptoms, forms of mass hysteria, and the like. There is also a unique new way of engaging with the actors on the screen, which Münsterberg struggled to articulate:

> The process which leads from the living men to the screen is more complex than a mere reflection in a mirror, but in spite of the complexity in the transmission we do, after all, see the real actor in the picture. The photograph is absolutely different from those pictures which a clever draughtsman has sketched. In the photoplay we see the actors themselves and the decisive factor which makes the impression different from seeing real men is not that we see the living persons through the medium of photographic reproduction but that this reproduction shows them in a flat form. The bodily space has been eliminated.

Screen actors, for Münsterberg, are simultaneously 'real', yet as images, incorporeal. Stars were already a major presence in American cinema when Münsterberg underwent his crash induction into the pleasures of cinema-going, and he refers to going 'with the crowd to [see] Anita Stewart and Mary Pickford and Charles Chaplin', while there is also a magazine photograph of an apparently starstruck 'Doctor Münsterberg' meeting Stewart.[15] His discussion in *The Photoplay* of the difference between stage and screen acting, where the former is helped by 'the content of the words and the modulation of the voice' to overcome the difficulty of feigning emotion physiologically, produced the observation:

> To the actor of the moving pictures, on the other hand, the temptation offers itself to overcome the deficiency by a heightening of the gestures and of the facial play, with the result that the emotional expression becomes exaggerated. No friend of the photoplay can deny that much of the photoart suffers from this almost unavoid-able tendency. The quick marchlike rhythm of the drama of the reel favors this artificial overdoing, too.
>
> [...] This undeniable defect is felt with the American actors still more than with the European, especially with the French and Italian ones with whom excited gestures and highly accentuated expressions of the face are natural. A New England temperament forced into Neapolitan expressions of hatred or jealousy or adoration too easily appears a caricature.

As a result, Münsterberg noted, many stage actors were 'more or less decided failures on the screen' compared with 'the specializing photoactor'; and despite his preference for European actors, Münsterberg contrasts two recent American versions of *Carmen* in terms of their editing rate, distinguishing them simply as the 'Theda Bara edition' and 'the Geraldine Farrar version'.[16] What we find, then, in this first major attempt to apply psychological science – the descendent of Ludwig Fechner's 'psychophysics' – to the developed feature film, is an implicit recognition of the centrality of stars, locating them as 'specialists' within the overall affective apparatus of film.[17]

Münsterberg died shortly after the publication of *The Photoplay*, and this aspect of his work was not carried forward during the period when Hollywood production and stars were conquering the world.[18] Indeed it was largely forgotten during the subsequent seventy years, until experimenters once again sought to investigate 'what psychological factors are involved when we watch the happenings on the screen'. When Münsterberg began to be rediscovered, he was seen by some, especially on the political left, as providing an early rationale for encouraging the consumption of film as 'escape' from the realities of working life; for creating a form of 'pseudo-consumption', which could be regarded as an immaterial equivalent of the consumerism promoted by modern capitalist society.[19] Only more recently, since the rise of experimental psychological approaches to film spectatorship, has his pioneering role begun to be acknowledged.[20]

Almost exactly contemporary with Münsterberg, another account of filmic fascination appeared in Europe, in the form of Luigi Pirandello's novel *Si gira*.[21] The title is a phrase that was used in contemporary filmmaking, meaning literally, 'turn over' (referring to the hand-cranked camera), or as it is usually translated, 'shoot'. Pirandello's narrator is an impassive cameraman employed at an Italian studio engaged in making the 'diva' films which had become Italy's most popular genre. Gubbio, the cameraman, observes an off-screen melodrama unfold, which will lead to the tragic death of the leading man while he is being filmed, in an ironic doubling of the 'real' and the fictive that anticipates Pirandello's most famous play, *Six Characters in Search of an Author* (*Sei personaggi in cerca d'autore*, 1921). His cameraman-observer is both fascinated and repelled by the off-screen drama he watches unfolding around him, and especially by the diva star of the Kosmograph studio, La Nesteroff, portrayed as a *femme fatale* who revels in her power 'at any moment, whenever the fancy took her, [to] tear from the side of any proud young lady and recapture for herself all the mad young men who threaten tragedies, *pst!*, by holding up a finger, and at once tame them, intoxicate them with the rustle of a silk skirt'.[22]

Despite this power, she is also, according to Gubbio, 'a bore', an empty and destructive force, who fatally exerts her influence over the young actor starring in her latest film and brings about his death. Such films, for the alienated cameraman, impassively turning the camera handle, are sadistic spectacles of primitive passion being played out for popular entertainment. And this would seem to have been the position of the Italian Marxist thinker, Antonio Gramsci, who was working as a theatre critic at the climax of the *diva* cult, when *Si gira* appeared. In 1917, Gramsci wrote of the original diva, Lyda Borelli: 'This woman is a primordial relic of prehistoric humanity. They say they admire her for her art. That's not true. No one can explain the art of a Borelli because it doesn't exist. La Borelli doesn't know how to play anyone but herself. (…) La Borelli is the artist par excellence of the cinema whose language is the human body in its perpetually renewed plasticity'.[23] The background to Gramsci's polemic was his criticism of a society which relegated women to the roles of 'plaything' or 'brood mare', within which the diva film was merely another unwelcome symptom of increased sexualisation, while cinema itself was a debased medium, cynically inflicting kitsch on its vast public.[24]

A more nuanced interpretation of *Si gira* is, however, also possible. Angela Dalle Vacche has argued that the novel does not simply condemn film as mechanical, but attributes this negativity to its protagonist, Gubbio, who 'feels insecure about relations between men and women in daily life',[25] and transfers this to his relations with the actors. Furthermore, Dalle Vacche observes, Pirandello is the first author to attempt to portray the inner life of a screen goddess, when he writes of Varia Nesteroff: 'She herself remains speechless and almost terror-stricken at her own image on the screen, so altered and disordered. She sees there one who is herself but whom she does not know. She would not like to recognise herself in this person. (…) She is really tragic: terrified and enthralled'.[26] Whether this was merely inventive speculation on Pirandello's part, or whether it had some basis in his familiarity with the film studios that he visited in Rome while writing *Si gira*, we cannot know. However, it supports Dalle Vacche's claim that we should not too hastily conflate Pirandello's supposedly negative view of cinema with that of his protagonist.[27]

After Pirandello's novel was reissued in the mid-1920s, Walter Benjamin would build on its diagnosis of the alienation supposedly felt by the diva – 'the feeling of strangeness that overcomes the actor before the camera, as Pirandello describes it' – as if this were fact, incorporating it into his essay *The Work of Art in the Age of Mechanical Reproduction*, where 'the film responds to the shrivelling of the aura with an artificial build-up of the "personality" outside the studio'.[28] And from Benjamin, it is a short step to the Frankfurt School's familiar critique of popular culture as a debased form of mass-manipulation, which effectively revived the position occupied by Gramsci and many other socialist intellectuals in the 1910s, and is still evident in much hostility to the commercialised culture represented by Hollywood. But if we set aside this familiar judgement and return to the begsinnings of the 'star era', we may discover *structural* reasons for the emergence of the 'human capital' that stars unquestionably came to represent.[29]

Pierre Sorlin has observed, in his study of Italian national cinema, that although it later became fashionable to decry or mock the diva era, in an Italy deprived of state ceremony, '*dive* made up for what was lacking in public life, ostentation, magnificence, theatrical excess – in a word, glamour'.[30] Sorlin tries to account for the specific form that early stardom took in Italy; and we can find similarly national characteristics among the earliest star cults in other countries. In Germany, Henny Porten performed anonymously in at least 22 of short *Tonbilder* between 1906 and 1910, when she made her feature debut. In 1911 she would appear in a short prologue to the dramatic film *Tragödie eines Streiks* (*The Tragedy of a Strike*), in which, as Martin Koerber puts it, she 'greets the audience like old friends'.[31] By the following year, Porten films 'sold themselves', and the star was featured in special trade press supplements 'expressing gratitude for all the attention she had been shown',[32] supported by lobby cards and the now widely circulating picture postcards (about which more below). Similar patterns can be found in most of the main producing countries, although there is a striking contrast in between the glamour expected of Italian *dive* and the humility and projection of ordinariness which was the key to stardom in Germany and in Britain, where Chrissie White had been promoted by her producer Cecil Hepworth, and was typically described as 'delightful' in reviews that stressed her 'genuinely English qualities'.[33]

White and Porten, like all the other 'first wave' stars, owed much of their fame to the explosion of photographic postcards which more or less coincided with the popularisation of cinema. Cigarette cards were the first of these new collectible images, and their manufacturers had traditionally included 'Beauties' and 'Actresses' among the regular subjects. But around 1900, new printing processes made photographic cards significantly cheaper to produce, and output rose steeply in almost all European countries after the introduction of the 'divided back' format spread from Britain in 1902 to France (1904), Germany (1905) and finally the United States (1907), offering a full 14 x 9 cm portrait on the reverse side.[34]

Film 'stars' or 'personalities' joined the repertoire of subjects, and producers such as Oskar Messter and Hepworth took full advantage of the new craze for sending and collecting such cards to promote their stars, as it reached extraordinary levels by 1914, with up to 20 cards per head of the total population being posted in Britain alone.[35] Looking at these portrait cards today, as displayed on the collectors' website European Film Star Postcards, the Portraits of stars could be published in any of the countries where their films were being seen, to satisfy local demand, and indeed their frequency could provide a proxy measure of star 'impact'. Equally clear, iconographically, is how such portraits tended to reinforce a relatively stable star image, with many variations on the same 'type' – except in the case of Asta Nielsen, who perhaps uniquely appears in a wide range of different roles, testifying to *versatility* and *variety* as defining features of her image, rather than repetition.

Nationality		d.o.b.	Prev. exp.	Age at film debut	Film career
Britain	Gladys Sylvani	1884	Stage	1910 26	Short
	Chrissie White	1895	none	1909 19	Long
France	Sarah Bernhardt	1844	Stage int'l	1912* 68	Short
	Gabrielle Réjane	1856	Stage int'l	1900* 44	Short
	Mistinguett	1875	Stage	1908 38	Long
	Suzanne Grandais	1893	Stage	1909? 16	Long [until d.1920]
Denmark	Asta Nielsen	1881	Stage	1910 29	Long
Germany	Henny Porten	1890	none	1906 16	Long
	Lil Dagover	1887	none	1913 25	Long
Italy	Lyda Borelli	1884	Stage	1913 29	Short
	Hesperia [Olga Negroni]	1885		1912 27	Long
	Pina Menichelli	1890	Stage	1913 23	Long
	Francesca Bertini	1892	Stage	1910 18	Long
	Leyda Gys	1892		1912 20	Long
Russia	Vera Karalli	1889	Stage	1914 25	Short
	Vera Kholodnaia	1893	none	1915 22	Short
USA	Anita Stewart	1885	?	1911 26	Long
	Florence Turner	1885	Stage	1907 22	Long
	Theda Bara	1885	Stage	1914 29	Short
	Florence Lawrence	1886	Stage	1906 20	Long
	Mary Pickford	1892	Stage	1909 17	Long
	Lillian Gish	1893	Stage	1912 19	Long

* Both the rivals Bernhardt and Réjane made early film appearances as theatre celebrities, but their main 'starring' roles came between 1911-16.[36]

Chrissie White, promoted as a star by Cecil Hepworth, appeared in many postcard images.

Female stars became both the expression of national ideals and a transnational phenomenon in the period 1911-15.[37] Similar patterns can be seen recurring across the emergent national industries, and as a step towards trying to understand this phenomenon, I propose here an approach based on the pioneering methodology of George Huaco's *Sociology of Film Art*.[38] Huaco wanted to explore three 'stylistically unified waves of film art' (German Expressionism, Soviet expressive realism, and Italian Neorealism) by comparing the social structures that underpinned them, in terms of personnel, industrial capacity and prevailing ideology. Without attempting a similarly comprehensive causal account of the emergence of the film star, I have borrowed some features of Huaco's methodology to create a preliminary framework for comparison among the early stars. The table on page 201 summarises the careers of 22 early female stars – in most cases the earliest in their respective national film industries – and tabulates four main features: whether or not they had previous stage experience; the date and age of their film debuts and the length of their subsequent careers.

The majority of these actresses became 'stars' between 1911 and 1914, benefitting from the rapid structural changes that had transformed the film business in the previous two years, creating a new demand for longer 'headline' films that earned substantial revenues by being shown as 'exclusives' in the new cinema palaces that were appearing in all major cities. Their fame was intricately linked to the new promotional pressures and opportunities that surrounded the programming of these venues. With the notable exception of the three older French actresses (all already famous), the two-thirds who had some stage experience did not have major reputations before their rapid rise to screen fame. Indeed, three of the most typically successful of the youngest cohort, those born in the 1890s – Vera Kholodnaia, Henny Porten and Chrissie White – had no stage experience at all before they were 'discovered' by filmmakers, and quickly recognised as favourites of the cinema-going public.

What also stands out in this tabulation is that Asta Nielsen was among the oldest of those who became international film stars, with only Borelli, Hesperia and Bara also gaining fame in their late twenties, and these within a relatively limited range of genre roles. Asta Nielsen, crucially, made her mark before these later 'divas' and 'vamps' appeared, and was already the first transnational European star by the time they emerged. Exceptionally, she continued to be hailed for her 'versatility' and range at a time when star identities were becoming fixed: a 1913 full-page trade advertisement by her British distributor, Walturdaw, featured both the 'truly brilliant comedy-drama' *In a Fix (Jugend und Tollheit)* and *The Heart of a Pierrot (Komödianten)*, a 'tragedy that will touch the hearts of all'.[39] Such comparisons help clarify the uniqueness of Asta Nielsen's reputation and commercial success – and also reveal the significance of its timing.

By the beginning of 1914, there were many newer and younger entrants to the screen pantheon, but Asta Nielsen's name and 'brand' was established. However, by the end of that year, the First World War had engulfed Europe, and although it did not immediately damage Asta Nielsen's popularity in other territories, the underlying changes that it would bring about in the structure of the international film business would ensure that in future only American-based stars could enjoy the same global appeal.[40] As the nascent Hollywood majors increasingly controlled distribution after 1916, so the European industries dramatically lost whatever international market share they previously had.[41] Henceforth, film stars would be quintessentially a Hollywood phenomenon, with the qualification 'local' or 'national' attached to all others. Asta Nielsen, meanwhile, continued her independent and innovative career, benefiting from the relative stabilisation of Weimar cinema, and, like Henny Porten and Lil Dagover, a loyal following.

An earlier version of this appeared in Martin Loiperdinger and Uli Jung, eds., *Importing Asta Nielsen: The International Film Star in the Making 1910-1914* (KINtop 2/John Libbey, 2013).

Sounds Familiar

17.
Early Synchronised Pictures

There is a spectre still haunting the study of early film – the spectre of sound. Ever since the 1998 Domitor conference in Washington, entitled The Sounds of Silence, we have known that early film shows were generally accompanied by live music and other sounds. But more broadly, it is also clear that film was born, so to speak, with the expectation that sound recording, an already accomplished technology, would now be supplemented by movement recording. Most who take an interest in early film surely know the famous Edison sound-bite, predicting 'an instrument which does for the eye what the phonograph does for the ear'. But how many have taken to heart the order of priority implicit in this?

Certainly there is now a level of routine acknowledgement of early sound accompaniment. At the Washington conference we witnessed the 'premiere' of W. K. L. Dickson's Experimental Sound Film, deftly restored by Walter Murch, so that it could be experienced as conceived, if not actually experienced, in 1894 (this remains available online).[1] Most accounts of early film technology and presentation are at least illustrated by the florid art nouveau poster for Clément Maurice's Phono-Cinéma-Théâtre, as presented at the 1900 Paris Exposition Universelle, although it was not until the Pordenone Giornate del Cinema Muto of 2012 that elements of this programme were heard as well as seen. However, the Maurice presentation was only one of at least three rival talking films exhibits at the 1900 Paris Expo (others were the Theatrescope and the Phonorama) which points to a high degree of interest in presenting synchronous performance, rather than an isolated experiment.[2]

More significantly, the two major systems of synchronised performances, Gaumont's Chronophone and Oskar Messter's Biophon, both of which lasted for over a decade, have been marginalised, if not wholly omitted from most synoptic film histories.[3] Yet as Alison McMahon argued in her biography of Alice Guy, 'the real extent of the relationship between Guy's *chronophone* production and Guy's career has not been understood'.[4] Guy not only directed over a hundred of the 150 *phonoscènes* produced for the Chronophone system during 1905-06, but, according to McMahon, it was these sound films that occasioned her partnership and marriage to Herbert Blaché, and took the pair to the United States, to launch the Chronophone there, before forming their independent Solax Company in New Jersey in 1910.[5]

Oskar Messter's Tonbilder catalogue began after his 1903 synchronised shows in Berlin, and eventually had 500 cinemas throughout Germany using the Biophon electromechanical synchronisation system by 1913.

The failure to mention Messter's Biophon and the 450 *tonbilder* he produced which showed at some 300 cinemas is to some extent symptomatic of a larger failure in Anglo-American historiography to explore early German cinema 'before *Caligari*'. It was not until a cluster of articles and references about Messter appeared in 1994-96 that his central role in establishing an early sound-cinema network was recognised.[6] In 1996, Frank Kessler and Sabine Lenk revealed negotiations between Messter and Gaumont to try to 'stabilise the market situation' for sound films as early as 1903, by making an agreement to distribute the other's films.[7]

While the Gaumont Chronophone (of which more later) and Messter's Biophon established substantial exhibition networks devoted to sound films, a second wave of synchronising systems appeared in 1907-09 which were aimed at occasional use, rather than requiring dedicated cinemas. In Britain, Hepworth's Vivaphone and Walturdaw's Cinematophone both appeared in 1907, while Barker and Jeapes' Cinephone was said to have been already installed in 1,000 British cinemas before its transatlantic launch in 1909, with the prefix 'American'.[8] Another British system, the Animatophone, reported by Rachael Low to have been 'greeted in some quarters as the first really successful [synchronisation] system', came onto the market in 1910.[9]

A more recent historian of film music has written about the 'meteor shower of sound-film devices' in this period, listing their 'colourful' names: 'the Animatophone; the Biographon; Biophon, the Biophonograph; the Chronophotographoscope; the Cinemacrophonograph; the Cinematophone, and Cineograph; the Graphophonoscope; the Kinematophone and Kosmograph; the Phoneidograph, Phone-Cinéma-Théâtre, and Phonoscope; the Photophone, Foto-Fone, and Photokinema; the Picturephone; the Synchrophone and Synchroscope; the Talkaphone and the Vivaphone'.[10] Such a list of elaborate variations on the basic sound-image concept can only make these devices sound like so many outdated contraptions, and, indeed, Wierzbecki concludes that, at least in the United States, Edison's 'improved' Kinetophone effectively swept aside all competition in 1913. But he does not deny that this was 'an obviously crowded field'.

In view of all this accumulated and undisputed empirical evidence, we might wonder why successive generations of historians of early cinema have never really taken on board the fact that *recorded* sound was an integral, even if not a universal, component of the moving picture experience in the 1900s. In fact, Ben Brewster noted in a review of the Washington conference that 'the role of the synchronised film was perhaps a gap in the conference's coverage'. Subsequently Rick Altman's *Silent Film Sound* provided a systematic and exhaustive survey of sound accompaniment practices.[11]

But I contend that the *performative* aspect of recorded accompanying sound has still not been acknowledged. A key to this may lie in the attitude of one of the early historians, Rachael Low, who included an appendix on 'Sound' in the second volume of her influential *History of the British Film*. Low duly listed some of the bizarre apparatus names (including the Replicaphone and Appollogramophone) and provided details of their cost, which was a mere £5 5s in the case of the Vivaphone, compared with £72 for the Cinematophone. But in dismissing 'films with disc accompaniment' as 'little more than novelties, increasingly isolated from the advance of film technique', Low not only ignored the sheer volume of such 'novelties' but betrayed a teleological prejudice from the 1940s, when she was writing, in favour of what was currently considered the 'truly filmic' fiction film.[12] Viewed from a later standpoint, the argument could be reversed: that such early performance-centred films anticipated not only a dominant trend in cinema since the 1930s, but also modern music-video culture. And it is indeed from a new generation of historians and collectors focused on early sound recording, such as Thomas Schmitt, that the impetus has come to reverse the condescension of film historians.[13]

Low's assumption was driven by the need to separate 'film' from its formative phase in music halls and vaudeville theatres, when it had been one among many 'acts'. A high proportion of early film subjects by both Edison and Paul (though not by Lumière) were indeed dancers, magicians and 'eccentrics' – such as Chirgwin, 'the White-Eyed Kaffir' – who usually performed novelty songs, but frustratingly could not be *heard* until the appearance of the first synchronisation systems. From this perspective, the desire to make audible popular performers, preferably by means of their already recorded songs, is entirely understandable. Rather than see such devices as 'adding' sound, they might be better understood as *restoring* sound to the new regime of audiovisual representation.

> **Singing and Talking Pictures**
> **"THE VIVAPHONE"**
> *Invented by Cecil M. Hepworth, London, England. Patented in U.S.A. and Canada*
> **INSTANTANEOUS SUCCESS**
> The Vivaphone has come to stay:—
> Read this:—Mr. Oldknow of Atlanta, Ga., after seeing the first picture run through, said "How much for my nine Southern States?" "So much." Answer "Right; you've sold 'em; supply me with 100 machines for a start and 2 film subjects per week for each State, 18 pictures each week."
> **"Blinkie Boy, you've got a winner"**
> Don't forget it is no resurrection. We started 5 years ago and have had continuous success in Great Britain and Ireland ever since
> **NOTE: More than 500 *New* Subjects and Records Ready**
> PERFECT SYNCHRONISM   INEXPENSIVE AND SIMPLE
> **STATE RIGHTS SELLING RAPIDLY**
> *Send for Prices and Descriptive Booklets*
> **ALBERT BLINKHORN**, Sole Agent for U.S.A. and Canada **Longacre Buildings, 1480 B'dway, N.Y.**

Many countries had their own local synchronisation systems. In Britain, Hepworth's Vivaphone was apparently successful.

Léon Gaumont's belief in synchronised film was fully equal to that of Edison, and the success of his Chronophone system occupied the period between Edison's first Kineto-phonoscope venture and the Kinetophone of 1913. After his early demonstrations in 1902, Gaumont built a Paris studio for sound film production in 1905, and in 1908 the American studio that Guy-Blaché managed. 1907 was the year that Gaumont made a determined effort in the British market, gaining valuable publicity for the *phonoscène* programme already running at the Hippodrome Theatre with a special presentation at Buckingham Palace on 4 April, attended by the Queen, the Prince and Princess of Wales and their children and a bevy of courtiers.[14] According to another report of the programme of five operatic 'singing pictures', 'the Queen showed her pleasure by commanding the putting on of extra pictures after the ordinary programme had been completed'.[15]

What the early synchronised film could offer was precisely what cinema and television have continued to provide: a visible performance synched most often to an optimised, pre-recorded soundtrack. When Léon Gaumont began issuing *phonescènes* for the Chronophone, an important consideration was how 'universal' in appeal these would be, hence an early bias towards popular classical music. The Buckingham Palace programme consisted of scenes from Verdi's *Il Trovatore*, Gounod's *Faust*, a song and dance from André Messager's operetta *The Little Michus* (*Les p'tites Michu*, 1897), which had recently enjoyed great success on the London stage, and two Gilbert and Sullivan numbers. The fourteen comic 'Savoy operas' written by W. S. Gilbert and Arthur Sullivan between 1871 and 1896 were by this time a cult attraction in Britain, and more widely across the Empire and English-speaking world, attracting a relatively wide class spectrum, and the ninth of these, *The Mikado*, became by far the most popular. Perhaps unsurprisingly, this became a focus of competition between rival sound-film systems. Gaumont produced the first series of *Highlights from The Mikado* in 1906, which Walturdaw then followed with another series using its Cinematophone system in July 1907, starring the baritone George Thorne, who had created the role of Ko-Ko on Broadway in 1885.[16]

Contemporary star performers offered the potential of attracting wide audience interest, and hence increased sales to exhibitors, even if there were issues of language and locality. Gilbert and Sullivan had at least guaranteed British and American appeal, while French singers were unlikely to appeal outside France, however popular they might be domestically.[17] In 1907, with the Chronophone business apparently prospering, Gaumont's British branch signed an exclusive deal with Harry Lauder (1870-1950), the Scottish ex-miner who had become a British and eventually international variety star, with a career that lasted until the 1940s. Lauder wore Highland dress and sported a distinctive twisted walking stick, while singing his own compositions, such as 'Roamin' in the Gloamin'', 'I Love a Lassie', 'A Wee Deoch-an-Doris' and 'Keep Right On to the End of the Road,' mostly about courtship, marriage and the stereotypical Scottish themes of drink and parsimony.

The Gaumont Chronophone system was patented in 1902, and used widely for the next fifteen years, signing many famous artistes, such as Harry Lauder, to exclusive contracts.

Lauder was reported to be the highest paid variety entertainer in the world between 1906-12, and his fee from Gaumont was rumoured to be 'four figures' for the seven songs which appear among the 75 Gaumont titles listed on Carl Bennett's 'Silent Era' website.[18] Gaumont's *Kine Weekly* advertisement of 16 July 1907 sheds some light on how the Lauder 'singing pictures' fitted into the evolving entertainment economy of the era, with 'pre-recorded' material gaining ground. These were clearly a major attraction at Gaumont's flagship London theatre, The Hippodrome, where they were 'fast approaching the 400th consecutive performance – playing, in fact, as if Lauder were appearing there in person. They are also advertised as being 'open to offers… in districts not affected by the Moss-Stoll circuits', which were presumably the music halls in which Lauder *was* actually appearing. The Chronophone titles were therefore envisaged as a kind of supplement to Lauder's main career as a performer, able to take him to an even wider range of venues. We do not, of course, have any idea of the scale of exhibitors' response to this offer, except for occasional mentions in *Kine Weekly*'s impressionistic survey of exhibitors around the country.[19]

But far away in Reno, Nevada, the Chronophone was billed as a major attraction in 1910, for the reopening of the Grand Theatre, where 'the perfected talking picture apparatus… will present such artists as Harry Lauder, Victoria Monks, Blanche Ring, Dan Michaels and other celebrated stars in their best sketches'.[20] This advertisement explains that 'the Chronophone is an electrically synchronised machine for the purpose of reproducing in sound and motion picture sketches by the greatest vaudeville artists in the world. It has been added to the equipment of the Isis company and will take the place of the illustrated songs, which have always been a part of the program heretofore'. The Grand's proposed programme of 'three reels of the high-class motion pictures and two reels of talking pictures' sounds like an unusually high ratio of synchronised to unsynchronised pictures, but there is no information to hand about its progress or success.

1913 seems to have marked the climax of aspiration, and perhaps also of exploitation of sound-film systems. In March, *Moving Picture World* offered a survey of 'talking picture' systems which concluded that Edison's Kinetophone had been 'instrumental in gaining recognition for the "talking pictures"'.[21] A report in the following month from Louisville indicated that, while the response was not universally enthusiastic, it was enough to support plans for a dedicated theatre:

> The Edison kinetophone has made its appearance in Louisville, B. F. Keith's vaudeville house presenting the latest device of the inventor to the public. Largely speaking, it may be said that the Louisville patrons of the theater enjoyed the talking pictures, even though some expressions of disappointment were heard. Devotees of the animated pictures, perhaps, had been led to expect too much, and the performance therefore fell a bit beneath anticipations. One of Louisville's amusement companies is now negotiating for the local rights of the kinetophone, and one of its houses will shortly be devoted to the talking pictures.[22]

Such plans did not come to fruition. Although confidence in the Kinetophone and other systems was at its height – Harry Lauder entering a new partnership with Selig Polyscope to make seventeen sound-films, to coincide with his latest American tour – Altman notes that 'as suddenly as they appeared, the ads for synch-sound systems disappeared'.[23] Why did this happen? Altman points to 'two devastating events' which affected the market. One was the outbreak of the Great War in Europe, which 'jeopard[ised] the Kinetophone's export income' – and would also affect drastically the fortunes of both Gaumont's multinational business empire and Messter's immediate market in German-speaking countries. The other was a major fire at Edison's West Orange plant in December, which 'destroyed every Kinetophone record and film master'.[24]

While these factors were clearly significant, especially for Edison, other explanations have been offered for the rapid decline of sound-films in 1913-14. The most common is an assumption that the systems were inherently fragile or unreliable, since they depended on operators' skills and on systems of signalling, or mechanical coupling between projectors and turntables. This can certainly be challenged by pointing to the considerable technical advances made by, especially, Gaumont and Messter in developing their systems. During the entire era of short-duration recorded discs, skills in moving between turntables were well-developed, and such equipment continues to be used in modern disc-based 'performance by DJs. Martin Loiperdinger has challenged this account of inherent technical and practical problems, as articulated by Thomas Elsaesser in several accounts of early German cinema, insisting that '*tonbilder* did not disappear due to technical problems... but because their production was no longer profitable'.[25] Messter's sound-films, according to this view, were the victim of their own success, with over-production leading to price-decline, making them ultimately unprofitable to produce, since they represented an 'advanced technology [requiring] an increased investment by producers, on which they could then expect a higher return'.

Loiperdinger's argument provides a valuable counter-balance to the familiar assumption that these were in some sense 'primitive', compared with later sound-on-film systems. But it needs to be supplemented by noting the parallel trends towards longer films (which would erode the market for all short films, including the more expensive synch-sound ones) and larger cinemas of 2,000 seats and more, which must have challenged sound amplification technology in 1913-14. The very low rate of survival of early sound-films, and the inability to play any of those elements that have survived – other than through digital restoration – have undoubtedly contributed to making this once-substantial and 'advanced' sector of early film experience largely unknown.[26] Both Gaumont and Messter operated sound-film successfully for most of a decade and by 1912-13, the idea of pre-recorded music and film was beginning to interest artists, notably Paul Klee and Arnold Schoenberg.[27] The most successful international variety performer of the era, Harry Lauder, continued to involve himself in sound-film ventures, making a demonstration for Orlando Kellum's Photokinema system in 1921.[28]

Rachael Low, as we have seen, set the tone for commenting on early synchronised sound, dismissing it as 'quite outside the general stream of artistic development',[29] and more recent historians, includ-ing Altman, Elsaesser and Wiertzbicki, have tended to adopt a similar position, albeit for different reasons. I want to argue that it is unjustified to write off what was a very substantial and persistent part of early film presentation, one which required 'performance' (which was undoubtedly both a problem and a challenge) but also offered cinemas 'the means to distinguish themselves from the competition'.[30] Very few participants or observers of the pre-1915 period seem to have thought it was undesirable or misguided, and many leading performers of the period were happy to participate, lending sound film their prestige. We know very little about how many such performances were in circulation and how they interacted with live and 'normal' recorded performances of the same songs. No doubt they were, in effect, the 'music videos' and proto-YouTube clips of the era. We can no longer regard these as 'outside' audiovisual culture. Nor do we know what part they played in developing the popularity of cinemagoing by making the new moving-picture venues seem more like variety theatres – an important link in the long-suppressed history of cinema as a hybrid form of entertainment, and one which is once again topical, with the rise of live performance being transmitted directly into cinema theatres.

A version of this appeared in the proceedings of the 2012 Domitor Conference in Brighton, published as *Performing New Media, 1890-1915*, ed. Kaveh Askari, Scott Curtis, Frank Gray, Louis Pelletier, Tami Williams, Joshua Yumibe (John Libbey, 2014).

18.
'Suitable Music':
Silent-Era Accompaniment Practices

I want to try to answer a basic question: what evidence do we have of accompaniment practice for early film screenings in Britain, and specifically in London, before the mid-teens?

There have been for some time two main assumptions about accompaniment in the early years of moving pictures. The most common is that 'the silents were never silent', which has been challenged by the claim that they *were* frequently unaccompanied, at least before about 1908.[1] This latter view was advanced by Rick Altman in his controversial 1997 paper 'The Silence of the Silents', arguing that many, if not most, early film shows only had music *between* rather that accompanying films.[2] But rather than start from either of these assumptions, I want to marshal what evidence is available and to look specifically at London, bearing in mind that practices may very well have been different in other cities and countries.

Immediately, we have to address the issues of prevailing practices and tradition, and of incomplete evidence. In terms of tradition, we can look back to the earliest self-proclaimed 'moving pictures' in London: the Eidophusikon of Philippe de Loutherbourg. According to the *Daily Universal Register* advertisement of 1 March 1786, this entertainment offered five items: Aurora, Sunset, A Storm and Moon Light, ending with 'a Grand Conclusive Scene', illustrating an episode from Milton's *Paradise Lost*, with Satan reviewing his troops before the Palace of Pandemonium.[3] The advertisement also stated that these would be given 'with suitable accompaniment'. A handbill for the Eidophusikon from the same year refers to 'the usual accompaniments' for the 'Grand Scene from Milton'.[4]

Despite various appreciative comments from those who saw De Loutherbourg's shows, the only evidence of what the accompaniment might have been is the *Daily Register* advertisement's reference to 'English readings and recitals' that will be given while scenery is being changed, and a harpsichord visible in Edward Burney's 1782 watercolour of the Eidophusikon.[5] Iain McCalmain noted that 'between scenes, painted transparencies served as curtain drops, and Mr and Mrs Michael Arne entertained the audience with violin music and song'.[6] This might suggest that the main purpose of the readings and music was to 'cover' the scene changes, much as Altman has claimed music was used to bridge across reel changes in early cinema exhibition. Certainly there were sound effects, since De Loutherbourg was already recognised for his mastery of 'the picturesque of sound' in his stage work for David Garrick. Ephraim Hardcastle's recollection of attending the Eidophusikon goes into considerable detail on how De Loutherbourg enhanced his vividly realised 'moving pictures'.[7]

Throughout the following century, three important trends would have a bearing on the place of music in relation to spectacle. One was the return of 'incidental' music to the English stage. Although theatre music had been commonplace in 17th-century London, with Henry Purcell writing music for over forty plays in the 1690s, musical fashion favoured operas and masques during the 18th century, with Thomas Arne and Handel among the most popular composers in Britain.[8] But by the mid-19th century, as the London theatre turned towards spectacle, incidental music became fashionable. An early example of the spectacle melodramas that would come to dominate Victorian popular theatre was *The Cataract of the Ganges*, staged at Drury Lane in 1823. The stage directions called for 'A field of battle near Ahmedabad by moonlight... After overture descriptive of a battle, the curtain rises and discovers wounded, dead and dying... Music expresses the groans of the wounded and dying, the retreat of the Mahomedan army at a distance'.[9]

By the mid-century, descriptive and evocative music had become integral, not only for melodrama but for the spectacular staging of classic works. Madame Vestris' *Midsummer Night's Dream* at Covent Garden in 1840 featured extensive musical accompaniment and ballets, using Mendelssohn's music.[10] And for his *Faust* at the Lyceum Theatre in 1885, Henry Irving increased the size of his usual orchestra to place even greater emphasis on the role of music, heard continuously throughout the performance.[11]

Another trend of the early 19th century was the rise of Romantic programme music. Again, there had been instances of narrative and scene painting in 17th- and 18th-century music: Kuhnau's Biblical Sonatas and various 'effects' in the symphonies of Haydn. But from Beethoven's *Pastoral* (Sixth) Symphony onward, by way of his *Battle Symphony* and Tchaikovsky's *1812 Overture*,[12] through Liszt's symphonic poems and piano landscapes, there was a growing recognition of the descriptive and evocative potential of music. And much of this would later be recycled in pot-pourri film accompaniment during the 1910s and '20s.

This last was an international trend, as was the emergence of popular music-based 'variety' entertainment aimed at a wider social spectrum than the audience for concert music. The success of such entertainment soon prompted building on a lavish scale, with London music halls leading the way, and often providing a model – as in the case of the Folies Bergère in Paris being inspired by the Moorish Alhambra in London. In post-Civil War America, the new vaudeville theatres catered to family audiences by prohibiting alcohol and stressing wholesome performances – very different from the raffish atmosphere of London's rapidly expanding network of music halls. But as the music halls and their equivalents became the first regular exhibition sites for film, so their existing practices became the earliest conventions for film presentation.

This strongly suggests that moving picture shows at the Empire and the Alhambra, the two Leicester Square music halls which were first to present this novelty, had musical accompaniment from the outset. According to various accounts, the Paris Lumière show that began at the end of 1895 had piano accompaniment, and the London Lumière debut at the Polytechnic on 20 February 1896 is reported to have been accompanied by a harmonium.[13] Although early Lumière Cinématographe shows at the Empire began in the Grand Foyer during the afternoons in March 1896 and may not have been accompanied, these proved so popular that they soon moved into the main theatre, and a playbill dated 8 March states that 'a selection of music will be played under the direction of Mr George Byng'.[14]

In the case of Robert Paul's rival Theatrograph, there are two valuable reviews that give some insight into just what early accompaniments were providing. Paul's Theatrograph made its debut at the Egyptian Hall on 19 March 1896, introduced by the magician Nevil Maskelyne, and a review from a month later reported 'The first moving scene announced by Mr Nevil Maskelyne is a band practice. The music of the march that one may imagine is being played is given on the pianoforte by Mr F. Cramer'.[15]

The other items in this programme of Edison Kinetoscope subjects – Highland dancers, a Serpentine dance and boxing cats – all suggest that Mr Cramer would have supplied appropriate music that 'one might imagine'. When Paul was booked by the Empire's near neighbour in Leicester Square, the Alhambra Music Hall, his projector was renamed The Animatograph and began a two-year run on 25 March 1896. There is no reference to musical accompaniment until June, when Paul filmed the Derby being won by Persimmon, a horse belonging to the Prince of Wales. Having captured the finish of the race and taken his film back to London for overnight processing, Paul was able to present it on the following evening at the Alhambra, where 'an enormous audience... witnessed the Prince's Derby, all to themselves amidst wildest enthusiasm, which all but drowned the strains of "God Bless the Prince of Wales", as played by the splendid orchestra'.[16] Another account describes the same film being shown at the Canterbury music hall, also 'to the strains of "God Bless the Prince of Wales", and at both venues it was apparently encored.[17]

These appear to be the only contemporary accounts of film screenings in London before 1900 that specifically refer to musical accompaniment. But they all indicate what seems to have been a normal practice in venues where music usually accompanied most performances. Is it imaginable that the Alhambra's orchestra, used to playing for a wide range of acts on the programme, would *only* have played for this single film, lasting less than a minute, and forming part of a series that normally included up to twenty titles? The 'Persimmon' case rather implies that such accompaniment was routine; and that it was likely to be based on verbal/ title association, as Altman has suggested.[18] It implies that early London film shows would follow the conventions of the place of exhibition. Where an orchestra was present there would be 'normal' accompaniment, most likely based on subject or title 'cueing', so that, for instance, another film by Paul of Henley Regatta would most likely have been accompanied by a relevant boating song, while mention of the sea might have invited such staples as 'Heart of Oak' (William Boyce, 1759), 'A Life on the Ocean Wave' (Henry Russell, 1838) or even something from the recent Gilbert and Sullivan operetta, *The Pirates of Penzance* (1880).

Many early films were in fact based on, and no doubt suggested by, popular songs. When the Alhambra manager invited Paul to add a fictional film to his repertoire in April 1896, the subject chosen, *The Soldier's Courtship*, seems to have been inspired by the popular figure of 'Tommy Atkins', celebrated in a recent music hall song, 'Private Tommy Atkins'.[19] It seems very likely, especially given the participatory habits of music hall audiences, that this would have been accompanied by the song's music, which the audience would have then taken up. An even clearer example of a film suggested by a song is Paul's *Come Along, Do!* (1898), in which an elderly couple are first seen outside an art exhibition, then inside, where the man is seen staring at a nude female statue while his wife tries to pull him away.[20]

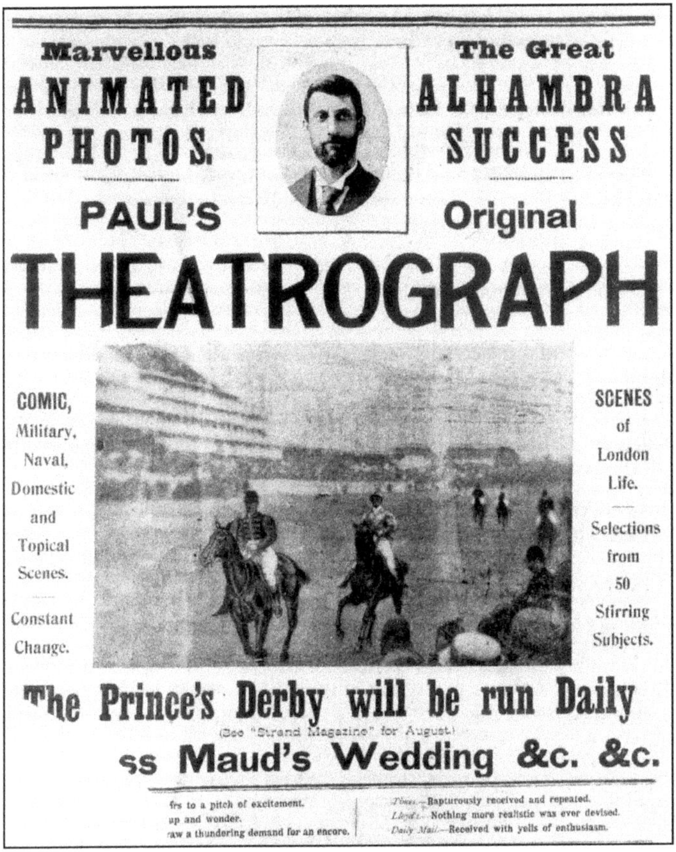

1896 advertisement for Paul's Theatrograph, featuring The Prince's Derby, originally accompanied by "God Bless the Prince of Wales".

This seems to be the earliest example known in filmmaking of two spatially distinct shots being joined to tell a story. But equally significant is the film's complex genealogy, stretching back some thirty-five years to a painting that narrativised and mocked the controversy caused by John Gibson's nude sculpture *Tinted Venus*, when this was exhibited at the 1862 International Exhibition. A song quickly appeared, using the same title and illustrated by a near-copy of the painting, with the refrain 'Come along do/What are you staring at?/You ought to know better – so come along do'.[21] In the 1870s, the anecdote was realised as a photographic stereo card, which was later republished in the 1890s, and presumably formed the immediate basis of Paul's filmed realisation. This chain inevitably recalls Martin Meisel's influential study of 'realisation' in 19th-century culture, whereby novels gave rise to illustrations, which in turn could become the basis of stage versions.[22] In the case of *Come Along, Do!*, a statue gives rise to an ironic anecdote, which mutates through four different media, acquiring in the process both a visual/dramatic form and a musical narrative, as a song by Walter Burnot and Jesse Williams, which is likely to have been available to both exhibitors and audiences for the film. In short, it is more than likely that screenings of the film would have prompted a knowing accompanist to 'quote' the song.[23]

Evidence of the kind of context where early film screening took place beyond music halls comes from reports of a mixed lantern slide and film presentation in the London district of Muswell Hill in December 1899, soon after the outbreak of the Anglo-Boer War.[24] Billed as 'A Trip to the Transvaal', this was a lantern lecture given to raise money towards building a new church in this developing suburb. It was given by a Mr Salmond, who had travelled widely in Southern Africa before the outbreak of the war, possibly as a missionary, in view of the venue for the lecture. In addition to the usual lantern slides, at least six films were shown, all apparently drawn from the Warwick Trading Company's extensive catalogue of non-fiction subjects.

What makes this suburban occasion particularly interesting in relation to musical accompaniment is a report of Mr Salmond performing two songs.[25] These are not identified, so we have no way of knowing if they were in any way related to the subject of the lecture. Perhaps more likely, in view of the setting, is that they were 'sacred songs' from the repertoire that was already common at non-conformist church social events.[26] Nor do we know if the Presbyterian Hall had a piano or the increasingly popular harmonium, which were common in such halls and could have been used to accompany Mr Salmond – and potentially also his slides and films. Live musical performance was indeed an integral part of much Victorian and Edwardian sociality. So rather than ask *if* films were accompanied, it makes more historical sense to ask: why would they *not* be?

The Magic Lantern show was an important tradition which 'incubated' moving picture exhibition in early hybrid or composite performances. Lantern shows took place in a wide variety of settings, ranging from the purely domestic to increasingly large halls, as new illuminants appeared in the later 19th century. Most lantern shows were broadly informative or educational, and therefore relied on the lecturer's voice alone.[27] But many 'life-model' lantern narratives had accompanying dramatic texts for recitation, often in verse, and would certainly have been accompanied by music performed on whatever instruments were available.[28] London's most elaborate lantern shows, known as 'dissolving views', were given throughout the mid-19th century at the Royal Polytechnic in Regent Street – which would also house the first Lumière demonstration in February 1896 – and these routinely had elaborate musical accompaniment, serving to emphasise their pictorial and 'aesthetic' content.[29]

We have one retrospective account of how such a composite slide and film show was presented with musical accompaniment. Cecil Hepworth was the son of a noted lanternist, T. C. Hepworth, and entered the film business in 1896, initially as an exhibitor. He continued as a director and producer until the 1920s and published his memoirs in 1951.[30] He recalled 'a little series' shown during the mid-1890s 'which always went down very well indeed. It was called The Storm and consisted of half a dozen slides and one forty foot film. My sister Effie was a very good pianist and she travelled with me on most of those jaunts. The sequence opened with a calm and peaceful picture of the sea and sky. Soft and gentle music (Schumann, I think). That changed to another seascape, though the clouds looked a little more interesting and the music quickened a bit. At each stage the inevitability of a coming gale became more insistent and the music more threatening; until the storm broke with an exciting film, of dashing waves bursting into the entrance of a cave, with wild music (by Jensen, I think)'.[31]

Martin Miller Marks has analysed this account from a musical standpoint, suggesting that Effie Hepworth may have played 'in an improvisatory fashion', to link the composed pieces she was drawing upon.[32] Like other commentators on Hepworth's recollection, however, he does not identify the film, which was almost certainly Paul's *Sea Cave Near Lisbon*, the most widely admired of his 1896 series *A Tour in Spain and Portugal*.[33]

After the first appearance of this series at the Alhambra, in October 1896, reviews described the *Sea Cave* as 'a picture of real beauty' and 'one of the most remarkable effects produced by any of the "graphies" yet put forward'.[34] Hepworth reveals that it could be used in quite a different way, to create the climax in a pictorial sequence, with still images as it were 'breaking into movement'. This not only suggests a continuity with the picturesque tradition that De Loutherbourg had helped inaugurate through his stage work and the Eidophusikon. It also draws attention to the influence of Symbolist culture at the *fin de siècle*, in which sound, word and image were closely intertwined, often to synaesthetic effect. A celebrated Russian music critic's reaction to his first experience of the Lumière film of children diving into the sea was to recall the musical representation of a similar effect: 'and then to watch the sea moving just a few feet away from our chairs – Mendelssohn's *Meerstille!* – yet this silvery movement produces a music of its own'.[35] Moving images, whether or not audibly accompanied, could create 'music of movement', just as the music of such Symbolist composers as Debussy and Skriabin aspired to evoke images, colours, and even perfumes.

There is further scattered evidence of early moving pictures being associated with contemporary music-making. During the second season of the popular Promenade Concerts at London's new orchestral concert venue, Queen's Hall in Langham Place, in September 1896, the magician David Devant showed Paul's Animated Photographs as an interval attraction in the upstairs 500-seat Small Hall, normally devoted to chamber music.[36] There is no mention of any musical accompaniment to Devant's shows, and there may well not have been any, since this was an interval in an orchestral concert, but the association between these pioneering concerts and the new experience seems significant.[37] However, the documented relationship that developed over the next ten years seems to have been less one of music accompanying film than the reverse. In 1907, Covent Garden Royal Opera House was reported to be using both lantern slides and, for the first time, in its new production of Wagner's *Ring of the Nibelungen*, film. The film of the 'Ride of the Valkyries', taken during a special rehearsal in Surrey, was, according to the *Kine Weekly*, 'generally admitted to be better than the old method' of presenting this popular episode from *Die Walküre*.[38]

In spite of the evocative associations between movement and music, the most obvious pattern was more or less literal illustration. Slides based on the stories told by popular songs, as well as those providing the words to be sung, were a familiar feature of the lantern repertoire. Why not, then, use film to bring familiar songs to life? The first to attempt this in England seems to have been Lewis Sealy, a pioneer exhibitor who later became an actor in America. Early in 1899, Sealy filmed 'dramatisations' of two songs, 'Tomorrow Will be Friday' and 'Simon the Cellarer', with the help of Esme Collings, and the latter was released in January as three films corresponding to each of the three verses, described as 'the latest sensation'.[39] A trade journal review praised the films, noting that 'when coupled with the singing of the song [they form] a spectacle of great interest'.[40]

Robert Paul was quick to adopt this new form, introducing four contrasting 'songs with animated illustrations' in his 1901 catalogue, 'on the basis of a large amount of experiment and trial'.[41] The songs are each characterised differently:

'Arry on the Steamboat – coster song [42]
Britain's Tribute to Her Sons – a patriotic song
Ora Pro Nobis – a sentimental song
The Waif and the Wizard – a descriptive song

Three of these were existing songs, two associated with relatively well-known performers,[43] while 'Britain's Tribute' was announced with some fanfare as 'a grand patriotic song... Specially written and composed for R. W. Paul by Clarence Hunt, with music by Frank Byng. Byng is described as 'of the Strand Theatre', where he was presumably music director or conductor; and his association with Paul had started a year earlier when he arranged a special score for *Army Life* in 1900.[44]

This ambitious documentary series, subtitled 'How Soldiers Are Made', consisted of 21 parts that covered the experience of joining up and 'training in the various branches of the service'.[45] Paul launched it at a special screening at the Alhambra on 18 September 1900, with an invited audience of officers, Chelsea Pensioners and schoolboys. Backed and facilitated by the Army's Adjutant-General, it was no doubt seen as a useful stimulus to recruitment as the South African War entered its second year. But it also seems to have been a distinctly personal project for Paul, whose brothers were serving in the City Imperial Volunteers, and who apparently served as his own cameraman for the series. The 1901 catalogue offered illustrated brochures for sale and 12-sheet posters to promote what was the longest film of the period, at nearly fifty minutes. A compilation of 'suitable music' was part of the exhibition strategy proposed, 'suitable for Sunday evening exhibition, with or without a lecturer'.

In this, as with the 'animated songs', Paul seems to have been an innovator. The song films, illustrating the songs' incidents word for word, were contrasted with 'phonograph accompaniment of the picture of a figure on stage'.[46] Clearly Paul envisaged live performance as an attraction, or a necessity, since phonograph technology at this time made filling any large space difficult, and he promised future illustrated songs: 'Particulars of new Christmas, Temperance and Religious Films, now in hand, will be announced shortly'. That these failed to appear suggests that the 'refined' audiences for which they were apparently intended had not responded or not been reached. However, one of Paul's other productions in 1901 pointed towards a new direction: *The Magic Sword* was billed as a 'medieval mystery' and uses stop-motion and multiple exposure to reproduce on film the kind of magic spectacle normally associated with pantomime.[47] There is no reference to any special music offered to accompany it, but its genre strongly suggests that Paul was aiming to provide a form of 'remediated' pantomime, for which music would have been expected. His other major production of late 1901, a multi-scene adaptation of Dickens' *A Christmas Carol*, entitled *Scrooge; or, Marley's Ghost*, also made use of the studio's growing skill with trick film effects, and had its premiere in the Promenade Concert interval at the Queen's Hall in January 1902.

Even if Paul's proposed series of 'illustrated songs' to perform did not find takers in 1901, recorded songs would become a staple with the various proprietary systems for synchronising recordings and films that proliferated towards the end of first decade of the 1900s. Having at least one synchronised item on the typical programme of seven to ten short films seems to have been as widespread in Britain as elsewhere.[48] These systems included the Vivaphone, developed by Hepworth in 1907, and Walturdaw's Cinematophone, launched in the same year.[49] Léon Gaumont had launched his Chronophone in 1902, but it was not until Gaumont introduced the Elgéphone in 1906, driven by compressed air, that the company's *phonoscènes* attracted substantial audiences.[50] In London, they enjoyed a successful run at the Hippodrome during 1906–07 under the anglicised name 'Chronomegaphone'. When Gilbert and Sullivan's popular *Mikado* was temporarily banned from performance in 1907, to avoid giving offence to visiting Japanese diplomats, Walturdaw issued a set of 12 Cinematophone numbers from it, while the trade press optimistically suggested that 'people will flock to hear the opera by cinematophone now that they cannot see it on stage'.[51]

Reports in the 'Round the Shows' pages of the *Kine Weekly* trade journal regularly note the inclusion of 'songs by the Cinephone'. This was a relatively simple device, developed by the pioneer cameraman and producer, Will Barker, and patented by Warwick in 1909. According to a present-day Australian collector, who owns one:

> Barker placed the playback gramophone in the corner of the shot with a speed indicator clearly in view while the players mouthed to the playing record. Later, when the film was shown to an audience, an identical gramophone, also with

an indicator, was placed on the stage. The projectionist had a control dial for the gramophone and all he had to do was ride herd on matching the two indicators. With the aid of a quick starting double spring projector, he could have the show in sync during the head leader and before the first image. The whole thing depended on the projectionist's skill.[52]

Despite, or perhaps because of, the performative element in presentation, Cinephone items on the programme were always said to be 'well received', although they continued to be supplemented by live 'illustrated songs' and variety acts. There are also occasional tantalising references to more ambitious presentations, such as a 'patriotic song scena "Invasion", illustrated by lantern slides' in 1909, which indicate that picture houses were still offering hybrid programmes of entertainment.[53]

But were the other films that made up the bulk of these programmes being accompanied? There is intermittent evidence from 'Round the Shows' that the bedrock of successful exhibition in this period was a capable improvising pianist. According to an experienced manager, quoted in 1909: 'too much importance cannot be attached to the music, and therefore it is necessary to have a competent pianist who knows how to improvise and 'fit in' as the phases of the pictures change'.[54]

This would suggest that such accompaniment was widespread, if not universal; although Jon Burrows has argued that trade press exhortation represented a 'blip' or aspiration against the reality of many exhibitors offering either only phonograph accompaniment or none at all.[55] Much reporting of the period is simply silent on the issue of music. For instance, the opening of the new 900-seat Brixton Cinematograph Theatre in March 1911, part of 'the ever-widening circle of Mr Montagu A. Pyke's high-class picture theatres', was greeted by *Kine Weekly* with a description of every aspect of the new cinema, except whether music accompanied the 'full two hours' show'. It seems highly unlikely that such a performance was viewed in silence, but we simply do not know what form or scale of accompaniment was usual in Pyke's cinemas. However, a year later, *The Bioscope* reported that 'the Islington Picture Palace has made a substantial addition, with an orchestra of five instrumentalists'.[56] Does this mean that this small theatre, seating just 120, had none before, or only a pianist?[57] We cannot be sure. Costs were a constant concern, even if, according to *The Bioscope*, a pianist was paid rather less than the projectionist in 1912, and in some cases less than £2 per week. Yet on the supply side, sheet-music albums of suitable mood and genre music began to appear with increasing frequency from 1909, along with advice columns in trade journals, and more comprehensive manuals, such as W. Tyacke George's *Playing to Pictures* (1912).[58]

Perhaps even more than music, sound effects played an important part in early film exhibition, as Stephen Bottomore has demonstrated, with the pianist often supplemented by a percussionist, who became responsible for a growing range of specialised effects. Effects machines began to appear around 1909, to automate what had become a demanding and expensive performance routine.[59] Electric pianos also came on the market, as a means of economically providing 'up to date' music in cinemas,[60] while in America theatre or 'unit' organs offered a versatile range of orchestral timbres and sound effects.[61] Amid all this technological innovation in an increasingly competitive marketplace, producers began to intervene in the chaotic variety of performance practices, in the case of Edison and Vitagraph, issuing their own recommendations for suitable accompaniment.[62] The Film d'Art company in France had led the way in 1908 by commissioning a small orchestra score from the doyen of French composers, Camille Saint-Saens, for their debut production, *The Assassination of the Duc de Guise*, although there is no evidence that this was used after its premiere. But Pathé's takeover of Film d'Art triggered an international movement that promoted cultural and historical subjects, and, together with the rise of the Italian 'epic', this undoubtedly helped promote a more 'symphonic' style of accompaniment.[63]

The seating capacity of new cinemas was also increasing, which called for more volume and perhaps variety in accompaniment. Super productions such as *From the Manger to the Cross* (Sidney Olcott, 1912) and *Quo Vadis?* (Enrico Guazzoni, 1913) were shown at the Albert Hall, and certainly had full-scale orchestral accompaniment with prepared scores accompanying both films. British 'features' aspiring to the same scale, such as *The Battle of Waterloo* (1913) and *Barnaby Rudge* (1915), would no doubt have met audiences' rising expectations that accompaniment should match spectacle. The earliest British medley or compilation score that has been reconstructed and performed from an original set of musical suggestions was prepared for *The Battle of the Somme* (1916), an official chronicle that proved unexpectedly popular in the months after the battle.[64] Using a variety of traditional and contemporary melodies, this confirms that close matching of mood was not expected in 1916.

The British film and music press have traditionally been regarded as taking little interest in cinema music during the 'silent' period, which has perhaps encouraged the belief that the British public was similarly indifferent. But there are in fact many clues scattered throughout the trade papers of the 1910s and '20s, which are beginning to be gathered and interpreted and which suggest that good local practice was appreciated. An example of this exists in a report on the presentation of Griffith's *Way Down East* in 1923 at the Tower Cinema in Peckham, which reveals that the intricate 'leit motif' [sic] style then favoured in Hollywood was not necessarily appreciated in a London cinema. Albert Marchbank, conductor of the Tower Cinema orchestra, took it upon himself to replace the supplied score by William Frederick Peters and Louis Silvers with his own, combining sound and visual effects with music in a performance that evidently thrilled the *American Organist* correspondent:

> The storm music provided the greatest sensation, and this, together with the wonderful effects supplied with the film, absolutely brought the house down. There were, for instance, realistic lightning effects for which a special electric installation had been laid on. This lightning, Mr Marchmont – like Zeus – controlled (from the organ), evoking thunderous replies form the lower regions of the orchestra. There were also ice-breaking machines, waterfall, rain wind effects and what not. All these effects, manipulated in the right way, combined with the wonderful setting of the music, as a musical illustration of the drama on the screen.[65]

As described, this accompaniment somewhat recalls both De Loutherbourg's Eidophusikon and the era of 'sensation' melodrama, to which Griffith's film properly belonged. In this sense, it would have been completely idiomatic, evoking the theatrical thrill of melodrama at Drury Lane a quarter of a century earlier. Such highly integrated performances may have been exceptional (the writer claims, in what is surely an exaggeration, that 'thousands of people had to be turned away from the Tower in Peckham' once the reputation of the show spread), but there is anecdotal and local press evidence that novel accompaniment could constitute a strong attraction.[66] Yet there were undoubtedly contrary views. In America, Vachel Lindsay argued in 1915 that 'the *perfect* photo play gathering place would have no sound but the hum of the conversing audience';[67] while in Britain, the heroine of D. H. Lawrence's novel *The Lost Girl* reaches her lowest ebb playing for a 'picture show' in a Midlands town, where she discovers that 'pictures don't have any life except in the people who watch them'.[68] For Lindsay and both romantic conservatives, the fusion of moving pictures and music that had created a deeply attractive new audiovisual form by the mid-'teens was a threat to be resisted. Yet for the mass audience, it had clearly become addictive.

Camille Saint-Saëns' commissioned score for *L'Assassinat du Duc de Guise* in 1908, probably the first accompaniment specifically written for a dramatic film.

The emergence of 'screen history' as a wider disciplinary frame than 'film studies' suggests that the 'early silent era' of cinema in Britain can usefully be seen as part of a continuum reaching back to the 18th century, with underlying practices and conventions often continuing into new technological regimes. Understanding contexts of presentation is vital and searching for the 'specificity' of the medium fatal. Within this continuum, mediated drama – or what the theatre historian Christopher Baugh has called 'technology-driven entertainment' – has been constantly refashioned, or 'remediated',[69] to maintain its appeal in a highly competitive market. Lacking confidence in the native quality of both music and film, British critics have consistently tended to underestimate the achievements of their compatriots, even though there is much to rediscover, and, no doubt, to celebrate.

This first appeared as a chapter in Julie Brown, Annette Davidson, eds., *The Sounds of the Silents in Britain* (Oxford University Press, 2012).

Time and Space Machine

19.
Bringing the Empire Home: Imperial Spectacle in Early Cinema

> The tumult and the shouting dies;
> The captains and the kings depart:
> Still stands Thine ancient sacrifice,
> An humble and a contrite heart.
> Lord God of Hosts, be with us yet,
> Lest we forget – lest we forget!
>
> Rudyard Kipling,
> *Recessional* (1897)

Consider a London film programme of August 1896: Robert Paul's Animatograph show at the Alhambra Music Hall in Leicester Square, a rival attraction to the Lumière Cinematograph at the nearby Empire. Among the 20 'animated photographs' at the Alhambra, one showed Princess Maud's wedding procession leaving Marlborough House. This is perhaps hardly surprising.

Paul had discovered two months earlier how popular royal association could be when his film of the Derby, won by the Prince of Wales' horse Persimmon, was cheered to the roof of the Alhambra and encored both here and at other music halls. Audiences seemed to have learned quickly how to focus on a film lasting less than a minute, and to associate its contents – however indistinct to our eyes – with contextual information. At a time before printed captions appeared on screen, they were often helped by a 'lecturer' identifying what they were seeing.[1] And they were very far from a passive audience: music halls were noted for the lively interaction between stage and especially the upper gallery. The Alhambra, in particular, had been the scene of frequent demonstrations and riots, often sparked by patriotic issues.

How might the short film of Princess Maud's wedding procession have been received? Maud was the daughter of the popular Prince of Wales (whose Derby win was still on the same Alhambra programme), and she married Prince Charles of Denmark on 22 July, at the height of a heatwave, with London gaily decorated and crowds out to see the procession. The *Illustrated London News* had already carried a double-page engraving of the wedding party, stiffly posed, and Paul's 'animated photograph' would have offered a livelier, less formal image, and almost certainly a closer view of the Princess than those lining the procession route had.[2] Maud's wedding may have been the first such informal royal film to be shown widely in Britain, but it was by no means the only departure or arrival on this Alhambra programme. There were passengers disembarking at Rothesay Pier and a ship leaving the same, more passengers landing from a small boat on Brighton beach, the Paris Express arriving at Calais, and Gordon Highlanders leaving their barracks in Glasgow.

Coming and going emerged very early as ideal subjects for 'animated photography'. Among its pioneers, Louis Lumière, co-inventor of the Cinématographe, was unusually well versed in the aesthetics of instantaneous 'still' photography and seemed to know instinctively the kind of diagonal movement towards the camera that would produce a strong sense of 'nature caught in the act'.[3] The first subject he took in 1894 was workers leaving the family photographic supplies factory, which produced a varied cavalcade of 'ordinary citizens', discreetly marshalled to make their entry onto the new stage of cinematography.[4] Another early Lumière subject in 1895, *Photographic Congress Disembarking*, allowed a succession of fellow-professionals to present themselves before the new apparatus as they came ashore from a boat. With these two markedly democratic films of 1895, which were included in almost every early demonstration of the Cinématographe, the Lumières inaugurated one of the great genres of the new medium: departures and arrivals.[5]

Why should this be thought of as a genre? Because a departure or arrival, when staged for display or recording, becomes a form of ritual, perhaps best described as a 'performative act'. (I am here adapting J. L. Austin's famous concept of 'performative utterance', which refers to statements that are also actions, or performances, as in betting, swearing or apologising.[6]) Departing or arriving is, of course, already an action of some kind, but to be considered 'performative' it would be one that is recognised by actor and audience as having symbolic significance. Thus, Columbus' departure in search of a new route to India or Prince Charles Edward Stuart's arrival in Scotland in 1745, like Caesar crossing the Rubicon, both announced intentions. Such celebrated departures and arrivals have long been recorded in paintings and illustrations that strive to condense their significance into a static image. Mantegna's late 15th-century series of paintings *The Triumphs of Julius Caesar*, long resident in Britain, have been credited with inspiring a revival of interest in the traditions of Roman Imperial ritual.[7] And the 19th century saw a rising level of public display that owed something to this tradition. After Nelson's unprecedented state funeral of 1806, the funeral of the Duke of Wellington in 1852 was planned on an even grander scale, with the design of his massive funeral car apparently modelled on Mantegna's victory carriage.[8]

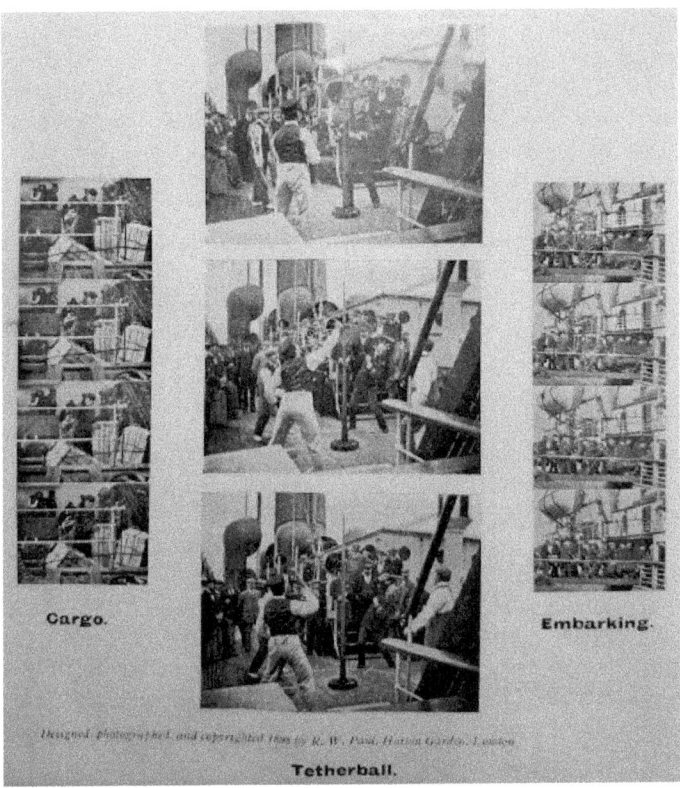

Display page from Robert Paul's 1901 catalogue,
showing how prominent sea travel films were.

In addition to the images of monarchs and national heroes, by the mid-century there was also a turn towards commemorating the departures and arrivals of ordinary, anonymous people: the emigrants setting off for a new life in Ford Madox Ford's painting *The Last of England* (1855), the shipwrecked sailor who eventually returns in Tennyson's narrative poem *Enoch Arden* (1864), and, in Russia, a political prisoner's arrival home in Ilya Repin's *The Unexpected Return* (1888).⁹ The first and last of these are elaborate tableaux that evoke the emotions surrounding emigration and political imprisonment, focused in the moment of departure and return.

Film would eventually take up this narrative tradition, creating extended portrayals of such emotion-charged departures and arrivals. But its first decades are rich in short films that seem merely to record the moment of departure or arrival. These films are so short, lasting between one and three minutes, that they are difficult for us to 'read' or to give due weight to. We are in danger of assuming that contemporary audiences might have considered them 'primitive' or fragmentary, although of course they stood for the exact opposite, demonstrating a miraculous new technology. But there seems to be another dimension to the frequent departures and arrivals, and it is the argument of this essay that the geography and panoply of Empire, which were fast approaching their climax in the last years of the century, provided an ideal subject for this new genre, helping to give its performances meaning and appeal.

But how can we gain insight into what the viewers might have made of these films as they saw them in the music halls, in fairgrounds and at a growing number of improvised venues? Raphael Samuel offered a striking demonstration of ways to connect individual experience with the overarching edifice of 'Empire' in his unfinished essay 'Empire Stories: The Imperial and the Domestic'.¹⁰ Noting that, *contra* Edward Said (or at least contra the wholesale generalisation of Said's thesis), '"Orientalism" was by no means necessarily a pathological affair', Samuel quotes a number of texts that convey the 'non-pathological' fascination of India for Victorians of many kinds. One of these is from Mrs Gaskell's novel *Cranford* (1851) and is the parenthetical story of an army wife who leaves her husband stationed in India to undertake a perilous journey home in order to save their latest baby from early death. He suggests that, 'in recounting the odyssey... Mrs Gaskell takes us to India itself'.

We have few ways of knowing if or how early films 'transported' their audiences to the remote places they portrayed. But one text from the period offers an imaginative insight into how an early encounter with film might have worked upon the individual psyche. Rudyard Kipling's story 'Mrs Bathurst' appeared in 1904 and turns upon the obsessive fascination that a film image can create. The narrator is invited by a warrant officer, Vickery, to accompany him to a film show in Cape Town, described as 'a new turn of a scientific nature called "Home and Friends for a Tickey"'. Another character in the conversation, Hooper, is already an initiate:

> 'Oh, you mean the cinematograph – the pictures of prize-fights and steamers. I've seen 'em upcountry'.
> 'Biograph or cinematograph was what I was alludin' to. London Bridge with the omnibuses – a troopship goin' to the war – marines on parade at Portsmouth, an' the Plymouth Express arrivin' at Paddin'ton'.
> 'Seen 'em all. Seen 'em all,' said Hooper impatiently.

Vickery forces the narrator to return night after night to the show, convinced that a woman on screen, seen arriving in Paddington station, is the Mrs Bathurst he previously knew in Auckland. She appears

> quite slowly, from be'ind two porters – carryin' a little reticule an' lookin' from side to side – comes out Mrs. Bathurst. There was no mistakin' the walk in a hundred thousand. She come forward – right forward – she looked out straight at us with that blindish look which Pritch alluded to. She walked on and on till she melted out of the picture – like – like a shadow jumpin' over a candle, an' as she went I 'eard Dawson in the tickey seats be'ind sing out: 'Christ! there's Mrs. B.!'

The ambiguities of this story continue to perplex Kipling critics, many of whom consider the film show as incidental to the central theme of Vickery's obsession with 'Mrs B'. But what strikes a film historian is that this appears to be the first fictional account by a major writer to describe the perceptual and psychological impact of the film image, which Kipling uses as the trigger for, or token of, Vickery's descent into madness and eventual death.

Inevitably we wonder: where and when had Kipling seen a film show, and what had he seen? There seems to be no definitive answer, except that it is likely he could have seen a show either on board a ship travelling to or from South Africa, in 1898 or 1900, or possibly in South Africa during one of his annual visits after 1900. What matters is that he clearly *had* seen a typical show of the period, with its London scenes, troops embarking and a train arriving at a station. As in another of his stories, 'Wireless', which appeared in the same collection as 'Mrs Bathurst', Kipling was quick to see the eeriness and poetic potential of new technology.[11] Whatever the sources of his intuition about film, 'Mrs Bathurst' strongly conveys not only the psychological impact of the film image – 'the real thing – alive an' movin'', as one of the characters says – but its emerging potential to connect the far-flung nodes of the Empire with affective imagery of 'home and friends'. Vickery's vision in Mrs Bathurst connects three continents, strongly suggesting what might have been the appeal of a film show for the seafarers who manned the far-flung Empire.

This was the 'rather brief period', as Samuel describes it, between about 1883 and the outbreak of the Great War, when 'Empire appeared in our school textbooks as a kind of ultimate fulfilment of our country's historic mission, and earlier periods were reinterpreted in the light of it. England was, quite simply, the greatest nation in the world'. However affecting or popular, none of the departure and arrival films of 1895-6 were truly 'imperial' until 1897, when Queen Victoria's Diamond Jubilee celebration provided an unprecedented spectacle in London that became moving pictures' first great international subject. This event was promoted by the dynamic Colonial Secretary Joseph Chamberlain as a 'festival of the British Empire', and instead of Europe's crowned heads, the governors and heads of state of all dominions and colonies were invited to take part in a great circular procession, which took the Queen from Buckingham Palace to St Paul's, where a brief service took place in the open air at the bottom of the steps (to avoid the elderly Queen having to ascend them). Detachments of exotically costumed servicemen, on horseback and on foot, accompanied the royal party and dignitaries, all in open carriages.

The result, helped by excellent weather, was an entirely outdoor spectacle, ideal for filming. Series of films were made by up to a dozen film companies, and subsequently shown throughout the UK and worldwide. The Lumière coverage, by its cameraman Alexandre Promio, began with two typical 'arrival' films, taken on Sunday 20 June, as Victoria arrived at Paddington from Windsor and her cortege was followed by crowds.[12] Two days later, the Jubilee procession was covered by cameramen stationed at many points along the route, among crowds that were estimated to total three million. A journalist, G. W. Steevens, saw clearly what Chamberlain and the organisers had achieved in this procession: 'Up they came, more and more, new types, new realms at every couple of yards, an anthropological museum – a living gazetteer of the British Empire. With them came their English officers, whom they obey and follow like children. And you begin to understand, as never before, what the Empire amounts to. Not only that we possess all these remote outlandish places… but also that these people are working, not simply under us, but with us'.[13]

Rudyard Kipling in 1895.

Other contemporary commentators understood that film would carry this spectacle to wider audiences. *The Era* urged: 'Those loyal subjects of her Majesty who did not witness the glorious pageant of the Queen's progress through the streets of London… should not miss the opportunity of seeing the wonderful series of pictures at the Empire, giving a complete representation of the Jubilee procession… by the invention of the cinématographe… our descendents will be able to learn how the completion of the sixtieth year of Queen Victoria's reign was celebrated'.[14]

A writer who interviewed Robert Paul about his filming of the Jubilee introduced his article in *Cassell's Family Magazine* with a similar eye on the future: 'This automatic spectator, who is destined to play an important part in life and literature by treasuring up the "fleeting shows" of the world for the delight of thousands in distant countries and in future ages'.[15] The processions had indeed been organised like a pageant or 'gazetteer' of the Empire, with highly recognisable figures from the dominions and detachments of their armed forces. What would the far-flung audiences make of this quintessentially imperial spectacle?

Guide to the 'Colonial soldiers of the British Empire', published in *Le Petit Journal*, 1897.

The Jubilee films also appear to have been popular and commercially successful in their new 'secondary markets'. Six weeks after the Jubilee, the Melbourne showman Harry Rickards, who had first presented animated photographs a year earlier, advertised on Friday 13 August that 'an enormous attraction will be announced tomorrow'. Monday's edition of the Melbourne *Herald* recorded 'one of the most thrilling spectacles ever witnessed, the appearance of Her Most Gracious Majesty on the Royal Carriage, drawn by six cream ponies, causing a perfect blizzard of LOYAL and Acclaimative ENTHUSIASM, the vast audience rising EN MASSE, cheering incessantly until the picture was reproduced'.[16] In Canada, the dominion's first premier of French ancestry, Sir Wilfred Laurier, was appreciatively recognised by local audiences, who would also have known that he had been knighted on the morning of the Jubilee procession. And in Melbourne, 'the waving arm of Sir George Turner', the Australian Prime Minister, was reported to be 'loudly applauded every evening'.[17]

The Diamond Jubilee had been staged to assert Victoria's and Britain's imperial power, and especially to display – visually and logistically – the extent and diversity of the Empire. In this, its organisers were able to draw on experience that had been accumulating since the success of the Great Exhibition of 1851, closely followed by the state funeral of the Duke of Wellington. For the latter, Prince Albert had asked that the design of the funeral car should be 'symbolic of England's strength and statesmanship, and also an expression of all the efforts of Victorian art'.[18] The result, although impressive, was also considered vulgar by many and backward-looking in its overloaded classicism.

During the intervening years, lessons had been learned, and the focus in the Jubilee procession was on a diversity of peoples united by the overarching concept of Empire. It marked the beginning of what David Cannadine has described as 'These new-old, royal-cum-imperial extravaganzas, which pulsed outward towards the localities of the imperial periphery, where they further strengthened and reinforced the community-based festivities from which they simultaneously drew their own inspiration and legitimacy. By these interconnected pageants and mutually reinforcing ceremonials, the British Empire put itself on display and represented itself to itself'.[19] Cannadine is even more sceptical than Samuel of Said's 'orientalism', maintaining that 'the British Empire was not exclusively (or even preponderantly) concerned with the creation of 'otherness', but was at least as much concerned with 'the construction of affinities'.[20] His riposte to post-colonial historiography argued that the 'ornamental' aspects of the British Empire were in considerable part its substance – or at least the visible expression of its connecting ideology.

Cannadine's subtitle, 'how Britain saw its empire', refers to the deliberate process of creating an elaborate system of honours and rituals which would confer rank on all those who formed part of the imperial 'family', and record their place in its hierarchy. Although many would question Cannadine's insistence that status mattered more than race in the Empire's 'system', his analysis of how its honours, costumes and rituals worked to bind together diverse peoples and to 'domesticate the exotic' is persuasive. Although he does not refer to film at all, the photographs that illustrate *Ornamentalism* are eloquent evidence of how important image-making was. And the examples of enthusiastic reception of Diamond Jubilee films quoted above confirm how the new medium of film allowed a greater degree of participation in collective imperial emotion.

Jubilees, funerals and coronations provided full-dress occasions when the 'gazetteer' of Empire was explicitly laid out. But what of the more mundane rituals of departure and arrival, and what I have termed their 'performative' dimension? The fact that these figured extensively in early film company catalogues is already evidence of their appeal, but further testimony about their reception is inevitably sparse. However, we have accounts of London audience reactions to films relating to Kitchener's defeat of the Mahdist army at Omdurman in the Sudan in 1898. First, one of seeing the return of troops involved in the battle: 'The American Biograph can accomplish wonders. For on Thursday night a picture was thrown on the screen at the Palace showing the Guards, home from the Soudan, marching just a few hours before to Wellington Barracks... The photograph was taken shortly after 2pm, and by 10.30 was being shown to prolonged applause... The enthusiasm was, of course, uproarious, breaking out as soon as the tablet announced "See the conquering heroes come! Welcome home"'.[21]

At this time, Kitchener held the rank of Sirdar, or commander-in-chief of the Egyptian army, and all contemporary coverage of his triumphs, including this report of a later Biograph show, refers to him as 'the Sirdar'.

> The Biograph at the Palace Theatre has out-biographed itself. Last night, through the medium of this wonderful invention, Londoners were able to look upon the idolised Sirdar, if not in the flesh, at least in the animated photographic representation of it. The strangeness of it all lay in the fact that the pictures shown were reproductions of scenes taken in France as recently as yesterday afternoon, and in England a few hours later. In the first instance the Palace audience saw the conqueror of the Soudan at Calais. They saw six feet odd of hard, wiry humanity, framed in an ordinary lunging suit of grey, alert and smiling. They saw him exchange a hearty shake of the hand with the steamer's skipper – and they rose to a man, aye, and to a woman – cheering loud and long. And when the cheers had died away, they were succeeded by volley after volley of vociferous and unmistakably genuine British 'hurrahs', which spread from floor to ceiling, from pit to gallery, from the back of the stage even into the fashionable areas of the tiers of boxes. The demonstration was renewed when the second scene was presented – representing the reception of the Sirdar, hat in hand, walking down the Admiralty Pier to meet the Mayor of Dover.[22]

The fact that this was quoted in a Biograph promotional brochure suggests it was recognised as an exceptional account of the impact of two of the company's films. But there is little reason to doubt its accuracy, in view of the extraordinary lionisation of General Kitchener. Paul would record a later stage of his triumphal reception: a distant figure seen arriving at a reception at the Guildhall, when he was given the freedom of the City of London, but no doubt equally capable of provoking patriotic sentiment.

Referring to Kitchener as 'the Sirdar' invokes an imperial code – he is the warrior-leader of an exotic army that has become part of the British imperial forces – and the 'Sirdar's Return' films also evoke a history of Britain's earlier humiliation, when the Mahdi's army took Khartoum and killed General Gordon in 1885, now avenged by decisive (and brutal) victory. Kitchener may be merely shaking hands, or appear small and distant on screen, but by seeing his reception, audiences are participating in a ritual of imperial acknowledgement. Within a year, the warning against hubris that Kipling had sounded in his 1897 poem *Recessional* – 'lest we forget' – would be put to the test as Britain faced the challenge of the Boer settlers of Transvaal at the end of 1899.

The outbreak of the Anglo-Boer War triggered a wave of departures and arrivals, and films of these doubtless played a part in fostering a sense of imperial unity in the face of widespread international hostility to Britain's war against the Boer settlers. Films of the City Imperial Volunteers (CIV) departing and returning showed Britain's business elite joining in the struggle against Boers. *Troops Boarding the Braemar Castle* (October 1899) is described in the Warwick Trading Company catalogue as 'an inspiring film', and the kilted Gordon Highlanders clearly symbolise Britain's military determination, as in *The Gordons Arriving at the Cape*: 'The arrival of the Gordon Highlanders was quite an event at the Cape, as it ensured lively action and daring deeds of these heroic troops at the front. A contingent of these stalwart Highlanders is seen marching down the street accompanied by the Pipers and Cycle Corps, all in the picturesque native uniform. They are lustily cheered and welcomed by the spectators lining the route'.[23]

Paul's 1901 catalogue included a section entitled 'Railway, Shipping and Marine Subjects. Arrival and Departure of Generals and Troops', which features both named figures and regiments that are associated with particular events of the war, such as *The Return of the Naval Brigade Which Saved Ladysmith*. As it wore on, with Britain's early reverses overcome under the command of Kitchener, the South African war would encourage film producers to innovate and produce many different kinds of war-related films, including patriotic tableaux and staged 'reproductions' of battlefield action.[24]

By the end of the conflict in 1902, after months of stalemate, there was little enthusiasm to record more war-related traffic, other than the arrival of Boer generals in Britain after the peace treaty had been signed.

Two 1903 films, however, demonstrate the ideological significance attaching to imperial departures and arrivals, even if not by 'captains and kings'. The catalogues of the period often refer to 'close' views and describe moments of informality; as statesmen enter or leave trains and wait on the quayside, they become briefly visible as travellers, sharing something of the experience of their ordinary viewers. As Joseph Chamberlain set off on a post-war visit to South Africa, Hepworth's *The Departure of Mr Chamberlain for South Africa* showed Mr and Mrs Chamberlain 'smilingly acknowledge the reception accorded to them', after which 'a close animated portrait is secured while the Colonial Secretary stands chatting to his friends' before boarding the ship. Much recent history is condensed into this brief scene, and in the liminal space of embarkation, the Chamberlains are revealed in a new, somewhat democratic light. Several months later, Paul's *The Return Home of the Rt. Hon. Joseph Chamberlain* shows 'four different views of the reception accorded to... Chamberlain after his tour in South Africa'. During two hectic months, Chamberlain had done much to reconcile former enemies and lay the foundations for political progress in South Africa, and the film ends with what sounds like an effective filmic flourish: 'the fourth view finishing with the departure of his train [from Southampton] for London. On the front of the decorated engine is seen a photograph of 'the Man of the Hour', which gets gradually larger as the engine approaches the camera until the front of the engine fills the whole of the picture, and Mr Chamberlain's photo forms a fine conclusion of a fine series'.[25] With the war concluded and reconciliation under way, the imperial spotlight began to shift from South Africa to India.

India was always an exception to generalisations about the Empire, being in many ways the cradle of a British concept of Empire. After the Mutiny of 1857, British policy turned away from replacing existing rulers and states towards supporting and guiding them. Indian ritual played a growing part in development of imperial spectacle, as monarchs from Victoria onwards were crowned its empresses and emperors. After Victoria's death, her son Edward was due to travel to India to be anointed emperor, but he refused to go, despite the two years of elaborate preparation that Viscount Curzon had put into organising a Coronation Durbar. His place was taken by the Duke of Connaught, Victoria's third son, who had previously served in India as an army officer. Curzon's chosen theme was 'joint Anglo-Indian sovereignty', and special prominence was given to the princely rulers and their retinues, who provided an exotic display of Cannadine's 'ornamentalism'. Paul's catalogue entry for his series of Durbar films emphasised spectacle, with 210 elephants 'of which a large number appear in the picture, each decked with chains of precious metals, and elaborately worked cloth-of-gold'.[26] The Duke and Duchess of Connaught were duly filmed returning from the event, with the now familiar ritual of scenes on-board ship, followed by a transfer to the London train in Southampton. Paul's catalogue suggests showing this film 'in conjunction with films of the Delhi Durbar', indicating the trend that now existed towards linking separate 80- and 100-foot films into travelogue-like narrative sequences, as tours of far-flung territories were 'bracketed' by quayside scenes, providing a metonymic allusion to the spaces and connecting trajectories of Empire.

We might wonder how these now routinely filmed subjects regarded their screen appearances. Royalty was certainly aware of the impact of film at an early stage, and were able to view their results 'by command'. Even officials seem to have been aware of their being filmed from a relatively early date. One instance appears in the 1910 memoir of a former senior member of the Bengal Civil Service, J. H. Rivett-Carnac.[27] Having been appointed an aide-de-camp to Queen Victoria, Rivett-Carnac was on duty at the coronation of Edward in 1903 and had been given a new charger to ride in the procession. He remembered rehearsing a dozen times 'to see how the horse would behave in a crowd and amidst traffic'. But on the day, a pipe band suddenly struck up nearby, so that 'the good horse stood straight up on his hind legs and it was quite as much as I could do to keep my seat'.

Rivett-Carnac remembered 'the expectant crowd' waiting to see 'an old gentleman a-comin'' off his ''orse', but he managed to hold on. Then comes a surprising observation to end the anecdote: 'although it was interesting enough to see oneself and show oneself to one's friends in the "living pictures" riding along in the procession, one did not want to be handed down to posterity coming off one's horse in an undignified attitude'. This aside from an old India hand provides a rare glimpse into the attitudes of both rulers and subjects: Rivett-Carnac's intense awareness of the crowd gleefully anticipating his fall, and the unexpected implication that he took his friends to see his appearance in films of the coronation. But this genre of the parade and procession was now being supplemented, and would soon be eclipsed, by the informality of the Chamberlain departure – seeming to allow viewers to eavesdrop on private con-versations – and the similarly informal quayside scene as the Duke and Duchess of Connaught's return.

'Seeing themselves as Centre of Great Imperial Pageantry': caption for engraved drawing of King George V and Queen Mary watching film of the Durbar in Calcutta in 1911. *Illustrated London News*, February 1912.

Rivett-Carnac's attitude might be distantly linked with the Russian Tsar Nicholas II's condemnation of moving pictures as 'empty, useless and even pernicious' in a note scribbled on a police report in 1913.[28] Although in private life he was an enthusiastic amateur photographer and organiser of home movies, Nicolas saw the potential for cinema shows to harbour and incite rebellious attitudes, and the strict controls imposed on Russian cinema were echoed in many censorship rules introduced around this time, including those of Britain's Board of Film Censors in 1912.

J. H. Rivett-Carnac, retired colonial administrator, who rode in the coronation procession for Edward VII in 1903 and was filmed.

By this time, there could be little doubt that film was playing a major role in amplifying imperial spectacle. When the newly crowned George V and his wife travelled to India in 1911, fulfilling the ambition that Curzon had in 1903 for a second coronation, Charles Urban's Kinemacolor process had developed to the point where it, too, needed an epic subject. The Delhi Durbar at which the king and queen were created emperor and empress of India provided a fitting subject for Urban's full-length documentary, which enjoyed wide commercial success.[29] It would prove to be the climax of what Samuel characterises as the period of Empire seen as Britain's manifest destiny, which did not survive the trauma of the war.[30] During the interwar years, Britain's commitment to Empire was no less profound; indeed, the Empire reached its greatest geographical extent in the 1920s and was celebrated in the massive British Empire Exhibition of 1924. But it had taken a new direction, more focused on trading relations, and on modernisation. The interwar years saw the rapid development of air travel and radio, both powerful media for shrinking distance and maintaining closer imperial connections, alongside the instrumentalisation of film as 'documentary' – with Empire a major theme of this new form.[31]

These developments have been well studied and are often seen as the main arena in which British film played its part in raising imperial consciousness. Historians of Empire have been slow, or reluctant, to recognise the early contribution that film made to popularising imperial sentiment in its first decade after 1896. I have tried to show that Empire was present from the outset in film's attraction for turn-of-the-century audiences. The colonial wars and conquests of the late 19th century predisposed them to read imperial significance in the first fleeting films – a glimpse of Kitchener or Chamberlain could spark emotional outpourings. And before films were expected to have diegetic structure, the short arrival and departure films created condensed signifiers of Empire as a matrix of *movement*.

Is it possible to go beyond noting a symbiotic relationship between the growth of the popular audience for film and the growth of imperial confidence in the early years of the 20th century? Harold Innis, the Canadian historian of technology, sought to relate the rise and fall of Empires throughout history to their command of new media technologies.[32] Media, he argued, offered ways of mastering time and space, and the success of Empires relies on a balance being struck between those that emphasise time, which favour decentralisation, and those that emphasise space, encouraging centralisation.[33] Innis' most famous disciple was, of course, Marshall McLuhan, who went on to analyse media according to what Innis called their 'bias'. Without wanting to follow McLuhan's often simplistic labelling of media, we can perhaps see that film, as a new medium around 1900, offered a striking new spatio-temporal experience – as when a recent moment of departure or arrival was represented to the Alhambra audience. Did this new mastery of space-time in miniature contribute to changing their sense of place in the world? We cannot know, except by proxy, as in Kipling's story, and by trying to interpret the surviving imperial performances that make up what P. D. Morgan has described as 'an entire interactive system, one vast interconnected world'.[34]

This first appeared in Lee Grieveson and Colin MacCabe, eds., *Empire and Film* (Palgrave/British Film Institute, 2011).

20.
Ancient Rome Revisited: Classical Subjects and Cinema's Expansion after 1910

The extreme admiration and excitement provoked between 1911 and 1915 by a group of films set in classical antiquity is difficult to evoke today. Partly this is due to a continuing critical disdain for the popular representation of the ancient world that began with 20th-century reactions to such painters as Jean-Léon Gérôme, Lawrence Alma-Tadema and Frederic Leighton, and reappeared in relation to the films of Cecil B. DeMille and other 'epics' of the 1950s.[1] A more specific strand in the 'condescension of posterity' also identified these films as 'uncinematic' at a crucial moment of critical stocktaking around 1930.[2]

As a result, little attempt has been made to recover the relatively rich history of critical and even personal response to other early landmark films, such as D. W. Griffith's *Birth of a Nation* (1915) or DeMille's *The Cheat* (1915). We know what wide and lasting cultural impact DeMille's film had in France, thanks to the writings of those celebrities who were happy to pay tribute to it. But if we look at early French critical writings on film such as those collected by Richard Abel,[3] we find no mention of Pastrone's *Cabiria* (1914) – despite the assurance of Bardèche and Brasillach, writing in 1935, that 'nothing else was talked of in France for years' after the film's triumphant opening in 1915.[4] They quoted *Le Cinéma* writing that 'M. D'Annunzio seems to have laid the foundation here for a new art which is perfectly in the spirit and to the taste of our times', and equally passionate and evocative praise dating from as late as 1920.

There is certainly evidence of an appreciative response to *Cabiria* in Britain, even apart from the film trade press, always ready to praise. The first *Times* review acknowledged its narrative accomplishment: 'merely as a spectacle the film would be an assured success – some of the scenes of the siege of Carthage are very effective – but it has the added advantage of a well-defined plot, the interest of which is sustained for a full two hours'. However, four months later, the response was more generic: '[*Cabiria* has been] received with much applause by large audiences. It is on a lavish scale, and is said to have taken two and a half years and cost £40,000 to prepare. Fire effects, a volcanic eruption, battles, thrilling adventures on land and water, crowds of actors make a kaleidoscope of action that lasts for more than two hours, and the incidents follow in a succession so rapid as to be sometimes a little confusing'. And yet another account, published two months later, suggested diminishing enthusiasm: '…that story of ancient Rome and Carthage which… takes its jerky way through almost unbelievable visions of Etna in eruption, destroying palaces and villas, of Hannibal crossing the Alps, of living sacrifices to a nightmare of a Moloch, of the court of Hasdrubal, and what not'.

Hannibal crossing the Alps, one of many spectacular sequences in *Cabiria* (1914).

The cursory tone of these comments is rather different from *L'Opinion* in France, which hailed the film's scenarist Gabriele D'Annunzio as 'the early master of a new art, the Giotto of the cinema'. It is also far from the enthusiasm of an eloquent personal response, free of hindsight and not intended for publication:

> I went to see *Cabiria*… last night and returned with a much fairer opinion of the artistic value of the movies. The picture is simply stupendous. The acting is excellent – far above any I have ever seen done by an American company – and the

scenery is wonderful. Hannibal's army crossing the Alps, the destruction of the Roman fleet at Syracuse by the reflecting mirrors of Archimedes, the temple of Moloch at Carthage, the desert expedition of the King of Cirta, the siege of Carthage by Scipio – all of these are done with the grimmest realism and are blood stirring in their gripping action... Of course it cost fifty centavos to view Cabiria from the ground floor and one rather expects the unusual, but I was enthusiastically surprised...

This was the future playwright Eugene O'Neill, writing in October 1914 to his girlfriend, while a mature student at Harvard.[5] The same highlights that were briskly noted by *The Times* clearly impressed O'Neill, but as a demonstration of film's artistic, rather than merely spectacular, potential. We might wonder if there are equivalent contemporary responses still to be found elsewhere, in letters or journals, but pending any such discoveries, it would seem that *Cabiria* did not make as great or lasting an impact in Britain as in France and the United States.

The main reason may simply be circumstantial: Cabiria opened in Britain relatively late, in mid-1915, when the Great War was under way and dominating both public and private attention. Another may be that, for all its novel qualities, it confirmed the cinematic appeal of the classical world, which had already been well proven by a series of successes that dated back as far as 1910. It is this series I want to examine, to test the proposition that such ancient world films, largely Italian, played a decisive part in transforming the film business in Britain.

We can construct a pre-history of such subjects in moving pictures, beginning with Georges Hatot's *Nero Trying Poisons on His Slaves* (1896–7) and Robert Paul's *The Last Days of Pompeii* (1900).[6] Although the latter is known today only from a catalogue image, it must have traded on the established appeal of Edward Bulwer-Lytton's 1834 novel which, as Maria Wyke has shown, enjoyed success in many different media throughout the 19th century, and had made the title-phrase synonymous with refined spectacle.[7] There was also much more classical-world spectacle on offer in turn-of-the-century Britain. Among many late Victorian painters drawn to this period, Lawrence Alma-Tadema's portrayal of a luxurious Roman world had been especially popular since his successful Grosvenor Gallery exhibition of 1882.[8] Lew Wallace's *Ben-Hur* (1880) and Henryk Sienkiewicz's *Quo Vadis?* (1896), both set in first-century Rome, were already hugely popular in cheap editions. And when a London stage version of the former opened in

1902, it attracted wide attention – for its extravagance of spectacle, if not for its dramatic subtlety.[9] Significantly, *The Sketch* noted 'several clergymen' in the opening night audience at Drury Lane, prefiguring the particular advantage that such religiously themed entertainment would continue to enjoy.[10]

Catalogue still from Paul's lost *The Last Days of Pompeii* (1900), a single-shot representation of the climactic eruption of Vesuvius as it alarms the citizens of Pompeii.

Paul's film was also perhaps most immediately inspired by the popular 'pyrodrama', or fireworks spectacle, loosely based on Bulwer-Lytton's novel, that was a popular attraction in the grounds of Alexandra Palace, near his North London studio.[11] Paul's short film, typical of the period at just over a minute, showed 'the interior of a Greek house, in which Ione is seated with Lydia, the blind girl'. While a dance is in progress, 'Vesuvius is seen in eruption… the volcano throws out lava, which rushes over the house, of which the pillars and walls fall in, making a complete wreck.[12] Realising that he could not compete with the spectacle of the pyrodrama's 'eruption' – the film frames a distant view of Vesuvius – Paul concentrated instead on the climax of the novel's narrative, when Glaucus escapes the eruption with his beloved Ione. This is perhaps an early example of what George Kleine, the American entrepreneur who popularised ancient world spectacle films, would later describe as film's ability to show 'the characters [as] living and breathing human beings'.[13]

Pain's Fireworks 'pyrodrama' of *The Last Days of Pompeii* was a reliable popular spectacle at Alexandra Palace, as at many other venues, which may have influenced Robert Paul's 1900 film.

Paul's film must have been predicated on a proportion of viewers knowing enough of the Pompeii story, in whatever form, to grasp what they were seeing – although the questions of to what extent, and precisely how, audiences knew what was being represented in such early films remain unanswered.[14] No doubt there was a 'lecturer' in some situations, and such commentary continued until at least 1912 in certain cinema halls.[15] But perhaps it was only solved by including title cards on films; and Paul was in fact a pioneer of title slides and titles printed on film, introduced in his 1901 catalogue. But he did not continue with 'classical' subjects, turning instead to Dickens adaptations in the following year. However, Pathé, which would soon become the first multinational producer and distributor, began to include subjects from antiquity in its catalogues as early as 1902. These sat alongside popular tales from all eras, some of them clearly offering a 'legitimate' excuse for female nudity – such as *Le jugement de Pâris* (*The Judgement of Paris*, 1902) – but after Pathé became closely involved with the 'film d'art' movement in 1908, there is a notable increase in classical subjects. Alberto Capellani followed his *Tarquin le superbe* (*Tarquin the Superb*, 1908) with *La vestale* (*The Vestal*, 1908), which has survived in a stencil-coloured print that emphasises the spectacle of its conclusion, as the temple flame neglected by the vestal virgin who has broken her vow is 'magically' reignited.[16] A similar eroticism runs through two films directed by the co-founder of the short-lived Film d'art company, André Calmettes: *Le retour d'Ulysse* (*The Return of Ulysses*, 1909), with Penelope besieged by her suitors, and especially *Héliogabale* (*Heliogabalus*, 1910), in which the depraved emperor tries to molest a vestal virgin he has abducted.[17]

Lurid poster for the U.S. release of Cines' *Quo Vadis?* (1913).

These films, running for about fifteen minutes each, were widely admired, and exported to many countries. In Britain they would form a featured attraction within the mixed programmes of between eight and ten short films which were standard until at least 1911–12,[18] often described in the trade press as 'headliners', indicating they were used to promote the programme as a whole.

So, for instance, in February 1912, the Empire Picture Palace in Finchley, North London, included Pathé's *The Vengeance of Licinius* (*La vengeance de Licinius*) – billed as a 'coloured drama' – in a programme comprising eight titles, of which four were comedies, one scientific, one a Western, and one other a drama.[19] But there were other cinemas in London that had already shown some of the longer Italian spectaculars. On looking closely at actual cinema programmes, we discover there is no straight line of 'progress' towards the feature-centred programme. Instead, there is a complicated ecology of halls of different sizes and levels of ambition that was in almost constant flux during the period between 1908 and 1915, and perhaps beyond. By 1912, two-hour programmes are the standard offer, but these could be made up in many different ways.

For as long as this remained the typical exhibition pattern, there is little point in trying to guess which types of film were most popular. The 'trade', comprising distributors and exhibitors, continued to insist that its audiences wanted 'variety' – although there was also mounting evidence of the popularity of longer films.[20] What complicates any analysis of cause and effect, or even of routine practice, is that films set in antiquity tended to be longer than the average, and more promotable as events. Their appearance also coincided with, and perhaps helped to drive, the new 'exclusive' film distribution pattern, which requires some explanation.

Before 1910, the film trade in Britain, as in all countries, operated on a free market basis, with 'renters' or distributors sourcing films from producers (who might also be distributors, as in the case of Pathé and Gaumont) and renting them to exhibitors for screening. In principle, there was nothing to prevent a renter providing the same films to neighbouring exhibitors, although there may well have been informal understandings to avoid such an occurrence. Equally, the same film might be available from a range of renters. This situation represented a transitional period away from the early economy of film that was based entirely on producers selling as many prints as possible – at first directly to exhibitors – and making whatever return and profit they could from the volume of print sales. The effect of this system was to discourage investment in more elaborate, and therefore more speculative, types of production. Producers' outlay per title and the prices of their films remained relatively low.

Around 1910, this distribution system began to change, although unevenly in different countries. The earliest mention of a film being offered 'exclusively' in Britain seems to have been Clarendon with *The Invaders* in 1909, but Rachael Low cited a

Danish film from Nordisk, *In the Hands of Imposters*, released by New Century Film Services in 1911, as 'the first film in this country specifically handled as an exclusive'.[21] Subsequently the shift towards exclusive contracts accelerated. Throughout 1911 and 1912, the trade journals carry numerous advertisements by renters urging exhibitors to 'boom' their show by securing an early booking of a new exclusive. The same film would then become available more cheaply for a subsequent booking in the same area, with the implication that the first booking would be the most profitable – although as we shall see, this might not always have been the case. Nor did the exclusive system appear in other countries at the same time: in the Netherlands, according to Ivo Blom, it did not start until 1913, by which time ancient world films were among the most eagerly sought for exclusive engagements.[22]

The first exclusives offered in Britain were mostly contemporary thrillers. But in March 1911, the Tyler Film Co. advertised Itala's *The Fall of Troy* (*La caduta di Troia*) as 'sole agents for the British Empire'.[23] Citing a 'special report' on this impressive production four weeks earlier,[24] Tylers emphasised the film's scale (over eight hundred actors), realism, length (2,000 feet, running approximately 30 minutes) and 'striking posters' – all of which they claimed would bring people back 'again and again' to see it. There had been a *Last Days of Pompeii* and a *Nero*, both from Ambrosio in 1908, as well as the Pathé subjects mentioned earlier. But by 1911, *The Fall of Troy* and Milano's Dante adaptation, *The Inferno* (*L'Inferno*, 3,950 feet, or 65 min. running at 16 frames per second) seem to have benefited from a conjunction of the exclusive system, with its need for prestige titles, and a growing willingness among exhibitors to show longer films. Production companies were now able to invest more substantially, and the costs of the Italian 'spectaculars' soon became a part of their publicity – a 1914 illustrated supplement on *Cabiria* carried the headline 'A £50,000 film: D'Annunzio's Cinema-Play'.[25] Exclusive territorial rights also created a new level of competition, with *Quo Vadis?* cited as 'the first film to be sold by auction in Britain... only ten years after £12 or £13 had been the price of a best seller'.[26]

It was not only the scale and value of films that were changing. The period 1910–12 saw a boom in building large and increasingly luxurious cinemas around Britain. In London alone, Montagu Pyke, added five new cinemas to his existing circuit of eleven between February and August 1911 – in Peckham, Brixton, Balham, Finsbury Park and Charing Cross Road. One of these, the Brixton Cinematograph Theatre, seated 'nearly 900 patrons in comfortable tip-ups',[27] while, in less than two years, the Maida Vale

Picture House would seat 1,500 and a year later, The Grange super cinema in Kilburn reached a capacity of 2,028. The audience for film shows was growing, exponentially it would seem; and there are reports from this period of prosecutions for overcrowding in the old, smaller picture theatres. But did the rate of cinema building simply reflect increased demand for film entertainment, or was there also a relationship between the vast number of seats now on offer and the scale of films being offered to fill them?

Two films shown within six months of each other in 1913 marked the decisive impact of ancient Roman spectacle in the new long format, as well as the link between these subjects and prestigious venues. Cines' *Quo Vadis?* opened at the Albert Hall on 26 April and was reported to have attracted 23,000 spectators on the May Bank Holiday two weeks later.[28] Then on 6 October, Ambrosio's new 6,000 feet version of *The Last Days of Pompeii* opened exclusively at the West End Cinema in Coventry Street, with 'specially composed music' performed by 'a full orchestra', and all seats bookable, at prices ranging from one shilling to ten shillings and sixpence. Schools and colleges were encouraged to inquire about special prices for group visits to 'Lord Lytton's classical masterpiece'.[29]

Both films set new records for the price required to secure exclusive British rights: the distributor Jury's paid £6,700 for *The Last Days of Pompeii* and Ruffells paid £8,000 for Cines' *Anthony and Cleopatra* (Guazzoni), the immediate successor to *Quo Vadis?* later in 1913. Having paid such sums, there was naturally pressure to secure returns, initially from prestigious central London venues, but also – in a new development – from a growing range of new suburban cinemas, as well as provincial cinemas. But before looking at how they performed in the new exhibition marketplace, it is worth considering what these films offered that was distinctive and appealing.

The first successful genre of the 'exclusive' era was the thriller, usually driven by a crime story involving theft or kidnapping, or by espionage. 'Nick Winter' and 'Nat Pinkerton' pitted their wits against highly organised gangs, reaching an apotheosis in the Zigomar, Fantômas and *Vampires* titles of 1911-15.[30] These series offered dynamism, speed, modernity and suspense with their characteristic cliff-hanger episode endings – very different qualities from those of the antiquity subjects. The appeal of these ancient world films lay in spectacle, with massed crowds of extras, period costume and architectural sets, while their typical plots veered between pomp and decadence, punctuated by scenes of combat, sacrifice and, of course, large-scale destruction.

These qualities clearly appealed, perhaps for the first time, to the 'better class' of patron that the burgeoning cinema business was trying to attract – sometimes described in Britain as 'the carriage trade', in a reference to traditional theatre parlance – although they seem also to have appealed to the popular audience. Moreover, films set in ancient Greece or Rome had distinctive commercial qualities, very different from those of the serials. With already familiar titles, they could be publicised in advance; ticket pricing could be higher, with pre-booked seats (rather like opera transmission today); and films could run for longer – a week or more, rather than the two or three days that had become common by 1914.

Above all, the antiquity films had moral as well as cultural appeal, like their theatrical precursor *Ben-Hur*. The two key source-texts, *The Last Days of Pompeii* and *Quo Vadis?*, were both popular 19th-century novels that portrayed the triumph of Christian values over pagan Rome.[31] Unlike their rivals (the thrillers that turned on kidnapping and torture, while hinting at other depravities), these Christian epics judiciously balanced their portrayal of decadence with the eventual triumph of Christianity. They also co-existed with a widely distributed series of explicitly biblical films – *From the Manger to the Cross* (Kalem, 1912), *The Bible* (Aquila, 1913), *The Messiah* (*La Vie et la Passion de Noître Seigneur Jésus Christ*, Pathé, 1913–14), *Daniel* (Vitagraph, 1914), *Christus* (Cines, 1916) – and with the success of Max Reinhardt's 1911 production of the pseudo-medieval religious play, *The Miracle* (*Das Mirakel*), staged at Olympia and followed by a British-financed film version of it in 1912.[32] A further source of cultural status was the Shakespeare connection: as early as 1909, Vitagraph was advertising its *Julius Caesar* as 'another Shakespearean headliner', while two of the most popular ancient world films of the early 1910s appear to have been Cines' *Anthony and Cleopatra* (1914) and *Julius Caesar* (1915) – the latter proclaimed in a trade advertisement as 'the most important event in Scottish pictures so far this year'.[33]

Quo Vadis? appears to have been the first extended film booking at London's Royal Albert Hall, announced as a two-week run on 26 April 1913, which was extended for a further two weeks on 7 May.[34] Jury's published a sixteen-page 'story of the play' brochure, which was also on sale at provincial venues.[35] In addition to admiring reviews, the film gained valuable publicity from a widely reported 'private' visit by King George V and Queen Mary to see it at the Albert Hall on 5 May.[36] This royal patronage was used to promote the film throughout the Empire. The film's New Zealand debut at His Majesty's Theatre in Wellington, on 17 July

1913, was advertised in fulsome terms: 'Its beauty, magnificence and grandeur; its mighty magnitude, artistic excellence, historical accuracy, and marvellous realism; its gorgeous accessories and startling depiction of BURNING ROME, THE MARTYRDOM OF CHRISTIANS thrown to the lions, in short ITS MERIT, which captures Europe, America and Australasia, has now captured Auckland and is sure to capture Wellington'.[37] And at Ashburton, on New Zealand's South Island, a 'special grand revival of the world's greatest picture success' on 31 December advertised 'the king of films / the film of kings', 'as honoured by King George V'.[38]

The opening of *The Last Days of Pompeii* in 1913, six months after its predecessor, attracted more critical attention than *Quo Vadis?* had. Launched with a special 'press view', it gained a highly supportive advance review in *The Times* which is worth quoting in full:

> The story of Lord Lytton's famous novel, with the fine spectacular setting of most of its central incidents, is peculiarly suitable for reproduction on the cinematograph. The film... has been made in Italy, the more important scenes having been enacted by the performers under the shadow of Vesuvius. The pictures have, in consequence, a brilliance of lighting and an accuracy of definition which would probably have been unattainable in our own latitudes. The film is also a striking example of the elaborateness of the preparations made for the production of modern cinematograph pictures. The number of the performers is enormous, and one tumultuous scene, 'in which the Senate's judgment on Glaucus is announced to an immense gesticulating multitude', extorted a tribute of warm admiration from the audience. The story is unfolded in a way which preserves the interest of the narrative throughout and works up to a dramatic climax. These closing scenes are a triumph for the maker of the film. The gladiatorial contests in the arena are suddenly interrupted by the eruption of Vesuvius, followed by the wild flight of the populace, whose frantic efforts to escape are reproduced with great realism. The story closes with some beautiful and striking scenes of the Bay of Naples, with the smoking volcano in the background.[39]

The cinema's advertisement on the opening day, also in *The Times*, went to considerable lengths to establish the film's credentials and status. Prices, as we have seen, were high, although patrons were assured that 'the Press has been unanimous in acknowledging this new film as the greatest actually on the market [and] as one of the most instructive Plays of today'.[40]

It was certainly significant that Bulwer-Lytton was a well-known English author: for the cinema trade, his novel was simply a 'classical masterpiece'. And, interestingly, his grandson gave a lecture for London University's Extension Guild on 1 November, while the film was still running, in which he defended Bulwer-Lytton, despite acknowledging that he was now 'out of fashion'.[41] Although ostensibly held to promote the forthcoming biography of his grandfather, could this event also have reflected the success of the film in bringing Bulwer-Lytton back to attention, if not fashion? If so, it would be an intriguing case of Boulter and Grusin's 'remediation' effect, whereby the spectacular use of a new medium to represent a venerable subject benefits both the status of the medium and the longevity of the source material.

How popular were the long films? There are few indications of audience size, apart from the Albert Hall figure quoted above, and no box-office statistics from this period. But we can find other indicators. One is the level of investment that distributors were willing to make, which can be judged from an Index of Exclusives published by *The Bioscope* in 1914. The Index lists over seven hundred titles, among which Pathé's 1912 *Les Misérables* is the longest (at 10,000 feet) and *Quo Vadis?* the second longest. The list includes a surprising number of films of less than 500 feet, all British, but largely consists of titles of between 1,500 and 4,000 feet. The implication seems to be that there was rising demand for longer films.

Another indicator of audience size is the place of classical-world films in local cinema programmes. To show *Quo Vadis?* or *Anthony and Cleopatra* in 1913–14 was to make a statement about a cinema hall's status, its confidence in its audience and ability to afford an 'exclusive'. An example of this dynamic at work can be found in the competition between two cinemas in North London: the East Finchley Picturedrome (which today survives as the Phoenix) and the Finchley Rink Cinema. On 15 August 1913, the Picturedrome advertised 'Coming! *Quo Vadis?* A completely new version'; and again on 22 August: 'Monday next – *Quo Vadis?*'[42] Meanwhile, the Rink Cinema was advertising *Ivanhoe* with 'the full Lyceum company', a reference to that theatre's reputation for spectacular productions under the direction of Irving and Beerbohm Tree. The film in question, made by Zenith at their Whetstone studio (dir. Leedham Bantock), used settings from the Lyceum, and appears to have held over, and is listed as still playing at the Rink on 29 August.⁴³ On 5 September, the Picturedrome struck back with *Ivanhoe* 'for three days only', but stated that this was the American IMP version, made by Herbert Brenon. The Rink countered with *1812*,⁴⁴ along with a Broncho Billy Western and a Nick Winter thriller. From 12 September, the Picturedrome showed one of Britain's few historical films made on a grand scale, British & Colonial's *The Battle of Waterloo* (dir. Charles Weston), for two weeks, against which the Rink offered *Fantômas*. But on 19 September, the Rink advertised that *Quo Vadis?* would be showing 'for one week only' from 29 September; and on 26 September, the film was further promoted as 'shown before their majesties the King and Queen'. The Picturedrome meanwhile showed *The Battle of Waterloo*.

What this short passage of exhibition history in a relatively affluent district reveals is the prestige attaching to *Quo Vadis?*, which was announced with more extensive press advertising than any other film during these months. Its value to exhibitors was confirmed by the results of a survey among managers, 'What does the public want?', published in *The Bioscope* in February 1914: the only film mentioned more than once was *Quo Vadis?* Later that month, a letter to *The Bioscope* referred to 'the immense success of *The Mysteries of Paris*, *Quo Vadis?* and several other masterpieces', originally regarded 'with suspicion' by exhibitors as being 'too artistic', which proved to the writer that 'the public is really interested in the technical and artistic development of the picture play'.⁴⁵

Elsewhere, in the Netherlands and in Poland, the Italian spectaculars were also major attractions. Ivo Blom has shown how the Amsterdam distributor and exhibitor Jan Desmet became embroiled in fierce battles over the Italian spectaculars in 1913, competing with his rival Anton Nöggerath to secure *Quo Vadis?*, after the success he had with *The Fall of Troy* in 1911.⁴⁶ When Nöggerath got the Dutch rights by outbidding Desmet, the latter retaliated by showing a cut-down version of the film, presumably pirated, under the title *Emperor Nero and the Fire of Rome*, which then provoked stern press denunciations of misleading the public.⁴⁷ With the success of this genre well established, Nöggerath found himself faced with further challenges. Having secured the Ambrosio version of *The Last Days of Pompeii*, another rival bought the Pasquali version of the same subject and launched this on the same day. Claims and counter-claims flew in the Dutch press over which was the 'real' *Last Days*. Although Nöggerath retained his lead, with *Antony and Cleopatra* in 1914, Desmet countered with *In Hoc Signo Vinces* (dir. N. Oxilio; known in Britain and the U.S.

as *By the Cross*), which dealt with the later Roman emperors and Constantine, and continued to rent the film to cinemas in Catholic areas of the Netherlands as late as the 1920s.[48] In Poland, where the author of *Quo Vadis?* and recent Nobel prize laureate, Henryk Sienkiewicz, was a national hero, the film broke all records – for attendance and prices charged by the cinemas.[49]

The Roman films of 1910-15 reached a world that was in many ways well prepared for them, with producers, distributors and, however reluctantly, exhibitors seeking ways of extending and holding their audiences' attention. They introduced new forms of publicity and promotion, with press shows, press books and souvenir brochures, all considered worthwhile investments for films that could compete in the cultural marketplace. Their scale and 'classical' associations helped neutralise opposition to the moving pictures as a corrupting influence; and they lent glamour and dignity to many of the new super cinemas that showed them. Above all, they appealed to a broad audience: those who were already confirmed filmgoers – described in a reflective *Times* article of 1913, 'the hall full of men and women, old, elderly, and young, paying their sixpences, listening intently, going away and coming again'[50] – and apparently also to a new influx of the more educated who had previously spurned the picture palaces, such as Eugene O'Neill. Occasionally we glimpse the place of these classical subjects within what Hugo von Hofmannsthal called the 'chaos of literatures' about cinema that flew past.[51] In an early novel entitled *Voyage in the Dark* (1934), clearly based on her own experiences in pre-First World War London, Jean Rhys evokes lively audience reaction in a Camden Town cinema to an episode of the adventure series *Three-Fingered Kate* (1909–12), which is followed by 'a long Italian film about the Empress Theodora, called *The Dancing Empress*'.[52] But there is no account of how this was received.

Part of the appeal may well have been erotic, since this had certainly been an important feature of much ancient world painting and sculpture from the *fin de siècle*. The hero of Joseph Roth's 1934 novel *The Antichrist* describes seeing naked women for the first time in a film about Moses, in which 'an Egyptian princess bathes naked in the Nile, with her naked servants', before finding the cradle containing 'the Jews' guide, the legislator of the world'.[53] The future literary scholar and Christian apologist C. S. Lewis, born in 1898, described in his autobiography how he had 'developed a great taste for all the fiction I could get about the ancient world: *Quo Vadis?*, *Darkness and Dawn*, *The Gladiators*, *Ben Hur*... Early Christians came into many of these stories, but they were not what I was after.

I simply wanted sandals, temples, togas, slaves, emperors, galleys, amphitheatres, the attraction, as I now see, was erotic'.[54]

Lewis' generation, already familiar with ancient world fiction in print and illustration, was the first to discover cinema as teenagers (although not apparently Lewis himself). They could now enjoy the panoply of popular antiquity 'put into action', as the *Times* advertisement for *Quo Vadis?* announced. But despite the vast numbers in Britain who flocked to see such action, there seems to be surprisingly little evidence of lasting cultural impact. By 1930, Paul Rotha could refer condescendingly to *Cabiria* as 'a remarkable feat for 1913 [sic], even though its cinematic properties were not pronounced', in a book that would become the vade mecum for a rising generation of cinephiles.[55] *Quo Vadis?*, *The Last Days of Pompeii* and *Cabiria*, once benchmarks against which British and American films were measured, seem to have been completely forgotten, until the new film history of the 1970s began cautiously to acknowledge their achievements.[56] *Sic transit gloria antiqui...*

Originally a chapter in Pantelis Michelakis and Maria Wyke, eds., *The Ancient World in Silent Cinema* (Cambridge, 2013).

21.
A 'Theatre of Memory'?
Screening Historic Literary London

> The art of memory, as it was practised in the ancient world, was a pictorial art, focusing not on words but on images. It treated sight as primary. It put the visual first. Outward signs were needed if memories were to be retained and retrieved. 'Something is not secure enough by hearing, but is made firm by seeing'.
>
> Raphael Samuel, *Theatres of Memory*[1]

British cinema has often been characterised as a cinema burdened by literary adaptation, with the implication that this tendency has diverted it from being 'truly cinematic'. The suggestion is that if it were more like American cinema, committed to character-driven action, or, like French cinema, a vehicle for personal expression, it would be truer to the medium's potential, and so more successful internationally. Despite these longstanding charges, the fact remains that many British films have maintained an international reputation precisely because of their 'literary' qualities, even if they are not actually adaptations – as in the paradigmatic cases of *The Third Man* (1949) or *Lawrence of Arabia* (1962), two films that are precisely *not* adaptations.[2] In the 1980s, a further generalised criticism was introduced with the concept of 'heritage cinema', applied to historical fiction 'fascinated by the private property, the culture and values of a particular class' – that class being the land-owning English aristocracy.[3] Henceforth many popular films and television series based on classic literature would be stigmatised as ideologically suspect, reducing 'the nation itself… to the soft pastoral landscape of Southern England untainted by… modernity'.[4]

So, for instance, the films of the producer-director partnership of Ismael Merchant and James Ivory were for long regarded with a kind of automatic disdain by many British film scholars.[5] Films such as *A Room with a View* (1985), *Howards End* (1992), *The Remains of the Day* (1993) and *The Golden Bowl* (2000) were dismissed as 'literary' and overly reliant on period costume and setting to be considered truly cinematic or relevant to the times in which they appeared.[6] Yet all of these films can also be seen as intelligent and purposeful adaptations of novels that are very much about themes of continuing relevance, especially the prejudices enshrined in the English class system and its relationship to the realities of the modern world, as well as issues of 'deviant' sexuality within a puritanical culture.[7] Nor should Ivory's ability to depict luxury and gracious living be taken for granted, as Martin Scorsese observed in the context of his own recreation of New York's 'gilded age' in *The Age of Innocence*.[8]

What was ultimately at stake in the 'heritage film' debate was perhaps more the collective prejudices of a post-war generation reacting against the portrayal of an 'Englishness' to which they felt instinctively antipathetic than a measured critical response to this upsurge of historical fiction. And it was a social historian, Raphael Samuel, who would provide a broader perspective on the 'heritage industry' to which these films related, discussing their role as a 'theatre of memory' for the 1980s and '90s, in which historical time itself is being restructured for a contemporary public.[9]

The rather confused and self-lacerating criticisms of English literary adaptation and 'heritage' cinema would not be worth resurrecting if they did not point to a number of underlying prejudices and misunderstandings that I will argue have long obscured the role of spatial and architectural imagination in cinema more generally – as well as reinforcing a domestic prejudice against some of the most widely admired British films.[10] Quite apart from their critical reputation, these are also works that have created the contemporary image of Britain, circulating around the world and playing an increasingly important part in defining how the nation's capital is perceived.[11]

New Theoretical Scaffolding
Although pre-occupied with issues of subject position and narrative discourse within the text, the new generation of semiotic theorists of cinema of the 1970s recognised the importance of the 'pro-filmic' in the overall process of filmic narration: 'The pro-filmic concerns the elements placed in front of the camera to be filmed: actors, lighting, set design, etc. These elements, rather than being seen simply as raw material, can be understood as narrative discourse by the fact that they have been chosen and selected to communicate narrative meanings'.[12]

With set design now assigned set least some narrative significance, the way was open for its theorisation by Charles and Mirella Affron in their ground-breaking study of 'art direction and film narrative'.[13] After noting the near-total absence of reporting on art direction in the popular literature of cinema during the 1930s and 1940s, the Affrons proposed a theoretical model which recognised five levels of set 'intensity', graduated from 'transparency' to 'opacity': 'From denotation, in which the set functions as a conventional signpost of genre, ambience, and character; to punctuation, where the set has a specially emphatic narrative function; to embellishment, where the verisimilitudinous set calls attention to itself within the narrative; to artifice, where the set is a fantastic or theatrical image that commands the centre of narrative attention'. The fifth level in this scheme is termed 'set as narrative', which refers to a relatively small number of films where 'the field of reading is composed of a single locale', as in, for example, Hitchcock's *Rope* and *Rear Window*, but also the village street of *How Green Was My Valley*.

Despite the obvious heuristic value of the Affrons' model, it cannot be said that the study of art direction has made rapid progress during the decades since their book appeared. Such relatively few works on production designers as have appeared are essentially tributes to leading figures in the profession.[14] My project here attempts to combine something of the Affrons' analytical approach with an overview of British filmmaking and the persistence within it of the literary-historical genre, in order to shed light on the distinctive contribution of some British production designers.

New Theory: New Histories
The semiotic theorisation of film not only provided an opening for the fuller understanding of film practice but led to a revaluation of early cinema during the 1980s.[15] And it has been from this new study of what had previously been considered 'primitive' that much evidence has emerged which enables us to trace the progress of design for film. Instead of considering the first films as mere recording of 'pre-arranged... pieces of dramatic action',[16] scholars of early cinema have firmly turned away from the teleological model of cinema's progress towards contemporary sophistication, seeing instead the persistence or recurrence of much older tropes, and also placing cinema in a wider field of media and entertainment – in contrast to the tradition of seeking 'specificity' at all costs.[17]

From this perspective, it has become clear that moving picture entertainment was much less of a break with previous forms of representation or a new beginning in the mid-1890s than had often been implied by film historians. Most of its conventions and subjects were in fact carried over from the variety stage and from other contemporary practices such as the posing of 'life models' for stereoscope pictures, then for lantern slides and eventually postcards. Indeed, during its hey-day in the later 19th century, the Magic Lantern brought into being a vast repertoire of literary, theatrical and even opera slide-sets, anticipating by some five decades the range of subjects that cinema would tackle. We should therefore not be surprised that early producers were quick to see the potential of representing already popular subjects. The issue was not whether the new medium of film was 'adequate' to portraying, say, a full-scale novel or opera (which it plainly was not in terms of duration, with individual films lasting only a minute or two) but rather that the new device could demonstrate its novel powers by presenting acknowledged cultural icons.

This process has been termed 'remediation' by Jay Bolter and Richard Grusin, who identify it as a key feature of how new recording media have sought validation, which is now carried into the digital era.[18] But it can also be explained in terms of 'intertextuality', a term imported into critical theory from the work of the Russian philologist Mikhail Bakhtin, who argued that all literature draws upon not only other literary works, but also on deep 'strata of the popular language'.[19] The cumulative result of this reshaping of the early history of cinema is a shift away from the ideas of novelty, specificity and evolution that were once so important, towards a much wider, more inclusive notion, sometimes termed 'intermediality', in which new media compete with older, established forms by emulation and hybridisation to produce what Bakhtin called 'the differentiated unity of [an] epoch's entire culture'.

Early Production in England

Early film production in Britain had a notably different character from that of other countries. While Edison was filming vaudeville stars for his Kinetoscope in 1894, the English pioneers Birt Acres and Robert Paul produced a scene of violent affray, *Arrest of a Pickpocket*, as an early Kinetoscope subject. Fights, robberies and knockabout scenes would continue in Paul's catalogue throughout the next decade, which it is tempting to link with a longstanding national reputation for aggression and violence.[20] Yet another distinctive feature of this early production was its emotional and even erotic frankness. Paul's first fictional film, *A Soldier's Courtship* (May 1896), had its principals, a soldier and his sweetheart, engaged in lively courtship before they are interrupted by a busybody, who is vigorously expelled from the scene. Later in the same year, Paul would film *2 a.m.; or, The Husband's Return*, taken from a London theatre production and with the original actors.[21] Both this scene of a drunken husband reeling around before being drawn into bed by his wife, and the earlier enthusiastic courtship are notably longer than most other films of the period, with naturalistic settings – unlike the detached 'close-up' of Edison's celebrated *May-Irwin Kiss*, also based on a popular play.

Three years later, the British Biograph company filmed scenes from Beerbohm Tree's production of Shakespeare's *King John*, advertising this exclusive as 'taken with all the scenery and effects of the original production', which strongly suggests these theatrical features were considered an attraction.[22] When Paul undertook a pioneering Dickens adaptation in 1901, *Scrooge; or, Marley's Ghost*, this unprecedented six-minute condensation of *A Christmas Carol* in thirteen scenes closely followed a long-popular stage adaptation, with a range of specially constructed sets. Like all Dickens' work, the original story had appeared with illustrations, establishing a visual tradition from the outset, which this latest 'remediation' would extend, with the benefit of filmed supernatural effects.[23] Another early Paul film, *The Hair's Breadth Escape of Jack Shepard* (1900), which is lost but known from a catalogue illustration, suggests that this pioneer studio was experimenting with the kind of dramatic effect created on stage in 'sensation melodrama', using a painted cyclorama of rooftops for a scene from the life of the notorious outlaw.

During the first decade of the following century, Britain's pioneer producers largely failed to adapt to rapidly rising audience expectations, as set by Pathé, followed by the Italian and Danish industries. While Paul and others abandoned the industry, others remained attached to shorter films, lacking large studios to create large-scale spectacle. According to British cinema's first historian, Rachael Low, discussing the period 1910-15: 'Even the biggest efforts of Barker, the London Film Company and Hepworth were dwarfed by the towering stature of Italian films like *Quo Vadis?* or *The Last Days of Pompeii*'.[24]

Writing in the late 1940s, as British cinema entered another period of crisis, Low may well have felt a sense of *déjà vu* when contemplating the period immediately before the First World War, when British producers saw their share of the domestic market plummet. However, her account of the earlier period also undervalues the efforts of those British producers who felt they could compete with Italian, American and Danish imports. Will Barker, in spite of his background in rapidly-made 'topicals', had realised the value of striking a patriotic note. His *Henry VIII* (1911) had capitalised on the fame of Sir Herbert Beerbohm Tree and his theatre company, and was widely regarded as the first British film to offer serious competition to imported historical spectaculars.

In a double irony, Barker's promotional strategy for this major production included burning all copies of the film after six weeks of screenings, in an effort to drive up its value, so that nothing survives to be compared with Alexander Korda's exploitation of the same subject for his debut film as British quality cinema's saviour in 1933. Yet the results of Barker's strategy were good enough to encourage him to persevere, and in 1913 he co-produced, with G. B. Samuelson, *Sixty Years a Queen*, a dramatised chronicle of the reign of Queen Victoria.

Only fragments of this ambitious film survive, but research has shown that it drew heavily on the tradition of 'illustrated news' from the time of Victoria's reign, and was highly successful in attracting a public avid for British historical subjects.[25] A 1913 adaptation of Walter Scott's *Ivanhoe,* filmed partly on location at Chepstow Castle in Monmouthshire, was apparently attractive enough for exhibition in the same years as *Quo Vadis?*[26] In 1915, Barker would produce an equally spectacular story set during the 15th-century Wars of the Roses, *Jane Shore*, about the mistress of Edward IV, who outlived him to become a celebrated courtesan. *Jane Shore* involved a large cast and spectacular action. It had two designers credited, indicating how vital this role had become in the era of historical fiction.

Yet Low's account of this rare surviving example of a British film of the period is preoccupied with doubt as to how properly 'filmic' it is, constantly noting issues of camera placement and editing, very much according to the canons of 'film appreciation' laid down in Lindgren's contemporary *Art of the Film*. One passage in particular is fascinating for its avoidance of any direct discussion of the film's actual design: 'It is possible… that the at the very size of the sets made possible a greater variety of angle from which they could be taken than the little two or three-walled rooms, the whole of which could clearly be shown from one camera position; while at the same time the size of the sets and the crowds made emphasis of detail a more pressing problem'.[27] Set design here is considered wholly in terms of how it facilitates camera angles and cutting, rather than for its contribution to the film's historicity, drama or atmosphere.

The main arena for British filmmakers, however, was their treatment of the second most important of all British authors:

Charles Dickens. While Shakespeare reigned supreme, he was also an international author, and many early Shakespeare adaptations were made outside Britain prior to the First World War. But Dickens remained very much an English speciality, and by 1912 he had become an important asset in the struggle against imported historical fiction. Cecil Hepworth's company produced three Dickens adaptations in rapid succession, all directed by Thomas Bentley, a former actor who had specialised in Dickens on stage. After *Oliver Twist* (1912), Bentley moved on to *David Copperfield* (1913) and *The Old Curiosity Shop* (1914). All were popular, but the last, according to Low, 'received such praise as had hitherto been reserved for foreign epics'.[28] In the absence of any surviving material, we can only guess at what was done to create the atmosphere of Dickens' 'repository for old and curious things'. But Bentley's *David Copperfield* has been preserved, and shows a strong emphasis on 'real' locations, ranging from the sea-front at Yarmouth and the cliffs near Dover, to David meeting Dan'l on the steps of St Martins in the Field in Trafalgar Square, and Steerforth's house in Highgate. For this last, the filmmakers used Church House in Pond Square, Highgate Village, which survives almost unchanged to the present day.

Dickens, of course, has long been celebrated for his emotional stories and sharply realised characters. But his novels also rely on a density of description and evocation, as well as a quite precise topography of London and its surroundings, which seems to have made his work highly suggestive for British filmmakers. In a famous essay, written while he was working on *Ivan the Terrible*, Sergei Eisenstein traced the influence of Dickens on Griffith, suggesting that the origins of the close-up and parallel action lie in these familiar novels, as Griffith himself acknowledged.[29] However what is most 'cinematic' about Dickens, Eisenstein suggests, is his 'creation of an extraordinary plasticity' and the 'optical quality' of his observation. The challenge for British filmmakers in the early 'teens was not only how to compete with the quality and scale of spectacle on offer from foreign producers, but also how to realise the cinematic potential of their greatest modern author.

The climax of this first period of engagement with historic literature was probably Hepworth's ambitious 1915 production of *Barnaby Rudge*, Dickens' novel set amid the anti-Catholic Gordon Riots of the late 18th century. The fact that this has not survived, like the majority of British films from the silent era, has undoubtedly limited its reputation, although at the time of its release, the quality of set construction and design was an important talking point in the trade press:

It is a wonderful piece of stage architecture, complete in every detail, and the illusion of solid realism, when viewed from the proper aspect, is quite perfect. The paved sidewalks, the cobbled roadway, the doors with their link-holders and extinguishers, the glazed windows with their neat white curtains – every tiny point has been remembered… Behind the streets, moreover, there is a magnificent reconstruction of Newgate Prison – an immensely lofty structure, grey, drab, and forbidding, with a sinister gallows before its outer wall. The whole of this marvellous city, we understand, was designed by Mr Warwick Buckland, and it is certain that he merits the very warmest congratulations [on] a remarkable piece of work.[30]

If *Barnaby Rudge*, with its 1,500 extras (or 'supers', as they were known at the time), and *Jane Shore* were the most spectacular British historical productions of this period, other producers were also active in bringing classic literature to the screen. The Ideal company launched a series of more modestly budgeted films aimed at discriminating audiences in 1916, which included versions of Oliver Goldsmith's *The Vicar of Wakefield* and Oscar Wilde's *Lady Windermere's Fan*. Ideal's energetic publicity campaigns, aimed at exhibitors and also at key opinion-shapers, stressed the idea of giving discriminating cinema customers the chance to see famous stage actors in films that bring out 'the great idea of the drama', with scenery and acting subordinated to this aim. A trade press story of 1917 is clearly contrived to support this policy, with a vicar reporting his admiration for *The Vicar of Wakefield*: 'I believe I am expressing the mind of many of my brother clergy when I say that if such pieces, accompanied by such acting, were more frequent, we should hear little of those well-founded complaints of the kinema, with its puerilities and inanities and worse'.[31] The same correspondent concluded that 'taste is much higher than managers would have us believe', obviously supporting Ideal's claim that their modestly budgeted 'quality' films could attract a new, discriminating audience to the cinema, as well as satisfying existing spectators.

The question inevitably arises: how can the apparent success on different levels of Barker's, Samuelson's, Hepworth's and Ideal's strategies, not to mention those of other companies such as London Films, Turner and Trans-Atlantic, be reconciled with conventional accounts of British cinema's abject failure during the 'teens and '20s? To a great extent the answer lies in the larger economy of the international film business, which saw an important shift of power during the First World War, giving American producers and their international agents effective control of the world trade.³² Certainly British producers had lost ground in their domestic market, and found decreasing export opportunities due to the cartel operated by American producers operating under Edison's Motion Picture Patents Company up to 1915. But against these very real business difficulties, the fact remains that British filmmakers made considerable headway in producing feature subjects throughout the 'teens which reflected national culture, drawing on a wide range of authors, both classic and modern, for their stories. Equally important, they had laid the foundations of a coherent approach to visual design in film, starting with the pioneer efforts of the painter Sir Hubert Herkomer, who took up filmmaking in 1913,³³ and continuing with the work of Mumford and Ambrose on *Jane Shore*, and Buckland on *Barnaby Rudge*.

Cecil Hepworth's *Barnaby Rudge* (1915),
set during the 1780 Gordon Riots in London (a lost film).

Similar developments were taking place across the Atlantic during the same period, although less in the monumental films of D. W Griffith, *Birth of a Nation* (1914) and *Intolerance* (1916), long considered the cornerstones of American cinema's critical and commercial success. However rich these were in spectacle and scale, they did not directly influence domestic filmmaking as much as the scenography of the *film d'art*. This influence came through Adolphe Zukor's success in 1912 with an imported *Queen Elizabeth*, starring Sarah Bernhardt. The great actress had achieved extraordinary international fame through her tours, but was understandably wary of appearing on screen in her late fifties, despite the attractions of capitalising on her reputation.[34] However, the failure of her Paris stage production *La Reine Elizabeth* in 1912 encouraged her to recoup the losses by undertaking a filmed version, which was shot in London by the aptly named Histrionic Film Company and co-financed by the American exhibitor Adolph Zukor. Such was Bernhardt's celebrity that Zukor was able to tour this somewhat old-fashioned *tableau*-based film around the United States with enormous commercial success, which laid the foundations for his Famous Players company that would merge with the Lasky Company in 1916 and later become Paramount, one of Hollywood's most successful studios. Cecil B. DeMille was already working for Lasky in 'a place called Hollywood' from 1913, and would become Paramount's most successful director during the late 'teens, due in part to his collaboration with the pioneer art director Wilfred Buckland between 1914 and 1919.[35]

DeMille came from a New York theatrical background, having worked with the master of spectacular melodrama, David Belasco, and he would soon infuse his filmmaking with a powerful integration of dramatic elements, paying particular attention to the role of controlled lighting in relation to cinematography and set design – an effect that became known as 'Lasky lighting', but was apparently much influenced by Buckland.[36] But what Zukor brought to the partnership was a shrewd sense of the need for filmmakers to make motion pictures 'as artistic, as high-class, and as notable things in [their] line of entertainment as such men as… Charles and Daniel Frohman were doing in high-class Broadway theatres'.[37] The choice of subjects that had established cultural appeal, which usually meant a literary and theatrical pedigree, was vital. Among DeMille's great successes of the period were *Carmen* (1915) and *Joan the Woman* (1917), both starring the Metropolitan Opera diva Geraldine Farrar, and both ingeniously adapted to make use of cinema's potential for new ways of staging the classics. Carmen benefited from *plein air* Californian landscapes before its denouement outside a superbly realised bullfight arena, while DeMille's account of Joan of Arc, prompted by America's recent entry into the Great War and with a contemporary framing story set in the trenches, showed a growing confidence in handling historical subjects in ways that communicated with cinema's vast and diverse audience.

The Struggle for England's Self-Image

America's military role was not its only contribution to reshaping Europe after the war. Indeed, the disruption of international trade caused by the war had already brought about favourable conditions for a reshaping of the film business, along with many other industries formerly controlled by London. With two important centres of film distribution, London and Paris, preoccupied by the war, the way was open for American companies to 'cash in on Europe's war'.[38] Kristin Thompson has identified the period from mid-1915 to early 1916 as the time when 'the American move to hegemony occurred', with a significant proportion of American exported film footage thereafter going directly to markets other than Britain.[39] Britain would continue to be American's largest external customer for film, with close links maintained by such figures as Charles Chaplin – London-born, yet launched as an international movie star by the dynamism of American producers – but increasingly American producers found they could supply the world's exhibitors directly, and on their own terms.

In this climate, British producers found themselves at a multiple disadvantage. Not only had the war drained Britain's economy and shattered its workforce, but British cinemas, like most others around the world, were now overwhelming committed to showing American films. Patriotism became an important theme in the trade advertising of British producers such as Ideal, who were trying to reinvigorate British 'quality' production in the later 'teens.[40] The strategy favoured by both Ideal and a new company, Stoll, which also had major theatre holdings, was to promote adaptations of popular contemporary 'British authors', relying on the familiarity of these names to help boost films which might otherwise be seen to lack the glamour of Hollywood.

Despite such well-conceived strategies, the Hollywood studios had achieved a dominance over the British distribution and exhibition market which made it increasingly difficult even to release domestic productions. While Ideal, Stoll and the long-established Hepworth studio all struggled, an expatriate Englishman returned to inject some American showmanship into the depressed domestic business, a pattern that would recur over subsequent decades. James Stuart Blackton had left Britain in his youth when his family emigrated, and his sketching talent led to early jobs in newspapers and on the vaudeville stage, as a 'lightning sketch artist'. After appearing in three early Edison films, he set up the Vitagraph company in 1900, which later pioneered an American form of *film d'art*, with a series of historical and literary subjects.[41] As new companies entered the business, Vitagraph lost ground and its founders parted company, with Blackton joining Famous Players briefly as an independent producer.

It was apparently a dinner in New York with Sir Thomas Lipton and the whiskey magnate Lord Dewar that persuaded Blackton to consider returning to England, as Lipton put it, 'to show our film chaps how to do a proper job'.[42] Whatever the precise motive, Blackton set up what was then a major production in British terms, which shrewdly combined a number of striking features. *The Glorious Adventure* (1922) was set during the Great Fire of London, in 1666, and wove its fictional story of society ladies thrown together with criminals from Newgate prison around historical events and characters of this major event, which appears not to have been treated before or for another seventy years.[43] As a showman, Blackton also believed in the need for novelty, and *The Glorious Adventure* demonstrated the latest colour process, Prizma Color, as well as boasting a notable society beauty, Lady Diana Manners, as its star.

Launched with a great fanfare at Covent Garden Opera House in January 1922, Blackton's film was soon at the centre of controversy: boosted by Blackton's lavish advertising yet suspect as a publicity stunt among many in the British film trade. Modern critics and historians had to wait until 1993, when the film was restored and shown at the London Film Festival, where it largely failed to impress, except as an early example of Victor McLaglen's earthy appeal. To complain, however, about a lack of 'modern' qualities is to ignore everything that might have impressed the audiences of 1922, seeing the first-ever 'colour feature', set in a Restoration London conceived for the screen for the first time. *The Glorious Adventure* did not reveal Blackton as a gifted director, but it staked out a territory for British production which will be mined intensively and sometimes brilliantly in future decades. Blackton meanwhile went on to make two further historical films in England, *The Gypsy Cavalier* (1922) and *The Virgin Queen* (1923). The former starred the French boxing champion Georges Carpentier and the latter Lady Diana, appearing as Queen Elizabeth. *The Virgin Queen* was entirely filmed at Beaulieu Castle and Abbey, with the whole cast and crew based there for two months, and whatever its dramatic qualities, it would mark an important milestone in the use of authentic historical locations.[44] Unfortunately, like the majority of British silent-era films, both it and *The Gypsy Cavalier* are lost, and their success or otherwise can only be conjectured.

A vision of London during the Great Fire of 1666: the climax of
James Stuart Blackton's *The Glorious Adventure* (1922),
starring Victor McLaglen and Lady Diana Manners, filmed in Prizma Color.

The Long Shadow of Caligari:
Continental Influences on British Cinema
Most design in cinema before the 1920s was essentially anonymous, organised by craft scenery specialists, who would have received their training in the theatre.[45] But change was under way in the American and German film industries. Wilfred Buckland is generally credited as cinema's first 'art director', and in Germany, the designers of *The Cabinet of Dr Caligari*, Walter Riemann, Walter Röhrig and Hermann Warm, were soon known by name. Production in Britain would benefit from these foreign developments towards the end of the '20s, when Andrew Mazzei came to Gaumont-British, having previously worked at Famous Players-Lasky, Alfred Junge arrived from Germany at British International Pictures and Vincent Korda came from Paris to join his brother Alex at their proudly named London Films.

Alfred Junge and the architectural imagination
Junge is often regarded as the father of serious art direction in British studios, which is perhaps more a reflection of the esteem in which German production personnel were held than the literal truth. BIP was established in the late '20s as the production arm of John Maxwell's expanding film empire, which also included a

cinema chain and distribution company. Part of the intention was to take advantage of Continental talent and prestige, so BIP made an approach to the German director E. A. Dupont, who had scored a major international success with *Variety* (Variétiés, 1925). Largely set in the world of fairgrounds and circus, *Variety* had impressed many by its intensely filmic qualities, in which atmospheric settings and elaborate chiaroscuro lighting played an important part. When Dupont arrived at BIP's Elstree Studios, he brought with him a group of German technicians who would leave a lasting impression on British filmmaking. Chief among these was Junge (1886-1964) who had originally trained in the theatre and opera house, starting as a scenic artist, before joining the Ufa Studio in 1920 and gaining experience during German cinema's most intensively creative period.

Multicultural Limehouse, as staged for *Piccadilly*, a British International Pictures production in 1929, directed by E. A. Dupont with a largely German crew, starring Anna Mae Wong and Jameson Thomas.

Having worked on *Variety* with Oskar Werndorff (who would also come to Britain), Junge became Dupont's sole designer for two of the three lavish films he made for BIP during 1928-29. The first of these, *Moulin Rouge* (1928), involved recreating the stage of the famous Parisian music, with its exotic sets, but comparatively little evocation of London. However, for *Piccadilly* (1929), set in both the West End and the multicultural dock area of Limehouse, Junge created some of the most remarkable settings that had yet been seen in British cinema. His nightclub is a blazing horseshoe-shaped arena, where glamorous reputations are made, and when Anna May Wong steps up form the scullery to take over from the club's former star, she is displayed to glittering, seductive effect. Yet when the club's manager, played by Jefferson Thomas, accompanies her to 'our Piccadilly' in a rowdy Limehouse pub, the atmosphere is even more electrifying, with a crowded saloon bar, seen in a single extended tracking shot, followed by a jostling dance-floor, on which racial tension explodes. For all the impact of these sequences, there is no attempt to impress with excessive decorative detail elsewhere: the coroner's courtroom in which the story ends is bare, allowing the actors to carry the climax of the drama.

Of course we cannot be certain whether either the dramatic atmosphere of Limehouse or the sparseness of the court were due solely to Junge's design decisions. They may have been decreed by the director, or by the film's budget, and they certainly involved the collaboration of the cinematographer and other members of the art department. But from what we know of Junge's later career, especially his collaboration on eight films with Michael Powell, we may be reasonably sure that his was at least a guiding hand in *Piccadilly*. After the Dupont films, Junge worked in Germany and France briefly, before returning to England and taking up permanent residence from 1932. He first became supervising art director for Gaumont-British, under the leadership of Michael Balcon, then from 1938 occupied a similar role at MGM's British studio, working on the major productions *The Citadel* (King Vidor, 1938) and *Goodbye Mr Chips* (Sam Wood, 1939).

In these roles, and in the many important films he oversaw at Gaumont-British, Junge was in effect the pioneer of modern studio design procedure in British cinema, during the crucial period when old silent-era practices were, of necessity, being replaced by the demands of shooting for sound. Quality, solidity and organisation were the Junge hallmarks, although these virtues could also prove restricting, as Powell increasingly felt after the Second World War, when he felt he had to breathe life into such Junge constructions as the heavenly amphitheatre of *A Matter of Life and Death* (1946). The partnership finally sundered on *The Red Shoes* (1948), when Powell's desire for a more expressive, less architecturally based design came to the fore, and led him to appoint the painter and former ballet designer, Hein Heckroth.

Vincent Korda: A Painter Among Producers

Another major Continental influence on British art direction arrived when Alexander Korda brought his brother Vincent to join London Films in 1932. Alexander Korda had already enjoyed a precocious early film career in his native Hungary, followed by successful periods in Vienna and Berlin, a humiliating three years in Hollywood and 'recovery' in Paris, before coming to England. With this wealth of international experience, Korda set about creating a new image for film production, deliberately aiming to raise its social and artistic status. He quickly made connections with English high society, which helped his negotiations with financiers, and his political connections (with Winston Churchill, among others) would stand him in good stead during the war and later years. But what Korda wanted, above all, was to create 'one big solid success to establish himself and open up the sources of finance he needed'.[46] The subject should be "national"... but sufficiently well known to have international appeal'; and drawing on Korda's previous experience with 'private lives', he settled on *The Private Life of Henry VIII* (1933). To realise this he needed trusted associates, including his younger brother Vincent, who had been painting in Paris before he was imperiously summoned to London to serve as set designer on this knowing account of England's most famous monarch, played with knowing panache by Charles Laughton.

Stories of Vincent Korda's dishevelled appearance and casualness are legion, suggesting a polar opposite to the elegant and highly organised disciplinarian Alfred Junge, although the two did in fact collaborate on the design of Alexander Korda's major French film, *Marius* (1931), which was also Vincent's debut in film design. Yet Vincent quickly became Alexander's most important associate, as London Films built on the vast success of *Henry VIII* with a series of calculatedly risqué exotic period pieces, starting with *The Rise of Catherine the Great* (1934) and *The Private Life of Don Juan* (1934), in which the gracefully ageing Douglas Fairbanks made his final appearance. The film that is probably Vincent Korda's masterpiece as a designer followed. In *Rembrandt* (1936), starring Laughton again, the two Kordas created a more intimate study of the vicissitudes of age and desire than their earlier success, which predictably had little popular appeal, despite its impeccable sets and deeply felt performances.

If *Rembrandt* clearly appealed to the painter in Vincent, his brother's other major project of 1934-35 made extraordinary demands on his ability to synthesise Modernist design. Conceived as a massive prestige project, *Things to Come* was based on H. G.

Wells' didactic novel, in which history is projected forward from 1930 to warn against the danger of another devastating war that will kill millions and virtually destroy civilisation.[47] Quite apart from the dramaturgical problems of turning Wells' tract into a workable script, the challenge for Vincent was to assimilate the work of prestigious Modernists that Alex had engaged – including Fernand Léger and Laszlo Moholy-Nagy – and produce a coherent futuristic design for the film. *Things to Come* was hardly more of a commercial success than *Rembrandt*, considering its high cost and practical problems, but the production of two such visually sophisticated works within the same year of release established London Films and Vincent Korda as forces to be reckoned with – and the equal of any Hollywood studio. Appropriately, the Kordas moved to Hollywood soon after the outbreak of war, initially to complete their Arabian Nights fantasy *The Thief of Bagdad* (1940), but then to continue to produce high-quality propaganda for American entry into the war, in such films as *That Hamilton Woman* (Alexander Korda,1941) and *To Be or Not to Be* (Ernst Lubitsch, 1942).

Vincent Korda had shown remarkable versatility during his first decade as a production designer, without perhaps revealing any distinctive personal style.[48] In his post-war work would reveal a distinct progression from the chocolate-box confection of *An Ideal Husband* (1947), swamped by the prevailing aesthetic of Technicolor,[49] to the taut drama of two collaborations with Graham Greene as writer and Carol Reed as director, *The Fallen Idol* (1948) and *The Third Man* (1949). In these latter, he would demonstrate a mastery of settings that are realist yet lend themselves to expressionistic interpretation, especially in the nocturnal Vienna, filmed on location, and studio-built sewers of *The Third Man*. And it was arguably these films, together with Powell and Pressburger's three Technicolor masterpieces and David Lean's Dickens adaptations, that gave a new status to British production during the years of postwar economic hardship.[50]

John Bryan
Much of Vincent Korda's best-known work was for 'exotic' films, such as *The Drum* (1938) and especially *The Thief of Bagdad* (1940), where he was able to unify a potentially fragmented potpourri of *Arabian Nights* motifs into a convincing, fabulous whole. One of his art department staff on *Things to Come* was John Bryan, who would go on to design the most famous of all sound-era Dickens adaptations, combining Korda's graphic fluency with

a solid architectural underpinning. This was no doubt due to his early experience working in a theatrical scenic artists studio, which led to jobbing film work in the early 1930s before he joined Korda's staff at Denham. His opportunity to shape a whole film came with two George Bernard Shaw adaptations, first *Pygmalion* (1938), a production on which David Lean was editor, then on the troubled *Major Barbara* (1941), where Korda stepped aside leaving Bryan in sole charge of designing this prestige production.[51]

Ronald Neame, later to become a producer like Bryan, was cameraman on *Major Barbara* and recalled Bryan's qualities as a designer: 'John Bryan quickly became the best designer I have ever met... He was the cameraman's dream boy, and the director's too. When one proposed a set to him, he would move to a sixteen by twelve drawing pad and with a few deft strokes in charcoal he would give you exactly what you had in mind. The moment John began his sketches the film came to life... His sets, when built, were always what one wanted. But he was a perfectionist and had no compunction about making changes if he felt they were needed, no matter what the cost... or aggravation he caused the construction department'.[52]

Bryan gained more experience designing Victorian London for the screen with the macabre melodrama *Fanny by Gaslight* (Asquith, 1944), but it was his two Dickens films for Lean that allowed his talents and personal style to emerge fully. For *Great Expectations* (1946), the unit was based at Rochester, closely linked with Dickens' own childhood, and Lean was determined to give the film a distinctive visual style. His solution was to use long lenses, thereby flattening the image, to which Bryan responded by using forced perspective, with foreground objects larger than life and furniture specially built in perspective, effectively reviving the tradition begun by *Caligari* and its Weimar successors, and for the same reason: to convey an intense subjective view of the characters' world. The effect is first seen in the churchyard, when Magwich startles Pip – and the audience – by appearing from behind a tombstone. The scene was built in the studio, with a church only ten feet high and a cloud painted on glass, but its atmosphere and drama are unquestionable. Bold stylisation continues throughout the film, after Pip comes to London and begins his gilded life, with Bryan making astute use of real locations. London, it should be remembered, often represented by the dome of St Paul's, had become a potent and frequently portrayed symbol of British resilience during the war.[53] So with the image of St Paul's, as well as elaborate studio sets, drawn in part from Cruikshank's original illustrations, *Great Expectations* became both a celebration of victorious 'Englishness' in the immediate aftermath of the war, and also a contribution to the climate of neo-romanticism then prevalent in English culture.[54]

After the immense success of *Great Expectations*, for which Bryan won an Academy Award, Lean wanted to change direction, but found himself obsessed by Dickens' other, much darker account of childhood, *Oliver Twist*, and so many of the same team found themselves plunged into creating the Victorian underworld. Lean encouraged Bryan to continue using forced perspective, especially to refresh scenes which were already visual clichés, such as Oliver asking for more in the workhouse. Overall *Oliver Twist* is literally darker, much of it taking place in squalid settings that had little natural or artificial light. Chiaroscuro effects, with light seeping through dirty windows, give the film an atmosphere that has since established a new benchmark for picturing the Victorian city, a classic in its own terms, and one that fitted well with the prevailing vogue for *film noir*.

David Lean's influential, though controversial, *Oliver Twist* (1948), was designed by John Bryan using photographs of Victorian London and images drawn from Gustave Doré's *London, A Pilgrimage*, such as the view of St Paul's from the Brewery Bridge.

Bryan also made use of Gustave Doré's famous etchings of London scenes and characters, basing much of the world of Bill Sikes and Fagin on these crowded images with their fantastic Piranesian tracery of arches and bridges and arches.[55] During the 1950s, Bryan would turn towards production, no doubt frustrated by the limited opportunities offered by the British industry at this time, but one of his last films as production designer was *The Magic Box* (1951), a biography of the controversial British cinema pioneer William Friese-Greene, to which all branches of the industry contributed as part of the Festival of Britain.[56] Despite its dubious veracity, this allowed Bryan to recreate the late Victorian world of photographers and passionate inventors in superb detail, along with London and its supposed earliest filmed images. Among his later productions, *The Horse's Mouth* (1958) offered a rare view of Bohemian London, seen through the eyes of the disreputable Gulley Jimson, an artist comically ruthless in pursuit of his vision, played by Alec Guinness who also scripted the film.

Carmen Dillon

The closest counterpart to John Bryan in British cinema during the 1940s was also its only female art director until recent times. Carmen Dillon (1908-1995) had trained as an architect before starting to work in cinema in the 1930s, during the production boom that followed the introduction of the British 'quota'.[57] An art director from 1937, she worked on many of Anthony Asquith's wartime films, before being nominated for an Academy Award for her contribution to Laurence Olivier's highly original *Henry V* (1943). The film that Olivier directed and starred in was partly inspired by Eisenstein's stirring evocation of medieval Russia in *Alexander Nevsky* (1938), and was originally conceived by an ex-BBC producer Dallas Bower.[58] But its greatest innovation was to recreate the Globe Theatre for its opening, before moving into heavily stylised scenes based on medieval illustration, and finally into a vivid naturalistic portrayal of the Battle of Agincourt. Dillon worked under Paul Sheriffs on this landmark Shakespeare adaptation, and went on to become production designer on all Olivier's subsequent films, winning the Academy Award in 1948 for *Hamlet*. While there is no single major 'literary London' film to her credit, her prolific forty-year career saw British cinema pass from a formulaic studio-based style through the bold experiments of the 40s, back to retrenchment in the 50s and early 60s (when she designed for both the popular 'Doctor' and 'Carry On' comedy series). Yet amid these often routine projects, she designed in rapid succession one of the few 1950s Dickens adaptations, Ralph Thomas' *A Tale of Two Cities* (1958), with Dirk Bogarde as Sidney Carton, and Basil Dearden's shocking exposé of London racism in the murder mystery *Sapphire* (1959), a harbinger of the new realism of the 60s. And many of the film designers who would make their mark in the 60s and 70s owed their training to Dillon's inspiring professional example.

The opening sequence, set in the Globe Theatre, of Lawrence Olivier's *Henry V* (1944), filmed in Technicolor at Denham Studio and at Powerscourt, Co. Wicklow.

John Box

John Box (1920-2005) considered Carmen Dillon and John Bryan the two formative influences on him as a production designer. Having served in the war as a tank commander, and qualified as an architect, Box started work in the studios during Britain's uncertain post-war years, but was lucky to gain wider experience from working in the art department on a number of American productions based in Britain, such as *Treasure Island* (Byron Haskin, 1950), *The Black Knight* (Tay Garnett, 1954) and *The Inn of the Sixth Happiness* (Mark Robson, 1958).[59] He is certainly best known today for his collaborations with David Lean, especially on *Lawrence of Arabia* (1962) – which he took over when Bryan fell ill – and *Doctor Zhivago* (1965), but I want to focus here on his two 1960s films that involved creating an historical London, *A Man for All Seasons* (1966) and *Oliver!* (1968), and which also offer an instructive comparison in scale.

A Man for All Seasons was closely based on Robert Bolt's 1960 play, which focuses on the moral struggle between Thomas More and his king Henry VIII over the latter's determination to ignore the Catholic church and change English law in order to divorce his wife and marry another. As a loyal Catholic, More cannot accept this and resigns as Chancellor, but is then accused of treason by Henry and, after refusing to give way, executed. The play had enjoyed great success, with Paul Scofield becoming closely associated with the part of More, striking a defiant note of conscience and sacrifice amid the hedonism of 'swinging London' in the mid-60s. Yet when it was acquired for filming by Columbia, the project was given a much lower priority than the studio's other current production, a James Bond extravaganza, *Casino Royale*.[60] As the director Fred Zinnemann explained, it was 'a very modest and, in a box-office sense, totally unpromising project... a costume movie [with] very little action, let alone violence, no sex, no overt love story and, most importantly, *no stars*... No wonder the budget was tiny'.[61] The low budget seems to have given all concerned an exceptionally clear sense of priorities. With most of the script's themes being conveyed by dialogue – the play has always lent itself to being staged in a bare Brechtian style – the film's makers had to consider how best to negotiate a balance between location and studio shooting, and what use to make of the considerable amount of surviving visual evidence of More's life and Tudor London.

Their solution involved focusing on three main settings, one of which would be realised by the use of different locations, and the two others constructed in the studio, with only a few brief exterior shots to 'place' one of them. More's house, supposedly beside the River Thames in a still rural Chelsea, where he first feels the force of the King's determination and which later becomes his retreat, was created by using the exterior of an historic house in Oxfordshire. For Henry's 'informal' visit, as part of his campaign to win over More, the filmmakers used a stretch of river on the Beaulieu estate in Hampshire, and lined the muddy water's edge so that King could stride ashore and leap over the wall, to arrive in More's garden – actually a hundred miles away – before entering the interiors skilfully constructed in Shepperton Studio. This scene, with Robert Shaw as a charismatic Henry VIII, remains one of the most memorable in the film.

The other key location was Hampton Court Palace, where More's predecessor as Chancellor, Cardinal Wolsey, wielded his power. This palace still stands, but the production could not afford extensive location shooting, so its façade was represented by a single exterior view, supplemented by John Box's false perspective rendering painted onto flats: 'Fortunately, one of the great production designers, John Box, was with us. Using three enormous flats raised in perspective, he built a replica of the palace at Hampton Court for £5000. When comparing photographs of the movie set and the real thing, no one could tell the difference'.[62] Wolsey's chamber is ingeniously made small to emphasise the menacing bulk of Orson Welles, with the walls painted in the same imperious red as his cardinal's robe. The other key setting is Westminster Hall, where More's trumped-up trial for treason takes place before Parliament. Here, director and designer were fully agreed that the setting should be spare as well as imposing – 'conceived by us as a kind of bullring' (Zinnemann) – relieved only by the red robes of the judges and the green silk costume of More's opportunistic accuser, Richard Rich.

Henry VIII visits Thomas More in *A Man for All Seasons* (1966), directed by Fred Zinnemann and designed by John Box.

There is a comparatively extensive iconography of More's life and martyrdom, which led to his being canonised by the Catholic Church, which the filmmakers used as a basis for the More family scenes and the trial. But Zinnemann resisted the temptation to 'open out' what is essentially a study of conscience resisting tyrannical power. The film's limited budget no doubt helped maintain this focus, avoiding any irrelevant period detail and ensuring that what visual spectacle there is serves a dramatic purpose. Even More's execution at the Tower of London is shown tightly framed, keeping the drama of conscience wholly at the centre of attention. As a film of theological controversy and of early Tudor London, *A Man for All Seasons* is notably austere, yet unquestionably all the more effective for its restraint.

By contrast, John Box's second essay in representing historic London counts as one of the most lavish and exuberant screen celebrations of the Victorian city. *Oliver!* (1960) was a successful musical version of Dickens' novel by Lionel Bart, originally nurtured by Joan Littlewood's East End Theatre Workshop (itself partly inspired by the British discovery of Brecht), which interpolated both lively and sentimental songs into the original story and created major roles for 'The artful Dodger', Fagin and Nancy. After its great success on stage, the film version was keenly awaited, but its progress to the screen was dogged with problems. John Box, already appointed production designer, was responsible for proposing Carol Reed as a last-minute choice for director, with the result that most of the key production personnel lacked any previous experience making musicals. This may account for a lack of slickness and the frank engagement with darker issues that makes *Oliver!* the equal of some major American musicals, and a major contribution to the long history of Dickens adaptations for stage and screen mentioned earlier.

Unlike *A Man for All Seasons*, *Oliver!* had a substantial budget for the construction of sets at Shepperton. Three of these are particularly interesting in relation to the iconography of Victorian London: the Covent Garden market in which Oliver first experiences London's excitement; the network of wooden walkways that provide entry to Fagin's attic den and to the waterside tavern where the underworld gather; and the crescent of luxurious new houses that represent the moneyed world to which he will finally escape. None of these depicts an actual city location: all are composites that combine accurate period detail with elements of stylisation and fantasy. The market scene into which Oliver emerges his ride into London in a produce wagon bears some relation to the Covent Garden fruit and vegetable market that has featured in many films as a signifier of 'historic London', centred around Inigo Jones' Piazza and church of St. Paul's.[63] But it is also an 'expanded' Covent Garden that includes some activity of the meat market of Smithfield, while the main street offers a perspective clearly inspired by Gustave Doré's etching, 'Ludgate Hill: A Block in the Street', with a train crossing overhead.[64] The wooden steps and the recurrent distant dome of St. Paul's also owe much to Doré,[65] and to the earlier *Oliver Twist* designs of Box's mentor John Bryan, but there is evidence of new research on historic London buildings, as Colin Sorenson demonstrated in his pioneering study *London on Film*.[66] For the later sequence, built around the song 'Who will buy?' and set in fashionable London, when Mr Brownlow has first rescued Oliver from the clutches of Fagin, Box designed and built on the Shepperton backlot a full-scale crescent terrace. Faced in brilliant white, with elaborate ironwork and a central garden, this may be more evocative of Bath, but it also corresponds to the elegant stuccoed crescents that were being built around London in the early 19th century.⁶⁷ And in dramatic terms, the contrast between the darkest London that Oliver has been incarcerated in and this shining vision of a new London of wealth and benevolence becomes a vital axis of the film, giving substance to both Dickens' and Bart's redemptive fantasy.

For Carol Reed's 1968 film of the Lionel Bart musical *Oliver!*, John Box created an extensive set at Shepperton studio, including a Covent Garden 'street'.

Reflecting on the Celluloid City

Can we draw any general conclusions from these few case studies? Rather than consider them in terms of 'accuracy', it is surely more fruitful to place the work of production designers in the wider context of the history of representing London – which has never been merely a matter topographic precision.⁶⁸ Between William Hogarth's well-known prints of the 1750s, including 'Gin Lane' and 'Beer Street', and Doré's portfolio of 1872, there was a rich tradition of London illustration, greatly supplemented by the engravings published by the *Illustrated London News* from the 1850s onwards.⁶⁹ Often the aim of such illustration was to convey an impression, or a judgement.⁷⁰ Doré was accused by at least one contemporary critic of 'inventing rather than copying' in his portrayal of a relentlessly gloomy, teeming metropolis.⁷¹ From the earliest moment at which they could escape the painted canvas of the studio and take to the streets, filmmakers have been seeking to convey what Samuel Johnson called 'the wonderful extent and variety of London'.

In doing so, they have been constrained by many factors, not least the ever-changing face of the city itself, driven by commerce, which has left few historic views unaltered and also made it immensely prohibitively expensive to shoot on location. *Pace* the art historian Erwin Panofsky and his faith in 'unstylised reality', this has meant that, paradoxically, many of the most 'authentic' screen representations of London have been created in the studio (albeit often a suburban London studio), using cinema's range of *trompe l'oeil* effects.

Nor has such authenticity usually been a matter of strict visual correspondence between image and reality, since the viewer's referent is more likely to be other representations of London. In terms of the Affrons' categorisation of set functions, London settings are usually both denotative *and* narrative, in that the location of characters within, or movement between, particular districts of the city constitutes a narrative in itself.[72] Thus, no less than any 20th-century London gangster moving from East to West or contemplating the disappearance of the 'old East End',[73] Thomas More commutes between his home in Chelsea and the centres of state power, Hampton Court, Parliament and the Tower, while the Oliver of the 1968 film is the first to traverse a richly textured, yet deterritorialised 'Dickensian' London conceived in colour.

The founders of the British school of production design were, perhaps unsurprisingly, both foreigners, central Euro-peans who made England their temporary home. But Alfred Junge and Vincent Korda brought with them international experience that British studios badly needed at the beginning of the 1930s, and both stayed long enough to train their native pupils and successors. Both believed implicitly in the professional principle that art direction should be 'invisible', yet both contributed to the rising prestige of the designer that would lead to their successors becoming highly influential in giving British films a distinctive stylisation, a creative intertextual relationship with the literary works that are often their premise.[74] What is more, these relationships and traditions have continued.

Most recently, Stuart Craig emerged from the Bryan-Box succession to design very different versions of Victorian London for *The Elephant Man* (David Lynch, 1980) and *Chaplin* (Richard Attenborough, 1992), before creating a paradigmatic version of contemporary London in *Notting Hill* (Roger Michell, 1999) and then embarking on the hugely popular Harry Potter series, rooted in the tradition of English juvenile fantasy fiction and combining British studio practice with the new graphic resources of CGI.[75]

Meanwhile, the process of reimagining an earlier London has also continued, with notable contributions from visiting designers. One of the most remarkable has been a rare vision of the 17th-century city, in *Restoration* (1995), Michael Hoffman's film based on a novel by Rose Tremain, designed by the Argentinian Eugenio Zanetti. An American critic's response encapsulates the sense of revelation that London films have been trying, and have occasionally managed, to produce for over a century: 'Never before in the movies have I seen such a riotous depiction of period London: The overwhelming excess of the royal court, the teeming traffic on the Thames, the bridges groaning with buildings and people, the streets jammed with life and lowlife, the delight in all the pleasures of the flesh – and then, like two grim wake-up calls, the Black Plague and the Great Fire. It is remarkable that this movie, which recreates a world, cost only about $18 million, and never seems to cut a corner'.[76]

The adaptation of Dickens for the cinema has also continued apace, despite the prevalence of television serial adaptation, which allows greater textual fidelity to the novels.[77] Alfonso Cuarón successfully transposed *Great Expectations* to an American setting in 1998, with his English designer Tony Burrough finding narrative equivalents to Dickens' Kent and London in modern Florida, Manhattan and Long Island. And Roman Polanski returned to the roots of the studio tradition with his *Oliver Twist* (2005), made at the Barrandov Studio in Prague, where the distinguished Polish production designer Alan Starski was able to create a more realistically squalid London than either Bryan or Box could have contemplated for this study of survival against the odds. If, as Grahame Smith has recently shown, 'visualisation' played a vital part in Dickens' imaginative life and works, and if his evocative power was readily compared with the new photographic media of the 19th century by his contemporaries, we should not be surprised that 'Dickens adaptation' continues to play a leading role in British, and indeed world, cinema.[78]

An earlier version appeared in Rumiko Handa and James Potter, eds., *Conjuring the Real: The Role of Architecture in Eighteenth and Nineteenth Century Fiction* (University of Nebraska Press, 2011).

22.
Who Needs Film Archives?
Notes Towards a User-Centred Future

National film archives have never had the status of documentary and written archives, despite the oldest among them approaching their centenary, and the existence of an international film archives association that implies uniform standards and coverage.[1] Only the Motion Picture division of the American Library of Congress belongs to its nation's authoritative central archive, with a record of collecting to establish copyright in the new medium that dates back to the 1890s. And thanks to successive stages of conservation, the incunabula of early American film have been preserved like no others.[2] Elsewhere, attempts to deposit films as historic documents were largely resisted – as in Britain, with only single frames imperfectly stored – until the 1920s saw a number of independent efforts to preserve copies of what remained from early film production, by which time many of the pioneer producers had ceased operation and retained no further interest in their pioneering work.

There were many disincentives for the early collectors. Film stock was highly flammable and prone to deterioration if not carefully stored. Nor would there be much point in preserving a used projection print, which would be unsuitable for making new copies; while preserving or making negatives would ignore the fact that film stocks were constantly changing, and by the end of the 1930s both colour and sound-on-film systems were gaining wide acceptance. Despite the appearance of histories of the medium, which identified already antique works as having historical significance, it required a rare confidence and vision in the early 1930s, when the first 'national archive' collections were formally established, to believe that this history of a fast-changing medium would matter to the future.

The inevitable consequence was a massive scale of loss from the early decades, estimated at approximately 80% of all pre-1930 production, which has become increasingly apparent as digital access to early film has begun to generate informed 'demand'. For it is one of the paradoxes of the digital era that, with film now widely experienced in digital formats, either online or via DVD and DCP, has come a range of 'archival' passions that have generated interest in many periods and genres of film long believed of little or no interest. The history of film in all its many aspects is almost certainly more alive today than at any period during the last century, which poses a special challenge, and perhaps opportunity, to traditional film archives.

Archival Activism
The new culture of 'cinephilia 2.0' was ably characterised by Laurent Jullier and Jean-Marc Leveratto in their contribution to an anthology on the current state of audiencehood.[3] Most of these new and often compulsive cinephiles have no training in the routines of the traditional film archive, and few would have any patience with their legal restrictions surrounding digital access to film, which are largely governed by commercial efforts to control digital consumption of entertainment content. The new connoisseurs and collectors of 'archival' film have been characterised as 'prosumers', referring to the fact that they are likely to make use of their findings in personal productions, making them in effect producers, although not necessarily with any commercial ambitions. The rapid growth of personal digital media, capable of manipulating moving and still images, has eradicated any sharp distinction between producers and consumers, giving enthusiasts efficient means to shape their archival compilations.

Access to these resources has created what could be considered a new golden age of archival activism. Where the efforts of the first generations of archivists were largely devoted to securing copies of canonic fiction films, film archives have increasingly sought to broaden their holdings of non-fiction and informal film, as well as related visual media and contextual data, with family films and local commemorations featuring strongly among the holdings of regional, if not national, film archives.

Once again, the American Library of Congress and Smithsonian collections pointed the way, with curated thematic displays and later online exhibitions demonstrating the potential of combining film to illuminate periods and themes in American history.[4] But others have followed and pioneered new ways of bringing the fruits of such activist archiving to wider audiences, as several contrasting case studies may make clear. An influential model emerged from French municipal library policy in the 1980s concentrating on developing 'médiathèques', which would combine traditional print-based libraries with a variety of disc-based media and films on video-tape. Out of this came the Vidéothèque de Paris, now known at the

Forum des Images, launched in 1988 as a promotional initiative by the mayor's office, in part to circumvent the restrictive practices then common in such official film archives as the Cinémathèque française or the CNC Service des Archives.[5] Offering direct viewing access on video to a wide range of films made in or about Paris, the Vidéothèque quickly established itself as a democratic new institution committed to catering to a wide variety of users and promoting access to many different kinds of film, including advertising, commercials, music promotion, all of which originated in Paris. While, traditionally, documentary enjoyed a quasi-artistic status within French cinema, the range of material now made available under 'subject' search criteria amounted to a revelation and undoubtedly helped advertise the potential of a user-oriented approach.

Archives and History Go Regional
Elsewhere, there have also been shifts in archival policy which would lead to a more 'de-centred' and responsive service. In the UK, the traditional structure of national archives was challenged during the 1980s by the creation of a network of regional film archives, many later renamed 'screen archives' to advertise their intention of collecting *all* screen media, from lantern slides to modern digital formats, and including television, which had largely been separated from film in earlier archiving practices. By collecting material from delimited geographical regions, such as the Southeast of England (excluding London), the new archives were joining a movement to de-centralise arts provision, and indeed many aspects of government, across the UK.[6] The result, although subject to many funding problems over subsequent years, has been a profound change in attitude towards what an audiovisual archive can be. The UK regional screen archives have created patterns of work and regional representation which brought archiving close to its constituency, and showed how audiovisual media could play a vital part a part in defining and preserving regional identity.

Two aspects of the UK and other regional archives' work has proved particularly important. One is the custom of showing curated selections of their holdings to local audiences, where the response has been typically lively and engaged, often leading to improved identification and future donations; and the other is collecting narrow-gauge colour film, as widely used by amateurs from the 1930s onwards. Television producers of such popular series as *The Second World War in Colour* (1999) and *The Thirties in Colour* (2008) found that much of their most vivid material came from regional archives' holdings, where traditional archival prejudice against reversal stocks and amateur formats had been ignored.

In many ways, regional archives were following the earlier growth of local and regional written histories – notably E. P. Thompson's *The Making of the English Working Class* (1963) and the work of the Annales group in France, especially Emmanuel Le Roy Ladurie's *Montaillou* (1975); and more recently Raphael Samuel's *Theatres of Memory* and Pierre Nora's *Lieux de mémoire*.[7] Where the new historians had made use of micro-histories, ephemera and oral records, the pioneer local film archivists took an interest in previously scorned genres and formats. While the new film archivists have rarely been radical in their politics, they were radical in their belief that film could have a closer relationship with people than being merely commercial entertainment, or the distant 'classics' of the cinema canon. So the valuation of local documentary and amateur film that began with regional archives has since flourished through television with the rise of social history programming, linked with such private initiatives such as Albert Kahn's The Archives of the Planet, the Internet Archive, and indeed with YouTube and similar direct-access sites.

This unplanned and often anarchic 'bottom-up' movement has in many ways left the official archives struggling to find their place amid a new, populist tide of interest in 'experiencing' the past. For example, the UK's 'Their Past Your Future' project of 2005, intended to mark the 50th anniversary of the end of the Second World War and communicate its importance to the young, funded a number of regional archives to produce local compilations. London's Screen Archives Network was able to digitise and compile an overview of the experience of the war and its aftermath in London, widely distributed to community groups and education users.[8]

The emergence of YouTube as a universal open-access archive has obviously brought a hitherto unimaginable quantity of moving image archive to everyone with an internet connection. And if much of this is parasitic on collections and even archives, it has also become an important site where hitherto inaccessible material may be quickly and informally accessed. One among many examples of the new 'archival' role of YouTube is its hosting of substantial portions of the otherwise lost multi-media production *The Photo-Drama of Creation* (1914).[9] But however beneficial, this is not without difficulties, the most fundamental being the issue of rights and ownership. While much of YouTube functions in an effective 'zone of tolerance', with many rights holders permitting and even encouraging material they 'own' to appear freely, some copyright regimes are more exacting, notably the French. With publications and 'creation' attracting multiple forms of protection under French law, few French film-texts are free to be made available online, and in other countries which offer complex safeguards against unauthorised publication, archives find that the new digital opportunities pose as much of a legal threat as an opportunity to create maximum access.

Long believed lost, film elements of the multi-media
Photo-Drama of Creation, 1914, appeared initially on YouTube
from a personal restoration project.

Faced with the challenge of making their collections regionally accessible, both the British Film Institute and the Australian National Film and Sound Archive have created networks of mediatheques, where pre-curated specialist archival programmes may be viewed, without the rights issues raised by physical copies being supplied to users or open online access.[10] Despite these restrictions, undoubtedly irksome to those used to the desktop freedom afforded by YouTube, the opportunity to book a viewing space for group use and to browse within a curated sub-collection does offer real advantages – especially compared with the cramped flatbed conditions of traditional film-based archival viewing.[11]

Such examples of state-funded film archives seeking to fulfil their statutory obligations in a seemingly permissive climate of universal digital access are indeed a far cry from the image of the archive as a place of ultimate authority, invoked by Jacques Derrida in his widely cited essay *Archive Fever: A Freudian Impression*.[12] The archive, Derrida recalled, was traditionally a site of power, containing titles and documents on which other powers and entitlements depended. But if all this is still true to some extent in the civic or state archive, it has rarely, if ever, been true of the film archive. The only near-exceptions would be the archives of ex-communist states, where images of canonic figures and events were once jealously preserved and guarded against corruption – having already been subject to brutal ideological pruning.[13] There may indeed still be scope in a number of state film archives for the forensic investigation of how cuts have been made, and compilations of fragments assembled, but in view of the poor state of documentation within most archives, it is highly unlikely that any substantive conclusions could be drawn about what may have guided these actions.

Unlike state archives, with their mass of legal and political documents, most film archives consist mainly of what were once commercial productions, which are still residually controlled by successor companies – even if these have only a nominal link with the historic company of a similar name. In a climate of vigorously asserted IP [intellectual property] law, where the latent value of rights and assets is routinely overestimated and fear of violating rights that are little more than theoretical often prevents sensible action in favour of the common good, many large archives find themselves paralyzed by the threat of potential litigation, while also obliged to preserve films which they do not 'own' – a very different situation from the equivalent museums and galleries of historic visual art, which are able to capitalise on ownership of their holdings.

Restoration as the New Archival Distinction

For many, the way forward in this unenviable situation has been to reinvent themselves as centres of expertise in reconstruction or 'restoration'. Even though much of the specialist photo-chemical and increasingly digital manipulation involved may be sub-contracted to commercial experts, archives increasingly distinguish themselves through authorship of restorations of important holdings. These may range from producing definitive editions of well-known films long available only in corrupted versions – such as Fritz Lang's *Metropolis* (1927)[14] – to curated presentations of neglected genres in 'DVD editions'. Among the latter have been such achievements as Czech animation, British documentary and many other such collections.

At a time when the popularity is growing of 'live' presentation of films from the silent era, often in festivals devoted to such reappreciation, such as the Giornate del Cinema Muto in Pordenone, and the Cinema Ritrovato festival in Bologna, both in Italy, archivists have been joined by a new generation of festival organisers and curators, in search of new discoveries among their holdings. And similarly, the growth of the specialist DVD and latterly Blu-ray market, setting store by quality of presentation and contextualisation rather than simply cheapness or rarity, has helped to create a 'secondary market' for restoration and curation in the form of albums and box sets, which can be seen as the audiovisual equivalent of historic music's extensive panoply of 'archival' box sets. Once again, an American project has set the standard, with the *Treasures from American Film Archives* collections, a series of seven boxed sets coordinated by the National Film Preservation Foundation since 2000, which has made available well-presented and annotated DVDs of American archives' early film holdings, initially circulated to interested parties on a non-profit basis through archival festivals.

There are indeed reasons to be optimistic that the sheer flexibility and economy of digital organisation and access has started to rescue film archives from their long subordination as the poor and unrespectable relations of paper archives; although this should not diminish respect for the extraordinary tenacity and ingenuity of their founders.[15] And it must be admitted that the very term 'film archive' has already begun to sound like a period concept. At a time when the majority of our film viewing needs are met by online or other forms of digital mediation, the archives that cater to surviving elements of film's material life have perhaps become closer to archaeological museums; and as such, they may finally gain a status as 'ultimate repositories' that they never enjoyed during film's uniquely photochemical era. Indeed, with the commercial film industry now far advanced in its conversion to wholly digital operation, the archives' specialist laboratories catering to archival work may well become the sole surviving sites capable of carrying out such photochemical operations.

A Future for Film Archives?
If film archives have ceded many of the functions that they were never well-equipped or funded to perform and have gained new conservation and curatorial roles in the digital era, as suggested here, the title question may perhaps need to be rephrased: do we *need* to have separate audiovisual archives in the digital future; and if so, what functions might they serve for future users?

As we have seen, the earliest film archives were created by those convinced that film had created a new cultural form, which was in danger of being lost due to its material and commercial fragility. For all the archival pioneers, educating and inspiring future generations was an essential part of their motivation, sometimes, as in the case of Henri Langlois, founder of the Cinémathèque française, taking precedence over prudent conservation.[16] But once there is no longer a link between creating and defending a collection, and making that collection a source of inspiration for others, there would seem to be no further role for charismatic archivists. Or perhaps even for separate film archives?

This would be an understandable, but I think premature conclusion. On the one hand, it risks assuming that the recognition of film culture that Langlois, Lindgren, Iris Barry and Jacques Ledoux and their many colleagues in the international archive movement fought for has been achieved. It also potentially places the existing film archives in a precarious position, at a time when large-scale digital storage and conservation seems to offer attractive economies of scale. Despite the evidence of film's presence at many levels of education, and a general level of 'film literacy' very different from the period when archives and their supporters were first active, there is still widespread resistance to recognising how projected pictures and cinema transformed the culture of the *fin de siècle*. Rather than portray film as a 'new art' in the early 20th century, as was common in early film education, it would be more accurate to show how cinema became part of an increasingly multi-media culture – in many cases helping to diffuse new tendencies in literature, fashion and music and so act as an engine of modernity.[17]

Film archives, during their foundational phase, were not ideally placed to portray film in this intermedial light, often tending to emphasise the exceptional, rather than to trace the shifting role of film within a new cultural ensemble. By contrast, a number of recent comparative studies have ranged beyond the vagaries of archival holdings to demonstrate the value of locating genres of early production within larger and more pervasive cultural trends. One such is the ongoing programme of studying filmic representations of the ancient world produced in the silent era, led by Pantelis Michelakis and Maria Wyke, which has involved a wide range of archives and given new currency to their holdings by showing how these films were often informed by revivalist painting, symbolist literature and archaeology itself – as well as promoting public screenings and seminars at the Cinema Ritrovato festival in Bologna and at academic venues.[18]

Another comparative project based in the same era has focused on one of the most distinctive features of early production: the creation and promotion of stars, who would develop loyal followings in many countries. Asta Nielsen emerged as a star of Danish films in 1909 and soon moved to Germany, where her many varied roles made her the most popular screen actor in the world before

Chaplin. An international conference, 'Importing Asta Nielsen', organised by the German film historian Martin Loiperdinger at the Deutsches Film Institute in Frankfurt, 2011, demonstrated how pervasive and also varied the impact of Nielsen had been, providing a focus for currents of modernism and feminism in many cultures.[19]

Neither of these projects would have been considered 'progressive' during the early years of Film Studies, often preoccupied with the progress of 'filmic language' and the medium's specificity. Yet both ancient world subjects and Nielsen's vehicles reached and influenced vast audiences before and even beyond the First World War. Indeed their impact, depending on much more than a growing mastery of filmic mise-en-scène, did much to establish the pervasive cultural presence of cinema by c.1912. But this cannot be understood by reference alone to the surviving copies. It needs more complex research that draws on newspaper, journal and ephemera archives, as well as a grasp of comparative social and cultural history.

Archives are not alone among institutions created during the era of collecting and classifying in having to rethink how to justify their existence, especially to economy-seeking paymasters. Museums and libraries face similar challenges – although in many ways they are better buttressed by core academic disciplines that value their collections and expertise, and by a wider public esteem for these. Many have also managed to reinvent themselves as 'destination venues' in the context of modern cultural tourism, in a way that relatively few film archives have yet managed.[20]

In earlier decades, film archives suffered from a disconnect between their often deficient collections and the generally ahistorical new academic field of film studies, which was more closely aligned with connoisseurship and latterly cultural studies. Most were founded within traditions of secrecy and defensiveness, often resulting from the early hostility of the industry, and in relative isolation from academic disciplines that might have influenced their direction. In consequence, they have continued to lack the support of film scholars, PhD researchers, or indeed historians of most kinds, especially as many of these now find their film sources and references online. But if we try to rethink the role of archives in the era of YouTube, a number of possible new constituencies emerge/appear:

There are surely opportunities to learn from how the regional and local archives have engaged with amateur family and community historians, joining this great popular movement – long shunned by academic historians, but beginning to attract recognition as a new form of 'participant history'.

The Danish Film Archive has pioneered putting early Danish films freely online and inviting viewer responses to clarify aspects of their production.

Historians interested in the 'pervasive' impact of film (and related media) in all its forms – 'the place of filmgoing/viewing in national life'; or in how film and television contributed to transnational themes, such as the world wars, de-colonisation, the Cold War, the post-communist world after the 1980s, space travel and exploration, etc.

Could archives do more to address and even anticipate these questions and discourses, through their own research projects? Can they join forces with the new user-friendly sources of visual history, and with the new providers of online historical source material – the databases, wikis and special-interest webs?

Those inspired by the new sub-divisions of history, such as gender history, histories of representation, emotions, work, the everyday, etc. In fact women's history has already been a powerful driver of interest in film history, as feminist historians have sought to challenge received canons and reveal the subordinated role of women – at all levels, from film-makers to film fans. Now gay and sexual minorities' history are starting to do the same, seeking out once-marginal, interstitial material.

The material and social histories of the media that were grouped under 'film', reaching back into earlier photographic and projection media and forward into the digital media of today and the future (following the lead of Frankfurt, Turin and the Cinémathèque française). Can they respond to the new interest that's emerging in 'obsolete' formats and technologies, from stereo and ML to 16mm,

8 mm and even 9.5mm – an interest that links car-boot sale collectors with contemporary visual artists and media archaeologists?

There are undoubtedly opportunities as well as challenges for film archives today, at a time when the very basis of their collections is shifting from photochemical to digital. They face a massive task: to explain that digital is not a preservation format, and that access, restoration and preservation are to some extent in conflict as priorities. However, a world with fewer and smaller screen archives would undoubtedly be a poorer place, while archives that had more users and supporters could potentially overcome the neglect that has long relegated them to the margins of intellectual and institutional life.

First appeared in print in the *Czech and Slovak Journal of Humanities*, 2015, no.1, 36-44.

Pivotal Portraits

23.
'A Very Wonderful Process': Queen Victoria, Photography and Film

Queen Victoria's Diamond Jubilee, celebrated in 1897, is generally agreed to have been the ceremonial climax to her reign, marking an unexpected return to public appearance after decades of self-imposed seclusion following the death of Prince Albert in 1861. Yet how much its impact owed to being the first major state event to be comprehensively filmed, with records of the procession being shown throughout Britain and the British Empire, as well as elsewhere, has hardly been assessed. Nor has the relationship between Victoria's long-standing interest in photography, still very much in evidence at the time of the Jubilee, and her response to 'animated photography'. While John Plunkett has argued convincingly for seeing Victoria as 'media made', his focus is primarily on 'the tremendous expansion of the market for newspapers, books, periodicals and engravings' that her reign witnessed.[1] And despite agreeing with Plunkett's claim that 'the royal image itself became photographic', at least one of his critics has drawn attention to an apparent lack of agency in his portrayal of Victoria's relationship to this process.[2]

My purpose here is not to adjudicate the degree of Victoria's involvement in her photographic or filmic representation – especially in view of the limited and somewhat selective evidence available from royal archives. Rather, it is to connect the scattered fragments of evidence, in order to offer an account that does not underestimate Victoria's active interest in the new photographic media, or create a false hiatus between still and moving pictures, while broadly agreeing with the many writers who have stressed how these reshaped the image of monarchy at the turn of the century.

A Passion for Photography
In one of the most vivid accounts of Victoria's involvement with photography, a pioneer historian of the medium, Bill Jay, claims that the Queen was viewing the first specimens of the daguerreotype to reach England on the very occasion that she effectively proposed to Prince Albert: 15 October 1839.[3] The story that Jay traces is one

of a shared enthusiasm for the new medium in its earliest formats, with Albert photographed by daguerreotypist William Constable in Brighton in 1842 and Victoria by her former drawing master, Henry Collen, who had taken up the calotype negative-positive process invented by William Fox Talbot, and produced a miniature portrait of her in 1844 or 1845.

Early photograph of Victoria and her family by Roger Fenton.

By the early 1850s, Victoria and Albert were recognised patrons and practitioners of photography. A private darkroom had been established at Windsor Castle, and the royal couple were reported by the *Illustrated Magazine of Art* as 'well known to be no mean proficient in photography'.[4] As patrons of the newly formed Photographic Society of London, they visited its first major exhibition in January 1853 and Victoria's journal entry reveals how engaged she was with the personalities and varieties of early photographic work: 'It was most interesting & there are 3 rooms full of the most beautiful specimens, some, from France, and Germany, & many by amateurs. Mr Fenton, who belongs to the Society, explained everything & there were many beautiful photographs done by him. Prof Wheatstone, the inventor of stereoscope, was also there. Some of the landscapes were exquisite, & many admirable portraits. A set of photos of the animals at the Zoological Gardens by Don Juan, 2nd son of Don Carlos, are almost the finest of all the specimens'.[5]

Roger Fenton, the Society's first secretary, would soon become closely involved with the royal family, photographing their children in early 1854 and taking formal studies of the couple, including the well-known double portrait in court dress of 1854. Later that year, he left for the Crimea, apparently at the prompting of Prince Albert (if not the Queen herself) to photograph the war, in the hope that his record would counteract reports appearing in the press about the poor management of the war. Also significant is Victoria's recognition of the polymath Charles Wheatstone, Professor of 'Experimental Philosophy' at King's College London, inventor of the telegraph and much else, whose explanation of binocular vision in 1838 introduced stereoscopy.[6] A commercial version of his stereoscope had been launched at the Great Exhibition in 1851, which was very much Albert's project, and the royal couple acquired their own early example of what would soon become a hugely popular instrument, although one often passed over in many histories of 'Victorian photography' in favour of the carte-de-visite craze of the 1860s.[7] Likewise, Victoria's reference to Don Juan indicates how widely photography was practised by the aristocracy by the 1850s.[8]

Victoria and Albert took steps to have their children given instruction in photography, with all the princes and princesses encouraged to use cameras and learn the still-complex 'wet' process.[9] Prince Alfred took his equipment on a tour of South Africa in 1860 and was backed up by a professional photographer, Frederick York. Albert, the Prince of Wales (known as Bertie, and later Edward when he became King), also learned photography, and was accompanied on a tour of the Middle East in 1862 by another professional, Francis Bedford. All the princesses practised photography, and made up albums, like their parents, while Albert's wife, Princess Alexandra of Denmark, eventually exhibited her work and published a *Christmas Gift Book* of family photographs in 1908 to aid charities.

Two major exhibitions have recorded the depth of Victoria and Albert's shared interest in photography: 'Victoria and Albert: Art & Love' (Queen's Gallery, 2010) included photographs among the other art they collected, while 'A Royal Passion: Queen Victoria and Photography' (Getty Center, 2014) focused on Victoria's lifelong preoccupation with the medium, as a family photographer herself, a collector and also in her extensive use of photography to memorialise Albert after his death. Jay notes that: 'Few days passed without Victoria sending for one volume [of photographs] or another, all of which were methodically catalogued with their contents arranged in systematic order. Photographs for these albums were commissioned, bought at auction, exchanged with related royal families abroad, or simply requested. The Queen even had a standing order with her favourite photographers for one print of every picture they made'. Even after Victoria's death, when Bertie undertook a draconian house-clearing exercise and 'thousands of loose photographs were burnt', what remained would illustrate 'the extent of the Royal passion for photography – over 100,000 photographs survived in 110 albums'.[10]

'Passion' is also used by Anne Lyden in the title of her Getty exhibition, and for once it seems to be deserved – this was far from a routine amassing of family photographs, even if many of the subjects were members of Victoria and Albert's extended family. It amounted to a serious and also passionately motivated collecting ambition. The technical-cum-aesthetic novelty that photography offered, which appealed to Victoria and Albert alike, led them to take a scientific interest in research to improve the fixing of the photographic image. (Jay cites Albert supporting several lines of inquiry into fading, and Victoria later 'having her most treasured prints copied by the stable carbon process'.[11]) After Albert's death, the multiplication of his image in a wide variety of photographic formats, on ceramic and enamel as well as in coloured prints, clearly served her mourning need, recalling one of the earliest drives that helped popularise photography.

But Lyden also cites another facet of Victoria's passion, which points towards a shrewd understanding of the power and status of the photographic image by the 1890s. In 1897, as the Diamond Jubilee approached, the Queen chose a photograph made some four years earlier and nominated it her 'official portrait', under specific conditions: 'She has the copyright removed from the photograph. The only stipulation being that whoever reproduces the image has to credit the photographer by name. Well, you can imagine what this does; it means that her image is on everything from biscuit tins to tea towels'.[12]

In his contribution to a 1997 television documentary on Victoria's Diamond Jubilee, David Cannadine insisted on her reluctance to take part in such ceremonial, and also paints a portrait of the elderly Victoria retreating into a romanticised imperial fantasy, with exotic décor inspired by India created at her Isle of Wight residence Osborne House, and a fondness for 'native' servants. What this account ignores is the evidence of Victoria's almost encyclopaedic collecting, and her deliberate amassing of photographic evidence, beginning with the extent of suffering in the Crimean War, all carefully recorded in albums: 'She had amazing albums compiled of the severely injured and maimed soldiers after they had returned. She met them and the photographs become a personal record of her interaction with these men. She had the photographers compile the soldier images for her with very detailed captions'.[13]

Even earlier, Albert had pioneered the use of photography to create a visual inventory of all of Raphael's known paintings and drawings, as an adjunct to cataloguing the Royal Collection, and had urged the Photographic Society to establish a reference collection of exemplary works.[14] Long before Albert Kahn's The Archives of the Planet project in the early 20th century,[15] Victoria and Albert clearly understood the documentary as well as the personal value of photography – a fact that apparently still needs to be asserted against the sentimentalising account of 'royal amateurs' recording their leisured lives.[16] In view of this long history of growing up with the medium, Victoria's overseeing an approved Jubilee image of herself, knowing this would become an essential imperial icon in the era of expanding 'mechanical reproducibility', seems like a farsighted recognition of the role of image in the interactive system that imperialism had become.[17]

The Moving Image
We have seen that both Victoria and Albert were well aware of innovation in photography from the 1850s onwards. So it would hardly be surprising that Victoria should show an interest in a subsequent development, which was widely advertised as 'animated photography'.[18] Equally, pioneer filmmakers, like many other inventors, were well aware of the potential value of royal 'patronage', which had already been conferred on many photographers during previous decades.[19] Birt Acres was the first British photographer to seek royal permission for moving pictures. His partnership with Robert Paul had produced a workable moving picture camera before they split acrimoniously in the spring of 1895, whereupon Acres travelled to Germany and filmed Kaiser Wilhelm (Victoria's grandson) opening the Kiel Canal, and in August took more films of the Kaiser reviewing troops in Berlin. This was before film projection had been developed, so they would have been seen on Kinetoscopes before the end of that year, when first the Lumières,

then Paul, took up projection (some of the Paul–Acres 1895 films were shown by Edison in New York in April 1896 at the launch of his projection system, the Vitascope).

During 1896, Acres continued to seek royal patronage, and gave a screening for the Prince of Wales at Marlborough House on 21 July 1896 'by royal request', where he was assisted by the future producer Cecil Hepworth. This resulted from Acres having filmed a visit by the Prince and Princess of Wales to the Cardiff Exhibition on 27 June, which he wanted permission to exhibit publicly.[20] According to the official British monarchy account, 'before giving his permission, The Prince of Wales asked Acres to bring the film to Marlborough House for inspection'.[21] There had been press reports of Acres having made a hole in the exhibition wall to gain a better view of the visitors – allegedly with permission, although not from the royal party – and in this (lost) film, the Prince of Wales was seen scratching his head. Despite this 'indiscretion', the royal couple were apparently happy to invite him to show the film, along with some twenty other subjects, in a marquee at Marlborough House, before forty specially invited guests.

The future Edward VII seems to have been aware of film's ability to capture the moment from an early stage, and visited the Alhambra Music Hall in June 1896 to see what had become the first major success of British 'animated photography': Robert Paul's film of the Derby, won by the Prince's horse, Persimmon. Having filmed the finish of the race at Epsom, when an enthusiastic crowd surged onto the course, Paul hurried back to London to develop and print the film, which he was able to show the following evening as a novel addition to his regular Animatographe programme: '[A]n enormous audience at the Alhambra Theatre witnessed the Prince's Derby all to themselves amidst wild enthusiasm, which all but drowned the strains of "God Bless the Prince of Wales", as played by the splendid orchestra'.[22]

Another report confirmed that the film was encored at the Alhambra, and also at another music hall which Paul supplied with a regular programme, the Canterbury.[23] Paul filmed the public procession that accompanied Edward's daughter Princess Maud marrying Prince Charles of Denmark on 22 July (another lost film), and it is likely that Paul's 'animated photograph film' would have offered a considerably livelier image than the formal group photograph published in the *Illustrated London News*.[24] It almost certainly offered a better view of the procession of carriages and Life Guards than many lining the procession route would have had, just as Acres' earlier film had offered unusual intimacy with royal personages.[25]

Scenes at Balmoral, filmed in October 1896 by William Downey, with Queen Victoria, her son Prince Arthur, Tsar Nicholas II and other family members.

Queen Victoria's own initiation into moving pictures came in early October 1896, when J. Downey was summoned to Balmoral to take photographs of a visit by the Tsar and his wife, Alexandra, who was Victoria's granddaughter and a frequent visitor to Britain in her youth before marrying Nicholas. This Downey was a son of William Ernest Downey, proprietor of the leading portrait studio W. & D. Downey in London, and already an official photographer to the Queen,[26] which helps explain why an otherwise obscure South Shields firm, J. & F. Downey, was given this commission. One of Downey's assistants, T. J. Harrison, had been working on a film camera of his own design, and Downey junior took the camera to Balmoral, along with his normal still equipment, and asked if he might also take some animated photographs. The Queen agreed, recording her own reaction in her journal: 'At 12 went down to below the terrace... & were all photographed by Downey by the new cinematograph process, which makes moving pictures by winding off a reel of films. We were walking up & down & the children jumping about. Then took a turn in the pony chair'.[27]

Victoria would not see the result until the following month, when an elaborate screening was arranged at Windsor Castle, probably as a treat to mark the tenth birthday of a grandson, Prince Alexander. The show on 23 November included lantern slides 'from some of the old Royal Photographs and the modern Art Studies', and a selection of ten films drawn from the Lumières' and Paul's catalogues, finishing with the now celebrated 'Prince's Derby', as it had become known.[28]

According to a report in the *Lady's Pictorial* in December, the audience at Windsor included 'the Duchess of Saxe-Coburg, the Duke and Duchess of Connaught and their children, Princess Christian and Princess Henry of Battenberg and her children', together with 'some forty or fifty ladies and gentlemen of the Royal household'. The Queen viewed the show with her opera glass, and was 'delighted with the animated photographs, wondering if it were possible to repeat the views'. When told that this would take time – since films were not wound onto take-up spools at this date – she 'was pleased to withdraw her request'.[29] Later, she wrote in her journal: 'After tea went to the Red drawing room where so-called "animated pictures" were shown off, including the groups taken in September [*sic*] at Balmoral. It is a very wonderful process, representing people, their movements & actions, as if they were alive'.[30] After she left, according to the *Lady's Pictorial*, 'some of the young Royal children came behind the screen and displayed much curiosity as to the working of the views and the lighting of the same by electric light and oxy-hydrogen'.

What the Windsor audience had seen was in fact an unusual and complex presentation, making use of two film projectors – one for the 70mm Balmoral films (only completed on the morning of the show) and a Paul Theatrograph for the others – with a magic lantern for photographs from the royal collection, many of which would have been taken by Downey senior. Three Balmoral films are listed in the programme, and presumably these are the source of three shots now extant: one of the donkey carriage, which had become Victoria's preferred vehicle in old age, turning; a second extended shot of the carriage amid a crowd of parents, children and dogs, including the Queen holding a white dog in her carriage; and a third of the carriage coming towards the camera, with guests walking alongside.[31] This appears to be the sole surviving footage of Victoria among her extended family, similar in form and content to the conventional family film that stretches from Louis Lumière to the present day. It is surely significant that Victoria recorded the audience as including 'we 5 of the family'.[32] Spanning three generations, from the matriarch to her grandchildren, it conveys a strong sense of the relative informality of life within the court family circle. And knowing that it was seen first by many of those who appeared in it brings it within the defining form of all family film, intended to be seen primarily or exclusively by those who appear in it.[33]

What differentiates the Balmoral film from other family records of the period, of course, is that it shows Victoria, Queen of Britain and Empress of India, in a 'domestic' setting, and to our eyes strongly reinforces the image that Victoria and Albert had created of a 'bourgeois' rather than a courtly lifestyle. It also makes visible the interconnectedness of European monarchy at this time, with Nicolas ('Nicky' in Victoria's journal), the recently crowned Tsar of Russia, wearing plain country dress and walking respectfully alongside his wife's grandmother. Nicolas had married Victoria's granddaughter, Alix, Princess Alexandra of Hesse-Darmstadt, in 1894, the same year that his father Alexander III died, but was not crowned Tsar until 1896. Downey and Paul were both quick to advertise that they had 'exhibited before Her Majesty at Windsor Castle',[34] but there is no evidence that this intimate family footage was widely, if ever, seen outside the royal family until modern times.[35]

Five months before the Balmoral film, in May 1896, Nicolas had his own first encounter with the new medium, which showed its power both to celebrate and embarrass. Two days after the coronation, which was filmed exclusively by Charles Moisson and Francis Doublier for Lumière, the new Tsar was to be presented to the ordinary people of Russia at Khodynka Field, a military parade ground outside Moscow. Some half-million people gathered from early in the morning to receive a souvenir package of food and gifts from the Tsar, but in the afternoon a rumour began to spread that there would not be enough for all. Panic spread as people began rushing towards the food and drink tables and over 1,300 were trampled to death – some estimates have claimed up to 5,000 – with another 1,300 injured. Nicholas had left the scene by this time, but when he was informed of the tragedy decided not to attend a banquet that night at the French Embassy, before being persuaded to do so by his uncles.[36]

The disaster had been filmed by Moisson and Doublier, but the film was taken from them and never seen again.[37] However, in July, another Lumière travelling operator, Alexandre Promio, managed to present a programme before the Tsar and Tsaritsa, and in the following year, Boleslaw Matuszewski, a Pole who had moved from Paris to Warsaw, became 'photographer to Tsar Nicholas' (although apparently only on a commercial basis), and took both still photographs and film of the imperial family, including the state visit by President Félix Faure of France in 1897.[38] When the former German Chancellor Otto Bismarck accused Faure of not showing respect by removing his hat in the presence of the Tsar, this slur was effectively refuted by Matuszewski showing his films of the visit in a special presentation at the Elysée Palace in Paris in January 1898.[39] Later in the same year, Matuszewski would publish two pamphlets arguing for the value of films as a 'source of history', now widely regarded as among the earliest documents to advocate film archiving.[40]

Compared with the short royal films of 1896, Victoria's Diamond Jubilee in June 1897 provided the first major spectacle of the film age, on a par with the passion plays and boxing matches that pioneered extended filmic presentation as a commercial proposition. The Jubilee was also credited, nearly forty years later, with helping to develop or revive interest in moving pictures, after film companies' operators lined the route of the procession and subsequently promoted their films.[41] Unlike Victoria's earlier Golden Jubilee, focused on the Queen herself and attended by fellow crowned heads of Europe, this was conceived by the dynamic new Colonial Secretary Joseph Chamberlain as a 'festival of the British Empire'. With the aid of Reginald Brett, then Secretary of the Board of Works, who had become close to both the Queen and the Prince of Wales, he ensured that 'the diamond jubilee of 1897 was showier, more triumphal, and more imperial than previous London ceremonies. The jubilee organisers also persuaded the queen to drive south of the river through Kennington. They were attempting to bring the monarchy into closer contact with both the empire abroad and the newly enfranchised working classes at home'.[42]

Governors and heads of state of the dominions and colonies were summoned to make up a great procession, which took the Queen from Buckingham Palace to St Paul's and back. But the major coup which made the Jubilee spectacular in a new way – and eminently filmable – was the massive cast of 50,000 servicemen, both mounted and on foot, many wearing exotic 'colonial' uniforms, that accompanied the royal party and dignitaries in open carriages. A journalist, G. W. Steevens, summed up what the organisers had achieved in this procession: 'Up they came, more and more, new types, new realms at every couple of yards, an anthropological museum – a living gazetteer of the British Empire. With them came their English officers, whom they obey and follow like children. And you begin to understand, as never before, what the Empire amounts to. Not only that we possess all these remote outlandish places… but also that these people are working, not simply under us, but with us'.[43]

There were, of course, dissenting views, from the likes of Beatrice Webb, Keir Hardie and other anti-imperialists.[44] But during the heady days of the Jubilee, when even the warm sunshine became known as 'the Queen's weather', much of the country seemed to enter into a delirium of self-congratulation and identification

'A Very Wonderful Process' 319

with the aged Queen, so little seen since the death of her beloved Albert in 1861. And if Victoria was initially reluctant to take part in a public celebration of her sixty-year reign, she could hardly doubt the affection of her people. She wrote in her journal: 'No one ever I believe, has met with such an ovation as was given to me, passing through those 6 miles of streets, including Constitution Hill. The crowds were quite indescribable, & their enthusiasm truly marvellous & deeply touching. The cheering was quite deafening, & every face seemed to be filled with real joy. I was much moved & gratified'.⁴⁵ To which a recent historian of the Jubilee year adds: '[A]t times the response overwhelmed her, and keen observers noted that she frequently wiped away tears as she received this thunderous ovation'.⁴⁶

Queen Victoria's Diamond Jubilee, June 1897,
filmed by many camera crews and widely distributed.

The Lumière coverage, by its star cameraman Promio, began with two films, taken on Sunday 20 June, as Victoria arrived at Paddington from Windsor and her cortège was followed by crowds. Two days later, the Jubilee procession was filmed by cameramen stationed at many points along the route, among crowds that were estimated to total 3 million. Robert Paul recalled: 'Large sums were paid for suitable camera positions, several of which were secured for my operators. I myself operated a camera perched on a narrow ledge in the Church yard. Several continental cinematographers came over, and it was related of one that, when the Queen's carriage passed he was under his seat changing film, and of another, hanging on the railway bridge at Ludgate Hill, that he turned his camera until he almost fainted, only to find, on reaching a dark room, that the film had failed to start'.⁴⁷

Contemporary commentators foresaw that film would carry this spectacle to wider audiences. The showman's paper *The Era* urged: 'Those loyal subjects of her Majesty who did not witness the glorious pageant of the Queen's progress through the streets of London... should not miss the opportunity of seeing the wonderful series of pictures at the Empire, giving a complete representation of the Jubilee procession... by the invention of the Cinématographe... our descendants will be able to learn how the completion of the sixtieth year of Queen Victoria's reign was celebrated'.⁴⁸

Throughout Britain, a variety of new exhibitors of moving pictures made the Diamond Jubilee the centrepiece of their programmes throughout the second half of 1897 and into the following year. Producers and distributors experienced a boom in sales, and even resorted to renting the most popular items to secure maximum returns. One pioneer itinerant exhibitor, William Slade from Cheltenham, had no prior entertainment experience, but toured throughout England and Scotland in 1897, featuring in all his shows five Diamond Jubilee subjects, with the Queen at St Paul's always considered the highlight.⁴⁹ A writer who interviewed Paul about his films of the Jubilee introduced his article in *Cassell's Family Magazine* with an eye to the value of moving pictures as a chronicle: 'This automatic spectator, who is destined to play an important part in life and literature by treasuring up the 'fleeting shows' of the world for the delight of thousands in distant countries and in future ages'.⁵⁰

The processions had indeed been organised like a pageant or 'gazetteer' of the Empire, with highly recognisable figures from the dominions and detachments of their armed forces. In Ireland, with its already long history of home rule and independence campaigns, the Jubilee films inevitably provided a focus for different factions to demonstrate their positions. While they played for substantial seasons in Dublin and Belfast, there were reports of vociferous hostility at the latter's Empire Theatre in November when the orchestra played 'God Save the Queen', after which a diarist wrote that he 'thought the angry gods and balconyites would tear down the house in their exceeding wrath'.⁵¹

Elsewhere across the Empire, the recorded responses seem to have been mainly appreciative, and often rapturous in the most distant countries. Six weeks after the Jubilee, the Melbourne showman Harry Rickards, who had first presented animated photographs a year earlier, advertised on Friday 13 August that 'an enormous attraction will be announced tomorrow'. Monday's edition of the Melbourne *Herald* enthused about 'one of the most thrilling spectacles ever witnessed, the appearance of Her Most Gracious Majesty on the Royal Carriage, drawn by six cream ponies, causing a perfect blizzard of LOYAL and Acclaimative ENTHUSIASM, the vast audience rising EN MASSE, cheering incessantly until the picture was reproduced'.[52] As the screenings continued in Melbourne, 'the waving arm of Sir George Turner', the Australian Prime Minister, was reported to be 'loudly applauded every evening'.[53] In Canada, where there were also no doubt mixed responses, especially in Quebec, the dominion's first premier of French ancestry, Sir Wilfred Laurier, was appreciatively recognised by local audiences, who would also have known that he had been knighted on the morning of the Jubilee procession.

Perhaps unsurprisingly, then, the Jubilee films provided a focus for displays of pro- as well as anti-British sentiment across the sprawling Empire, with these demonstrations most vociferous where there were active independence movements, and equally strong loyalist communities. We might wonder how aware the participants in the Jubilee procession were of these reactions. One of the earliest presentations of the Jubilee films to those who had taken part in the procession must have been the royal command performance at St James' Palace on 20 July, when the British Mutoscope and Biograph Company was invited to give a 'special exhibition' after a banquet celebrating the Prince of Wales' appointment as Grand Master of the Order of the Bath. On show were the Diamond Jubilee procession, along with the associated naval review at Spithead and military review at Aldershot, all filmed in Biograph's impressive 68mm format: an appropriately ceremonial and martial programme for this all-male company.

In November, however, a selection of Lumière films was presented to a mixed audience at Windsor by H. J. Hitchens, the manager of the Empire, with the theatre's full orchestra accompanying, conducted by Leopold Wenzel. The Queen recorded the occasion in her journal: 'After tea went with the children to the Green drawing room, where the Ladies & Gentlemen were assembled, & where we saw Cinematograph representing parts of my Jubilee Procession, & various other things. They are very wonderful, but I thought them a little hazy & rather too rapid in their movements'.[54] Victoria's comment on the quality of the presentation, which suggests that the projector set-up was less than ideal, and that the films were shown too fast, demonstrates that the 78-year-old Queen was still a photographic enthusiast, as well as a shrewd judge of quality.

The British Mutoscope and Biograph, an offshoot of the original American company, started operations early in 1897 and appears to have adopted a deliberate policy of courting royal relationships, possibly in order to counteract the dubious reputation of its Mutoscope subjects, which often featured titillating images of glamorous women.[55] In the summer of 1897, their record of *Afternoon Tea in the Gardens of Clarence House* showed three generations of the royal family at a garden party with what Richard Brown and Barry Anthony term 'startling informality'.[56] British Bioscope's relationship with the royal family continued to bear fruit after the St James' Palace showing. They filmed the Queen laying the foundation stone of the Victoria and Albert Museum on 17 May 1899, while a Biograph show was given at Sandringham on 29 June.[57] And in the summer of 1900, Biograph filmed what is probably the most important of the early 'intimate' royal films, *Children of the Royal Family of England*, which showed 'our future king at play' – namely Prince Edward of York, later Edward VIII.[58] This two-part film, made over two mornings, was a major success for the company, becoming an extremely popular item in Biograph programmes at the Palace Theatre, and later on their home-viewing system, the Kinora.[59] And Biograph's relationship with the future king, Prince Albert, soon to be Edward VII, would continue, as they filmed many events throughout his reign.

The Diamond Jubilee was the last great public occasion of the Queen's long reign. However, the outbreak of the Anglo-Boer War late in 1899 led to Victoria not visiting France, as was her springtime custom, but instead travelling in April to Ireland, where at least four companies filmed her procession in Dublin and reception by the city's Corporation, followed by a review of troops in Phoenix Park and a large children's party.[60] With various currents of nationalist and home rule sentiment running high, following the centenary of the 1798 United Irishmen uprising, there were inevitably protests during the visit. As Kevin and Emer Rockett note, some members of the Corporation boycotted the Queen's reception, while the nationalist leaders Maud Gonne and James Connolly 'organised a nationalist riposte, the "patriotic children's treat", for 15,000 poor children'.[61] If the extant footage of the visit does not register the dissent it provoked among Irish nationalists and home rule campaigners (although a man visibly appealing to the crowd near the Queen's carriage could conceivably represent some protest in progress[62]), neither does it reveal the equivalent enthusiasm that greeted the films in loyalist quarters. One of the two Belfast-based cameramen who filmed Victoria's visit to Dublin, John Walter

Hicks, who also carried on his film activities as 'Professor Kineto', improved on Paul's Derby coup by having his coverage of the Queen's arrival ready to show by the same evening a hundred miles away at the Empire Theatre in Belfast, where it was reportedly 'cheered to the echo', in striking contrast to the Jubilee response three years earlier.[63]

By Christmas Victoria's health had begun to decline and she died at Osborne House on 22 January 1901. She had left detailed instructions for the detail of her funeral (to include mementoes of Albert and of her loyal Scottish retainer John Brown), but the actual procession followed a similar pattern to the Jubilee after her coffin reached London, with many film cameramen seeking the same camera positions they had used for the Jubilee. The funeral films were also widely shown, although the grey winter weather made them considerably less striking than those of the Jubilee.

Two anecdotes from early in the new century reveal how rapidly awareness of the role of film in portraying royal ceremonial was advancing. The best known of these comes from the memoir by the pioneer producer Cecil Hepworth, who had positioned three cameras along the route of Victoria's funeral procession. He operated one of the cameras, positioning himself inside the railings of Grosvenor Gardens, opposite Victoria station. As the procession approached, headed by the new King, Edward, Hepworth began to crank his camera, and was horrified by the noise this made in the prevailing silence. He later wrote: 'If I could have had my dearest wish, then the ground would certainly have opened at my feet and swallowed me and my beastly machine'.[64] However, the noise of the camera attracted Edward's attention, and he halted the procession for a moment so that a 'cinematograph record' of the procession could be preserved for posterity. Another anecdote appears in the memoirs of an ex-India civil servant, J. H. Rivett-Carnac, who had been an aide-de-camp to Victoria, and rode in the procession for her son Edward's coronation in 1903. Rivett-Carnac recalled how 'a pipe band suddenly struck up nearby, so that the good horse stood straight up on his hind legs and it was quite as much as I could do to keep my seat'. He added: 'Although it was interesting enough to see oneself and show oneself to one's friends in the "living pictures" riding along in the procession, one did not want to be handed down to posterity coming off one's horse in an undignified attitude'.[65]

Edward's coronation was extensively covered by all leading film companies, in marked contrast to the relatively modest occasion of his mother's, sixty-four years earlier, on the threshold of the era of photography. An indication of the level of filmic interest was also provided by one enterprising producer's decision to commission a fake film of the Westminster Abbey event. Charles Urban, manager of the Warwick Trading Company in London, commissioned Georges Méliès, already known for his trick films, to solve the problem of not being able to film inside Westminster Abbey by staging a film of it in Paris in time for the scheduled date of the coronation, 26 June. However, due to Edward's illness, the coronation was delayed until 9 August, when the film played as a headliner at the Alhambra Music Hall (where the Persimmon Derby had been shown six years earlier) before touring the world as the first 'royal documentary'.[66] Urban's investment in this coverage, and that of the other companies, confirm that the advent of the photographic image, both still and moving, had made the British monarchy a highly marketable spectacle.

Posterity

What we can discover in the filming of Victoria and her children between 1896 and 1900 are two primordial film genres in their earliest form. One is the 'family film' that would become central to amateur practice during the 20th century, even if Victoria's family films were very different from those of her subjects. For the British branch of the 'family' of Hanover (later changed to Saxe-Coburg and Gotha), film 'could break down barriers of social etiquette… and present a vivid glimpse of their private life to their subjects'.[67] That such glimpses were contrived could hardly be doubted, even if the journalistic context surrounding *Children of the Royal Family* was at pains to stress the 'courtesy and thoughtfulness of the Royal trio', as well as their 'unaffectedness', during the two mornings that they were filmed by Biograph, after being shown several of the company's Mutoscope subjects as an induction into what filming would involve and produce.[68] These are the prototypes of what would become the British royal family's most potent mode of communication with its subjects: the occasional and partial 'glimpse' of informal family life, away from the official news media, yet communicated by these same media in 'special' documentaries.[69]

The other genre, raised to a new level by the large-scale filming of the Diamond Jubilee, is the ceremonial procession. While processions quickly became a staple of early film programmes, usually structured around military formations passing the camera, the Diamond Jubilee procession also brought together a number of significant narratives, which help explain its wide popularity.[70] One was the intended 'gazetteer' of the British Empire, with its exotic diversity made visible in the ethnic variety of those processing, condensing into a dynamic yet disciplined image of the very concept of the Empire.⁷¹ A second, however, was the appearance, after long seclusion, of the sovereign at the centre of this mighty web. The contrast between Victoria's small, elderly figure, in simple widow's clothing, and the vast spectacle surrounding her struck many spectators at the time.

One observer was the American writer Mark Twain, hired for the occasion by the *New York Journal*, who offered an intriguing comparison between processions as 'shows' and 'symbols', comparing the Jubilee procession with Henry V's London victory procession after Agincourt, and describing it as 'a symbol, and allegory of England's grandeur'.⁷² While criticising the composition of the procession for what it omitted – the sources of British power and prosperity – Twain also concluded that the Queen 'was the procession itself, all the rest was mere embroidery'.⁷³ This seems to express what many contemporaries also felt, that the figure of Victoria somehow eclipsed the pageantry all around it. Through film this microcosmic image of the Queen, always seen distantly by the lenses of the time, circulated globally. The contrast between such an image and the 'official' Jubilee close-up portrait photographs could not be greater.

Before 1896, Victoria had already lived through fifty years of still photography, as an early adopter and connoisseur of the successive processes and formats, an important collector, and patron of the leading photographic society in Britain. Encountering 'animated photography' in her old age, she seems to have retained her earlier interest in new techniques and subject matter, and a willingness to assess their quality. As Twain observed, she had witnessed almost every technology of modern life develop during her reign, and on the morning of the Jubilee, she pressed a button that sent a telegraphic message around the world.⁷⁴ Seeing and sharing the response to these first family and procession films, she may well have guessed that animated photography was about to create a new paradigm by 'representing people and their actions as if they were alive' far into the future.

Originally a chapter in Mandy Merck, ed., *The British Monarchy on Screen* (Manchester University Press, 2016).

24.
Thomas Edison:
The Media Wizard of Oz

If there is any common image of Thomas Alva Edison today in Europe, it's probably as the grumpy old man who organised a group of fellow American film pioneers into 'The Trust' – a turn-of-the-century cartel aimed at monopolising the motion picture business.

There is a photograph of The Trust, taken at the 1908 meeting where agreement was hammered out between those who had until recently been bitter rivals. Everyone wears bowler hats except Edison the Great Inventor, already a legend in his own lifetime, who wears a German-style cap which clearly sets him apart from these businessmen gathered at his West Orange base to claim this young industry as their own.

For most of the previous eight years Edison had harried these same men, claiming that almost everything they did infringed at least one of his 1,093 patents. Now he had suddenly decided to make them an offer they couldn't afford to refuse. Taking the same route as other great American robber barons – Carnegie, Rockefeller, Frick – he proposed a trust which would 'protect' its founder members and fight off newcomers. But this final role, as Godfather to the American movie industry, was also Edison's most improbable and indeed mysterious.

Invention, for Edison, was a religion. In the terms of his Scottish-American Protestantism, it was a spiritual quest to discover the 'divine plan' and to apply it more efficiently to human needs. And as the Frontier gave way to America's new dynamic capitalism, it also became a kind of patriotism: making American destiny manifest through profit and monopoly. Finally, it became his identity, his being: I invent therefore I am. And the number of his patents bears witness to a terrifying rapacity in claiming for himself what his assistants had played an increasingly major part in creating.

Edison's early inventions had sprung from first-hand experience. He had started his working life as a railway telegraph operator, where he saw the potential of automating parts of the sending process, and had set up his first laboratory in a railway goods wagon – so that he could continue working round the clock, or so the legend claims.¹ Edison's involvement with electric light – he is credited with inventing the modern lightbulb, as well as storage batteries and large-scale distribution systems – had both a commercial and a symbolic significance, lighting the darkness of the late 19th century's 'cities of dreadful night'.² His work on sound, which led to the carbon microphone used by Alexander Bell for the telephone in 1876 and the phonograph in 1877, may have had a more personal motive as he started to become deaf.

Certainly Bell and the French moving picture pioneer Georges Demenÿ had both started work on sound reproduction as an offshoot of their interest in improving methods of teaching the deaf to speak: an initial interest in making good impaired human faculties became for them, in Marshall McLuhan's classic definition of modern media, a dream of extending them. And the phonograph would embed Edison definitively in the history of 'new media', with a long tail stretching forward from 1878 into the mid-20th century.³

By the late 1870s Edison had become a worldwide celebrity and a new kind of prophet. Having established himself as the master inventor, he increasingly used his predictions to set the agenda for what would come next – which he then magically made happen. In 1878, long before he had started to work on reproducing images, the English magazine *Punch* had foretold in its almanac for the following year, 'Edison's Telephonoscope (transmits light as well as sound). The cartoon shows an English couple talking to their distant children in Ceylon 'every evening' by means of 'an electric camera-obscura over their bedroom mantel-piece'.⁴ Today we can only see this as an astonishingly confident anticipation of the wall-sized flat screen videophone, only two years after the invention of the telephone and a year after the phonograph.⁵

Edison had perfectly good reason to believe his own publicity. It seemed that whatever he predicted could somehow be made to happen. Meeting the English photographer Eadweard Muybridge in 1888 inspired him to announce the idea of a 'phonograph for the eye'. It would take four further years of work (mostly by assistants) to realise it; but the key idea, of recording images like sound, brings us right to the heart of Edison's genius as an inventor. It was both a straightforward extension of something that already worked, the phonograph, and a leap into the dark, literally. Moving pictures would take Edison far from the drawing room and the factory floor, into another important Victorian space, the shadowy world of eroticism and commercialised pornography.

At the very moment that Edison was reaching the end of his work on the 'phonograph for the eye', he had also become a character in someone else's erotic fantasy. The French Symbolist writer Villiers de l'Isle-Adam's drama *Axel* had defined the languorous, archaic, 'decadent' sensibility of the 1890s. Villiers was no enthusiast for progress, but in his fantasy *L'Eve future* – about an artificial 'ideal' woman created to satisfy a man's desires, the *fin de siècle* counterpart to Mary Shelley's high Romantic Frankenstein – he made Edison the woman's creator.

Punch Almanach for 1879. 'Edison's Telephonoscope', predicted by George du Maurier, just months after Edison had launched his Phonograph in 1978.

In Villiers' novel, Edison is an out-and-out alchemist, with all the picturesque trappings. We first meet him at sunset, wrapped in a magician's cloak, tobacco smoke wreathing his head like incense. The decor is pure hokum, but the essence of Villiers' Edison is strangely plausible – indeed it helps us see what was in contemporary eyes truly magical about the Wizard of Menlo Park.[6] This fictional Edison is ready to create an android to satisfy the desires of a lovesick friend – one of those perverse English aristocrats cherished by French writers.[7] This android is a fantastic extrapolation from the phonograph and an anticipation of the fantasy that millions would soon experience before the cinema screen. Its memory bank of speech, culled from the best of world literature, ensures that Lord Ewald never has to endure 'normal' female banality when 'conversing' with his robot. And Villiers wasn't alone in his fantasy.

Even Jules Verne, normally more robust about matters of the heart, included in his 1892 novel *The Carpathian Castle* a dead diva recreated by one of her lovers via recorded sound and projected moving image, which looks suspiciously holographic in the contemporary illustration (and remember, this is two years before Edison's Kinetoscope appears in public).[8] Already Edison and his inventions were linked, in fiction writers' minds, with do-it-yourself gratification – and even with the final blasphemy, that of creating the illusion of life itself.

As it happened, the official debut of the Kinetoscope couldn't have been further removed from such hints of licentious 'entertainment'. It formed the climax to a reception for the National Federation of Women's Clubs, given by Mrs Edison on 20 May 1891. After lunch at their mansion, Glenmont – which remains today a perfectly preserved monument to Mrs Edison's Victorian tastes – visitors were taken to the nearby laboratory.[9] There, according to one newspaper report, 'Edison chuckled,' as he demonstrated 'the picture of a man which bowed, smiled, and took off its hat with the most perfect naturalness'.

The well-mannered image was almost certainly of his assistant, the Scottish-American W. K. L. Dickson, who had actually done most of the work in Room Five at West Orange. However, only Edison featured in the carefully orchestrated press coverage of the next few weeks. All the examples he gave to the press of the Kinetoscope's potential were of subjects that would certainly not have offended the clubwomen: a senator introducing the explorer Henry Morton Stanley at the Metropolitan Opera House, as well as recordings of plays and operas. The setting Edison initially envisaged was clearly domestic – 'you can sit in your parlour and look at a big screen' – although he had only a peep show with a few seconds of action to demonstrate it. Even in his practised supersalesman mode, Edison was still speculating like a Sunday School superintendent about bigger and better forms of 'improvement'. Could he have known that in the place of such pieties he was about to unleash the first 'virtual reality' machine, a means of transporting audiences into a collective dream where intense visual stimulation would overwhelm their normal inhibitions and create a new sphere of imaginary immorality beyond even Villiers' or Verne's powers of imagination?[10]

Perhaps he had some inkling. The subjects chosen for the first Kinetoscope loops included exotic dancers – at least one of whom, Annabelle Moore, was soon linked with a stag-party nude dancing scandal – as well as musclemen, magicians and such ambiguous icons of Americana as the Wild West sharpshooter Annie Oakley. Did Edison personally choose which performers were to be invited to West Orange and filmed in the tar-paper structure that served as a studio, soon nicknamed the 'Black Maria'? Did he have – as many of his contemporaries did – a 'secret life' frequenting New York music halls, and other place of ill repute far from Glenmont? If he did either, there is no evidence of it. But he certainly knew what was being sold in his name, succeeding like many of his position and generation in retaining a high-minded image while allowing his business to follow its own seamier logic.

Advertisement for the Kinetoscope, which would draw Paul, the Lumières and the public into a new culture and business of moving pictures.

Edison had been forced into the public arena by dramatic developments in Europe. He had failed to patent the Kinetoscope abroad, considering the move an unnecessary extravagance, or possibly foreseeing complications due to earlier patents.[11] This was a fateful decision, because it allowed Robert Paul in London and the Lumières in France to benefit from studying Edison's machine without worrying that they might be infringing his patent. And it was as a direct result of these successful European experiments that the 'social' practice of projecting on a screen – rather than privatised coin-in-the-slot solo viewing – became the preferred mode of movie consumption. Characteristically, Edison promptly bought up a projector patent already held by Thomas Armat, along with the right to call it the 'Edison Vitascope'. On 23 April 1896, he relaunched his moving picture business two years after the Kinetoscope had started it, with a much-heralded show at Koster and Bial's Broadway music hall. Although the programme consisted mainly of recycled Kinetoscope loops, the biggest hit was Paul and Acres' kinetoscope loop *Rough Sea at Dover*, sent by Paul to Edison, who simply kept it, and now praised as 'the closest work of nature that any work of man has yet achieved'. Ironically, of course, Paul's film would never have existed had not Edison's original invention drawn him into this novel business.

What happened or failed to happen next is puzzling, and perhaps a sign of Edison's deep ambivalence about the Pygmalion he had created. For while others jumped enthusiastically into the new medium, he held back, starving his production company of resources or encouragement. His energies went instead into an endlessly tangled legal battle, ultimately futile, to claim nothing less than a patent on all moving pictures in America. The courts were reluctant to concede his claims, especially when it became clear that assistants like Dickson had been forced by the terms of their employment to give false credit to Edison for aspects of the invention. As the suits continued into 1900, Edison contemplated selling all his moving picture interests to his arch-rival, American Mutoscope and Biograph, for which Dickson now worked.

The deal was ready to sign when, in a Kane-like act of defiance, he drew back at the last moment and returned to the patent war which would continue until 1908. But even during this period, when little about moving pictures except litigation seems to have interested him, there were two projects that show Edison still trying to assert 'Protestant' seriousness against a rising tide of mere entertainment. The first was the remarkable series of films which began at the Buffalo Exposition in 1901. The previous year, the Paris Exposition

Universelle had yielded a popular series of subjects, and Edison had an exclusive contract to film at an equivalent exposition in Buffalo in the United States. President Mckinley was due to visit on 5-6 September. Edison's crew had already taken some twenty views of various pavilions, when their coverage became suddenly and horribly newsworthy. An anarchist shot and fatally wounded the President in the Temple of Music pavilion, while Edison's cameraman happened to be filming the crowd waiting outside as word spread among them. This record of a dramatic non-event was starkly named 'Mob Outside the Temple of Music', and the camera crew was instructed to follow subsequent events, filming McKinley's coffin leaving Buffalo, his funeral procession in Washington and his burial at Canton, Ohio.

Edison with his most famous early invention, the Phonograph.

It was not the first film coverage of a state occasion: a Lumière operator had recorded the celebration of the coronation of Tsar Nicholas II of Russia in 1896, and Queen Victoria's Diamond Jubilee had been filmed in the following year. But the Buffalo-McKinley series created a sequence of events from discrete items which looks forward, beyond the selectivity of newsreels, to modern extended coverage of events in the cinema and especially on television.

Did Edison play any part in deciding to follow the McKinley story? Evidence of his direct involvement in the Kinetograph Department of the Edison Manufacturing Company is elusive. But we can speculate that he had some personal involvement in the second of his projects 'against the grain' – the filming in 1904 of scenes from Richard Wagner's final music-drama *Parsifal* – since the idea of combining motion pictures with sound recording to preserve an opera had turned up more than once in his promotion of the Kinetoscope. In May 1891 newspaper interviews, he spoke expansively of recording an opera in complete 30-minute acts. '"I can put a roll of gelatine strip a mile long into it if I like," said the inventor yesterday'. The *New York Sun* reporter was apparently sceptical: 'Taking 46 photographs per second in half an hour there would be 82,800 photographs on the gelatine strip. If the photographs were half an inch square and half an inch apart, the strip of film used in taking a 30-minute act of an opera would be 6,900 feet long and Mr Edison would need something more than his "mile of gelatine"'.

And again, in a book written to order by Dickson, *The History of the Kinetograph*, Edison had returned to the idea of recording performances by stars of the Metropolitan Opera, and storing them long after their deaths. This appeal to opera as potential 'quality' entertainment might have been no more than a reflex attempt to talk the Kinetoscope up-market, of course: but the filming of *Parsifal* in 1904 suggests otherwise. Wagner had intended his last 'sacred' music drama for performance at Bayreuth only, and so his widow tried, unsuccessfully, to ban the Met from mounting its production in late 1903. The resulting controversy and respectful coverage led to a dramatic (i.e. spoken) version being launched, which Edison contracted to film. The total length of the eight scenes is about thirty minutes. There were apparently plans for an elaborate musical presentation using lantern slides to fill out the narrative.[12]

This unlikely project needs to be understood in the context of a turn-of-the-century culture which had a somewhat less rever-ential attitude (though no less starstruck) to opera, and which naturally wanted to link the new marvel of moving pictures with its favourite dramatic medium. Opera singers were already becoming the first recording stars thanks to the phonograph, and both Gaumont in France and Messter in Germany would soon have catalogues boasting many hundreds of popular and operatic synchronised sound films.[13] In 1915, Cecil B. DeMille would make the Metropolitan Opera diva Geraldine Farrar one of Hollywood's first stars in a remarkable adaptation of Bizet's *Carmen*.[14]

But in 1904, Edison was too far ahead of his time. Even in the year that followed the success of his *The Great Train Robbery*, very few prints of the highly priced *Parsifal* were sold. Edwin Porter, who directed both, managed to keep Edison's output competitive until around 1907. But there was clearly little encouragement from above for the film department. Starved of investment, it was still being run more like a service necessary to sell equipment than a fully-fledged production company. And despite Edison's harassment, other American producers were belatedly starting to forge ahead and challenge the European companies who had a major share of the American market. Biograph, which Dickson had helped found, was encouraging a talented young actor turned producer named D. W. Griffith. And Vitagraph had decided to beat the Europeans at their own game by making its own classics, with a string of Shakespeare and Dante adaptations for 1908.

Edison was increasingly out of step with an industry he still aimed to control. The solution, recognising the fact that he alone could not satisfy the market that 'his' invention had created, lay in forming a cartel. And so on 18 December 1908, after a year of tough negotiations, the founder members of the Motion Picture Patents Company (MPPC) gathered at West Orange. The next seven years saw American production develop rapidly. These were the glory years of Griffith at Biograph, which also saw the start of the great American genres, the Western and the gangster film, and of comedy, with Mack Sennett providing a school for all future slapstick. European imports began to lose ground, at least until the appearance of the Italian epics – *The Fall of Troy*, *Quo Vadis?*, *Cabiria* – set a new benchmark in the teens.[15]

But none of these developments interested Edison. Even while longer films were sweeping the board, he insisted that the public in fact wanted short subjects and insisted on persevering with these, possibly as a way of avoiding the investment that major production would require. The truth was that he had never been interested in fiction, regarding it as at best a necessary extravagance to maintain equipment sales, and he was certainly not about to compete with the new breed of producer – many of them with immigrant backgrounds – in this speculative and perhaps for him immoral trade.

However, even this rear-guard action against new trends sometimes bore fruit. A 1912 experiment linking a series of short films, *What Happened to Jane*, with a parallel series of short stories in the *Ladies' World* magazine suggests the influence of Mrs Edison. But it also anticipated the whole growth of serials and print tie-ins which would revolutionise film-going habits over the next two decades (although Edison would play no part in this). Ever the prophet of multimedia, he remained obstinately true to his original interests in later years, still trying to perfect synchronised sound and image, and trying to return his 'phonograph for the eye' to a domestic setting. The Kinetophone sound-film system was leased to theatres with a regular supply of vaudeville acts and extracts from plays. And in 1911, Edison launched the 'Home PK' (PK: Projecting

Kinetoscope). Neither of these was exactly successful, but as with so many of Edison's 'inventions' the aim was true. His friend in later life, the photographic pioneer George Eastman, would in the end accomplish with the Cine-Kodak 16mm system and emulsions such as Kodachrome and Kodacolor what Edison only dreamed of: home movies in full colour.

Edison and members of his Motion Picture Patents Company trust at its foundation in 1908. The trust would attempt to control the whole industry that has grown up since Edison's launch of the Kinetoscope in 1894, before it was dissolved in 1917.

Meanwhile, government anti-trust proceedings against the MPPC started in 1912, and succeeded in dissolving it in 1915. In 1918, Edison sold his Bronx studio and ended his formal connection with an industry to which he had never really belonged. Eastman had long urged him against trying to control an invention as far-reaching as moving pictures, but Edison had been unable to shake off the domineering, acquisitive habits of a lifetime, until he was effectively forced to concede defeat. Nonetheless, he remained a visionary to the end, and in the late '20s was claiming – in the sweeping terms the media had loved for over fifty years – that films would soon replace books.

Looking back from the start of the CD-ROM era, we can see he was basically right.[16] The potential for encoding large amounts of information on mass-produced, machine-readable supports had been born with the phonograph, the true forerunner of all modern mass media. He grasped this intuitively, putting it across in what must have been wonderfully seductive interviews, and cumulatively awakening the 19th century to what lay ahead, even if not in the terms he proposed.

Edison's Home Projecting Kinetoscope, launched in 1912, and essentially a commercial failure, despite pointing toward the future of domestic film consumption.

Edison was both a driven and a divided man. The incentive he admitted to the outside world was industrial success – power, wealth, monopoly. He harnessed science to industry with electrical generating stations, iron-ore milling machinery and cement manufacture. But his bravado may have masked the insecurity of a self-educated man, who regularly advised parents not to send their sons to college. This same insecurity played into Edison's popular persona as 'the Wizard'. It was perhaps a strange role for a Protestant taskmaster to accept, but it may have been the only way he could deal with the godlike power that invention brought. Edison was already established in the popular mind as 'the Wizard' long before L. Frank Baum wrote *The Wizard of Oz*, but it's tempting to recast him in the same mould as Oz, the medicine-show fake who hides behind the mystique he's created. When X-rays became a popular craze in 1896, Edison climbed aboard the bandwagon. Having announced 'improvements' to Röntgen's apparatus, he opened a fairground X-ray show in New York, decked out in spooky mock-Egyptian decor. And, rather as Walt Disney used to visit Disneyland incognito, Edison apparently went to watch the punters. We can perhaps imagine him, Oz-like, hiding behind the curtain and spying on the customers, watching them pay for a glimpse of their own mortality.

For decades, in the labs and workshops of Menlo Park and West Orange, he wrestled furiously with the many stubborn mechanical problems that barred the way to an automated utopia. Today, a poignant corner of the lab still houses a bizarre collection of animal horns and hooves, which were collected during his search for recording materials in the pre-plastic era. For a moment we're back in the world of the medieval alchemist. So long as invention played its part in the businesslike American scheme of things, Edison could reconcile the contradictions of his position. But once the alchemy of moving pictures had started, he could no longer control a monster that threatened the sanctity of the traditional hearth. And so all his positive energies were directed towards putting the genie back in the bottle: re-domesticating the movies.

Why did he so want to control something he seems always to have despised? What had drawn him into a mode of trickery that went against the deepest beliefs of his Protestant culture? Was it this realisation that led him to allow it to die through neglect? The answers to these questions take on a new significance when we compare the 1890s with the 1990s. For what makes the 'centenary of cinema' more than an excuse for showbiz nostalgia is the disturbing realisation that history is repeating itself. The media explosion we're living through parallels almost exactly the first communications revolution that Edison started in the 1880s. And just as such media pioneers misunderstood what they had started, so we too may be misreading what is happening around us. Above all – and this is the truly eerie part – the revolution that Edison originally imagined but didn't live to see, is what's happening to us today.[17]

First appeared in *Sight and Sound*, May 1996.

25.
Robert and Ellen: Inventing Cinema

Who invented cinema? For most of the last century, this was very much a international competition. If you were American, it was self-evidently Thomas Edison, or more correctly his employee, W. K. L. Dickson, with their Kinetoscope. If you were French, it was equally obviously the brothers Lumière, playing down their debt to Edison's example, and lack of interest in anything other than actualities, with a nod to fellow countrymen Étienne-Jules Marey and Georges Demenÿ. Meanwhile, Germans argued there was a strong case to be made for the brothers Skladanowsky, who screened moving pictures to a paying audience before anyone else.

In Britain, the story was more complicated. Until the 1960s, it was a matter of national pride to point to William Friese-Greene as the true visionary, who first patented and perhaps even demonstrated moving pictures, but had his glory stolen by Edison (and Dickson). His monument in Highgate Cemetery still declares him to be 'the inventor of kinematography'. And the Boultings' film *The Magic Box*, made for the Festival of Britain in 1951, duly toed the party line, with Robert Donat an irresistibly moving incarnation of the reckless inventor – in the same vein as John Mills' gallant Scott of the Antarctic (both films incidentally shot by Britain's Technicolor virtuoso Jack Cardiff). But after the claims made for Friese-Greene were derided in 1960, Brits generally withdrew from the field, preferring to honour a galaxy of quasi-pioneers, ranging from Louis Le Prince to Wordsworth Donisthorpe and ultimately Paul's early collaborator, Birt Acres.

Of course, the idea that any single person 'invented' cinema is essentially absurd. So the correct answer should be 'no one'. It was a relay race, a group effort, a product of 'the spirit of the age' that had created photographic images, projected them through magic lanterns, discovered how to give them stereoscopic depth, and finally wanted to have them move.

But one name has rarely been promoted as the British entry in this contentious race. And yet, if there was any single figure who foresaw the potential of 'animated photography' to become something much more than a sideshow or a passing novelty, it was Robert William Paul – certainly supported and very likely encouraged by his wife Ellen, who had been on stage at the Alhambra when they first met in 1896. So convinced was Paul, after three hectic years at the heart of the new business, that he built a studio in Muswell Hill, then on the outskirts of London, during 1898, and placed a bold advertisement in the showman's paper, *The Era*. First, the problem: 'The public have been surfeited with Trains, Trams and 'buses, and… the capacity of animated pictures for producing BREATHLESS SENSATION, LAUGHTER AND TEARS has hardly been realised… Exhibitors have been asking for something New, Distinctive, Telling and Effective'. What he went on to offer customers was 'A staff of Artists and Photographers [who] have been at work in North London, with the object of producing a series of animated Photographs (Eighty in number), each of which tells a tale, whether Comic, Pathetic, or Dramatic… with such clearness, brilliancy and telling effect that the attention of the beholders should be riveted'.

Very little survives today of the slate of films that supported Paul's vision. Even what was almost certainly the world's first two-scene film, *Come Along, Do!*, somehow lost its second shot on the way to the National Film Archive. However, the pay-off interior scene – when the husband taking a close interest in a nude statue is chided by his wife – has now been reconstructed digitally from another of Paul's innovations, the illustrated catalogue.

Among the films from that extraordinary autumn for which we only have catalogue stills, *Our New General Servant* tells a complete story in four spatially and temporally distinct scenes. A wife engages a new servant. Her husband is found dallying with the maid in the garden and the maid is sent packing. It is of course a familiar Victorian tale, told in many media, but here making a sensationally early appearance on film. The great French cinema historian Georges Sadoul read Paul's catalogues carefully in the 1940s, and concluded that he was ahead of everyone else, and a major influence on French filmmakers, such as Ferdinand Zecca, who are today much better known. Ironically, however, Sadoul's volume has never been translated into English!

The pioneer English film historian Rachael Low was studying this period at the same time as Sadoul, and they shared some of their research. But Low seems not to have appreciated Paul's narrative ambition, even going so far as to prudishly accuse him of 'bad taste' and an excessive concern with 'marital discord' – especially when compared with the wholesome family life portrayed in her favourite early British film, the 1905 *Rescued by Rover*.

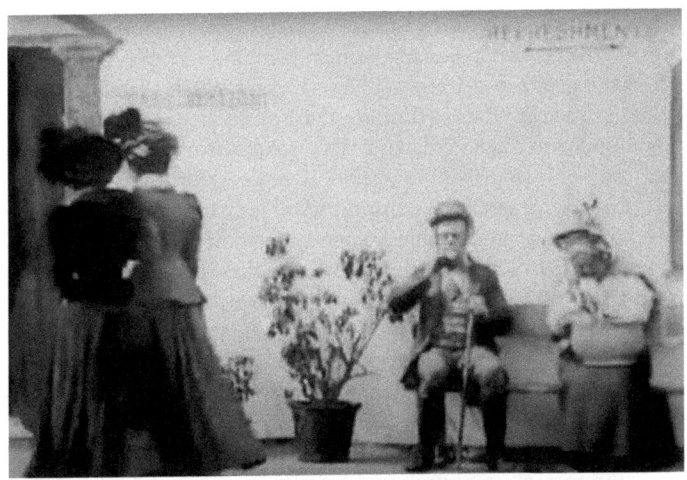

In 1898, their new suburban studio enabled Robert and Ellen Paul to experiment, in a series of eighty films, all of which are lost apart from *Come Along, Do!*, which may well be the first two-scene production, with Ellen as the wife calling her husband to order after they enter an art exhibition.

Robert and Ellen

Perhaps Low would have thought differently about Paul's storylines if she had realised how much the output of his studio owed to his wife Ellen. The traditional history of pioneer filmmaking spoke only of men, which made the 'discovery' of Alice Guy – originally Léon Gaumont's secretary, but actually responsible for many of his company's early films – a tremendous boost for feminist film history. But most of the many women who undoubtedly made early filmmaking possible were not 'directors.' Indeed, that title really belongs to a later phase of the industry. The most telling revelation of how important Ellen Paul was to Paul's Animatograph Works came in a 1943 obituary, from an electrical engineer colleague: 'his wife was producer, stage manager or principal lady in many a playlet for which her expert knowledge eminently fitted her'.

Ellen Daws was the niece of Britain's first female theatre proprietor, at the Theatre Royal in Brighton, and had enlisted her aunt's support for a career on the stage. She was a member of the Alhambra ballet company when Robert's 'animatographe' became an act on that famous music hall's programme in early 1896, and played the character role in his first fiction film, *The Soldier's Courtship*, in April of that year. An anonymous note on a BFI record card suggests that she appeared in a number of his films – including *Come Along, Do!* – but her real contribution, as the obituary made clear, was more likely to have been managing the studio. And this may well have included proposing 'playlets' or new directions for its output, as competition from other producers increased.

In fact there is more circumstantial evidence of Ellen's involvement in other films. So, for instance, Bryony Dixon was recently able to identify Paul's 1897 *Fun on the Clothesline* because it 'stars' a popular slack-wire artiste Harry Lamore. But the man and woman larking with him around the clothesline look very much like Robert and Ellen. Likewise, in one of Robert's films from the following year, recording the launch of the cruiser *HMS Albion* on the Thames, the camera pans quickly past a well-dressed woman in the boat. Because this event became a tragedy, with many onlookers drowned by a large wave, we know much more about the circumstances of filming than usual. When Paul had to defend his showing the film against accusations of profiting from a disaster – made by his one-time collaborator Birt Acres – he explained that the camera was electrically powered and running automatically, enabling him to rescue survivors from the water. And if it is Ellen that we see fleetingly, this would be because it was a royal occasion, for which Robert had hired a boat, with no expectation of any mishap.

The full extent of their professional partnership will probably never be known, in the absence of any surviving letters or relatives (their three children died in early infancy). But the scattered evidence we have is already enough to suppose that it was extensive, and to deepen our understanding of 'women in early cinema'. The obituary already quoted, and the testimony of a younger family friend, Irene

Codd, both point to Ellen playing a major part not only in Robert's film business, but also in helping manage his parallel and more substantial scientific instrument business.

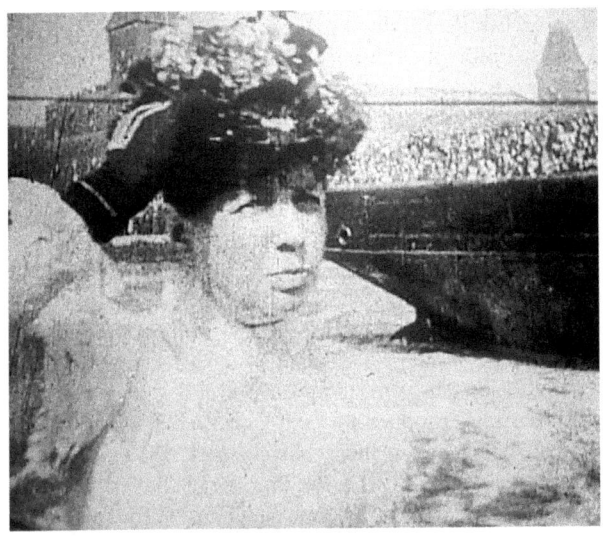

In Paul's *Launch of H.M.S.Albion*, 1898, the electric camera inadvertently catches what is probably the only close-up of Ellen Daws, now Ellen Paul, anticipating a royal occasion which would become a tragedy, when many spectators of the ship launch were drowned.

Spreading Cinema Across the Map
The Pauls' inventive fiction in 1898 gave them a commanding position as suppliers to the burgeoning exhibition business. Their catalogues briefly carried titles in French and German, which suggests they already had, or were, seeking wider international sales. But what would take the British film business in unforeseen new directions was the war in Southern Africa at the end of the following year.

Two other companies, British Biograph and Charles Urban, acted as quickly as Paul, all three sending cameras to the Cape in the hope of gathering first-hand material to satisfy a home audience. In the event, it proved almost impossible to get close enough to any action to produce what might have been expected by viewers familiar with vivid graphic representations of battle. In spite of Paul producing a vivid colour poster of a mounted soldier on the veldt, which advertised 'living photos', very few of his or others' managed more than distant views of troop movements.

Yet even some of these – such as the image of a captured Boer general being taken into captivity, or Scots Guards marching triumphantly into the Boer stronghold of Bloemfontein – seem to have been popular with a public avid for some contact with the distant war. But Paul realised that more was wanted, and responded with another remarkable burst of innovation. A group of battlefield 'reproductions' were staged on Muswell Hill's new golf course (and soon exuberantly imitated by the new Blackburn firm of Mitchell and Kenyon). Elaborate allegorical tableaux were filmed in the studio, mocking Boer leaders and invoking traditional images of Britannia. A wounded soldier's dream of his mother, seen in a vignette insert, added pathos to the films on offer. But most ambitious of all was Paul's own contribution to the national war effort: a comprehensive 25-part guide to *Army Life*, endorsed by the War Office and no doubt intended to boost recruitment, yet running almost as long as a modern feature, with a specially compiled music score for accompaniment.

Once again, almost nothing beyond a few fragments survives of this wartime production, although Paul's now voluminous illustrated catalogues can still evoke cinema's first engagement with a national emergency. With fewer than 80 of the roughly 800 films that Paul produced over fifteen years still extant, the catalogues offer a tantalising record of continuing ambition. The Boxer Rebellion in China would inspire political satire, and the Russo-Japanese War of 1904-5 three dramas. Perhaps most unexpectedly, his *Goaded to Anarchy* shows surprising sympathy for the plotters of the 1905 Russian revolution.

What has survived Paul's destruction of his stock in 1909, after deciding to exit the industry he had helped create, tends to favour his 'trick films'. Using stop motion and multiple exposure, like his early customer, Georges Méliès, Paul and his collaborators, including the conjuror Walter Booth, apparently hoped to create a market for distinctively 'English fantasy'. His surviving 1901 film *Scrooge*, even in its incomplete state, is the closest link we have with the era of original Dickens stage productions, and a *tour de force* of early special effects. In the following year, *The Magic Sword* tried to create the equivalent of a miniature Christmas pantomime, complete with a gallant knight, his lady love, a witch, a good fairy and even more 'magic' effects.

There would be more new genres, such as the 'day in the life' documentary and location-based crime dramas (as reported in *Sight and Sound* in 2016), reinforcing Paul's claim to wider recognition as a true pioneer of the cinema we know. And 1906 saw his anticipation of the spirit of Toad of Toad Hall, or indeed of *Back to the Future*, with *The '?' Motorist*. Probably his best-known work today, thanks to YouTube, this features a mystery couple who defy police and magistrates to fly freely through the solar system, before touching back down in Muswell Hill and making their final, shape-shifting escape.

Anticipating *Toad of Toad Hall*, or even *Back to the Future*, *The '?' Motorist* (1906) features a mystery couple defying police and magistrates to navigate the solar system, before they return to Muswell Hill. Robert and Ellen's fantasy life?

Its anarchic fantasy seems to express something quite personal. Paul was a keen pioneer motorist, who had already made a speeded-up *Runaway Car Through Piccadilly Circus* in 1899, and would himself be fined for speeding in North London the year after his film, in the same car we see in this film. Like fellow-motorists Arthur Conan Doyle and his Muswell Hill neighbour, the poet W. E. Henley, he was impatient with police 'ambushing' drivers. Later accounts of his activities during the First World War, working on scientific gadgets for air and sea warfare and mobilising his work force for war work, reveal a forceful, impatient character – as enigmatic as the ? motorist himself.

Time Machines
How did Paul come to be omitted from the list of 'usual suspects' credited with inventing or creating cinema, despite remaining centrally involved for much longer than many others? The main

reason is probably that he wasn't a failure or a casualty, but a very successful producer and technologist, who also judged his exit shrewdly. But another seems to have been temperamental. Despite being a frequent letter writer to newspapers and journals, and having gifted much of his equipment to the Science Museum, he seems to have been genuinely averse to personal publicity. Another obituarist wrote of him having a strange talent for 'melting away'.

Paul's fluctuating reputation through the writing of early cinema history is traced in my forthcoming book. But his odd relationship with two better-known figures is revealing. One is William Friese-Greene, his apparently discredited forerunner. Since the demolition of Friese-Greene's reputation by Brian Coe in 1960, a much more creditable record has recently emerged; and Peter Domankiewicz has convincingly shown that the older man did indeed succeed in shooting moving pictures.

However, the most famous story about Friese-Greene, brilliantly dramatised in *The Magic Box*, has him demonstrating his eventual success to a suspicious patrolling policemen, played in the film by Laurence Olivier. Bizarrely, while this didn't happen to Friese-Greene, it actually did to Robert Paul, who first recounted it as an after-dinner anecdote to film industry colleagues. Yet after Friese-Greene's destitute death in 1921, it was strangely 'transferred' to him, and the device upgraded to a projector. What really happened, in Paul's workshop in Hatton Garden, early in 1895 when he was still collaborating with Acres, was a noisy midnight celebration of their first trial film for a Kinetoscope viewer – which did indeed attract police attention.

The other strange relationship was with H. G. Wells. Terry Ramsaye told the story of 'Paul's Time Machine' in his 1926 popular history *A Million and One Nights*, although Paul's preliminary patent for an entertainment inspired by Wells' breakthrough novella *The Time Machine* was no secret. It's easy to understand why neither of these young-men-in-a-hurry took it any further in 1895. To create the theatrical spectacle of time travel would have needed resources and experience that neither had – more like the spectacles that Imre Kiralfy was presenting at Earls Court, where Paul's Kinetoscopes had made their debut as a sideshow.

Much less well known, however, is that Wells seems to have appreciated the potential of this new medium as fully and quickly as Paul did. In the year following Paul's advertisement, 1899, he wrote what would long remain his most comprehensive envisioning of the technological future. *The Sleeper Wakes* is a time travel story about a man who wakens from a coma after two hundred years, to discover that purchases can be previewed on portable gadgets like a small Kinetoscope, and books have been replaced by cylinders that offer screen versions of novels he already knows. And Wells' *Story of the Days to Come* (also 1899) even predicted giant moving-picture advertisements in a future London.

Paul's 1895 patent for a Time Machine entertainment, after his meeting with H. G. Wells, was never developed. But it seems to have influenced Wells' visionary novel *When the Sleeper Wakes* (1899), which envisioned a London with giant public screens in 2100.

Wells' own relationship with cinema would remain complex, and largely unsuccessful. One book was based on a rejected film script (*The King Who Was a King*), and even when Alexander Korda recklessly gave him free rein with *Things to Come*, the result proved spectacular, although dramatically disappointing. But for both Wells and Paul their early encounter, and the dream of cinema as time-travel, remained a vivid memory. In 1941, while the war that Wells had desperately warned against raged, he reminisced in the scientific journal *Nature* about the project, exclaiming 'we would have become ground landlords of the entire film industry'. Paul was quick to reply, observing that the impact of 'the simplest scenes, coupled with the novelty of seeing photographs moving, sufficed to attract the public and establish the new art of cinematography'.

Paul remained a realist. By then he considered himself primarily an electrical scientist, with his contribution to the 'childhood' of cinema a distant memory, even though he played an active part in starting the Cinema Veterans organisation. If he and Ellen did see Wells' *Things to Come* in 1936, we might wonder what they made of it. And he wasn't going to let even the great guru Wells get away with overselling their bright idea of 1895.

First appeared in an earlier version in *Sight and Sound*, 2019.

26.
Fred Karno's Fun Factory

Is the name 'Karno' still evocative today? It made a rare appearance in recent political polemic, with the British prime minister Theresa May described by one critic as 'more at home in Fred Karno's Circus than leading her party or Brexit negotiations'. May is also recorded mentioning it herself twenty years earlier in a parliamentary debate about railway privatisation. But these are a far cry from Karno's heyday, at the beginning of the First World War, when he was widely enough known to headline the popular troops' song: 'We are Fred Karno's Army/Fred Karno's infantry/We cannot fight, we cannot shoot/So what damn good are we?' (sung to the tune of 'The Church's One Foundation', in an era when hymns were also widely known). So, a rather fusty byword for disorganisation, apparently with both army and circus associations?

David Crump's painstaking 600-page tribute to 'the legend behind the laughter' aims to strip away a century of accumulated misinformation and scandal, and restore Karno to his rightful place in entertainment history. Just why we might be expected to appreciate this labour of love is shrewdly signposted by his book's cover. Charlie Chaplin is shown peering cautiously round one side of a portrait of Karno which casts him as a pillar of the establishment, while at the opposite corner Ollie Hardy gives Stan Laurel a leg up. Mock-heraldically, these supporting figures signal what must be Karno's lasting claim to legendary status – to have 'discovered' both Chaplin and Laurel, and given them the solid early training in physical comedy that would take them to worldwide stardom. Ironically, and there are many ironies along the way, their success would come through a medium in which Karno himself had little or no success.

In many respects, it's a typical story of earnest Victorian endeavour, of building a mighty business empire through diligence and sheer hard work, with the advantage of starting at a crucial period in British imperial history. The key to Karno's success lay in that peculiar institution, the British music hall; and perhaps even further back in Britain's ambivalent attitude to theatrical entertainment. Theatres offering spoken drama had been limited in number, and subject to a strict censorship enforced by the Lord Chamberlain, since the early 18th century. When pressure to relax this straitjacket produced a new Theatres Act in 1843, one of its unintended consequences was to open the way for a parallel network of 'saloon theatres' and 'song and supper rooms', which unlike the theatres could serve alcohol. Any drama in these would still require the Lord Chamberlain's prior approval, but song, dance and physical performance were exempt.

Hence the flourishing of what became legendary 'halls', not only in London, but soon in every major city and town. Their steeply tiered auditoria, and bars, could accommodate audiences of all classes, from the 'swells' promenading at lower levels to the masses cheering on their favourites from the upper reaches. Among those who fondly recalled their youth at the halls were such varied figures as Rudyard Kipling, Winston Churchill, and T. S. Eliot, who wrote admiringly about one of the stars, Marie Lloyd, at her death in 1922. Singers, dancers and acrobats were the main stock-in-trade of the halls, and it was as an acrobat that young Fred Westcott made his debut, having exchanged a plumbing apprenticeship in Nottingham for joining a circus act in 1881, which would provide his performing name of Karno. The lives of circus and music hall performers were hard, made even more hectic by the comprehensive Victorian railway network that allowed them to travel to widely separated bookings, and Crump's exhaustive research spares no detail in chronicling Fred's early years. He and his wife Edith, also a performer, would lose two babies in rapid succession under gruelling professional pressure.

But Crump also identifies the early ambition that drove Fred to create what was essentially a new stage genre: an extended panto-mime sketch with a loose narrative framework, which depended on individual and group virtuosity from a company that could soon number as many as seven acrobatic comedians. One of his earliest successes was called simply *Hilarity*, and Crump quotes an appreciative 1899 review of the 'graceful and artistic tumblers... surrounded by rustic scenery, who fall from a balcony outside a dainty cottage, go through doors, disappear with alarming alacrity and dodge one another with marvellous dexterity'. *Hilarity* would remain popular on the music hall circuit and was soon joined by an expanding repertoire of increasingly elaborate pantomimes, all intensively rehearsed and creating openings for new recruits. Soon, bookings on the music hall circuit were enough to justify Karno launching additional companies under his 'brand', allowing him to take a managerial perspective and create a base in Camberwell, where sets and props could be made. This would pass into legend as The Fun

Factory, while Karno found his own escape from an unhappy marriage on a houseboat which he moored at an island in the Thames, making possible a new social life, with a young mistress and opportunities to mix with show-business grandees and bohemian aristocrats. By 1903, the strain had become intense, and his family acrimoniously disintegrated, his wife moving out with their surviving children, and his mistress arriving at the Fun Factory.

Advertisement for Karno on Tour in the U.S., with Chaplin featured in a 'drunk' sketch.

Meanwhile Karno's pantomime creations had become ever more elaborate. *Jail Birds*, dating from 1895, signalled a new level of complexity, which Crump suggests may have germinated from its author observing convicts while doing a plumbing job at Nottingham jail. In the sketch, no fewer than twenty performers enacted an extraordinary sequence of scenes from prison life, starting with work in a quarry, climaxed by the destruction of a bridge by dynamite. Next came scenes from many departments of the prison, including inedible food that had to be sawn up. Then a prisoner manages to steal a warder's keys and liberate his fellows, leading to a spectacular finale in which 'walls and floors open as if by magic, to make way for pursuers and the pursued, and finally the curtain falls on an effective tableau'.

Today, we can perhaps only imagine a spectacle like this in filmic terms – like a frenetic version of the stylised prison sequence in Wes Anderson's *The French Dispatch* – even if it was performed throughout Britain by countless Karno employees over more than a decade. And Crump is well aware that screen success stalks his narrative. The crucial juncture comes with a 1904 sketch titled, somewhat mysteriously to modern ears, *Mumming Birds*. Fortunately, we can experience at least a screen version of this, thanks to Richard Attenborough's 1992 *Chaplin*, with Robert Downey Jr. giving an extraordinary impersonation of the young Chaplin. In this, we see Downey perform in one of the actual venues that Chaplin played as a leading Karno employee, the Hackney Empire.

What's not apparent from the condensed film version is that the original sketch involved the front theatre boxes as part of the on-stage set, in an astonishing *mise en abyme*, which is also the substance of the act. And even more remarkably, this remains the longest-running sketch in music hall history. The essential idea is simple: a series of typical stage acts are disrupted by interventions from the boxes. On one side, a youngster in an Eton collar uses a pea-shooter, while on the other, a 'drunken swell' interrupts the stage acts, while also falling out of his box. It was in this role that Chaplin first emerged as a star, which led to him heading of one of Karno's North American tours in 1910, where the sketch was retitled *A Night in an English Music Hall*. One of the many ironies Crump reveals is that the future Stan Laurel, also a Karno graduate, had been successfully playing the 'swell' before Chaplin arrived, at which point he had to hand over the costume. A decade later, Stan Jefferson would briefly scratch a living on the American vaudeville circuit as a Chaplin imitator, after Charlie's career had taken off on screen in 1914, and four years before his own would begin under a new name.

An engaging feature of Crump's book is his rueful awareness that many reading it will be Chaplin or Laurel and Hardy fans. Hence the careful unpicking of legend and contradictory information about its hero is laced with admonitions to 'wait for the moment' when these figures make their debuts. There's also patient clarification of many assumptions which have been widely accepted as fact, such as Chaplin breaking his contract with Karno to sign a lucrative film deal with Mack Sennett at Keystone in 1913. The truth appears to be that a handwritten phrase, 'by mutual consent', allowed him to do so legally. Both Chaplin and Laurel would continue to assert, as their cinema careers prospered, that Karno had taught them at least most of what they knew about comedy. Above all, as Laurel insisted, 'he taught us to be precise'.

Yet, while his protégés prospered in the new world that cinema had opened up in the 1910s, especially after the Great War enabled American studios to assume control of the worldwide film business, Karno had little luck in this 20th-century medium. Before the war, he had invested heavily and unwisely in creating a pleasure garden on Tagg Island in the Thames, which would remain a drain on his resources. His sporadic attempts to break into film in Britain during the 1920s would suffer from the depressed state of the local industry. Then, in 1929, came the summons that many around the world were awaiting. The mighty William Morris Agency wired to invite him to contribute to the next production by a new sensation, the Marx Brothers.

Karno's business card, listing his most popular 'speechless' sketches, devised to avoid English stage censorship.

The story of Karno's return to the scene of his former triumphs makes sad reading. After kicking his heels in New York, he headed west with no firm promise of work. And despite a fulsome welcome from Chaplin, there was no further contact, with his former protégé immersed in producing *City Lights*. Believing he had been hired to advise on productions by Hal Roach, he discovered that the studio was about to feel the impact of the Depression. Back in England, he had further misfortune in cinema, when the film he produced in 1936, *Don't Rush Me*, proved a humiliating failure, even as another of his music hall protégés, Will Hay, was emerging as Britain's new comedy star. Appropriately, Karno's last success, rarely attributed to him, was to have inspired Britain's new comedy group, the Crazy Gang. With their surreal antics, Nervo and Knox, along with Flanagan and Allen and others, could be seen as the homegrown seeds of Britain's later comedy successes, up to the sketch format of *Monty Python*. But for Karno, facing bankruptcy again, it would be a retreat to his native Southwest, where he ran a modest off-license in Dorset until his death in 1941.

David Crump's book presents a formidable amount of detailed original research, much of it in the local and ephemeral press that is now accessible online. One of his aims is to rescue Karno's personal reputation from the opprobrium cast by a 1971 biography by J. P. Gallagher, apparently based on scant first-hand research, which has been widely referenced in many accounts of both Chaplin and Laurel. Clearing Karno of charges of cruelty to his first wife Edith, and of neglect of his family, is certainly worthwhile. But perhaps more important is restoring the vanished world of music hall, which was to have a vital influence on the early decades of cinema. Indeed – although Crump doesn't press this claim – it could be argued that without the 'silent pantomime' pioneered by Karno in the Edwardian halls, cinema would not have reached its global audience. But to say this is, once again, to cast Karno in a supporting role.

Perhaps the most eloquent expression of what music hall meant before 1914 was Eliot's pean of praise for Marie Lloyd and her significance for working class audiences: 'in the music hall comedians they find the artistic expression and dignity of their own lives; and this is not found for any life in the most elaborate and expensive revue'. Nor was it to be found in 'the cheap and rapid-breeding cinema', according to Eliot, reflecting the long-standing cultural prejudice against cinema in his adopted country. Yet today we might reflect on the paradox that it was the explosion of silent-era film comedy that would ultimately destroy music hall, while also giving its Karnoesque pantomime a lasting afterlife. The figure that emerges from behind the legend – stoic, sometimes spendthrift, yet eternally optimistic – was apparently given to wishing colleagues 'better luck with the second house'. Here, he has been lucky enough to secure a posthumous return engagement that lives up to the high standards he passed on to his myriad protégés.

This originally appeared in the *Times Literary Supplement* in December 2022 as a review of David Crump, *Fred Karno: The Legend behind the Laughter* (Brewin, 2022).

What Cinema Made of Us

27.
New Windows on the World

Over a century ago, moving pictures opened new ways of seeing and experiencing the world for audiences. In 1900, watching lifelike images from near and far in a darkened space was a new experience, and one that quickly attracted audiences everywhere. For those not living in crowded cities, movies offered a taste of city life. And for those far from centres of innovation, they brought modernity and new styles of life. They also created a new kind of encyclopaedia, displaying wonders of nature and science for the masses. And they created new kinds of glamour in the images of stars on-screen and in the picture palaces where these were seen. Today, digital access is giving us more ways of accessing this culture of the moving image, with new tools and sources that take us closer to what enabled movies to make the modern world.

Beginnings
There can be little doubt that we are currently beginning to enjoy a golden age of online access to early cinema. Thanks to digitisation and online archival resources, such as the Library of Congress Paper Print and American Memory collections, and those of other archives, such as the BFI National Archive, Eye Filmmuseum in the Netherlands and the Danish Film Archive, each of us can individually call up a range of films that were impossible to see until recently. In 1978, the International Federation of Film Archives (FIAF) had the unprecedented idea of bringing together all the archived films dating from 1900 to 1906 for screening. The resulting FIAF conference held in Brighton effectively launched early film as a dynamic new component of film studies, which had only recently emerged as an academic subject.

The Brighton screenings and discussions involving a new generation of scholars demolished many long-standing myths about early film being 'primitive' and launched a new understanding of its variety and close relationship with other media of the late Victorian period.[1] But outside archives, relatively few of the actual films were available to view in this pre-video and pre-internet era. Seen on 16mm film in classrooms, they were often shown at the wrong speed and invariably without the musical accompaniment we take for granted today.

Yet despite the current ease of digital access, many myths persist and are entrenched through online repetition. For instance, the Lumières' *Train Entering a Station* was not part of their earliest programmes, and there's no evidence of spectators being terrified by it, apart from journalists talking up the idea to enliven their copy. Nor indeed were the Lumière films the first to be seen by most audiences. So online access of the range provided by the Media Ecology Project (MEP) Compendium is a great opportunity to correct continuing misconceptions and open up a much wider understanding of the contexts in which moving pictures first appeared.[2] And context is the most vital issue. Seeing these films today online gives little sense of where and how they were first received.

Early shows took place in every possible darkened space, from lecture theatres and church halls to cafés and fairgrounds. But the most influential context was the variety theatre. This took different forms in different countries – vaudeville in the U.S., music hall in Britain, cabaret and *café chantant* in France – but everywhere, its essence was a fast-moving, varied programme of live acts. And it was in this context that early one-minute films found their first audiences as a minority component of larger, predominantly live performances.

The business that took shape during 1896 was also inherently international. Audiences were largely unaware of the sources of their entertainment, and there were no effective copyright laws to prevent producers from copying or remaking their rivals' subjects. Films were bought and sold as physical copies, to be used for as long they lasted, until hire and licensing became the dominant terms of business some fifteen years later.

Two of London's largest music halls, the Empire and the Alhambra, joined battle early in 1896 with rival film offers. A Lumière programme at the Empire was initially presented by the popular impressionist Félicien Trewey, while the Alhambra had Robert Paul showing his locally made films. Within a month, Paul was persuaded to star two of the Alhambra's popular dancers in an acted sketch, *The Soldier's Courtship*. Meanwhile, in New York, Edison realised that he had to catch up with this new trend, and in April he launched his Vitascope projector at a Broadway music hall with a programme that included Paul and Birt Acres' *Rough Sea at Dover* as its most popular item, a film they had made a year earlier to show on Paul's British version of the Edison Kinetoscope, which had been sent to Edison as part of an invitation to cooperate.

Robert Paul and Birt Acres' *Rough Sea at Dover* (1895), an unacknowledged hit for Edison in New York.

What Happens in the Dark
Actuality films, taken in the streets of cities around the world, remained an important part of programmes for the rest of the decade, even though Edison realised that performance was a key attraction for his first Kinetoscope programmesm, which had included subjects featuring two lively dancers, Carmencita and Annabelle Moore. In April 1896, he filmed a moment from a contemporary play featuring two actors in what we would term a close-up, *The Kiss*, around the same time that Paul had staged *The Soldier's Courtship* on the roof of the Alhambra. The theatrical context in which films were widely seen also became a framing feature of a number of subjects: as in Paul's *The Countryman and the Cinematograph* and its remake by Edwin Porter for Edison as *Uncle Josh at the Moving Pictures*. Eventually this framing device would suggest more elaborate narratives that dramatised moviegoing as a new leisure pastime, with a hilarious example of its social pitfalls from D. W. Griffith, *Those Awful Hats* (1909), which also shows us what a nickelodeon interior was like and includes the future pioneer of slapstick comedy, Mack Sennett, among its still-anonymous cast.

Moviegoing, which introduced the novel experience of an audience sitting close in darkness, was understood from the outset to have erotic implications. An ingenious twist on this is the subject of American Mutoscope and Biograph's *The Story the Biograph Told* (1904), in which adultery is revealed on-screen. But even earlier, G. A. Smith, a member of what became known as the Brighton School of pioneers in Britain, hinted at the voyeuristic implications of film in *As Seen Through a Telescope* (1900).³ And Pathé, set to become cinema's first multinational company, further developed the voyeuristic theme with Fernand Zecca's *Through the Keyhole* (1901), in which an inquisitive hotel porter spies on guests and discovers more than he bargained for in one, as a female impersonator removes 'her' disguise.

As the study of early cinema has developed since 1978, historians have identified intricate patterns of influence and – certainly – barefaced plagiarism among the first producers. So Zecca's keyhole drama is now recognised as owing much to Smith's earlier film, while many of Paul's innovations soon found their way across the English Channel and the Atlantic. Perhaps the most significant of these were the multiscene productions that Paul and his wife, Ellen, produced in their new London studio during the summer of 1898 – films that Paul announced would replace the plethora of everyday scenes with 'comic, pathetic or dramatic tales' that were guaranteed to 'rivet the attention' of audiences. Sadly, like much of early cinema, almost nothing of this bold venture survives. But one of the eighty films released by the Pauls in 1898, *Come Along, Do!*, has been reconstructed to demonstrate its innovative two-scene structure.⁴

Chases and Acrobatics

Paul and fellow English pioneers based in Brighton and Sheffield were active in launching many influential genres, although this early lead was not maintained. Probably the most important was the chase structure, which began modestly with films such as James Williamson's *Stop Thief!* (1901), Paul's *The Unfortunate Policeman* (1903), and his former employee Frank Mottershaw's *A Daring Daylight Burglary* (1903). This last is now widely believed to have influenced Edwin Porter's celebrated *The Great Train Robbery*, made later in the same year. As the French industry began conquering markets internationally, its leading companies, Pathé and Gaumont, pushed the chase form to new heights of ingenuity in such zany comedies as Pathé's *The Runaway Horse* (*Le cheval emballé*, 1908), and Gaumont's *The Pumpkin Chase* (*La course aux potirons*, 1908). With its delirious pursuit of pumpkins escaping through Paris streets, this film would later be discovered and admired by French Surrealists, who were among the first to celebrate early cinema.[5]

By 1910 American producers had begun to consolidate their dominance of international distribution, with Sennett's troupe of energetically bumbling Keystone Cops making their 1912 debut in a folksy comedy, *The Bangville Police*. The cops would sometimes accompany Charlie Chaplin in his first great comedy series for Keystone, and elements of their acrobatic style reappear in his subsequent Essanay and Mutual series: for instance, his 1917 masterpiece *Easy Street*. By the time a slightly later generation of screen comics appeared, led by Buster Keaton, the legacy of the early chase format had been well learned. Keaton's *Seven Chances* (1925) climaxes in an epic chase sequence, with a mob of hopeful brides pursuing the hapless Keaton in the hope of snaring his fortune.

Rebellious pumpkins in Gaumont's delirious chase comedy *The Pumpkin Chase* (1908), greatly admired by the Surrealists.

Ghosts and Miracles
If the chase provided cinema's most fundamental narrative structure – still in use, with ever more elaborate variations (think of George Miller's *Fury Road*) – it was the 'trick film', starting around 1900 that laid the basis for all subsequent fantasy and illusion. At its simplest, this could involve merely stopping and restarting the camera after adjustments, demonstrated as early as 1895 in Edison's *Execution of*

Mary Queen of Scots, made for the Kinetoscope, and Georges Méliès' *The Vanishing Lady* (1896), or inverting it with trompe l'oeil scenery, as in Paul's *Upside Down; or, The Human Flies* (1899). Stop-motion, along with the superimposition of multiple exposures to create ghostly effects, provided the bedrock of trick film technique up to around 1910, often in the service of popular supernatural stories, such as Dickens' *A Christmas Carol* in Paul's *Scrooge; or, Marley's Ghost* and Cecil Hepworth's *Alice in Wonderland* (1903). These techniques were taken to new heights in the increasingly elaborate fantasies of Méliès, such as *A Trip to the Moon* (*Voyage dans la Lune*, 1902), *The Melomaniac* (1903), and *The Fantastic Voyage* (1904), which were widely recognised as a genre in their own right. But American cinema would also make use of these techniques in comedies such as James Stuart Blackton's *The Haunted Hotel* (1907), now widely considered a founding work of stop-motion animation, and in early science fiction, often drawing on Jules Verne's fantastic journeys, as in Universal's *20,000 Leagues Under the Sea* (1916).

Méliès' *The Fantastic Voyage* (1904).

Nor were trick film techniques only used for comedy and adventure. They were crucial for many of the popular early biblical cycles, such as Pathé's and Gaumont's enormously popular series. For example, *The Life of Christ* (Zecca, 1903), which vividly dramatised New Testament miracles such as Christ walking on water, as well as creating the scenes of the Annunciation – a major subject for Renaissance artists – and the Ascension. Such 'miraculous' effects would eventually be incorporated into longer narratives, becoming what are known as special effects, to enhance key moments in essentially realist narratives, as in the dream sequence of August Blom's *Atlantis* (1913) or the volcanic eruption that opens Giovanni Pastrone's epic of the war between ancient Rome and Carthage, *Cabiria* (1914). These films from emerging European industries played an important part in leading the transition from cinema programmes based on varied short films to full-length features.[6]

Early Cinema and the Wider World
We might assume today that film played only a small part in the turbulent world from which it emerged. This may be true, insofar as it was only part of the busy entertainment spectrum for *fin de siècle* audiences, which included elaborate magic lantern shows, and such domestic entertainments as stereoscopic views and early phonograph sound recordings. But like many of these media, early film also reflected that world with often surprising topicality.

Picturing War – by any mean
Two major conflicts that broke out very soon after regular film screening began would decisively shape the 20th-century geopolitical world, and also have a dramatic impact on the status of film. The earliest conflict to engage film producers was the Spanish-American War, which broke out in 1898 after the sinking of the USS *Maine* in Havana Harbour and led to United States intervention in the Cuban War of Independence against Spain, initiating its quasi-imperial involvement in Caribbean and Pacific territories. In the following year, another rebellion, by the Boer republic of Transvaal in South Africa, would precipitate the second Anglo-Boer War, pitting Dutch settlers against the British Empire.

Both of these conflicts, initially local, developed into extended wars that attracted wide international interest. And both offered early film producers tantalising subjects to portray on-screen, despite the impossibility of filming actual combat. The Library of Congress' special feature on the Spanish-American War collects sixty-eight subjects produced between 1898 and 1901, which display the variety of techniques and forms used, ranging from troop parades and embarkation actualities and portraits of the leaders involved to reenactments of often questionable authenticity and outright appeals to patriotic sentiment.[7]

Films from the Anglo-Boer War of 1899–1902 have not been collected as conveniently in one site, but examples can be found of a similar range of responses, with some additional novelties.

Among these were the large-format 68mm films taken on location by W. K. L. Dickson for the Biograph Company. Dickson had been instrumental in creating Edison's original Kinetograph camera and Kinetoscope viewer, but left Edison soon after to co-found the American Mutoscope Company, which made flip-card viewers – soon known as 'what the butler saw' machines due to their often risqué subjects. In 1896 the company launched its Biograph camera and projectors, using 68mm film to give a remarkably large and steady image – superior to any other early format – and Dickson became the leading operator for the company's British branch.

Wreck of the Maine.

After a publicity coup with his films of Pope Leo XIII in 1898, Dickson travelled to the scene of the Anglo-Boer War in South Africa, filming extensively around the battlefields. The book he published chronicling his exploits, *The Biograph in Battle*, has kept this dimension of Boer War coverage visible, although little was seen of actual Biograph films until the collections held by Eye Filmmuseum in the Netherlands and the British Film Institute National Archive were recently restored and shown digitally at many venues, revealing how spectacular the Biograph format must have been.[8]

More substantial coverage of the war came from the two largest British producers of the era, Robert Paul and the American Charles Urban, fast becoming the most dynamic figures in pre-1914 British cinema. Both Paul and Urban offered films of troops embarking for the voyage to South Africa; Paul sent two cameras, entrusted to serving officers, which secured a lively scene of British troops triumphantly entering the Boer stronghold of Bloemfontein, and one of a captured Boer general, seen in the distance, which underlines how difficult it was to film action in the field at this time. Faced with strong demand for films of a war that was testing Britain's imperial confidence, Paul also produced a series of reproductions of scenes from the war, filmed on a golf course in North London, which he realised would likely be presented by showmen as authentic battlefield scenes.[9] A similar approach was followed by the Edison Company, which produced its fictional Boer War scenes in New Jersey, like *The Capture of a Boer Battery by the British*.

Historians of early cinema, notably Charles Musser in the U.S. and John Barnes in Britain, have argued that the level of audience response to film coverage of these wars played a major part in boosting national film industries at this early stage in their development.[10] At this distance in time, it may be hard to believe that films offering such scant representation were so enthusiastically received, yet the evidence is clear from contemporary newspaper accounts. 'A howl of enthusiasm went up at Hopkins' Theater at the initial appearance in this city in the evening of the Biograph picture of the battleship Maine which was sunk in Havana harbor… Many of the patrons rose to their feet. There was a yell of three cheers for the United States navy. Men whistled and yelled. There was a stampeding of feet, and women waved their handkerchiefs'.[11] The film that so moved this 1898 Chicago audience actually showed two other battleships but had been opportunistically retitled by Biograph to link it with one of the most famous incidents of the war. As Stephen Bottomore has observed, this and all subsequent war films have often traded on audiences' willingness to accept what they are told.

Film certainly seems to have stimulated patriotic fervour in both the Spanish-American and Anglo-Boer Wars, producing new levels of identification and emotion. Bottomore quotes an intriguing account of audience response to a film of the funeral of victims of the Maine sinking. 'There seemed to be miles of that grim procession of the dead. It was not mere photographic reproduction; the crowd soon saw that. It was the real thing and as the full horror of that cowardly murder swept through the theatre a sigh went up that not even the lighter pictures which followed could change to a smile'.[12]

'Photographic reproduction' might refer here to lantern slides, contrasting the still with the moving image. But what if the war being shown was not one in which the audience had an obvious stake? The 1904 war between Russia and Japan would demonstrate that filmed conflict itself seemed to have a permanent appeal for film audiences.

As news of this distant war reached the United States and Europe, film companies resorted to the now-familiar strategy of recreating episodes on home territory. After Biograph staged a version of *The Battle of the Yalu* in Syracuse, New York, purporting to show a major naval engagement in the Japanese-Chinese War, the film was reported to be 'running at all the leading Vaudeville houses, cheered from start to finish'.[13] Edison took note of this success and made its own version of the battle at Forest Hill, New Jersey.

Meanwhile, in Britain, while Urban sent cameramen to record episodes of the war, Paul produced a series of dramatic films inspired by it – none purporting to show specific events, but all claiming to use authentic uniforms and insignia.[14] Recognising a clear business opportunity, Edison assembled a diverse collection of material to meet the demand coming from exhibitors. This included a relatively elaborate production representing the sinking of two Russian ships by the Japanese fleet using studio reconstruction and miniature ships, which proved highly profitable. Also on offer were battle reenactments staged using American military personnel, and news and travel films bought in or simply copied from foreign sources.

Henceforth, armed conflict has remained a subject of permanent fascination for cinema, even after television took over much of its topical reporting during the 1960s, with a variety of genres in play. Actuality film depended on signposting, which might be more or less scrupulous in its accuracy. Producers looked for human interest stories, which might be extracted from real events, or constructed to appeal to prejudices and emotions. And increasingly, audiences throughout the world would have their attitudes to war and conflict powerfully shaped by its screen presentation.

Topical Events

War may have been the most reliable crowd-pleaser in early cinema, but many other topical events, especially of national significance, prompted responses by enterprising producers. As early as June 1896 – less than six months after regular public screenings began – Paul filmed the annual Derby horse race, and managed to have his record ready to show at the Alhambra the following evening, titling it *The Prince's Derby*. The fact that the race had been won by a horse belonging to the popular Prince of Wales made this a joyous event, and the packed house demanded that the film be rerun at least twice, accompanied by the orchestra playing 'God Bless the Prince of Wales'. Paul was brought on-stage to take a bow, and the Prince later came to see the film in person.

Less than a year later, a marathon championship boxing match between James Corbett and Bob Fitzsimmons, held in Carson City Nevada, was filmed in its entirety. The fourteen rounds, with breaks, ran for one hundred minutes, making this the longest film produced anywhere up to this time, although only fragments have survived. Prizefighting was banned at this time in many U.S. states, which undoubtedly contributed to the film's commercial success, since there was no prohibition on its screen portrayal. But its producer, Enoch J. Rector, had already discovered the attraction of boxing on-screen with a six-minute film of Corbett fighting the outsider Peter Courtney, made for the Edison Kinetoscope in 1894.

Sports events had the advantage of being predictable, with guaranteed audience interest, and remained a staple of cinema for decades until the advent of television. However, unforeseen current events could also acquire a new immediacy on-screen. Among pioneers, Méliès is best known today for his fantasy films using elaborate trick photography. But he responded to the political furore of the Dreyfus Affair, which had convulsed France since 1894, when Dreyfus was brought back from imprisonment on Devil's Island for a new trial in 1899. Departing from the pantomime style of his fantasies, Méliès told the story of Dreyfus' original trial and imprisonment in twelve crisp tableaux that have all the immediacy of modern news reporting, including one where journalists rush from the packed court towards the camera.

Another milestone in early film reportage occurred in the United States in 1901, during the Pan-American Exposition in Buffalo, New York. An Edison crew was filming President McKinley on his tour of the exhibits, and after his review of a guard of honour they were waiting for him to emerge from the Temple of Music. Suddenly word spread among the assembled crowd that the president had been shot by an assassin inside the temple. The cameraman filmed a panoramic shot as word spread, and the resulting *Mob Outside the Temple of Music*, as it was titled in the Edison catalogue, became an eerily poignant record of the shooting's impact.

Edison cameramen also continued to film the events that followed. The first stage of McKinley's elaborate funeral took place in Buffalo before continuing to Washington and finishing in his hometown in Ohio. This brought the total coverage of the exposition and its tragic aftermath to eleven films, all of them actualities until what should have been the climax of the series, the execution of the president's assassin, the anarchist Leon Czolgosz. When Edison's cameramen were refused permission to film the execution at the

Albany jail, they resorted to staging it themselves, setting the scene with a shot of the jail's exterior.

The filmic treatment of this event also gives us real insight into customs of film exhibition at this period. Exhibitors were encouraged to end a sequence with a wholly manufactured item, *The Martyred Presidents*, which showed memorial portraits of Lincoln, Garfield and McKinley flanked by a mourner and the allegorical figure of Justice. The gravity of the occasion had apparently triggered a response from Edison's production department that instinctively drew upon magic lantern conventions, where allegorical compositions of this kind were common.[15]

Bringing It All Back Home

The McKinley sequence of films is notable for another reason. Among the mourners can be seen Vice President Theodore Roosevelt, already famous for his public relations skills. Early in 1901, he inspired what is probably the first political satire on film, Edison's *Terrible Teddy, the Grizzly King*. A burly rifleman hurries through a forest, accompanied by figures labelled 'My Press Agent' and 'My Photographer', before making a ceremonial kill for the camera. Two years later, Roosevelt was president, and films were issued by AM&B showing his Rough Riders cavalry unit, originally formed to serve in the Spanish-American War.

Roosevelt would become the most filmed of all statesmen in the years before 1914. Traveling to Africa in 1908 on a big-game hunting expedition, he hired the English cameraman Cherry Kearton to accompany him, and the resulting coverage entered his personal film library, while also forming part of a 1910 Pathé commercial release, *Roosevelt in Africa*. This was welcomed by the trade press with enthusiasm: 'not an uninteresting foot in the two reels', declared *Motion Picture World*.

The coverage of Roosevelt's game hunting might seem merely a publicity stunt, which it clearly was. But it also contributed to an important genre in the early decades of cinema – the travel film – and to the emerging subgenre of expedition films. Kearton would film elsewhere in Africa and in India, Borneo, and South America, contributing his films to Charles Urban's growing library. Urban's belief in non-fiction film as a new educational medium was reflected in the full title of his impressive catalogue: *Urbanora: The World's Educator*. Films of exotic locations, natural features and animals in the wild filled the catalogues of most early producers and made up an important part of the programmes shown in cinema theatres up to 1912.[16]

Expedition films became major feature attractions after Robert Falcon Scott's Antarctic Expedition of 1910–12 was filmed by Herbert Ponting for Gaumont. The first part of Ponting's coverage was shown in Britain and elsewhere in 1911, when Scott and his comrades were already in difficulty in their final trek to the Pole. By the time the second part was released in 1912, they were dead, although this was not discovered until months later. Ponting would devote the rest of his life to commemorating the Scott expedition as an example of heroism in adversity, first in slide and film lectures during the First World War, then in a feature-length documentary, *The Great White Silence* (1924), and finally in a sound version, *90° South* (1933). Tracing the different forms that Ponting's memorialisation took over twenty years provides a timeline and taxonomy of the emergence of what we know as 'documentary'.[17]

The Great White Silence (1924).

During this period, films recording exploration in remote places became a major attraction. Frank Hurley's *Endurance* (1919) recorded another Antarctic expedition, by Ernest Shackleton in 1914, which included an impressive drama of survival and rescue. Robert Flaherty's gently humorous account of Inuit life in northern Canada, *Nanook of the North* (1922), proved a surprise worldwide box-office success, and two films of tribal life by Merian C. Cooper and Ernest Schoedsack, *Grass* (1924) and *Chang* (1927), were similarly successful as theatrical releases. The cost of later expeditions, such as those to climb Everest or penetrate distant lands, could henceforth be partly covered by the anticipated returns on film releases. Eventually television would adapt the forms of these pioneer works to its programme formats.

Street Scenes

Cinema and city life were closely linked from the outset as regular venues developed in large population centres. The Russian poet Alexandr Blok confessed to an early fascination when he wrote to a friend in 1904 to apologise for missing an appointment: 'Yesterday I set off for your place, but suddenly I noticed that cinema on the Liteyny, and went in and watched the pictures for about an hour... There is a kind of city mystery here, like hidden ambushes'.[18] What those 'ambushed' in this way initially saw were the city streets they had just left. The marvel was that this kaleidoscope of action could be captured in all its detail and played back in an eerie silence or with musical accompaniment. Street scenes were among the Lumières' and Paul's first subjects. Taken initially in Lyon and Paris and in London, these were enough to fascinate the first viewers.[19]

Such city scenes came later in America due to Edison's early reliance on his Black Maria studio in West Orange, but soon there were evocative images of American city streets.

Some of these were so striking that they were restaged decades later, such as the Biograph view of a teeming *Lower Broadway* (1903), which would inspire a scene in Martin Scorsese's *The Age of Innocence*. Edison's *What Happened on 23rd Street, NYC* (1901) is clearly contrived to show a young lady who suddenly finds her skirt lifted by a draft from a sidewalk grating – an image that irresistibly recalls the gag with Marilyn Monroe in Billy Wilder's *The Seven Year Itch* (1955). And when we discover that Biograph's *At the Foot of the Flatiron* (1903) was taken at this notoriously windy Manhattan location to produce a similar view of women's ankles, there is clearly more staging involved in these early street scenes than modern viewers realise.

A theme that was discussed in one of the earliest studies of urban life was the city dweller's rapid assumption of a condescending attitude towards his country cousin.[20] Making fun of 'rubes' was indeed a frequent theme in early American comic-strips as well as films. *Rubes in the Theatre* (Edison, 1901) shows two countrymen overreacting to a show and being laughed at by their neighbours, while *Rube and Mandy at Coney Island* (Edison, 1903) offered a tour of the amusement park in the company of a couple who stuff themselves with hot dogs.

Like the rube, new immigrants were also regular figures of fun at the turn of the century, resulting in films such as *A Gesture Fight in Hester Street* (Biograph, 1900), where two peddlers fight for the same pitch, and *Levi and Cohen, the Irish Comedians* (Biograph, 1903), in which the aspiring performers are pelted with tomatoes.

More brashly insensitive humour based on ethnic stereotypes appears in Biograph's *Hot Mutton Pies* (1903), in which two boys discover that what they have just bought from a pig-tailed Chinese man are 'cat pies', while the gruesomely comic explosion in *A Catastrophe in Hester Street* (Biograph, 1904) appears to have been caused by drunken foreign anarchists. In 1975, Joan Micklin Silver could recreate this epicentre of Eastern European immigration in her *Hester Street*, based on a novella subtitled 'A Tale of the New York Ghetto'.[21]

What Happened on 23rd Street.

The Fascination of Lowlife

A sub-genre that seems to have been unique to early American cinema was the 'tourist view' of New York's sordid under-world. *Rube in an Opium Joint* (Biograph, 1905), made by D. W. Griffith's future cameraman Billy Bitzer, showed a middle-aged couple being ushered into an opium den by an enthusiastic tour guide with a megaphone. After a trial puff on an opium pipe, the man prefers his own pipe, and the pair leave. This turns out to be a scene from a longer film released in the same year, *Lifting the Lid*, which starts with a busload of sightseers in a busy New York street. Their guide then takes a couple through a series of lowlife encounters, each arranged as a studio-based set piece, of which the opium den is one.

Such tours did, in fact, take place, not only in New York, but in Paris and London, offering 'respectable' visitors a chance to observe the decadent pleasures of the metropolis in safety. But that they should have been staged as films in the United States perhaps underlines the gulf between country and city in this largely immigrant society. On a more traditional moral plane, Biograph's *The Downward Path* (1902) chronicles a country girl being dragged into big-city vice, as her aged parents try to rescue her. By the end of the decade, innocents being trafficked and recruited into prostitution had become a major theme under the generic term 'white slavery', with a succession of films seeking to exploit prurient interest under the guise of exposing its operation. One surviving title from this genre, *Traffic in Souls* (George Loane Tucker, 1913) has attracted extensive scholarship, focused on its innovative ways of showing police wiretapping and surveillance techniques to gather evidence against the traffickers.[22]

Crime Pays
Many of the earliest fiction films were in fact portrayals of crime, reflecting a late 19th-century trend in popular fiction. In Britain, Birt Acres made *Arrest of a Pickpocket* for the Kinetoscope in 1895, while his erstwhile partner Robert Paul made a number of crime subjects – often with a comedy twist – as in *Robbery* (1897), where a man is forced to hand over his clothes at gunpoint, and *His Brave Defender* (1900), in which a wife tackles a burglar while her husband hides. But two genres dominated early screen crime portrayal: detective heroes and criminal gangs. The fictional American private detective Nick Carter became the protagonist in three French series between 1908 and 1909, starting with Victorin Jasset's *Nick Carter, King of Detectives* (1908), while France also launched the urban crime syndicate mystery with Jasset's *Zigomar* (1911), followed by Louis Feuillade's *Fantômas* series, both of which enjoyed wide international success and influenced the rising generation of filmmakers and avant-garde artists.

The models pioneered by Jasset and Feuillade were also taken up and soon imitated elsewhere in Europe: *Dr. Gar El Hama* (1911) in Denmark; *Lieutenant Daring* (1911) *Three-Fingered Kate* (Martinek, 1909-13) and the *Ultus* series (Pearson, 1916) in the UK; *Tigris* (1913) and the *Za La Mort* series (1914-24) in Italy. But it was Pathé's American branch that took the multipart serial to new levels of worldwide popularity with its production of *The Perils of Pauline* (1914), followed by many successors featuring plucky heroines, making the cliffhanger serial a key American export during the 1910s and 1920s.

Postwar Germany saw the emergence of its own distinctive crime syndicate genre headed by Fritz Lang's *The Spiders* (1919-20) and *Dr. Mabuse, the Gambler* (1922). And perhaps surprisingly, early Soviet cinema also bore the imprint of French and American serials in such films as Sergei Eisenstein's *The Strike* (1924) and Lev Kuleshov's *The Extraordinary Adventures of Mr. West in the Land of the Bolsheviks* (1924), as well as the first projects of a Petersburg group, the Factory of the Eccentric Actor (FEKS).[23] Today the eerie worlds of Feuillade's and Lang's thrillers, in which surreal events unfold in banal settings, are probably best known from their reimagining in such René Magritte paintings as *Le barbare* (1928) and *Le retour de flamme* (1943).

Gender Trouble

The rise of cinema coincided with changing attitudes towards women's rights on many levels. While the earliest moving pictures showed traditional images of female dancers (Moore, Carmencita), there would soon be subjects reflecting what Britain's *Daily Mail* described in 1900 as 'the athletic young woman'. While Biograph's *The Physical Culture Lesson* (1906) ended with an instructor embracing his student, *The Athletic Girl and the Burglar* (Biograph, 1905) showed the girl knocking out an intruder.

Alongside such light-hearted treatments of women's new lifestyles – women cycling was another popular subject – campaigns for political rights attracted notably hostile treatment in a number of early films. A British film from 1900 showed a pair of young men clandestinely nailing the skirts of two women to a fence, and catalogue text reveals this was a satire on women's militancy: 'Now behold the champions of women's every right'.[24] In France, Alice Guy, widely celebrated today as a pioneer female filmmaker, made a 1906 satire, *The Consequences of Feminism*, which mocked gender roles being reversed. And with a militant suffrage campaign under way in Britain that included Emily Davison throwing herself under the king's horse in a race in 1913 (widely seen in newsreel coverage), a comedy made in the same year, *Milling the Militants* (Clarendon, 1913), has a man dreaming of setting suffragettes like his wife to work mending roads.

It would be unwise to draw general conclusions from such pointed examples, considering how many titles from the early period have been lost, but there can be no question that 'the woman question' was reflected in much production of the pre-1914 period, both satirically and, less often, sympathetically. The suffrage movement in Britain made considerable use of films of its spectacular demonstrations as publicity. And the sheer volume of images of 'new women' to be found across the production of every country – from Biograph's *Gibson Goddess* (1909) to Asta Nielsen's many 'modern' roles – made cinema an important forum for displaying and perhaps debating this worldwide social movement.

Moving, Making and Microscopes

Film emerged simultaneously with the beginnings of revolutionary new forms of transport that would shape the 20th century. Both automobiles and flying machines made early screen appearances, and the new perspectives they offered – the speeding vehicle and the aerial view – would become an essential part of the new medium's visual rhetoric.

Processes of manufacture were also undergoing dramatic change in the early period of film production – indeed, film itself was an early part of that third industrial revolution, using new materials and machinery to create a distinctive new business based on selling experience. Films showing new processes of construction and production were widely seen in the years before 1914; the Westinghouse series of actualities made in 1904 is an early example of a major company displaying its industrial wares on film, showing these at various expositions as well as to employees and the public. From Europe there were notable early 'industrials', such as *A Visit to Peak Frean & Co's Biscuit Works* (1906) and a large number of films that showed modern methods transforming traditional industries, such as fishing, in *Fish Factory in Astrakhan* (Russia, 1906; imported by Pathé to the US), and *Whaling Afloat and Ashore* (Paul, 1908).

Popular science films were an important early genre that gained wide exposure in entertainment programmes. The technique that produced especially spectacular results was photomicrography, making minute organisms and processes visible on the large screen. Urban's series *The Unseen World* pioneered this genre in 1903, with its presenter, Francis Martin Duncan, delivering *Cheese Mites,* 'the sensation of the first public programme of scientific films at the Alhambra Music Hall in 1903'.[25] Another key technique that made scientific film widely attractive was stop-motion, used to show natural processes 'accelerated'. Again, it was Urban who realised the appeal of these subjects and recruited the naturalist Percy Smith to produce such films as *The Acrobatic Fly* and *The Birth of a Flower* (both 1910). After his early association with Urban, Smith went on to produce his hugely popular *Secrets of Nature* series in the 1920s. Like sports and travel, this important early genre would pass over to television to become a staple of factual programming.

The World That Movies Made
What did the coming of cinema mean at the start of the 20th century? One consequence, widely realised towards the end of the first decade, was connecting and even synchronising habits and interests around the world. Audiences in widely separated continents might be watching the same images and sharing the similar emotions. Pathé, which had established branches in many countries that would soon promote local production as well as bringing its own French output to a global audience, had as its trademark an image of the founders 'conquering the world'. Soon the baton would pass from Pathé and Gaumont to companies such as the Danish Nordisk and Italy's Ambrosio and Cines,

before American producers decisively took control of world film distribution networks around 1916.[26]

Robert Paul's *Whaling Afloat and Ashore* (1908), about the Norwegian whaling industry off Ireland, looks forward to future documentary and 'industrial' films.

Creative artists in other media began to realise the potential of this upstart new industry. The Russian dramatist Leonid Andreyev wrote in 1911 about how it had long been scorned by intellectuals and sophisticates, while embraced by the masses. But it was time to recognise what cinema had become, he argued:

> If the highest and most sacred aim of art is to instigate contact between people and their individual souls, then what an enormous, unimaginable socio-psychological role is destined to be played by this artistic Apache of the present! What is there to compare with it: aerial flight, the telegraph and the telephone, even the press itself?... Having no language, being equally intelligible to the savages of St. Petersburg and the savages of Calcutta, it truly becomes the genius of international contact, brings the ends of the earth and the spheres of souls nearer and gathers the whole of quivering humanity into a single stream.[27]

A year earlier, Leo Tolstoy had confessed to Andreyev that he was 'thinking about cinema', and had decided that, if he had time, he wanted to write for it because it was 'understandable to huge masses of all nations'.[28] And Tolstoy was not alone among established authors in believing that the future of reaching large audiences lay with cinema: in Britain, for instance, H. G. Wells, H. Rider Haggard, George Bernard Shaw, John Galsworthy, James Barrie and many other writers were all looking forward to the possibility of writing for the screen – or being able to sell their existing work for adaptation.

By 1920, in the aftermath of the Great War, cinema's foundational place in modern life across the globe was assured, and the dominant producers were based in America. The films of Chaplin, Griffith, and Cecil B. DeMille were seen and admired worldwide. Other national industries had to adjust to surviving in the shadow of the American studios' massive presence on their screens.

Material Traces

As we trace the progression of early moving pictures to the mainstream international cinema that had emerged by 1920, it's important to recall the spatial and material contexts in which this took place. From around 1907, buildings dedicated to showing film programmes began to appear all over the world. What had previously been variety or vaudeville theatres became cinemas, and in the U.S. movie theatres, often operating twelve or more hours per day and catering to exceptionally diverse audiences. Children and immigrants were among the new audiences, attracted to the anonymity and easily understood entertainment cheaply on offer. The rapid increase in scale of newly built urban 'picture palaces' is astonishing; from capacities of less than five hundred in the nickelodeon era, new theatres were seating over two thousand by the time super-productions such as *Quo Vadis?* and the film it inspired, Griffith's *The Birth of a Nation*, arrived in the early teens.[29]

Few of these structures survive today, except where they have achieved heritage status, like the Tuchinski in Amsterdam (1921) and Grauman's Egyptian Theatre in Los Angeles (1922), or have been converted to other uses.[30] But the construction of increasingly lavish movie theatres during the first half of the 20th century had a significant and lasting impact on the urban landscape of many countries. London's West End Leicester Square, which saw the first Lumière and Paul screenings in its major music halls in 1896, has remained the focus of screen entertainment in the city, with redeveloped venues catering to new styles of programming in multiplexes, and the Odeon Leicester Square (1937) remaining as a monument to the heroic age of cinema-building.

Cinema-going, however, has always encompassed much more than customers and buildings. Aspects of décor, ancillary products (snacks and drinks), and audience behaviour have been central to the experience and its legacy in 20th-century culture. While these elements have formed the subject of important studies, such as Robert Allen's *Going to the Movies: Hollywood and the Social Experience of Cinema*, they are more adequately covered in online resources, such as Allen's *Going to the Show*, an online digital resource documenting the history of moviegoing in North Carolina, and Luke McKernan's wide-ranging anthology of cinema experience, *Picturegoing*.[31]

Star Values
Filmgoers, unsurprisingly, were attracted to many of the figures they saw on-screen from an early stage. Traditionally the emergence of 'film stars' has been dated to around 1910, when American producers began to identify their actors by name and promote their popularity in pictorial media. The classic text on this phenomenon is Richard deCordova's *Picture Personalities: The Emergence of the Star System in America* (1990), which focused on the promotion of Florence Lawrence, the Gish sisters, and Mary Pickford. However, deCordova's account clearly needs some updating in at least two respects. Long before 'the first film stars', many figures already famous for various reasons appeared in early film, lending prestige and popularity to the medium. Many of these were established actors, vaudeville and music hall stars, who were often paid large sums to appear on-screen. One early example is Harry Lauder's lucrative 1902 contract with Gaumont for films synchronised with disc recordings. Secondly, while American films were fast becoming the most widely shown around the world from 1910 to 1914, there is a good case for identifying the Danish actor Asta Nielsen as the first truly global film star. An international research project led by Martin Loiperdinger brought together data from many countries around the world to reveal Nielsen's extraordinary popularity.[32]

Paper Cinema
The publicity culture of cinema played a major part in the wider media revolution that began around 1900, extending far beyond the attraction of the films themselves. Picture postcards, cigarette cards, posters and lobby-cards, and fan magazines – all of these new graphic media of the era catered to a growing population of movie-obsessed young people. The case of picture postcards is particularly significant, as this was a new medium that emerged at almost the same time as film, and 'star portraits' was one of its most popular

genres. I have suggested in a comparative study of postcards of early stars that the numbers of these images may be a way of estimating relative popularity in the early years of cinema.[33] Many such items have since become valuable collectables, and for years they remained unseen in private collections. But today they are widely viewable online, making accessible the culture of cinema at the peak of its influence.

Digital History
Digital resources not only make large amounts of cinema heritage material newly accessible, they have also made much of the industry's material residues more visible than most cinema museums created during the 20th century. See, for instance, the searchable collection at Exeter University, UK.[34] For periodicals, see the large digitised and searchable holdings of the Media History Digital Library.[35] Digital techniques are also central to most restoration of early film, allowing fragmentary and fragile material to be widely shared – and even sometimes projected on the scale that it was originally shown, as in the case of the large collection of Biograph 68mm titles held by the Dutch Eye Filmmuseum archive, material that has been shown in many festivals around the world in recent years.

Perhaps the most important revelation of the twenty-first century, as far as cinema is concerned, has been that the celluloid medium's early decades are now best displayed and studied by digital means. Thanks to searchable online collections of films, along with associated paper documentation and publicity materials, new kinds of empirical study are possible, in place of what were often impressionistic assertions during the early decades of cinema studies. Film has always been a complex phenomenon, with its material elements forming only part of the wider cultural impact that it has exerted for more than 120 years.

Assembling the elements for serious study has always been difficult, with materials held in a wide variety of collections and archives, or seemingly lost. Now coordinated online access, such as that provided by the MEP Early Cinema Compendium, promises exciting new opportunities for empirically grounded study and research, based on the consultation of digitised original materials. The challenge will be to frame new hypotheses and to challenge long-held assumptions and prejudices, just as FIAF's Brighton congress of 1978 – but now to make full use of the wealth of historical evidence and digital resources we have, to deepen and refine the history of the medium that mirrored and shaped the modern world.

Epilogue

28.
Strange Meeting:
They Shall Not Grow Old

Re-presenting archive film has always been risky, except when it's too dull to stir any emotion. I remember the condescension that hung over the first presentation of Kevin Brownlow's reconstructed *Napoleon* in 1982, when the idea of piecing together this battered and much-reviled carcass, with a patchwork orchestral score, seemed absurd to many. But as one of the visiting archivists, Jacques Ledoux, said: 'It shouldn't work, yet somehow it does'. And later, Bill Morrison's and Peter Delpeut's first films collaged from decaying nitrate fragments could rouse archivists to fury, for celebrating the decay they deplored.[36]

Now Peter Jackson's strange, experimental collage of First World War footage faces a new scepticism on many fronts. Few critics I've read (and many are friends and respected colleagues) want to disapprove outright of digital colourisation (which of course destroys nothing) – but they find it 'badly done', even 'disrespectful', and many disapprove strongly of Jackson's zooming in on detail, and overall reframing. Much of the criticism argues that this treatment of the archival footage renders it 'less real' than in its more familiar black and white academy ratio forms.

I beg to differ. Seeing *They Shall Not Grow Old* in a public screening at the Phoenix Cinema in North London (in 2D, and after a heated meeting to debate the cinema's future), I found myself launched on a reflective journey into another distant realm that Jackson has created. We begin in a simulated 'archival' register, with monochrome footage imperfectly speed-corrected on a small screen, recalling how most will previously have seen such material. There's nothing 'real' about it, except that this is how such footage has been shown during the last fifty-odd years. In fact, if you want to come close to the 'reality' of the Western Front, the numerous stereo photographs taken in the trenches will still take you there with a shocking immediacy.

But after this prelude, accompanied by voices reminiscing about the build-up to embarkation for the front, we too are transported to this ghastly, yet mundane world. It's not grey and silent, as Gorky described the eeriness of his first encounter with film in 1896. It's a world we are visiting, with the filters of monochrome and archaic framing removed, and within a sound tapestry that includes both the 'real' (even if not contemporary) and the revoiced reminiscent. More like Virginia Woolf's account of the eeriness of being present in scenes which are independent of us, while their denizens constantly acknowledge our presence by performing to camera.[37]

Jackson has fashioned his film as a visit to this distant world, in which too many of our forefathers spent months and even years. By the time we leave it, in the film's coda, we understand all too well why few of the returning ghosts wanted to speak of it. They quickly discovered that no one who had not been part of it could understand the experience, and, in fact, that few wanted to know, before the first round of filmic recreation began a decade later. But we have been on a surreal visit, sharpened and enhanced by the novelty of flesh, dirt and the blood and mutilation that we were long shielded from by censorship (although not always in painting, as the 2018 Tate Britain exhibition *Aftermath* revealed).

What seems strange to me is the concentration in commentary on pseudo-technical criticism, avoiding the larger issues of how we can relate to this distant era that clearly intrigued its maker. Blood, flesh and grass the 'wrong colours'? Snide remarks about Jackson as a 'fantasy' filmmaker. More relevant would be considering the very different status of First World War memorialisation in his native New Zealand, where it remains a cornerstone of national identity. And even more relevant would be the considerations that emerge from Catherine Russell's important new book *Archiveology*, which takes Walter Benjamin as its guide through the varieties of contemporary archival practice.[38] Few of the filmmakers discussed by Russell – ranging from Angela Ricci Lucchi and Yervant Gianikian, creators of *From the Pole to the Equator*, to such diverse figures as Joseph Cornell, Morgan Fisher, Harun Farocki and Gustav Deutsch – have considered archival material a sacred text. Instead, they treat it as 'second nature', material traces of the past that are available for contemporary renegotiation, making use of what Jaimie Baron has termed 'the archive effect'.[39]

Tellingly, Russell pinpoints the difficulty in classifying the diverse forms of 'archival effect' films that digital production offers us. 'Compilation', 'found footage', 'collage' – all invoke historic moments in working with pre-existing footage. Currently we favour 'essay' as a capacious category, with the option of a qualifying 'avant-garde' or 'experimental'. But the truth is that we are living in an age of proliferating formal invention, although the circumstances of Jackson's project seem to have limited discussion of the film's form as other than 'memorial'.[40]

'Reaching through the fog of time'. Promotional image for Peter Jackson's elaborate reworking of World War One footage in *They Shall Not Grow Old*, (2018), which controversially colourised archival material and added sound, 3D and dubbed speech based on lip-reading speakers in the original footage.

Russell's stimulating survey is laced with quotations from Benjamin's never-completed archival project 'The Arcades', and one of these seems apposite to *They Shall not Grow Old*: 'At any given time, the living see themselves in the midday of history. They are obliged to prepare a banquet for the past. The historian is the herald who invites the dead to the table'. Jackson's project seems to me truly phantasmagoric, in Benjamin's terms. A 'strange meeting', to invoke Wilfred Owen's unforgettable image, with archival ghosts in our digital midday.

Originally in *Sight and Sound* online Digital Bulletin, 2018.

Endnotes

Online links were included when many of the essays in *What Made Cinema?* were originally published. While some of those specific URLs are by now inaccessible and so not included in the notes that follow, readers should nonetheless be able to find online many of the films discussed in this book. Notable resources include the BFI Player, The Media Ecology Project at Dartmouth College, my Gresham College lectures, from 2017-21 (https://www.gresham.ac.uk/speakers/professor-ian-christie), and, of course, on YouTube.

Introduction: Back to the Future

1   See 'Immersion – new media and old ambitions', *Journal of the British Academy*, vol. 12, issue 1-2, 2004.
2   I hope that work related to this, and to other interests in European and Russian cinema, will appear in further collections of essays.
3   Accompanied by a book, *The Last Machine* (BFI/BBC, 1994), the series was co-produced by the BFI and Illuminations, in partnership with VPRO Netherlands, and transmitted in various countries..
4   For a summary of this work at Birkbeck see REF Impact statement, 'London Screen Studies Collection: bring London's film heritage to light'.
5   See essays in two books I edited for the Key Debates series with Amsterdam University Press, both on open access at www.aup.nl: *Audiences* (2012) and *Stories* (2018).
6   Walter Benjamin, *The Arcades Project*, trans. Howard Eiland and Kevin McLaughlin (Cambridge, MA: Belknap Press, 1999)., 481.

1. Toys, Instruments, Machines: Why the Hardware Matters

1   Hollis Frampton, 'For a Metahistory of Film,' in *Circles of Confusion: Film, Photography, Video, Texts 1968-1980* (Visual Studies Workshop, 1983), 112.
2   One of the many virtues of Yuri Tsivian's study of the cultural reception of early cinema in Russia is his treatment of 'the reception of interference, covering film damage, breakdown, extraneous noise and the like', revealing that this was as much a part of the experience as supposedly seamless illusion. See Tsivian, *Early Cinema in Russia and its Cultural Reception* (Routledge, 1994), chapter 4.
3   This essay was based on a presentation given in 2003, as part of a conference at the University of Exeter, organised by the AHRB Centre for British Film and Television Studies. The university houses the Bill Douglas Museum, which has a fine collection of kaleidoscopes among many other historic 'toys' and gadgets, some of which were displayed on the occasion of the lecture. The essay first appeared in in a collection: James Lyons and John Plunkett, eds., *Multimedia Histories: From the Magic Lantern to the Internet* (Exeter, 2007).

4   On early conceptions of the phonograph, see Ian Christie, 'Early Phonograph Culture and Moving Pictures', in Richard Abel and Rick Altman, eds, *The Sounds of Early Cinema* (Indiana, 2001), 3-12. On electricity as a spectacle, see Carolyn Marvin, *When Old Technologies Were New* (Oxford, 1988).
5   'The Cinematograph', *The Times*, 22 February 1896, 15.
6   'The Month: Science and Arts', *Chambers' Journal*, 25 April 1896.
7   'Lantern Mems', *The Lantern Record, Supplement to the British Journal of Photography*, 1 May 1896, 33.
8   After the original launch of the phonograph in 1878, Edison relaunched this as the 'Perfected Phonograph' in 1888, stimulated by the appearance of a rival sound recording system, the graphophone. See Paul Israel, *Edison: A Life of Invention* (John Wiley, 1998), 288-302. He would subsequently appropriate other inventions by claiming to have 'perfected' these, as in the case of x-rays (Israel, 309) and the projector acquired from Thomas Armat and renamed the Edison Vitascope, publicly hailed in The New York Herald (4 April 1896) as 'the Kinetoscope perfected'. Quoted in Terry Ramsaye, *A Million and One Nights* (1926) (Simon and Schuster, 1986), 227.
9   The phrase appears in a report on Edison's Vitascope by Joseph MacMahon in the *Sidney Bulletin* of 12 September 1896, quoted by Deac Rossell in his introductory notes to the invaluable 'Chronology of Cinema 1889-1896', *Film History*, 7:2, Summer 1995, 118. Later updated and published as *Chronology of the Birth of Cinema 1836-1896* (John Libbey, 2022).
10 'Edison's Vitascope Cheered', *The New York Times*, 24 April 1896, 5; quoted in Charles Musser, *Before the Nickelodeon: Edwin S. Porter and the Edison Manufacturing Company* (California, 1991), 61.
11 'Instrument', *Oxford English Dictionary* (1910), Vol. 5
12 *Webster's Revised Unabridged Dictionary* (1913).
13 See Jim Endersby, 'Classifying Sciences: Systematics and Status in mid-Victorian Natural History', in Martin Daunton, ed., *The Organisation of Knowledge in Victorian Britain* (Oxford, 2005), 61-85.
14 Toy, II. 6, *Oxford English Dictionary* (1910), Vol. 10.
15 John Baptist Porta (Giambattista della Porta), *Natural Magick* (Thomas Young and Samuel Speed, 1658), First Book, chapter 2, 'What is the nature of Magick?' This was the first English edition of della Porta's *Magia Naturalis*, originally published in Naples, 1558. For biographical and bibliographic clarification, see Louise Clubb, *Giambattista della Porta, Dramatist* (Princeton, 1965), chapter 1.
16 See, for instance, Yates' essay 'The Hermetic Tradition in Renaissance Science' (1967), in Frances A. Yates, *Ideas and Ideals in the North European Renaissance: Collected Essays* (Routledge, 1984), 227-46.
17 Anon., 'A True Description and Direction of what is Most Worthy to be Seen in all Italy, in W. Oldys (ed.), *The Harleian Miscellany* (R. Dutton, 1810), Vol. 5, 31. Quoted in Vaughan Hart, *Art and Magic in the Court of the Stuarts* (Routledge, 1994), 93.
18 On these automata, see Shelby T. McCloy, *French Inventions of the Eighteenth Century* (Kentucky, 1952), 108. On automata, see Silvio A. Bedini, 'The Role of Automata in the History of Technology', *Technology and Culture*, 5:1 (1964), 24-42; also Bedini, *Patrons, Artisans and Instruments of Science, 1600-1750* (Ashgate, 1999) and Dan North, 'From

Android to Synthespian: The Performance of Artificial Life', in *Multimedia Histories*, 93-96.

19 Derek J. de Solla Price, 'Automata and the Origins of Mechanism and Mechanistic Philosophy', *Technology and Culture*, 5:1 (1964), 9-23

20 Daniel Tiffany, *Toy Medium: Materialism and Modern Lyric* (California, 2000), 44.

21 Reading this in 2024, I would want to qualify referring to magic lantern images as 'static'. Moving elements within them, in 'slipping slides', and the slides as a whole, was and remains an integral part of magic lantern performance. Looking at peep-shows also invol. ves movement of hand and head. So early kinetic toys should properly be regarded as expanding what was already inherent in the tradition.

22 Roget's paper was read to the Royal Society of London in December 1824 and published in the Philosophical Transactions, 115 (1825), 131-40; Faraday's paper to the Royal Institution was given on 10 December 1830 and published as 'On a peculiar class of optical deceptions', in the *Journal of the Royal Institution*, 1 (1831), 205-23. For a discussion of these, and of the intervening contribution of Joseph Plateau, see Laurent Mannoni, *The Great Art of Light and Shadow*, trans. Richard Crangle (Exeter, 2000), 199-220.

23 Charles Wheatstone, 'Description of the kaleidophone or phonic kaleidoscope: a new philosophical toy, for the illustration of several interesting and amusing acoustical and optical phenomena', *Quarterly Journal of Science, Literature and Art*, 23 (1827), 344.

24 David Brewster, 'A Treatise on the Kaleidoscope (Archibald Constable and Co., 1819), 1.

25 Brewster *Treatise*, 133.

26 Nicholas Jardine notes that 'there are... remarkable continuities over several centuries in the traditions of practices and competences associated with microscopes, telescopes and surveying instruments'. See Jardine, *The Scenes of Inquiry: On the Reality of Questions in the Sciences* (Oxford, 1991), 166.

27 Jonathan Crary, *Techniques of the Observer: On Vision and Modernity in the Nineteenth Century* (MIT, 1992), 116.

28 Carpet making was an important industry in Kilmarnock, Dundee, Glasgow and other Scottish towns and cities in the eighteenth century, before Joseph Marie Jacquard's invention of the mechanical loom in 1801, controlled by punched cards, ushered in a new vogue for complex patterns.

29 Lecture by Helen Weston on the image of the lantern in 18th-century France at the 'Lantern Projections' symposium, British Academy, February 2001; and in a paper, 'Magic Lanterns in Revolutionary France: Where Street and Salon Intersect', Association of Art Historians Annual Conference, 2004.

30 Karl Marx and Friedrich Engels, *The German Ideology* (1846), quoted in Crary, *Techniques of the Observer*, 114.

31 Charles Baudelaire, 'The Painter of Modern Life' (1859-60) in P. E. Charvet (ed. and trans.), *Baudelaire: Selected Writings on Art and Artists* (Penguin, 1972), 400. Also quoted, in a different translation, by Crary, 113.

32 The concept of *mentalité* was central to the work of the *Annales* historians of cultural and material history in France. For a brief account and guide to further reading, see Peter Burke, *What Is Cultural History?* (Polity, 2004), 4.

33 Charles Baudelaire, Morale du joujou' [Moral of the toy] (1853), in Baudelaire, *Œuvres complètes* (Gallimard, 1961), 527-28.

34 Crary claimed that the phenakistoscope and stereoscope 'eventually disappeared' (*Techniques of the Observer*, 132), apparently ignoring the persistence and constant reinvention of such devices which continues today. Most museum and art gallery shops still sell versions of the stereoscope and Kinetoscope. I have before me a 'Naturescope', manufactured by Werkhaus Gmbh in Germany in 2001.

35 André Gide, *If I Die: An Autobiography* (*Si le grain meurt*, 1926), trans. Dorothy Bussy (Random House, 1935), 6-7.

36 On optical aspects of Proust's *A la recherche du temps perdu* (1913-27) and James Joyce's *Ulysses* (1922), both set at the turn of the century, see, most recently, Sarah Danius, *The Senses of Modernism: Technology, Perception and Aesthetics* (Cornell, 2002).

37 Dolf Sternberger, *Panorama of the Nineteenth Century* (1955), trans. Joachin Neugroschel (Urizen, 1977), 131-63. Sternberger's focus is on the German interior, but see also research undertaken under the auspices of the AHRB Centre for the Study of the Domestic Interior.

38 Robert-Houdin was the stage name of Jean Eugène Robert (1805-71), the son of a watchmaker and one of the pioneers of modern, technologically enhanced magic. His 'light and heavy chest' trick, used to trounce the Algerian Marabout folk magicians, relied on a concealed electromagnet. For an effective fictionalized account of this episode, see Brian Moore's novel *The Magician's Wife* (Flamingo, 1998).

39 The monologue was first published in Browning's collection *Dramatis Personae* in 1864, which followed the death of his wife Elizabeth Barrett Browning, who had been a believer in spiritualism.

40 E. Jentsch's work on the uncanny was Freud's starting point for a psychoanalytic interpretation of the sources of this feeling. See Sigmund Freud, 'The Uncanny', in James Strachey, ed. and trans., *Standard Edition of the Complete Psychological Works of Sigmund Freud* (Hogarth, 1955), Vol. 17, 217-56. See also my discussion of Freud's essay in a later essay, 'Unhoused: On the American Spaces of *Nomadland*' (Amsterdam, 2024), 121-22.

41 All recorded as actual or potential responses to the 'realism' of the new media of the late 19th century.

42 Price, 'Automata', 15.

43 See introduction to Paul's catalogue, *Apparatus for the Elementary Electrical Laboratory*, London and New York, 1914, Section S. Also on his career in general, Christie, *Robert Paul and the Origins of British Cinema* (Chicago, 2019).

44 Many of Paul's electrical instruments were made for the growing science education market, rather than for industrial use.

45 On other aspects of his career, see R.W. Paul, contribution to 'Before 1910: Kinematograph Experiences', *Proceedings of the British Kinematograph Society*, 38, 1936, 6.

46 Jules Carpentier (1851-1921), who began his engineering career in railways, also manufactured the first Branly radio-wave detector tubes in 1900. For a brief account of his career and relationship with Louis Lumière, see *Auguste and Louis Lumière, Letters: Inventing the Cinema*, trans. Pierre Hodgson, with annotation by Jacques Rittaud-Hutinet (Faber, 1995), 26.

47 André Bazin, 'The Myth of Total Cinema' (1946), in A. Bazin, *What Is Cinema?*, ed. and trans. Hugh Gray (California, 1967), 17 Bazin's essay was

actually a review of the first volume of Georges Sadoul's *Histoire générale du cinéma*, which countered Sadoul's "Marxist views' by proposing a 'paradoxical' reversal of 'the order of historical causality, which goes from the ideological infrastructure to the ideological superstructure' (17). Apart from caricaturing Marxist thought, Bazin's now-canonic essay misrepresents many cinema pioneers and completely ignores the continuum of illusory arts.

48 Christian Metz, 'On the Impression of Reality in the Cinema', in C. Metz, *Film Language: A Semiotics of the Cinema*, trans. Michael Taylor (Oxford, 1974), 4.

49 Laurent Mannoni, 'The Art of Deception', in *Eyes, Lies and Illusions*, eds. Laurent Mannoni, Werner Nekes and Marina Warner (Hayward Gallery and Lund Humphries, 2004), 41-52.

2. Moving Picture Media and Modernity: Taking Intermediate and Ephemeral Media Seriously

1 http://www.deadmedia.org/notes/0/004.html.

2 The five-part series, presented by Terry Gilliam and co-produced by the British Film Institute and Illuminations, with VPRO Netherlands, was transmitted on BBC 2 in 1995. The related book was Ian Christie, *The Last Machine* (BBC/BFI, 1994).

3 The phrases come from the Introduction to such a wide-ranging survey: Leo Charney and Vanessa R. Schwartz, eds., *Cinema and the Invention of Modern Life* (California, 1995), 1

4 Tom Gunning, 'Then Whole Town's Gawking: Early Cinema and the Visual Experience of Modernity', *Yale Journal of Criticism*, Vol. 7, no. 2, 1994, 189-201.

5 Gunning's widely quoted 'The Cinema of Attractions: Early Film, Its Spectator and the Avant-Garde' first appeared in *Wide Angle* Vol. 8, no 3/4, Fall 1986, 63-70; and is most easily found in Thomas Elsaesser and Adam Barker, eds., *Early Cinema: Space, Frame, Narrative* (BFI, 1990), 56-62.

6 Gunning, 'The Whole Town's Gawking', 192

7 David Bordwell, *On the History of Film Style* (Harvard, 1997), 125-127, 144-149.

8 See for instance, the discussion of its influence, in Wanda Strauven, ed, *The Cinema of Attractions Reloaded* (Amsterdam, 2007).

9 As example of spectator-based work, see Luke McKernan, "Only the Screen Was Silent": Memories of Children's Cinemagoing in London before the First World War', *Film Studies* 10, Spring 2007, 1-20.; also *Going to the movies: Hollywood and the Social Experience of Cinema*, eds Richard Maltby, Melvyn Stokes and Robert C. Allen (Exeter, 2007).

10 While this was a mainstay of earlier histories of film, it also reappears in one of the key texts of the 'new film history', Noël Burch, *Life to Those Shadows*, trans. Ben Brewster (BFI, 1990), 9.

11 The Dead Media Project (http://www.deadmedia.org/index.html). From internal evidence, this appears to have been created largely between 1999-2001.

12 The catalyst of much modern 'media theory' was Marshall McLuhan, especially in his *Understanding Media: The Extensions of Man* (Routledge, 1964). The German media theorist Friedrich Kittler has also been influential, since the translation of his *Gramophone, Film, Typewriter*, Stanford, CA: Stanford University Press, 1999. The science-fiction writers William Gibson

and others have fostered a genre known as 'cyberpunk', in which media theory, new technology and social dislocation come together. Examples are Gibson's novel *Neuromancer* (1964) and Ridley Scott's film *Blade Runner* (1982).

13 Indeed, there has been a reduction of these, at least in the UK, with the closing of the British Film Institute's Museum of the Moving Image, and the move of the Science Museum's pre-cinema display from London to Bradford's National Science and Media Museum in 2005, as well as the sale of the Barnes Collection to Turin's Museo Nazionale del Cinema.

14 An example of such displays would be the Early Photography section of the Science Museum in London, set up in the early 1970s. The British Film Institute's Museum of the Moving Image (1988-99) also essentially endorsed this 'story of cinema'. It is an account that was labelled 'the Basic Story' in David Bordwell, *History of Film Style*, Chapter 2.

15 The Bill Douglas Cinema Museum at the University of Exeter houses the Bill Douglas/Peter Jewell Collection . Most national cinematheques display similar collections, including the Cinémathèque française, Filmoteca Español, the Cinémathèque Royale de Belgique, Eye Filmmuseum, Amsterdam, Deutsches Filmmuseum et al.

16 McLuhan acknowledged that an important source of his claims about media 'influence' was the work of the economic historian Harold Innis, as in his studies *Empire and Communications*, Oxford: Clarendon Press, 1950 and *The Bias of Communication* (Toronto, 1951).

17 'The fantasy of a class became the fantasy of a culture to extend "the conquest of nature" by triumphing over death through an Ersatz of life itself'. See Burch, *Life to Those Shadows* (BFI, 1990), 7.

18 E. P. Thompson, *The Making of the English Working Class* (Penguin, 1968), 16.

19 On Reynaud's life and inventions, see Dominique Auzel, *Emil Reynaud et l'image s'anima* (Editions du May, 1992).

20 Both of these enhancements seem to have appeared in 1878-9, together with a 'toy Praxiniscope' (Praxiniscope-jouet) and an electrical version of the Praxinoscope-Théâtre, with a motor to rotate the drum and an electrical bulb. Auzel, *Emil Reynaud*, 42-6.

21 The first book in England to do so appears to have been Olive Cook, *Movement in Two Dimensions* (Hutchinson, 1963), followed by the English translation of C. W. Ceram, *Archaeology of the Cinema* (Thames and Hudson, 1965). Interestingly, Terry Ramsaye's popular history, *A Million and One Nights* (1925) (Simon & Shuster/Touchstone, 1985), made only passing – and confused – reference to Reynaud (40).

22 Auzel, *Reynaud*, 75

23 On the 'philosophical toy', see Christie, 'Toys, Instruments, Machines: why the hardware matters' (2007), Chapter One in this collection.

24 Baudelaire compared the Phenakisticope to the better known Stereoscope, describing its simulation of movement, performed with 'a fantastic precision', as 'equally marvellous'. *Morale du joujou*' (1853).

25 R. L. Stevenson, 'A Penny Plain, Twopence Coloured', in *Memories and Portraits*, 1887.

26 Auzel reproduces pages from the catalogues of the department stores *Au Bon Marché and Le Printemps*, showing in 1902 the Praxinoscope on sale alongside a toy version of the Cinematograph, and a plagiarised version in 1905.

27 'I do not see there's anything to be made out of it. I have been largely influenced by sentiment in the prosecution of this design', 'Thomas. A Edison. His Latest Invention', *Newark Daily Advocate*, 9 April 1894.
28 Notably Reynaud's Théâtre Optique and Etienne-Jules Marey's *'fusil photographique'* (chronophotographic gun). The intermittent illumination principle had already been used by Ottomar Anchütz in his Tachyscope of 1887.
29 $1400 gross revenue = 28,000 viewings at 5¢ or c.1,000 per day per month.
30 Georgiades and Trajidis were responsible for mounting Kinetoscope shows in Paris and London in 1894-5, which were responsible for drawing both the Lumiere family and Robert Paul into the nascent moving picture business. See Christie, *Robert Paul and the Origins of British Cinema*, 259.
31 His 1894 catalogue was named 'Edison's Latest Wonders'.
32 Cock fighting was banned in Britain in 1849, and was illegal in most US states.
33 *Syracuse Daily Standard*, 25. 12. 1894, 3
34 *Middletown Daily Argus*, 20. 3, 1895, 7. Reprinted from the *Atlanta Constitution*.
35 *Coshocton Democratic Standard* [Ohio], 21. 12. 1894, reprinted from the *New York Herald*.
36 'The Wonders of the Kinetoscope', *Bradford Daily Argus*, 20 December 1894, 3. Quoted by Richard Brown, 'The Kinetoscope in Yorkshire', Simon Popple and Vanessa Toulmin, eds., *Visual Delights* (Flicks, 2000), 112-13.
37 Although most accounts of the Kinetoscope have concentrated on well-documented instances of exhibition in major cities in the United States, Britain and Australia, there was a wider history of its spread to smaller communities, as described in Brown's pioneering study of Yorkshire.
38 Wells' description of how the Traveller appears and disappears seems to be based on his experience of the Kinetoscope, see H. G. Wells, *The Time Machine* (1895). On Wells and Paul's 'Time Machine' project, see Christie, *Robert Paul*, Ch 4. Proust *A la Recherche du Temps Perdu* includes many references to optical devices, ranging from the magic lantern to the Bioscope. See for example the opening pages of *Swann's Way* (1913), with mention of a Kaleidoscope (2), Bioscope (6), magic lantern (9-10). Scott Moncrieff trans, *Remembrance of Things Past* (Chatto & Windus, 1925). See also Jack London, 'Two Gold Bricks', *The Owl*, Boston, New York, v. 3, September 1897; and *Martin Eden* (Macmillan, 1909).
39 Martin Loiperdinger, 'Ludwig Stollwerck, Birt Acres and the Distributors of the Lumiere Cinématographe in Germany', in Cosandey and Albera, eds., *Images Across Borders, 1896-1918* (Payot, 1995), 167-77.
40 Pascal Fouché (http://www.flipbook.info/index_en.php).
41 Three early films known only from their Filoscope versions are included in the BFI DVD compilation, *R. W. Paul: The Collected Films 1895-1908* (2007), namely *Westminster Bridge*, *Andalusian Dance* (filmed by Henry Short) and *Chirgwin the White-Eyed Kaffir* (all 1896).
42 André Bazin, 'The Myth of Total Cinema' (1946), in *What Is Cinema?*, vol. 1, ed. and trans. Hugh Gray (California, 1967), 17-22.
43 Burch, *Life to Those Shadows*, 7.
44 Richard D. Altick, *Victorian People and Ideas* (Norton, 1973), 252.
45 Hampshire Museum Childhood Collection.
46 Auzel, *Emil Reynaud*, 41, 43. The illustration first appeared in *La Nature* in 1881.

47　Lewis Carroll, *Through the Looking Glass* (1897), in Martin Gardner, ed., *The Annotated Alice* (Penguin, 1965), 217.
48　Writing in 1926, Woolf recalled above all the discontinuous experience of early film shows, with unrelated scenes following in rapid succession. 'The Cinema', in Rachel Bowlby, ed, *The Crowded Dance of Modern Life* (Penguin, 1993).
49　Wanda Strauven has rescued and discussed a speculation by Thomas Elsaesser on the 'perversions' of cinema in her article 'S/M', in Jaap Kooijman, Patricia Pisters, Strauven, eds., *Mind the Screen* (Amsterdam, 2008), 276-87.
50　Bordwell, *Film Style*, 154.
51　Fernand Leger, 'Autour du *Ballet mécanique* (1924-25), in Léger, *Fonctions de la peinture* (Gallimard, 1997), 133-39.
52　Yuri Tsivian, '"What is Cinema?" An Agnostic Answer', *Critical Inquiry*, Vol. 34, no. 4, Summer 2008, p. 775.

3.　Not Only 'King of the Vast': John Martin and 19th-Century Visual Spectacle

1　William Vaughan, 'Turnabouts in Taste: the case of late Turner', Romanticism and postmodernism, ed. Edward Larrissy (Cambridge, 1999).
2　'Noctes Ambrosianae', *Blackwood's Magazine* 32, 1832, 857.
3　Richard D. Altick, *The Shows of London* (Belknap, 1978), 243.
4　Altick, 410. Géricault's canvas was even larger than Haydon's, measuring just under five metres, and Altick notes that its display in London was initially boosted by the staging of a melodrama dealing with the shipwreck that inspired the painting, *The Shipwreck of the 'Medusa'*, possibly organised by the Egyptian Hall's founder and impresario, William Bullock.
5　Altick, 414.
6　Altick, 414.
7　Richard and Samuel Redgrave, *A Century of Painters of the English School*, 2 vols (Smith, Elder, 1866), 396. Altick, 414.
8　*Book of Daniel II*, ch 5.
9　On the Diorama, see Chapter 4, 'Screening the City'.
10　Altick, 414-5. Martin was an early campaigner for artists' copyright. See Chapter 15: 'What is a Film?'
11　Sally Rush, 'Seeing Red', 19: *Interdisciplinary Studies in the Long Nineteenth Century*, Issue 30, 2020.
12　Rush specifically cites two articles, one by a Russian film historian and the other by an English Victorianist: Mikhail Yampolsky, 'Transparency Painting: From Myth to Theater', in *Tekstura: Russian Essays on Visual Culture*, ed. and trans. by Alla Efimova and Lev Manovich (Chicago, 1993),127-51; and John Plunkett, 'Optical Recreations, Transparencies, and the Invention of the Screen', *Visual Delights – Two: Exhibition and Reception*, ed. by Vanessa Toulmin and Simon Popple (John Libbey, 2005), 175-93 (176-79).
13　The glass *Belshazzar's Feast* belongs to the Duke of Northumberland's collection at Syon House, and is apparently the only surviving original work linked to Martin in this medium. It appears that Altick was misled by Richard and Samuel Redgrave's *A Century of Painters of the English School* (1866), which opined that 'the effect was startling, but surely allied more to the diorama than to fine art' (Vol. 2, 429).
14　Jonathan Crary, *Techniques of the Observer* (MIT, 1990), 2, 14, 129-31.

15 Eavan O'Dochartaigh, *Visual Culture and Arctic Voyages* (Cambridge, 2022), 181-231
16 *Observer*, 2011.
17 Spaightwood Galleries, Inc., 2019. http://www.spaightwoodgalleries.com/Pages/Martin.html
18 As an example of this, see Ivo Blom, *Quo Vadis?, Cabiria and the 'Archaeologists'* (Edizioni Kaplan, 2023).

4. Screening the City: The Long History of London Screen Entertainment

1 This essay originated in a lecture given at the 2008 Sorbonne Nouvelle-Paris 3 Summer School. A shortened version appeared in the collection of presentations, *Extended Cinema*, eds. Philippe Dubois, Frederic Monvoisin, Elena Biserma, Campanotto Editore, 2010.
2 Major contributions to establishing the pre-history of cinema range from C. W Ceram, *Archaeology of Cinema*, translated by Richard Winston (Thames & Hudson, 1965) to Laurent Mannoni, *The Great Art of Light and Shadow*, translated and edited by Richard Crangle (Exeter, 2000).
3 A key work for London entertainment history is Richard D. Altick, *The Shows of London* (Belknap, 1978), Unfortunately, although understandably, Altick's great trawl ends in the mid-19th century. A new account, focused on the rise of 'screen shows' should be informed by something like De Certeau's 'practices of everyday life', Michel de Certeau, *L'Invention du quotidian*, Vol. 1, *Arts de faire*, Paris: Gallimard, 1998.
4 *Punch*, July-December, 1851; quoted at http://www.victorianlondon.org/districts/leicestersquare.htm.
5 See Robert Hooke, writing about the value of the lantern in the Royal Society's *Philosophical Transactions*, vol. 3, 17 August 1668, 741-743; also in the history of the Royal Society.
6 Athanasius Kircher has traditionally been credited as inventor of the Magic Lantern, due to his account in the 1671 edition of his *Ars Magna Lucis et Umbrae*. But Christiaan Huygens had built a lantern by 1659, and Reeves was manufacturing them from 1663. See 'History of the Magic Lantern', Magic Lantern Society (UK). See also Chapter 9, 'Something to Look At', in this book.,
7 The elaborate Greek-inspired name, from *eidoion* ('image' or 'apparition'), *phusis* ('nature' or 'natural appearance') and *eikon* ('image'), indicates that it was certainly not intended as popular entertainment, but rather for the genteel figures seen in the sole surviving illustration, a watercolour sketch by Edward Burney. See Ann Bermingham's account in 'Technologies of Illusion: De Loutherbourg's Eidophusikon in Eighteenth-Century London'.
8 Alongside John Bunyan's near-contemporary *Pilgrim's Progress*, scenes from Milton's *Paradise Lost* were already canonic in Britain, even before the series of engraved illustrations commissioned from John Martin in 1822. On Martin, see also Chapter 3, 'Not Only "King of the Vast"'.
9 See Chapter 1, 'Toys, Instruments, Machines."
10 De Loutherbourg's 1801 painting *Coalbrookdale by Night* (owned by the Science Museum) has come to represent the Romantic appeal of the Industrial Revolution, showing the flaring iron works at night. A set model for his 1793 pantomime interlude, *The Wonders of Derbyshire*, also survives.
11 Information on Barker's and other panoramas predominantly from Ralph Hyde, *Panoramania! The Art and Enterainment of the 'All-embracing'*

View (Trefoil/Barbican, 1988), 57-64. See also Bernard Comment, *The Panorama* (Reaktion, 1999), 23-26.

12 On the experience of visiting a surviving panorama, see Luke McKernan's account of the Mesdag Panorama in Den Haag, in Christie, ed, *Spaces* (Amsterdam, 2024).

13 Heard, in D. Robinson, S. Herbert, R. Crangle, eds., *Encyclopedia of the Magic Lantern* (Magic Lantern Society, 2001), 228. The most familiar illustration of a *Fantasmagorie* and account by David Brewster refer to Robertson's presentation in Paris at various Gothic locations.

14 See *The Regency Redingote* website (https://regencyredingote.wordpress.com/) for Kathryn Kane's detailed account of the London panorama business and its rivalries.

15 *Punch*, July-December, 1851; quoted at http://www.victorianlondon.org/districts/leicestersquare.htm.

16 Although Barker's Panorama closed in 1863, its site was acquired for a new Roman Catholic Church, Notre Dame de France, which can still be visited to get an impression of how the interior of the panorama would have appeared, and its site viewed remotely on Google maps.

17 Confusingly, the term 'diorama' has since developed a second usage, almost contrary to its original form. According to Wikipedia, 'the current, popular understanding of the term "diorama" denotes a partially three-dimensional, full-size replica or scale model of a landscape typically showing historical events, nature scenes or cityscapes, for purposes of education or entertainment'. This form of diorama appears to have begun in museums such as the Stockholm Natural History Museum in the 1890s, and quickly became common in museums of many kinds.

18 The Pantheon had opened in 1772, as lavishly decorated public assembly rooms, architecturally inspired by the Pantheon in Rome and Santa Sophia in Constantinople. After burning down in 1792, it had a chequered career until being adapted to become the Royal Bazaar in 1833. Its site is now occupied by Marks & Spencer. The Queen's Bazaar opened almost directly opposite, on the north side of Oxford Street, in 1828, and also housed a diorama before it was converted into the Princess Theatre in 1836.

19 See Chapter 3, 'Not Only "King of the Vast"', on Martin's contested reputation.

20 Benjamin Read's fashions were displayed in the Queen's Bazaar in 1833 (Hyde, 121) and the Colosseum in 1836 (Hyde, 92). See Ralph Hyde and Valerie Cumming, 'The Prints of Benjamin Read, Tailor and Printmaker', *Print Quarterly*, Sept 2000.

21 John Timbs, *Curiosities of London*, 1867, quoted at http://www.victorianlondon.org/entertainment/egyptianhall.htm.

22 For an account of the Polytechnic's attractions and spectacular dissolving views, see Jeremy Brooker, *The Temple of Minerva* (Magic Lantern Society, 2013).

23 Henry Mayhew, *London Labour and the London Poor*, vol. 3, 1851.

24 See Ch. 5, 'The Anglo-Boer War in North London'; also Chapter 25, 'Robert and Ellen: Inventing Cinema'.

25 On the growth of cinemagoing in London, see Luke McKernan, 'Diverting time: London's cinemas and their audiences, 1906-14, *The London Journal*, Vol. 32, no. 2, July 2007. This resulted from The London Project, part of the AHRB Centre for British Film and Television Studies: see also the database

on early London cinema businesses maintained at http://londonfilm.bbk.ac.uk/. (This database is currently being relocated.)

26. Jon Burrows, 'Penny Pleasures: Film exhibition in London during the nickelodeon era, 1906-1914', *Film History*, Vol. 16, 2004, 60-91.
27. Luke McKernan, 'Unequal Pleasures: Electric Theatres (1908) and the early film exhibition business in London' (2006).
28. For detail on this and other pre-1930 cinema, see the London's Silent Cinemas website, https://www.londonssilentcinemas.com/westendexhibts/west-end-cinema-theatre/
29. On classical subjects and cinema's changing image, see Chapter 20, 'Ancient Rome Revisited',
30. On the New Gallery, see https://www.londonssilentcinemas.com/westendexhibts/new-gallery-kinema.
31. François Truffaut, *Hitchcock* (Granada, 1978), 141.
32. See Hale's Tours entry by Lauren Rabinowitz in R. Abel, ed., *Encyclopedia of Early Cinema* (Routledge, 2005), 293-4.
33. The ex-Astoria, later Rainbow, is a listed building.
34. The first IMAX theatre in Europe opened in 1983 in Bradford, at what was then the Science Museum's Museum of Photography Film and Television (now National Media Museum). The BFI IMAX was designed by Bryan Avery, previously responsible for the BFI's ground-breaking Museum of the Moving Image (1988-1999), the closure of which paved the way for the BFI's investment in the Waterloo IMAX rotundal
35. On Trafalgar Square screenings, see Chapter 6, 'The Ghosts of Cinema Past'.
36. These have included films ranging from *Lawrence of Arabia* and *The Battle of Algiers* to *The Red Shoes*, *The Third Man* and *The Grand Budapest Hotel*.
37. On the concept of remediation, see David J. Bolter, J. David and Richard Grusin, *Remediation: Understanding New Media* (MIT, 2000). See also my article 'Immersion – new media and old ambitions', *Journal of the British Academy*, vol. 12, Issue 1 & 2.

5. The Anglo-Boer War in North London: A Micro-Study

1. *The Boer War*, produced by Twenty Twenty Television, was shown on Channel 4 in 1999. Lewis' observation appears in his introduction to the accompanying book by Tabitha Jackson, The Boer War (Channel 4/Macmillan, 1999), 6.
2. The Boer War: The First Media War, produced and directed by William Cran, BBC, 1997.
3. John Barnes, *Filming the Boer War* (Bishopsgate, 1992) and *The Beginnings of the Cinema in England 1894-1901* (Exeter, 1997), vols. 4 and 5; Luke McKernan, *The Boer War (1899-1902): Films in BFI Collections, National Film and Television Archive* (BFI, 1999); Richard Brown and Barry Anthony, *A Victorian Film Enterprise: The History of the British Mutoscope and Biograph Company, 1897-1915* (Flicks, 1999); Elizabeth Grotttle-Strebel, 'Primitive Propaganda: The Boer War Films', *Sight and Sound*, 46: 1, Winter 1976/77, 45-7; Stephen Bottomore, 'Frederic Villiers, War Correspondent', *Sight and Sound*, 49: 3, Autumn 1980, 250-5; and (on Joseph Rosenthal) Stephen Bottomore, "The Most Glorious Profession', *Sight and Sound*, 52: 3, Autumn 1983, 260; Simon Popple, '"But the Khaki-Covered Camera is

the Latest Thing" The Boer War and Visual Culture in Britain', in Andrew Higson, ed., *Young and Innocent* (Exeter, 2002), 13-27.
4   Harold Innis, *Empire and Communications* (Clarendon, 1950). Innis is probably best-known today as a major inspiration of Marshall McLuhan's theories of media.
5   On Robert Paul's move to Muswell Hill, see Chs. 11 and 12.
6   On the travelogue lecture, see Theodore Barber, 'The Roots of Travel Cinema: John L Stoddard, E Burton Holmes and the 19th Century Illustrated Travel Lecture', *Film History*, 5:1, March 1993, 68-84.
7   According to the *Hornsey Journal*, 9 December 1899: 'every seat was occupied long before eight o'clock and late-comers were lucky if they obtained standing room'.
8   See, for instance, numbers 54, 69-71 of the Warwick listing given by Barnes (1997), Vol. 4, 283.
9   Khama, together with two other Tswana chiefs, paid an extended visit to Britain in 1895 as part of a campaign orchestrated by non-Conformist missionaries to bolster opposition to Cecil Rhodes' plan to annex Bechuanaland to Cape Province. See Neil Parsons, *King Khama, Emperor Joe and the Great White Queen* (Chicago, 1998). It is possible that a coloured glass lantern slide of Khama by the London Missionary Society, held by the National Portrait Gallery, is what Salmond showed.
10 Reviewed in the *Yorkshire Post*, 20 March 1900, quoted in Popple, 25.
11 The Tees' poster – dated 'Tuesday Feb, 27 1899', clearly due to a printer's failure to set 1900 – advertises a mixture of Cape actualities and 'reproduction' scenes, together with 'A Selection of Dissolving Views' (Barnes 1997), Vol. 4, 82.
12 *Hornsey Journal*, 16 December 1899.
13 On the siting of Paul's studio, see my article about Percy Baralet's photographs in Janet Owen, ed, *100 Stories from the Archive*. Hornsey Historical Society, 2023.
14 Paul's brothers, Arthur Lyon Paul (born 1873) and George Herbert Paul (born 1877) both survived the Anglo-Boer War, although both died relatively young (1922 and 1919, respectively). The City Imperial Volunteers (CIV) was a 1,000-strong force raised and funded by the City of London, where the younger Paul brothers both worked in their father's shipping business. Although Paul sent two cameras, one with a CIV member and the other with Colonel Beevor of the Scots Guards, he only mentions usable material resulting from the latter. (Letter of 20 September 1937 to Thelma Gutsche, kindly made available by John Barnes). Gutsche would use this in her *The History and Social Significance of Motion Pictures in South Africa 1895-1940* (Howard Timmins, 1972).
15 See Adrian MK Thomas, 'Walter Calverley Beevor, the Tirah Campaign and the Origins of Military Radiology', *Topics in the History of Medicine*, vol. 3, 2023, 63-76.
16 R. W. Paul et al., 'Before 1910: Kinematograph Experiences', *Proceedings of the British Kinematograph Society*, 38, 1936, 5.
17 See Chapter 19, 'Bringing the Empire Home'.
18 Discussed briefly in Ian Christie, *The Last Machine* (BBC, 1994), 127-8, and dramatized in the television series this accompanied. Kipling was a regular visitor to South Africa from 1898.
19 Ken Gay, *A History of Muswell Hill* (Hornsey Historical Society, 2000), 70.

20 At the time of writing, in 2006, only one of Paul's Boer War 'reproductions' was known to exist, having been found in the New Zealand Film Archive. Since then, another has been discovered, *Attack on a Piquet*, which shows Boer group overwhelming English soldiers. The action is certainly more restrained, and antiheroic, than in Mitchell & Kenyon's *A Sneaky Boer* (1901). Both films are available on YouTube.
21 From Paul's 1901 catalogue description, held at the BFI. Only one part of *Army Life* exists at present.
22 Only one of these trick-based films has so far been found: *Kruger's Dream of Empire*, which is held by the Imperial War Museum Archive.
23 Rudyard Kipling, 'Recessional' (1897).
24 'The Victory of Peace', *Hornsey and Finsbury Park Journal and Islington Standard*, 7 June 1902, 3.

6. The Ghosts of Cinema Past: Screen Heritage in Australia

1 See https://www.samnightingale.com/projects-works.
2 See https://www.nfsa.gov.au.
3 See Raphael Samuel, *Theatres of Memory* (Verso, 1996) and Island Stories (Verso, 1998).
4 In July 2014, as part of the Australian National University Humanities Research Centre conference organized by Jill Julius Matthews, the artist and historian Martin Jolly presented a number of life-model slide sets, accompanied by Kate Bowan and Peter Tregear. See also Jolly's article, '*Soldiers of the Cross*: Time, narrative and affect', *Early Popular Visual Culture* 11, 2013, 293-311.
5 Richard Alan Nelson, 'Propaganda for God: Pastor Charles Taze Russell and the Multi-Media *Photo-Drama of Creation* (1914),' in Roland Cosandey, André Gaudreault, and Tom Gunning, eds., *Une Invention du diable? Cinéma des premiers temps et religion/An Invention of the Devil? Religion and Early Cinema* (Laval, 1992), 230-255.
6 *Hantologie* (or 'hauntology') was a punning term coined by Jacques Derrida in his *Spectres de Marx* (1993), published in English as: *Spectres of Marx* (Routledge, 1994), For a discussion, see Colin Davis, 'Hauntology, spectres and phantoms', *French Studies* 59, July 2005, 373-379.
7 Keith Moxey, *Visual Time: The Image in History* (Duke, 2013).
8 See bbb.co.uk report on this from 23 October 2008, 'Capital visions', with a mention of *Living London* as a special attraction.
9 The London Project database is at http://londonfilm.bbk.ac.uk. This database is currently being relocated.
10 Luke McKernan, '"Only the screen was silent…": Memories of children's cinema-going in London before the First World War', and Simon Brown, 'Flicker Alley: Cecil Court and the emergence of the British film industry', both published in *Film Studies*, No. 10, Spring 2010, 1-20, 21-33.
11 The XIII Biennial Conference of the Film and History Association of New Zealand, held at RMIT in Melbourne.
12 Chris Long's series of articles on 'Australia's first films' included much valuable work on the early impact of visiting showmen and filmmakers. See *Cinema Papers*, Nos. 91-4, 1993-5.
13 On 'The Marvellous Corrick Family Entertainers' and films drawn from their collection, see catalogue of the Giornate del Cinema Muto, Pordenone, 2008, 140.

14 After Urban established The Charles Urban Trading Company in London in 1903, specialising in non-fiction film, he published an ambitious catalogue titled Urbanora, with the promotional by-line 'We put the world before you'. For more about Urban, see Luke McKernan's website, especially https://www.charlesurban.com/history.html.
15 *Urbanora* catalogue, 194. By courtesy of Stephen Herbert
16 Urban was already a specialist in London material, having advertised such permutations as Living *London Today*, *Living in London Today*, *Around London* and *'Round About London*.
17 See Sally Jackson, 'The Living London boom', *Senses of Cinema*, 2009.
18 Programme note by Leslie Anne Lewis, catalogue of Giornate del Cinema Muto, 148.
19 At the time of writing these included early websites devoted to exploring film locations and itineraries. Among those online in 2024 are *Film Locations in London* https://www.visitlondon.com/things-to-do/sightseeing/film-locations/top-10-film-locations-in-london; Secret London's list at https://secretldn.com/famous-film-locations-visit-london/; and *London's Silent Cinemas* at https://www.londonssilentcinemas.com/londons-silent-cinemas-map/.
20 *The City of the Future* formed part of the AHRB Centre for British Film and Television Studies programme 2001-6, and was shown as an installation at BFI Southbank Gallery in February 2008. See chapter in Keiller, *The View from the Train. Cities and Other Landscapes* (Verso, 2014), pp.131-145. Also Keiller, 'Sequence and Simultaneity: Critiquing English Spaces with a Cine Camera', in Ian Christie, ed. *Spaces* (Amsterdam, 2024).
21 See Chapter 14 'Fumbling towards some new art' in this book.
22 For a more recent example, making use of XR, see my account of *Ghosts of Solid Air*, an AR app created for the 2023 London Film Festival, in *Sight and Sound*, Winter 2023.

7. The Tarnished Myth of British Precedence: Friese-Greene, Paul and Will Day

1 A reference to the biblical parable of the vineyard workers, Matthew 20:1. Laurent Mannoni, *The Great Art of Light and Shadow*. Translated and edited by Richard Crangle (Exeter, 2000).
2 Stephanie Barczewski, *Heroic Failure and the British* (Yale 2016).
3 Interview with Will Day quoted in 'Inventor of the Cinema. Tragic life story of Mr W F Green', *South Shields Daily News*, 7 May 1921
4 The biography *Friese Greene: Close Up of an Inventor* was published in 1948 under a pseudonym, Ray Allister.
5 Sees https://www.britishcinemaandtelevisionveterans.org.uk/about-us/our-history/.
6 *Kine Weekly*, Jan 21, 1909.
7 Talbot, *Moving Pictures* (Lipincott, 1912), 39
8 Wood, *Romance of the Movies* (1937), 27.
9 Thus giving his book its title. Leslie Wood, *Miracle of the Movies* (Burke, 1947), 83
10 On Friese-Greene's evidence given in the US, see Raymond Spottiswoode, 'The Friese-Greene Controversy: The Evidence Reconsidered,' *The Quarterly of Film Radio and Television*, Vol. 9, No. 3 (Spring, 1955), 226.
11 Kristin Thompson, *Exporting Entertainment* (BFI, 1985).

12 Terry Ramsaye, *A Million and One Nights* (1926) (Simon & Schuster, 1926).
13 Geoff Brown, 'Did Britain Really Invent Film Sound?', 29 May 2018. http://iamhist.net/tag/william-friese-greene/
14 Alan Wood, *The Miracle of the Movies* (Burke, 1947), 129.
15 The British government's attempt to stem the outflow of earning by US studios in 1948 precipitated retaliation by the studios, and a climb-down by the Labour government. See, among various accounts, David Puttnam and Neil Watson, *The Undeclared War: The Struggle for Control of the World's Film Industry* (HarperCollins, 1977), 202-215.
16 Le Prince's success in photographing moving sequences in the late 1880s had already been publicised by a Leeds businessman, Ernest Kilburn Scott, in a 1931 article published in the *Photographic Journal*, and reprinted in Raymond Fielding's *Technological History of Motion Pictures and Television* (Berkeley and Los Angeles: University of California, 1967). Le Prince appears first in Low's 'Recorded or Claimed Demonstrations' list, although misdated to 1899!
17 Roger Manvell and Rachael Low, *History of the British Film* (Allen & Unwin, 1948), vol. 1, 5
18 'First Recorded or Claimed Demonstrations and Public Performances in Great Britain of Motion pictures Projected on to a Screen', Manvell and Low, 113
19 The story of how George Georgiades and George Trajedes hired Paul to manufacture Kinetoscopes was first told in print by Talbot, *Moving Pictures*, in 1912, and repeated by Ramsaye in 1926. See discussion of it and the aftermath in my *Robert Paul and the Origins of British Cinema*, 15-26.
20 Acres' annotated copy of Talbot is held by the BFI Library.
21 *The Magic Box* review, vol. 18, no. 213, October 1951, 342 Reviews were unsigned at this time.
22 Bosley Crowther, '*The Magic Box*, British Film on Early Movie Experimenter, Arrives at the Normandie.' *The New York Times*, 24 September 1952.
23 Ramsaye described the film as a 'romantic fabrication', and went on to accuse its financial supporter, the National Film Finance Corporation, of being politically motivated, 'socialist big-foot-in-the-door in the direction of nationalising the [film] industry for Britain'. *Motion Picture Herald*, 28 April 1951, 23.
24 Lindgren, *Sight and Sound*, January/March 1952.
25 Possibly contained in correspondence with Thorold Dickinson?
26 Howard Cricks, review of *Historique et developpement de la technique cinématographique*, ed. Jean Vivié. *British Kinematography*, Vol. 10, no. 3 (1947), 120.
27 Georges Sadoul, *Histoire générale du cinéma*, Vol. 1 (Denoel, 1946), 92-96.
28 R. Howard Cricks, 'The Place of Friese-Greene in the Invention of Kinematography', *British Kinematography*, 1950, Vol. 16, 156-163. Cricks admitted to doubts as to whether Friese-Greene's camera would have produced usable images, adding diplomatically (and tortuously?), 'one finds it difficult to believe that Friese-Greene did not give way to optimism in some of his statements'.
29 Raymond Spottiswood, 'The Friese-Green Controversy: the evidence reconsidered', *The Quarterly of Film Radio and Television*, Spring, 1955.
30 Spottiswood, 227, 225

31 Brian Coe articles: "The Truth About Friese-Greene', *The British Journal of Photography*, 1955, 448. (1955); 'William Friese-Greene and the origins of cinematography', over three issues of Screen, 10/2 (March-April 1969), 25-41; 10/3 (May-June 1969), 72–83; 10/4 (July-Oct 1969), 129-47
32 In *The British Journal of Photography* and then *Screen*.
33 I am particularly grateful for Peter Domankiewicz's assistance in locating documents that helped create the 'myth' of Friese-Greene. See his blog: William Friese-Green & Me blog, at https://friesegreene.com.
34 Raymond Durgnat, *A Mirror for England* (Faber, 1970), 17
35 Michael Chanan, *The Dream That Kicks* (Routledge, 1980), 86-93.
36 The fullest account of Paul's career in Barnes' history appears in the final volume, devoted to 1905. *The Beginnings of the Cinema in England 1894-1901* (Exeter Press, 1997), 1-21.
37 Deac Rossell, *Living Pictures* (SUNY, 1998), 106-07.
38 Currently 32 such comments (at 19 August 2019)
39 Scorsese does not refer to the policeman episode, but describes Friese-Green 'flipping a series of drawings in the margins of a book' to explain how individual images 'miraculously move'. Foreword to David Robinson, *From Peep Show to Palace* (Columbia, 1996), xi-xii. In *Hugo*, for essentially dramatic reasons, he would show Méliès discovering film at a fairground, rather than being present at the Lumière show in the Salon Indien in Paris, as he actually was. The intention of referring to Paul's role in enabling Méliès to get started in film, by selling him equipment when the Lumières refused, was shelved for similar reasons.
40 Reed Paper Group advertisement, Punch, May 1952.
41 W. H. Eccles, 'Robert W. Paul, Pioneer Instrument Maker and Cinematographer', *Electronic Engineering*, August 1943.
42 The figure of Paul and his early projector, standing on a pedestal and driven by a handcranked flywheel, are surprisingly accurate, indicating careful research.

8. 'Everyday Life' in Early Cinema

1 *Blackfriars Bridge* (Robert Paul, 1896). c.2009, 224,000 views, 199 comments (at 18.12.2024), https://www.youtube.com/watch?v=fABILtla_lE. This film is also posted on many other YouTube channels, most versions deriving from the BFI video *R. W. Paul. Collected Films*, curated by Ian Christie (2007).
2 See Ian Christie, *Robert Paul and the Origins of British Cinema* (Chicago, 2019), 167-69.
3 Jean Pierre Carrier, 'L comme Lumière Louis', Le cinéma documentaire de A à Z (2019), https://dicodoc.blog/2019/08/27/l-comme-lumiere-louis.
4 Thierry Lecointe, 'La sonorisation des seances Lumière en 1896 et 1897', 1895 *Mille huit cent quatre-vingt-quinze*, no. 52, 2007.
5 *Blackfriars Bridge*, VisitingLondonGuide, https://www.youtube.com/watch?v=Ig-8pSOYNNg&ab_channel=VisitingLondonGuide.
6 This quotation from Goffman's *Frame Analysis* (1974) serves as an epigraph to a review article by Nick Coudry,'Everyday life in cultural theory' (review article). *European Journal of Communication*, 18 (2), 2003, 265-270. http://eprints.lse.ac.uk/17653/1/Couldry_Everyday_life_review_2003.pdf.
7 Walter Benjamin, Charles Baudelaire. *A Lyric poet in the Era of High Capitalism*. Trans. Harry Zohn (Verso, 1973), 35.

8 Benjamin, *Charles Baudelaire*, 37.
9 *Charles Baudelaire*, 48.
10 *Charles Baudelaire*, 49.
11 Quoted in 'History of Periodical Illustration', North Carolina State University, Digital Humanities.
12 Jean-Jacques Meusy, *Ecrans français de l'entre-deux-guerres*, vol. I, Paris: AFRHC, 2017, 232- 237.
13 René Clair, *Cinéma d'hier, cinéma d'aujourd'hui* (Gallimard, 1970), 155-156.
14 Virginia Woolf, 'The Movies and Reality', *The New Republic*, 4 Aug 1926, 309.
15 Laurent Mannoni, *Le grand art de la lumière et de l'ombre: archéologie de cinema* (Nathan, 1995). English trans. Richard Crangle (Exeter, 2000).
16 'Une simple caméra capable de prendre la vie sur le vif et de la projeter à son tour'. This text has acquired an official status, repeated in a French Government commemoration of the first public presentation of moving pictures to a paying public. 28 décembre 1895: Première projection publique du Cinématographe Lumière au Grand Café de Paris. https://www.gouvernement.fr/archivesgouv.
17 See Peter Domankiewicz, 'Whatever happened at Clovelly Cottage?', talk given at Kings College Silent Film Symposium, 2019. See also: Christie, *Robert Paul and the Origins of British Cinema*, 26-29.
18 What is known about the production of individual Lumière subjects is detailed in *L'œuvre cinématographique des frères Lumière*, an online catalogue edited by Manuel Schmalstieg, based on Michelle Aubert and Jean-Claude Seguin, *La production cinématographique des Frères Lumière*, 1996, at https://catalogue-lumiere.com.
19 The initial Grand Café programme had two clowning routines, filmed at troop encampments, *La Vol. tige* and *Le Saut a la couverture*, but did not include *Train Entering Station at La Ciotat* or *The Card-Players*, later to become signature subjects.
20 The Lumières launched their Autochrome process in 1907. For a concise overview, see https://blog.scienceandmediamuseum.org.uk/autochromes-the-dawn-of-colour-photography/. Louis Lumière demonstrated his successful 3D process in 1935-6. See Miriam Ross, *3D Cinema* (Palgrave-Macmillan, 2015), 3.
21 It now appears that the Kinetoscope presentation Lumière saw in Paris may have been by the same Greek-American entrepreneurs who commissioned Paul to manufacture machines for them in London. See Georgiades, *Who's Who in Victorian Cinema*, https://www.victorian-cinema.net/georgiades.php.
22 I have commented on this as an example of the rowdiness in English behaviour previously noted by foreign observers. See Christie, *Robert Paul and the Origins of British Cinema*, 66.
23 Op cit, 27-29.
24 In 2019, I made a video advertising my lecture on Paul for Gresham College, with the camera placed where Paul's would have been. The small number of 'chance' passers-by is notable. See 'London's First Filmmaker' on YouTube. Paul is also mentioned this location as the scene of his first abortive attempt to film with Acres in 1895, which may have motivated his return to the same scene.
25 The Filoscope was a flipbook device, patented by Henry Short, a friend and associate of Paul's, from which several other films were also 'reanimated' for the BFI Collected Films DVD.

26 Gustav Dore, *On London Bridge*, 1872. See http://www.victorianweb.org/art/illustration/dore/london/7.html.
27 Photochrome print Collection.
28 Lumiere Catalogue, https://catalogue-lumiere.com/danseuses-des-rues.
29 Like many of the pioneer generation, Louis Lumière hoped that moving pictures could be stereoscopic, and many systems and patents were proposed in the late 1890s. However stereo projection proved a major problem, which Lumiere did not solve until 1936.
30 *Women Fetching Water from the Nile* (Henry Short, 1897).
31 Reproduced in Paul and the Origins, 80.
32 Op. cit, 65.
33 *An Extraordinary Cab Accident* (1903).
34 For instance, in Richard Taylor and Ian Christie, eds., *The Film Factory* (Routledge and Kegan Paul, 1988), 25. Gorky's phrase has also provided a title on several occasions, as in Simon Popple and Colin Harding, *In the Kingdom of Shadows: A Companion to Early Cinema* (Cygnus Arts, 1996).
35 L'œuvre cinématographique des frères Lumière, no. 115.
36 The alleged 'panicking spectators' at the screening of first screening of *Arrival of a Train at La Ciotat* has given rise to a large and continuing volume of discussion. For an overview, see Martin Loiperdinger and Bernd Elzer. 'Lumiere's Arrival of the Train: Cinema's Founding Myth,' *The Moving Image*, 4, no. 1 (2004): 89-118.
37 For these and many other early responses to early film shows, see Daniel Banda and José Moure, eds., *Le Cinéma: Naissance d'un Art* (Flammarion, 2008), 39-41.
38 Ibid. 43.
39 O. Winter, 'The Cinematograph', *The New Review*, May 1896, 507-513. This text was discovered by Stephen Bottomore.
40 Paul's film is only partly preserved, with its end missing; although a remake by Porter for Edison, *Uncle Josh at the Moving Picture Show* (1902), is more complete. It is possible that Paul's film was inspired by one of the books of 'sketches' mentioned earlier, in this case James Spilling's Giles' *Trip to London*, first published in 1872, in which a Norfolk farm labourer marvels at the attractions of the metropolis, including a visit to a 'camera' or Camera Obscura. Facsimile edition of the 1896 edition, Jarrold Publishing, 1998.
41 Jay Bolter and Richard Grusin, *Remediation: Understanding New Media* (MIT, 1999), 59.
42 Ibid, 272.
43 Michael Baxendall, *Painting and Experience in Fifteenth Century Italy* (Oxford, 1972).
44 *The Passagenwerk* or 'Arcades project' was never completed, but his extensive research and material have been published. Walter Benjamin, *The Arcades Project*, trans. Howard Elland, Kevin McLaughlin (Harvard, 2002). See also Benjamin, *Berlin Childhood circa 1900*, trans and ed. Carl Skoggard (Publication Studio, 2010).

9. 'Something to Look At': On the Disappearing History of Lantern Slides

1 The conference *Screen Culture and the Social Question: Poverty on Screen 1880-1914* was organised by the Screen1900 research group at the University of Trier. An earlier version of this essay formed an Afterword

2. Details of some of the historic slide collections of the British Museum could be found among the archives of the Natural History Museum in 2013. But attempting to do so in 2024 reaches a 'dead link.
3. 'The physical removal of about 60,000 books, thousands of slides, photographs and furniture followed, and on December 12th, 1933, the little steamers *Hermia* and *Jessica* with 531 boxes aboard moved slowly down the Elbe… When the two small steamers docked in the Thames, the Institute had reached what proved to be its new permanent home'. See https://warburg.sas.ac.uk/about-us/history-warburg-institute/transfer-institute.
4. Aby Warburg, 1866-1929. See https://warburg.sas.ac.uk/about-us/history-warburg-institute.
5. From the Wikipedia page 'Timeline: Development of Visual Resources in the U.S.', under 'Slide library' (https://en.wikipedia.org/wiki/Slide_library).
6. I raised the question of the lantern as a 'medium' at a conference I helped organise at the British Academ, Lantern Projections, in February 2001. See Ian Christie, 'Through a Glass Brightly: the Magic Lantern in History', *British Academy Review*, 5, 2001, 21-23. But an equally appropriate concept might also be 'format'; see for instance Jonathan Sterne, *MP3: the Meaning of a Format* (Duke, 2013).
7. The Secretary of the National Education Association, reported in *The Bioscope*, 11 February 1909, quoted in Rachael Low, *History of the British Film 1906-1914*, London: Allen and Unwin, 1948, 41-42.
8. McAllister, "To assist in the pictorial teaching of Temperance": the use of the Magic Lantern in the Band of Hope', in *Screen Culture and the Social Question*. 'Eyegate' and 'Eargate' are two of the five gates of the city of Mansoul in John Bunyan's allegorical novel *The Holy War* (1682), which followed his more famous *The Pilgrim's Progress* (1678).
9. John Locke, *Some Thoughts Concerning Education* (1693), para. 156.
10. John Ruskin, *Mornings in Florence* (1881) (Echo Library, 2007), 21.
11. Quoted in David Peters Corbett, *The World in Paint* (Manchester, 2004), 24.
12. John Ruskin, 'Benjy in Beastland', in *King of the Golden River and Other Stories* (1841) (Kessinger, 2003), 171.
13. See Ch. 1 here, 'Toys, Instruments, Machines'. Also: 'the vagueness built into the concept of media', in 'Addressing Media', W. J. T. Mitchell, *What Do Pictures Want?* (Chicago, 2005), 204-05.
14. All references to chapters in *Screen Culture and the Social Question*.
15. Jean-Louis Baudry's influential 1970 article, 'Ideological Effects of the Basic Cinematic Apparatus' posited cinema as an Althusserian 'ideological apparatus', melding technical, psychological and political concepts.
16. See for instance, the special issue of *Film History*, 19:4, 2007, edited by Dan Streible, Martina Roepka snd Anke Mebold. Also Gregory Waller, 'Locating Early Non-theatrical Audiences', in Ian Christie, ed., *Audiences* (Amsterdam, 2012), 81-95.
17. Recent work in this area includes Nick Couldry, *Media, Society, World* (Polity Press, 2012); Nanna Verhoeff, *Mobile Screen* (Amsterdam, 2012); and Roger Odin, *The Spaces of Communication* (Amsterdam, 2022). All three books are on open access.

18 When Paul offered to deposit some of his films in 1896, the Museum could not decide which department might house them and so never responded. See Christie, *Robert Paul and the Origins of British Cinema*, 63-64.

10. A 'Stagey Marvel': The Genealogy of an Early Trick Film

1 The BFI National Archive's print of The Magic Sword lacked a concluding scene, until discovery of a fragment at what was then the New Zealand Film Archive enabled the reconstruction of the complete film, in time for its publication on the BFI DVD, *R. W. Paul: The Collected Films* in 2007. My thanks were due to Cushla Vula and Bronwyn Taylor at what is now Ngā Taonga Sound & Vision.
2 Paul Hammond, 'Georges, this is Charles', *Afterimage* (UK) 8/9, Spring 1981, 39-49.
3 André Gaudreault, 'Theatricality, Narrativity, Trickality', *Journal of Popular Film and Television* 15, 3, Fall 1967, 113-119.
4 Elizabeth Ezra, *Georges Méliès: The Birth of the Auteur* (Manchester, 2000).
5 This 'Theatrograph Mk 2, no.1' is preserved in the collection of the Cinémathèque française (Inv. 1450.). See also Christie, *Robert Paul and the Origins of British Cinema*, 60-61.
6 Frederick A. Talbot, *Moving Pictures* (William Heinemann, 1912), 199.
7 R. W. Paul, 'Before 1900: Kinematograph Experiences', *Proceedings of the British Kinematograph Society* 38, 1936, 6.
8 As claimed by Talbot, presumably on Paul's advice, Moving Pictures, 200.
9 Information deduced from 'Chronologie bio-filmographique' in Georges Sadoul, ed. Bernard Eisenschitz, *Lumière et Méliès* (L'Harmattan, 1985), 257-259.
10 Talbot, 200-201. This sounds unnecessarily cumbersome, since vertical panning would have achieved a similar effect, but Paul may have modified his studio for other purposes. And unlike other European pioneers, he had a well-equipped mechanical workshop at his disposal, thanks to his parallel instrument-making business.
11 *The Era*, 2 November 1901, 32.
12 Since this article was first published, Walter Booth has been identified as the protagonist in *Upside Down*, *The Waif and the Wizard* and a number of other Paul productions. This has led to him being called their 'director', although I have argued that this is an unwarranted and anachronistic assumption for the period.
13 Katherine Singer Kovacs, 'Georges Méliès and the Féerie', in John Fell, ed., *Film Before Griffith* (California, 1963), 260.
14 Phyllis Hartnol, ed., *Concise Oxford Companion to the Theatre* (Oxford, 1972), 418.
15 Pollocks Toy Museum in London reprinted a selection of Green's Juvenile Dramas, as sold by J. Redington in Hoxton in the 19th century. For a history of English toy theatres, see https://www.pollockstoytheatresltd.com/copy-of-general.
16 On Planché, see the 'Extravaganzas and revues' section of his Wikipedia page.
17 In Walpole's 1764 novel, the giant ghost of a poisoned prince haunts the castle.
18 Georges Moynet, *La Machinerie théâtrale, trucs et decors*, Paris: 1893. Translations here by Christopher Baugh, to whom I am indebted for this source and for his advice on 19th-century theatre historiography.

19 Allardyce Nicholl, *A History of English Drama, 1600-1900*, Vol. 4 (Cambridge, 1952), 154.
20 Michael Booth, *Victorian Spectacular Theatre 1850-1910* (Routledge & Kegan Paul, 1981), 9.
21 On the Polytechnic's place in a range of Victorian phantasmagoric media and forms, see my 'Contextualising Paul's Time Machine', *Cinema & cie*, 3, Fall 2003, 49-57. Also, Jeremy Brooker, *The Temple of Minerva* (Magic Lantern Society, 2013).
22 Richard Grusin and Jay David Bolter, *Remediation* (MIT, 2000), 44-50.
23 George Pearson, *Flashback* (George Allen and Unwin, 1957), 13-14.
24 Robert Louis Stevenson, 'A Penny Plain and Twopence Coloured', first published in *The Magazine of Art*, April 1864; collected in *Memories and Portraits* (Chatto, 1887), 134.
25 Stevenson, 'A Penny Plain', 136.

11. Now You See It... From 'Tricks' to 'Effects'

1 Tom Gunning, 'The Cinema of Attractions: Early Film, its Spectator, and the Avant-Garde', *Wide Angle* Vol. 8, no.3/4, Fall 1986. Reprinted extensively, with references here to its appearance in Thomas Elsaessar, Adam Barker, eds, *Early Cinema* (BFI, 1999).
2 Charles Dickens, 'Not a new "Sensation"', All the Year Round, 25 July 1863, quoted by Annemone Ligensa, in 'Sensationalism and Early Cinema', Andre Gaudreault et al, eds., *A Companion to Early Cinema* (Wiley-Blackwell, 2012), 165.
3 Walter Benjamin, *The Arcades Project*, quoted in Ligensa, 171.
4 Nordisk familjebok: Konversationslexikon, 1917, quoted by Ligensa, 164.
5 For a comparison of different styles of trick film, see Chapter 10, 'A "Stagey Marvel"'.
6 Barry Salt, *Film Style and Technology: History and Analysis* (Starword, 1983), 70.
7 Quoted by Richard Abel, *The Ciné Goes to Town* (California, 1998), 361.
8 Vicki Callahan, 'The Innovators 1910-1920: Detailing the Impossible', *Sight and Sound*, June 2012
9 Federico Pagello, 'Transnational Fantômas: The Influence of Feuillade's Series on International Cinema during the 1910s', Belphegor. Litteratures populaires et culture mediatique, Dossier Fantômas.
10 Bulwer-Lytton's *The Last Days of Pompeii*, published in 1834, pioneered a distinctive kind of fiction, in which historical and archaeological detail supported a romance plot, embedded within strong Christian moralising, as in Lew Wallace's *Ben-Hur* (1880) and Henryk Sienkiewicz's *Quo Vadis?* (1895). *The Last Days of Pompeii* was filmed, albeit in a single shot film, as early as 1900 (by Robert Paul), and thereafter with increasing spectacle in 1908, 1909 and 1913.
11 On the exhibition of the ancient world spectaculars, see Chapter 20, 'Ancient Rome Revisited'.
12 Georges Méliès soon became and remains the most celebrated of early 'trick' filmmakers, with his Star Films releases commanding high prices and wide admiration between 1900 and around 1906. But the English-born James Stuart Blackton, active as a producer in the United States as co-founder of the Vitagraph company, scored a major success with stop-action animation in *The Haunted Hotel* (1907), before moving into historic dramas and 'classical' subjects from 1908 onwards.

13   *Times*, 15 May 1915.
14   Letter from O'Neill to Beatrice Ashe, 7 October 1914, quoted in Hayes (2001) For O'Neill's full report see p.385.
15   See Margarita Landazuri on *The Thief of Bagdad*, 'The Magic of the Magic Carpet', in the San Francisco Silent Film festival archive, at http://silentfilm.org/archive/the-magic-of-the-magic-carpet.
16   Percy Day (1878-1965) began his career as a matte painter in French filmmaking of the 1920s, and came to Britain at Alexander Korda's invitation, to work on London Films productions from *The Private Life of Henry VIII* (1933) onwards. He is perhaps best known today for work on many Powell-Pressburger films from *The Life and Death of Colonel Blimp* (1943) to *The Elusive Pimpernel* (1950). Significantly, the bulk of Day's filmography on IMDb lists him as 'uncredited'.
17   Michael Powell, *A Life in Movies* (Faber, 2000), 311
18   *A Life in Movies*, 494
19   Ibid, 493.

12. Staffing an Early Film Studio

1   Richard Brown and Barry Anthony, *A Victorian Film Enterprise* (Flicks, 1999), 37, n.2.
2   Albert E. Smith with Phil A. Koury, *Two Reels and a Crank* (Doubleday, 1952).
3   Simon Brown, *Cecil Hepworth and the Rise of the British Film Industry 1899-1911* (Exeter, 2016), 10-12.
4   Brown and Anthony, *Victorian Film Enterprise*, 64
5   W[illiam] G. Barker, C[ecil] M. Hepworth and R[obert] W Paul, 'Before 1910: kinematograph experiences,' *Proceedings of the British Kinematograph Society* 38 (1936).
6   W. H. Eccles, "Robert W. Paul: Pioneer Instrument Maker and Cinematographer," *Electronic Engineering*, August 1943.
7   Irene Codd, a family friend of the Pauls, left an unpublished memoir, which I have used in my work on Paul. See also a rare report of social activity outside Paul's studio, 'Animatograph Jollies', in *Optical Lantern and Cinematograph Journal*, 1906.
8   Advertisement in *The Era*, 8 October 1898.
9   See Christie, *Robert Paul and the Origins of British Cinema* (Chicago, 2019), 50.
10   44 Hatton Garden, where Paul was based, is not today the original structure, which may well have been demolished after damage by an explosion at a nearby paint factory in 1917.
11   Equivalent to £120 in 2017, according to the UK National Archive Currency Converter. Historical wage and price comparisons are notoriously difficult to provide, but 'a guinea a week' (21 shillings) was considered a reasonable wage.
12   Paul's surviving catalogues are held in the BFI National Library, with the 1901 edition the largest.
13   For comparison, Pathé's 1907 catalogue boasted that its factories at Vincennes and Joinville employed nearly 800 workers and produced over 40 kilometres of film per day. See Laurent Le Forestier, "Serial Production Discourses and Practices," in *A Companion to Early Cinema*, ed. André Gaudreault, Nicolas Dulac and Santiago Hidalgo (Wiley-Blackwell, 2012), 186.

14 This estimate is based on Paul's instrument business staffing, scattered evidence from his catalogues, and occasional references in trade journals to new appointments and special assignments. It seems likely to be conservative, and total staff probably rose sharply in the early 1900s.
15 Brown, *Cecil Hepworth*, 45.
16 Quatercentenary of Aberdeen University production.
17 Martin would join another Paul alumnus, G. H. Cricks, to form Cricks and Martin in 1908. See Rachael Low, *History of British Film, Volume 2: 1906-1914* (Routledge, 2011), 106.
18 Ray and Sylvia Spare have been researching Alf Collins' legacy, and were able to identify him in a number of Paul's films, including *Pocket Boxers* and *A Chess Dispute*. A surviving telegram confirms when he should report to Muswell Hill for filming the former.
19 Cecil M. Hepworth, *Came the Dawn* (Phoenix House, 1951), 68.
20 Brown, *Cecil Hepworth*, p. 50.
21 Ibid.
22 The Internet Movie Database (IMDb) currently records Booth as director of 40 of Robert Paul's films.
23 Barker, Hepworth and Paul, "Before 1910," 5-6.
24 Gifford was a pioneer researcher of British film history, best known today for his two-volume *The British Film Catalogue, 1888-1994* (Fitzroy-Dearborn, 1973-2000).
25 See Denis Gifford's revised entry on Walter R. Booth in the *Who's Who in Victorian Cinema* website https://www.victorian-cinema.net/walterbooth.php (2017).
26 Janet Staiger, 'The Director System', in David Bordwell, Janet Staiger and Kristin Thompson, *The Classical Hollywood Cinema* (Columbia, 1985), 117.
27 Le Forestier, 'Serial Production Discourses and Practices', 184.
28 Georges Méliès, 'Cinematographic Views' [1907], trans. Stuart Liebman, in *French Film Theory and Criticism, Volume 1: 1907-1929*, ed. Richard Abel (Princeton, 1993), 41; quoted by Le Forestier, 'Serial Production Discourses and Practices', p.184.
29 Catalogue Pathé 1907, 3-4.
30 Luke McKernan, *Charles Urban: Pioneering the Non-Fiction Film in Britain and America, 1897-1925* (Exeter, 2013), 35.
31 'By late 1909, Selig had four director-producers in three permanent locations… In 1911, D.W. Griffith, Frank Powell, and Mack Sennett all directed units for Biograph'. Bordwell, Thompson and Staiger, *The Classical Hollywood Cinema*, 117.

13. The Lost World of Early North London Filmmaking

1 For details, see https://www.victorian-cinema.net/georgiades.
2 This restoration was carried out in 2011, but not seen in Britain until 2019. *The Soldier's Courtship* can be viewed online as part of my lecture for Gresham College, 'Robert Paul Shows his Native City in Motion', at https://www.gresham.ac.uk/watch-now/robert-paul-native-london.
3 See also, for another side of Sims, his role in launching *Living London*, Ch 6.
4 Some 80 of an estimated 700 films from Paul's Animatograph Works are currently known to exist. But there are undoubtedly many more, still unidentified, in archives around the world.

5 Thanks to the research of local historian, the late Roland-Francois Lack, https://www.thecinetourist.net/my-local-filmmaker.html.
6 More detail about estimating Paul's workforce compared with other studios in Chapter 12, 'Staffing an Early Film Studio'.
7 Georges Sadoul, *Histoire générale du cinéma*, vol. 2, 1948, 238-40.
8 Christie, *Robert Paul*, 111.
9 The site of Paul's studio, and factory for electrical instrument manufacture, lay between Newton Avenue and Cambridge Gardens, both created and named by Paul.
10 Kirk, 'Films in Walthamstow', 41.
11 *Ultus and the Grey Lady* (1916) is on the BFI Player.
12 See Lynda Nead's article in Art History (2003), 'Paintings, Films and Fast Cars: A Case Study of Hubert von Herkomer' and the chapter on Herkomer in her book *The Haunted Gallery* (Yale, 2008).
13 On Barrie's extensive, and largely frustrated film activity, see Luke McKernan's account at https://thebioscope.net/2008/05/30/pen-and-pictures-no-3-jm-barrie.
14 Rachael Low, *History of the British Film*, vols. 1, 2 and 3 (George Allen & Unwin, 1948).
15 *Lady Windermere's Fan* was published on BFI video, and is the subject of a major dossier by Charles Musser, published in *Film Studies* in 2003 and available on his website.
16 *The Life Story of David Lloyd George*, directed by Maurice Elvey, was restored and widely shown with a new score by Neil Brand in the 1990s. On its suppression and rediscovery, see my chapter in Sarah Barrow and John White, eds., *Fifty Key British Films* (Routledge, 2008). A DVD is available from the National Library of Wales.
17 See a review of part of *Ultus, the Man from the Dead* (1915) at https://www.imdb.com/title/tt0007491/. Much of the evidence will be documentation, now increasingly accessible due to digitisation of newspapers and journals.
18 The Leavesden studio was created by Warner Brothers specifically for the filming of the cycle of Harry Potter adaptations, which took place between 2000 and 2010. It now houses an elaborate 'studio tour' visitor attraction.

14. 'Fumbling Towards Some New Art': The Structure of Cinema Programmes c.1909-13

1 George Stigler, 'The division of labour is limited by the extent of the market', *Journal of Political Economy*, 1951, no.59, 185-193.
2 Terms used by, respectively, Charlie Keil, 2001 Eileen Bowser, *The Transformation of Cinema, 1907-15*, 1990.
3 Bowser, *Transformation*, 6, 18.
4 At least longer secular narratives, since multi-part Biblical narratives were already in circulation by 1905, and presumably presented no difficulty to audiences who already 'knew the story'.
5 Bowser, *Transformation*, 57-58.
6 Janet Staiger, in Bordwell, Staiger, and Thompson, *Classical Hollywood Cinema* (Routledge, 1985), 87.
7 David Bordwell, *On the History of Film Style* (Harvard, 1998).
8 *KLW*, 11 July 1907.
9 Robert Allen, *Film History*, 1985, 57.

10 On this period, see inter alia Richard Abel, *The Ciné Goes to Town* (California, 1994); Kathryn H. Fuller, *At the Picture Show* (Smithsonian, 1996); (1994); Rachael Low and Roger Manvel, *The History of the British Film, 1896-1906* (Allen and Unwin, 1948); Vanessa Toulmin et al, eds, *The Lost World of Mitchell and Kenyon* (BFI, 2004).
11 Abel, *The Ciné Goes to Town*, 35-6.
12 See first Lumière programme in Paris, December 1895, reproduced in Georges Sadoul, *Lumière et Méliès*, Paris: Editions Pierre Lherminier, 1985, 34. A Robert Paul Animatographe programme of 31 August, 1896 has been preserved as a handbill and lists 20 subjects (Barnes Collection).
13 A 1912 manual for exhibitors explained the value of the 'feature film' in attracting audiences. James F. Hodge, *Opening and Operating a Motion Picture Theatre*, New York: Scenario, 1912.
14 Such as Williamson's *The Tower of London* (1908)
15 Based on reports in 'Around the Shows', a regular column in The *Kinematograph and Lantern Weekly* (hereafter *KLW*), in which the Prudential Hall, South Shields, was reported regularly – apparently on the basis of the manager sending full programme details – while only highlights are noted from other shows. The programme reproduced here was accompanied by Cinephone, one of a number of mechanical synchronisation systems in wide use during the 1900s, providing the experience of recorded music accompanying film as a special feature, before this became routine with sound-on-film systems after 1927.programme reported in *KLW*, 15 April 1909.
16 Gifford's 1973 catalogue did not include films of 'interest' – travel, education, primitive documentary- 'and 'actualities' – news and events. However, he later added non-fiction.
17 The demand for novelty – a characteristic that appears to be an inalienable aspect of the demand for film – meant that exhibitors could not continuously rescreen particular film products, without driving audiences away. See the discussion of film as a commodity in the Introduction to John Sedgwick, *Popular Filmgoing in 1930s Britain* (Exeter, 2000), and Chapter 1 of John Sedgwick and Michael Pokorny eds., *An Economic History of Film* (Routledge, 2005).
18 Not surprisingly this is reflected in the greater average length of films classified as dramas. Using the entries in Gifford's Catalogue, the average length of all British entertainment films was 386 feet, while the mean length of films classified as dramas was 524 feet.
19 See Abel, *The Red Rooster Scare* (California, 1999).
20 The estimate is derived by scaling down the mean length of films recorded in Table 1 for 1908 (based on entertainment films only), so as to reflect the relatively shorter length of interest and news films. Table 1 records the mean length of 'entertainment' films in 1908 as 386 feet. Table 2 indicates that News and Interest films comprised 25 per cent of the films put on the market in 1907-8. Hence, the mean length of all films for that season can be estimated at 300 feet. By multiplying the number of films released in the 1907-8 season, 1,107, by 300 feet per film provides a rough estimate of the aggregate length of all new films.
21 Rachael Low, *The History of the British Film, 1906-1914* (George Allen & Unwin, 1948), 45-48. Low gives 9 March as the date of this offer.
22 Film rental, rather than outright purchase, had begun as early as 1901,

according to Richard Brown, 'War and the Growth of Rental in Britain: An Economic Perspective', *Film History* 16, 2004, 28-36. However it did not become general trade practice until the end of the decade.
23 Low, *History of the British Film*, 46. Low gives 9 March as the date of this offer.
24 Low, *History of the British Film*, 95. Apparently this promise included burning the negative.
25 Cricks and Martin tried to launch exclusives, as did Cecil Hepworth, with *The Deception* in 1912.
26 The report of a new cinema opening by Montagu Pyke in Brixton in 1911 mentioned 'a full two hour programme'. *The Bioscope*, 16 March 1911, 59
27 'Cinematograph – Truth and Fiction', *The Times*, 9 April 1913, 11.

15. 'What is a Film?' Legal Controversy and Cases Before 1910

1 *The Era*, 17 Oct 1896
2 Stephen Bottomore, 'The Collection of Rubbish: Animatographs, Archives and Arguments: London 1896-97', *Film History*, vol. 7, 1995, 291-297.
3 This collection, transferred from Stationers Hall to the Public Record Office, and thence to the National Archives in Kew, was reported in 1993 by Richard Brown.
4 Under French law, the Lumière films are still 'protected' by a variety of rights – patrimonial rights (until 2039), rights of artistic property, and moral rights, which are vested in the 'Lumière succession' of descendents.
5 Luke McKernan, ed., *A Yank in Britain* (Projection Box, 1999), 57-59.
6 Ibid.
7 Brown mentions an earlier case of 'unauthorised use of a registered trademark' in Koopman v The Manchester Palace Theatre of Varieties (K. 365 of June 1897), in 'The British Film Copyright Archive', 241.
8 Urban, *A Yank in Britain*, 58.
9 Richard Brown, 'The British Film Copyright Archive', in Colin Harding and Simon Popple, eds., *In the Kingdom of Shadows* (Cygnus Arts, 1996), 240-45.
10 André Gaudreault, 'The Infringement of Copyright Laws and its Effects (1900-1906)', first published in *Framework* 29, 1985; reprinted in Thomas Elsaeser and Adam Barker, eds., *Early Cinema* (BFI, 1990), 115.
11 Brown, 'The British Film Copyright Archive', note 6, 244.
12 On Edison's unscrupulous use of European films in his Vitascope screenings, see Charles Musser, *The Emergence of Cinema* (California, 1990), 118.
13 Turner v. Robinson, 10 Ir. Ch. 121, 510
14 Additional information on this celebrated early case in photographic history from Heinz K. Henisch and Bridget Ann Henisch, *The Photographic Experience, 1839-1914* (Penn, 1994), 306.
15 "'The Death of Chatterton'" *Athenaeum* 1652, 25 June 1859, 841-842.
16 Ibid.
17 Judgement in Turner v. Robinson, 10 Ir. Ch. 121, 510.
18 Edison v. Lubin, 122 Fed. Rep. 240.
19 Brown, op. cit., 242-43.
20 See Charles Musser, *Before the Nickelodeon* (California, 1991), 421, 552. See also I. Trotter Hardy, 'Copyright and "New-Use" Technologies' (1999), https://scholarship.law.wm.edu/facpubs/187. I am also grateful to Jon Solomon for shedding further light on the significance of this case.

21 Copyright Act, 1911, Part III, Section 35: '"Dramatic work" includes any piece for recitation, choreographic work or entertainment in dumb show, the scenic arrangement or acting form of which is fixed in writing or otherwise, and any cinematograph production where the arrangement or acting form or the combination of incidents represented give the work an original character' [my italics]

22 The United States remained outside the Berne Convention until 1952, when a special Universal Copyright Convention was created to meet its requirements. This was then overtaken by America's Implementation Act in 1988, when brought the US fully into the Berne process, and led eventually to the foundation of the World Intellectual Property Organisation in 1996.

23 As long films became central to exhibition, and were sold at auction to distributors for unprecedented sums, so efforts to 'pass off' inferior or pirated copies occurred. For an account of this practice in the Netherlands in 1913-14, see Ivo Blom, *Jean Desmet and the Early Dutch Film Trade*, (Amsterdam, 2000), 228-232.

16. Measuring Early Screen Stardom in Europe

1 Hortense Powdermaker, *Hollywood the Dream Factory* (Little, Brown, 1950); Edgar Morin, *Les Stars* (Editions du Seuil, 1957); Alexander Walker, *The Celluloid Sacrifice* (Michael Joseph, 1966); Richard Dyer, *Stars* (BFI, 1979).

2 Richard deCordova, for instance, writes of 'a cinema completely without stars' before 1910, before going on to discuss rival theories of what brought about 'a cinema wholly dependent on them'. *Picture Personalities* (Illinois, 1999), 1.

3 On Messter's Biophon system and the Tonbilder boom in Germany, cf. Martin Loiperdinger, 'German Tonbilder of the 1900s: Advanced Technology and National Brand', in Klaus Kreimeier and Annemone Ligensa, eds, *Film 1900: Technology, Perception, Culture* (John Libbey, 2009), 187-199.

4 A Gaumont advertisement boasted: 'We are fast approaching our 400th consecutive Chronophone performance at the London Hippodrome where Harry Lauder is still going strong'. It also invited 'offers for the hire of this highly Popular star Comedian's most favourite productions (of which we have the entire rights as Chronophone subjects for Exhibition) in districts not affected by the Moss Stoll circuits' – an indication of the contractual problems being caused the same performer becoming available in two media. *KLW*, 16 July 1907, 152.

5 Martin Loiperdinger, 'The Kaiser's Cinema: an archaeology of attitudes and audiences', in Thomas Elsaesser and Michael Wedel, eds, *A Second Life* (Amsterdam, 1996), 41-50, here 47; Martin Loiperdinger, '"Kaiserbilder". Wilhelm II. als Filmstar' in Uli Jung, Martin Loiperdinger, eds, *Geschichte des dokumentarischen Films in Deutschland. Vol. 1: Kaiserreich 1895-1918* (Philipp Reclam, 2005), 253-268.

6 See Herbert Campbell as 'Little Bobby'(1899) on the BFI Player.

7 Terry Ramsaye, *A Million and One Nights* (Simon and Schuster, 1926); Benjamin Hampton, *A History of the Movies* (Covichi-Friede, 1931).

8 deCordova, Picture Personalities, 2-7; David P. Marshall, *Celebrity and Power* (Minnesota, 1997), 79-81.

9   'La fabrication (...) de scènes établies sur scénarios signés d'auteurs contemporains, avec le concours d'artistes connus', quoted in *Dictionnaire du cinéma français des années vingt*, 1895, no. 33, 2001, 198.
10 Jon Burrows, *Legitimate Cinema* (Exeter, 2003), 46.
11 Advertisement by Walturdaw Co., *Kinematograph Weekly*, 20 July 1912. The other adjective regularly used in advertisements for Asta Nielsen films was 'incomparable', while adjacent reviews of *Retribution* (Nachtfalter, 1911) and *A Beast at Bay* (Griffith, 1912), refer to 'that versatile Norwegian [sic] actress, Miss Asta Nielsen' and 'Miss Mary Pickford, the well-known charming actress now with the AB company in America', *Kinematograph Monthly Film Record*, July 1912, 108.
12 Gabriel-Maximilien Leuvielle (1883-1925) made his screen debut as 'Max Linder' in 1905 and was internationally famous by 1911. The French comedian André Chapuis (1879-1940) starred first in numerous Pathé comedies as 'André Deed', before moving to Italy in 1909 to become 'Cretinetti', known as 'Foolshead' in Britain and America. Another French comedian, Charles Prince Seigneur (1872-1933) started working for Pathé in 1909, and also became internationally recognised – as 'Rigadin' in France, 'Moritz' in Germany, 'Whiffles' in Britain and America, 'Tartufini' in Italy, etc.
13 Hugo Münsterberg, *The Photoplay* (Appleton, 1916). 'Photoplay' had become the accepted term for feature-length filmed drama in the United States by the early 'teens.
14 Münsterberg, *The Photoplay*. See the online Project Gutenberg edition.
15 Hugo Münsterberg, 'Why we go to the movies', *The Cosmopolitan*, December 1915.
16 Ibid. 31. *Carmen* (dir. Raoul Walsh, Fox, 1915) and *Carmen* (dir. Cecil B. DeMille, Lasky, 1915)
17 Gustav Fechner (1801-1887) was a German psychologist and philosopher who established 'psychophysics' as the science of measuring mental responses to physical stimuli (*Elemente der Psychophysik*, 1860), and laid the foundations for an experimental approach to aesthetic preferences.
18 Münsterberg's foundational work in forensic and industrial psychology has long been recognised. But an aggressively pro-German stance during the years leading up to the outbreak of World War One made him an unpopular figure within the American academic community, according to Allan Langdale, the editor of *Hugo Münsterberg* (Routledge, 2002), 5-6.
19 See, for instance, George Mitchell, 'The Movies and Münsterberg', *Jump Cut*, no. 27, July 1982, 57-60.
20 Compiling the index for my book Audiences in 2012, it was salutary to discover how many of the contributors had mentioned Münsterberg.
21 The first version of the novel, entitled Si Gira, appeared in 1916, but this was superseded by a revised edition, known as *The Notebooks of Serafino Gubbio Operator* (*Quaderni di Serafina Gubbio operatore*) from 1925. The differences between the two do not seem to have been established.
22 Luigi Pirandello, *Shoot!: The Notebooks of Serafino Gubbio*, trans. C. Scott Moncrieff (E. P. Dutton, 1926), 292
23 "In principio era il sesso", Avanti, 16 February 1917, quoted in Gian Piero Brunetta, *Storia del cinema italiano 1895-1945*, Rome: Editori Riuniti, 1979, 79-80; also in P. Adams Sitney, 'The Autobiography of a Metonymy', afterword to the Chicago University Press reprint of *Shoot!*, 224.

24 Later, in his influential *Prison Notebooks*, Gramsci would rethink the progressive potential of popular culture and it is this later position that was widely embraced in the 1970s.
25 Angela Dalle Vacche, *Diva: Defiance and Passion in Early Italian Cinema* (Texas, 2008), 56.
26 Ibid.
27 Sitney, in 'The Autobiography of a Metonymy', also attributes some complexity to Pirandello's view of cinema in the novel.
28 Walter Benjamin, 'The Work of Art in the Age of Mechanical Reproduction' (1936), in *Illuminations*, ed. Hannah Arendt, trans. Harry Zohn (Fontana, 1970), 232-233.
29 'Stars are human capital': so begins John Sedgwick's chapter 'Stardom and "Hits"' in his economic analysis, *Popular Filmgoing in 1930s Britain* (Exeter, 2000), 180.
30 Pierre Sorlin, *Italian National Cinema 1896-1996* (Routledge, 1996), 32.
31 Martin Koerber, 'Oskar Messter, Film Pioneer: Early Cinema between Science, Spectacle and Commerce', in Elsaesser and Wedel, *A Second Life*, 51-61, here 57.
32 Koerber, 58.
33 Review of *Drake's Love Story* (Hepworth, 1913), *The Bioscope*, 27 February 1913, 673.
34 On the history of picture postcards, see Tonie and Valmai Holt, *Picture Postcards of the Golden Age* (McGibbon & Kee, 1971); Paul Hammond, *French Undressing* (Bloomsbury, 1988).
35 Figures of national card postage levels from Hammond, *French Undressing*, 9, who observes that many cards were also being kept in albums. It is impossible to know what proportion of postcards were of film stars, but analysis of current market values among collectors could provide an interesting comparative framework.
36 On the contrasting careers of Bernhardt, Réjane and Mistinguett, see Victoria Duckett, *Transnational Trailblazers of Early Cinema* (California, 2023).
37 There were internationally known early male stars, apart from the comedians already noted, such as Broncho Billy Anderson, René Nararre and Emilio Ghione. But the era of male stars with the same impact as the female stars of 1911-14 began towards the end of the 1910s, with Douglas Fairbanks turning to swashbuckling roles and the emergence of the 'Latin lover', heralded by Rudolf Valentino and Ramon Novarro.
38 George Huaco, *The Sociology of Film Art* (Basic, 1965).
39 *Kinematograph Monthly Film Record*, March 1913, 63.
40 Kristin Thompson, *Exporting Entertainment* (BFI, 1985).
41 Gerben Bakker, 'The Economic History of the International Film Industry' (2008).

17. Early Synchronised Pictures

1 See http://filmsound.org/murch/dickson.htm.
2 See Emmanuelle Toulet, 'Cinema at the Universal Exposition Paris 1900', in *Persistence of Vision* 9, 1991.
3 David Robinson dated Messter's 'experiments' with sound film to 'around 1908', in his *World Cinema* (Eyre Methuen, 1973), 87. Most single-volume histories made no mention of Messter's Biophon system.

4 Alison McMahon, *Alice Guy Blaché* (Continuum, 2002, 64.
5 Ibid.
6 These included: Martin Loiperdinger, ed., *Oskar Messter: Filmpionier der Kaiserzeit* (Stromfeld/Roter Steren, 1994); Ian Christie, *The Last Machine* (BBC/BFI, 1994); Jan-Christopher Horak, 'Oskar Messter: Forgotten Pioneer of German Cinema', *Historical journal of Film, Radio and Television*, 15.4, October 1995.
7 Frank Kessler, Sabine Lenk, 'The French Connection', in T. Elsaesser, ed., *A Second Life* (Amsterdam, 1996), 67-68.
8 Cinephone claim recorded by Rick Altman, *Silent Film Sound* (Columbia, 2007), 164.
9 Rachael Low, *The History of the British Film 1906-1914* (George Allen & Unwin, 1948), 266.
10 James Wierzbicki, *Film Music* (Routledge, 2009), 76.
11 Rick Altman, *Silent Film Sound*.
12 The aesthetics of the period are laid out in Ernest Lindgren, *The Art of the Film*, London: George Allen & Unwin, 1948, exactly contemporary with Low's history, in which the Cinephone, Chronophone and Vivaphone are described as 'a fashionable novelty' (97-8).
13 See, for instance, Thomas Schmitt, 'The Genealogy of Clip Culture', in Henry Keazor and Thorsten Wübbena, eds., *Rewind, Play, Fast Forward* (Bielefeld, 2010).
14 'An afternoon entertainment of "Singing Pictures" at Buckingham Palace afforded much enjoyment. The Queen's command was received at the Hippodrome yesterday morning, instructing a private exhibition… to be given in the Palace, commencing at three o'clock.…[T]he instrument, placed in the [throne room], cast the pictures through the folding-doors [into the Green Drawing Room] upon a screen hung behind a bank of palms', *Daily Telegraph*, 5 April 1907.
15 *Daily Mail*, 5 April 1907
16 Another case of Walturdaw duplicating a previous Gaumont release is their rival version of the 1906 song 'Beside the Zuyder Zee' for the Cinematophone. There is no information to hand about the kinds of legal agreements that might have underpinned the early sound-film releases, which are likely have been regarded as experimental – especially at a time when the whole issue of film-related copyright was unclear. See Chapter 15 here, 'What is a Film?; Marta Braun et al, eds., *Beyond the Screen* (John Libbey, 2012), 78-84.
17 Gaumont made nearly forty phonoscènes starring three popular French singers, Polin, Mayol and Dranem, according to McMahon, Alice Guy, 322-23. But these were unlikely to have been released outside France and Belgium.
18 If the fee was at least £1,000, this would be the equivalent of $114,000 today.
19 *KLW* ran a regular column, 'Around the Shows', which reported impressionistically on various UK exhibitors' programmes – clearly depending on those who sent in information most assiduously.
20 *Reno Evening Gazette*, Reno, Nevada, Tuesday, 5 April 1910, 4c. Reported at http://footlightnotes.tripod.com/ArchivePressText2008/20080510.html.
21 'Talking Picture Devices', *Moving Picture World*, 29 March 1913.
22 G. D. Crain, Jr., 'Correspondence: Louisville', *Moving Picture World*, 12 April 1913.

23 Altman, *Silent Film Sound*, 177.
24 Altman, 178.
25 Martin Loiperdinger, 'German Tonbilder of the 1900s', in Annemone Ligensa and Klaus Kreimeir, eds., *Film 1900* (John Libbey, 2009), 194.
26 Thomas Schmitt noted that of the 774 phonoscènes produced by Gaumont between 1902 and 1917, only about 20 are currently accessible.
27 See Ian Christie, 'Before the Avant-Gardes: Artists and Film, 1910-1914', in The Tenth Muse, ed. *Leonardo Quaresima and Laura Vichi* (Udini, 2001), 368-70.
28 As did D. W. Griffith, who made a sound version of *Dream Street* for Photokinema.
29 Low, *History of the British Film*, vol. 2, 267.
30 Loiperdinger, 'German Tonbilder', 195.

18. 'Suitable Music': Silent-Era Accompaniment Practices

1 Like many early cinema researchers, I am indebted to Stephen Bottomore, who laid the empirical foundations for much that has been attempted later – including this essay. He recalls the nostrum that 'the silents were never silent' (originally attributed to Irving Thalberg) in his pioneering essay, 'An International Survey of Sound Effects in Early Cinema', *Film History*, 11, 1999, 485-498.
2 Rick Altman, 'The Silence of the Silents', *Musical Quarterly*, 80/4, 1997, 648-718. Altman reiterated this claim in his contribution to the 1998 Domitor Conference in Washington. See his notes on 'The Living Nickelodeon', in the conference proceedings: *The Sounds of Early Cinema*, eds. Richard Abel and Rick Altman (Indiana, 2001), 232-240.
3 *The Register* was the forerunner of *The Times*, which it became in 1790.
4 Reproduced in Richard Altick, *The Shows of London* (Belknap, 1978), 142.
5 Edward Francis Burney, *The Eidophusikon Showing Satan arraying his Troups on the Banks of a Fiery Lake with the Raising of Pandemonium from Milton*, 1782.
6 Iain McCalmain, 'The Virtual Infernal: Philippe de Loutherbourg, William Beckford and the Spectacle of the Sublime', in *Romantic Spectacle* (Special Issue), Romanticism on the Net (Montreal) 46, May 2007. See also: Christopher Baugh, 'Philippe de Loutherbourg: Technology-Driven Entertainment and Spectacle in the Late Eighteenth Century', *Huntington Library Quarterly* 70/2, June 2007..
7 Ephriam Hardcastle, *Wine and Walnuts* (Longman, Hurst, Rees, Orme, 1824), 297.
8 Only the 'patent theatres' could put on spoken drama, so other venues resorted to mime accompanied by music. Michael R. Booth, *Victorian Spectacular Theatre 1850-1910* (Routledge & Kegan Paul, 1981), 60.
9 Quoted by Booth, *Victorian Spectacular Theatre*, 62.
10 Only the Overture would have been available at this date, written as a concert work in 1826, since Mendelssohn did not write the rest of his incidental music for the play until 1842.
11 Booth, *Victorian Spectacular Theatre*, 97.
12 Both of these originally and subsequently performed with added live artillery effects.
13 Countless texts on early cinema, film and music refer to the Lumière presentation on 28 December in Paris 1895 being accompanied by a pianist,

although the evidence for this is, at best, debatable. Certainly the 'pianist-composer' Émile Maraval accompanied later screenings, but it seems unlikely that he was present on this occasion. See Thierry Lecointe, 'La sonorisation des séances Lumière en 1896 et 1897', 1895. *Mille huit cent quatre-vingt-quinze*, 52, 2007. The report of harmonium accompaniment at the London Lumière shows is quoted in Roger Manvell and John Huntley, *The Technique of Film Music* (Focal, 1957), 211, and seems to have originated with Hepworth's memoir, *Came the Dawn* (Phoenix House, 1951).

14 Manvell and Huntley, *The Technique of Film Music*, 17. Strictly speaking, this does not confirm that the music accompanied the films, but we might wonder what its relationship was if not to accompany them?
15 The Era, 18 April 1896, 16; quoted in John Barnes, *The Beginnings of the Cinema in England 1894-1901, Vol. 1: 1894-1896* (Exeter, 1998), 134-5.
16 *Strand Magazine*, Aug 1896; quoted Barnes, *Beginnings of Cinema, Vol. 1*, 130.
17 Canterbury report, *The Era*, 6 June 1896, 16.
18 Altman, 'The Living Nickelodeon', 234.
19 'Private Tommy Atkins', with lyrics by Henry Hamilton and music by S. Potter, was published in 1893, possibly inspired by Rudyard Kipling's invocation of the typical solider in his 1892 ballad 'Tommy'. Although the 1896 film made no specific reference to 'Tommy Atkins', when Paul remade it in 1898, he titled the new film Tommy Atkins in the Park.
20 The second shot is lost, but its contents are known from frame stills printed in Paul's catalogue,
21 I am grateful to David Robinson for first introducing me to this history and subsequently supplying detailed references from his collection.
22 Martin Meisel, *Realizations* (Princeton, 1983).
23 As Stephen Horne does in his accompaniment to the film on the DVD *R. W. Paul: The Collected Films, 1895-1908*.
24 See Chapter 5 here.
25 *Wood Green Weekly Herald*, 9 December 1899, 5.
26 Many of these were collected in Ira D. Sankey's *Sacred Songs and Solos* (1873), published after the American evangelical singer had first visited Britain, and which has remained a popular source of quasi-religious music.
27 For an overview of Magic Lantern lecture practice, see Richard Crangle, "'Next Slide Please': the Lantern Lecture in Britain, 1890-1910," in *The Sounds of Early Cinema*, eds. Abel and Altman, 39-47.
28 A practice revived in the annual shows given by Jeremy Brooker and the author at Birkbeck College, accompanied by Stephen Horne and Costas Fotopoulos, since 2006.
29 For details of the Polytechnic's practice, see Jeremy Brooker's PhD research at Birkbeck, published as *The Temple of Minerva: Magic and the Magic Lantern*, Magic Lantern Society 2013.
30 Hepworth, *Came the Dawn*.
31 Hepworth, *Came the Dawn*, 31-2.
32 Martin Miller Marks, *Music and the Silent Film* (Oxford, 1997), 247.
33 A sequence of 18 films shot by Henry Short for Paul in August-September 1896, and premiered on 22 October at the Alhambra. For details, see Barnes, *Beginnings of Cinema, Vol. 1*, 256-258; also Christie, *Robert Paul and the Origins of British Cinema*, 125-128.

34 *Daily Telegraph*, 23 October 1896; *Morning Post*, 23 October 1896. The latter comment refers to the profusion of terms being used for moving pictures, often mocked in the contemporary press.
35 Vladimir Stasov, writing to his brother after attending a screening with the composer Glazunov on 30 May, 1896, printed in *Iskusstvo kino*, 1957, quoted in Jay Leyda, *Kino* (George Allen and Unwin, 1960), 18.
36 Reported by John Barnes in an addendum to Vol. 1 of his *Beginnings of Cinema in England*, with a reproduction of the original handbill from the Barnes Collection, 136a.
37 The 1896 Promenade Concert handbill also advertised a new 'piano resonator', with an endorsement by the famous Polish virtuoso Paderewski.
38 *KLW*, 6 June 1907, 54. Covent Garden's performance history records that there were additional performances of *Die Walküre* in 1908, outside the then-yearly Ring cycle.
39 Simon the Cellarer was advertised by Philipp Wolff in *The Era* on 21 January 1899. Details in Barnes, *Beginnings of Cinema in England, Vol. 4*, 29 and 407.
40 *Optical and Magic Lantern Journal*, 10/117, February 1899, 118. Cited in Barnes, *Beginnings of Cinema in England, Vol. 4*, 31.
41 Robert W Paul, 1901 Catalogue, 10.
42 'Coster' is an abbreviation for costermonger, or street-seller of fruit and vegetables in the Victorian era. By the late 19th century, the 'coster' was famous for his street cries and songs, and as a music hall character, notably performed by stars such as Albert Chevalier and Gus Elen. On costermongers, see Henry Mayhew, *London Labour and the London Poor* (1851), ed. Victor Neuburg (Penguin, 1985), 12-14.
43 I am grateful to David Robinson for identifying these three songs and their authors. ''Arry on the Steamboat' (c.1895), with words by Harry Grattan and music by Albert Maurice, was sung by E. J. Lonnen (1860-1901), a performer in stage musicals, who seems to have done music hall work as well. 'The Waif and the Wizard' was written in 1898 by Edward Kent, who also performed it, and was taken up by Mel B. Spurr (1852-1904), 'pre-eminent society entertainer at the piano'. 'Ora Pro Nobis', music by M. Piccolomini with words by A. Horspool, was popular from the 1880s to the First World War. Copies of all three are in the British Library. For a performance of 'Ora Pro Nobis' by musicologist Derek Scott, visit https://victorianweb.org/victorian/mt/parlorsongs/29.html.
44 The Royal Strand Theatre, as it then was, had had a chequered history throughout the 19th century, being rebuilt a number of times, before a musical, A Chinese Honeymoon, settled in for a record run of 1075 performances, after which the theatre was demolished and its site used for the Aldwych underground station.
45 Only one of these parts is currently known to exist, but a detailed programme brochure illustrates the whole series.
46 Music for *The Waif and the Wizard* has been put online from the Davenport Collection, at https://www.davenportcollection.co.uk/item/the-waif-and-the-wizard-song-sheet-dedicated-to-david-devant-esq. The film, clearly based on the sheet music illustration, is accessible on the BFI DVD.
47 See my detailed discussion of this film Chapter 10, 'A "Stagey Marvel"'.
48 See Chapter 17 on these synchronisation systems.

49 Other synchronisation systems in use in Britain included the Filmophone, Replicaphone, the Simplex and the Appollogramophone. See Rachael Low, *The History of the British Film, Vol. 2, 1906-1914*, 265-269.
50 Laurent Mannoni, "Phonoscènes," in *Encyclopaedia of Early Cinema*, ed. Richard Abel (Routledge, 2005), 518.
51 *KLW*, 16 May 1907, 10.
52 See the YouTube page 'ABC show collectors'.
53 At the St James' Hall, Kingston, *KLW*, 1 April, 1909, 1365.
54 Mr J. S. Bainton, who has had thirteen years' experience in 'kinematography' after previous 'connection with lantern shows, etc'., quoted in *KLW*, 6 May 1909, 1556.
55 Jon Burrows, 'The Art of Not Playing to Pictures in British Cinemas, 1906 to 1914', in *Sounds of the Silents in Britain* (Oxford, 2013), 111-125.
56 *The Bioscope*, 7 March 1912, 663.
57 Information on The Islington Picture Palace from The London Project database, part of the London Screen Study Centre, based at Birkbeck College's Centre for Film and Media Research. Not currently accessible.
58 For a recent survey of this evolution, see *Celluloid Symphonies*, ed. Julie Hibberd (California, 2011).
59 Stephen Bottomore, 'An International Survey of Sound Effects in Early Cinema'.
60 See, for instance, an advertisement by the Harper Electric Piano Company, *KLW*, 1 April 190, 1366.
61 Robert Hope–Jones was an English organ builder who developed the 'unit orchestra' electric organ in the 1890s, before emigrating to the United States in 1903, where he eventually joined the Wurlitzer company in 1910 and began to install organs in cinemas as well as churches from 1911 onwards. See, Q. David Bowers Nickelodeon Theatres and their Music (Vestal Press, 1986), 180. Although Low refers to 'an outburst of organs, zithers and bells from about 1910', it is not clear how many of these expensive instruments were installed in British cinemas; and most would have been substantially later (Low, vol. 2, 286)
62 Gillian Anderson, *Music for Silent Films*, 1894-1929 (Library of Congress, 1998), xxix.
63 Ambrosio's *The Last Days of Pompeii* was advertised on its premiere run at the West End Cinema in 1913 as being accompanied by 'full orchestra, with specially arranged music', *The Times*, 6 October 1913.
64 Performances of the original compilation by J. Morton Hutcheson have been given by Stephen Horne and John Sweeney. See Toby Haggith, 'Reconstructing the Musical Arrangement for *The Battle of the Somme* (1916)', *Film History*, 14, 2002, 11-24.
65 M. M. Hansford, "Picturegraphs" The American Organist, 6/24, 1923, 234; quoted in Anderson, *Music for Silent Films*, xxxvii. The author appears to have been a regular contributor to this journal, and was presumably American – as well as an organist.
66 In North London, a 1913 advertisement for the East Finchley Picturedrome announced 'the special engagement of the 'Nella' Bijou Orchestra, conducted by Mrs Cecil Allen', *The Finchley Press*, 3 January 1913: 11; and later in the same year, the rival Finchley Rink Cinema advertised a film of Max Reinhardt's great stage success, *The Miracle*, as 'with chorus', *The Finchley Press*, 5 December 1913, 11. On these, see Chapter 20 here.

67 Vachel Lindsay, *The Art of the Moving Picture*. See the 1922 edition online at Project Gutenberg.
68 Lawrence began what became *The Lost Girl* in 1913, and his account of the 'Woodhouse' variety show 'going over' to showing only films is likely to have been based on his own observation of the that period. D. H. Lawrence, *The Lost Girl* (1920) (Penguin, 1995), 116.
69 On the concept of "remediation," see Jay Boulter and Richard Grusin, *Remediation: Understanding New Media* (MIT, 2000).

19. Bringing the Empire Home: Imperial Spectacle in Early Cinema

1 Robert Paul introduced titling, first on slides, then printed onto the film around 1900. A reference to to a 'lecturer' being optional in 1900-01 (to present his recruiting film series *Army Life*) indicates this was still common practice, as it would continue to be until around 1909. However, it is not clear if lecturers were common in music halls, or whether the subjects of films were displayed on boards alongside the stage. See note 21 below for 'the tablet' greeting the appearance of Kitchener.
2 See an eyewitness account of the wedding procession from Mary H. Krout, *A Looker-On in London* (1899).
3 'La nature prise sur le fait': the phrase used by several early viewers of the Cinématographe, noted by Georges Sadoul.
4 On the organisation and filming of *La sortie de l'usine Lumière a Lyon*, see Chapter 8, '"Everyday Life" in Early Cinema.'
5 Showing a cross-section of society was a feature of the Lumière brand: their earliest illustrated advertisement for the Cinématographe features a 'family' audience watching the *Gardener Watered* comedy.
6 'Performative Utterances', in J. L. Austin, *Philosophical Papers* (Oxford, 1961).
7 Mantegna's nine paintings date from the last decades of the 15th century, and were brought to Britain in 1629 by King Charles and hung at Hampton Court, where they have remained ever since.
8 Peter W. Sinnema, *The Wake of Wellington: Englishness in 1852* (Ohio, 2006), 75-76.
9 The Last of England exists in two versions, in Birmingham Museum and Art Gallery and the Fitzwilliam Museum, Cambridge. Tennyson's Enoch Arden has served as the basis of many films, beginning with D. W. Griffith's 1911 version. Ilya Repin's *They Did Not Expect Him* (1884-88), is in the Tretyakov Gallery, Moscow.
10 In Alison Light, ed., *Island Stories*, vol. II of *Theatres of Memory* (Verso, 1998), 74-97.
11 After their magazine appearances, both stories were collected in *Traffics and Discoveries*, 1904.
12 On the films of the Diamond Jubilee, see text of Luke McKernan's 2012 presentation.
13 *Daily Mail*, quoted by McKernan.
14 *The Era*, quoted by McKernan.
15 John Munro, 'Living Photographs of the Queen', *Cassell's Family Magazine*, July 1897, 327.
16 Opera House advertisement, *The Herald* (Melbourne), 14 August 1897.
17 *The Sun*, Melbourne, 27 August 1897, 5.

18   Leopold Erdiger, 'The Duke of Wellington's Funeral Car', *Journal of the Warburg and Courtauld Institutes*, 3, 1939; quoted in *Sinnema*, 76, 144
19   David Cannadine, *Ornamentalism: How the British Saw their Empire* (Allen Lane, 2001), 111.
20   Cannadine, xix.
21   *The Era*, 18 October 1898, 19a; quoted in Barnes, vol. 3, 157.
22   *Morning Leader*, 28 October 1898, originally quoted in *The Mutoscope* (American Mutoscope Co, 1898), 8; quoted in Richard Brown and Barry Anthony, *A Victorian Film Enterprise* (Flicks, 1999), 51.
23   Warwick catalogue, quoted by Barnes, vol. 4, 288-89.
24   See Chapter 5, 'The Anglo-Boer War in North London'.
25   The film is lost. Description from Paul's Films. Supplementary List, April 1903, BFI Special Collections.
26   Only fragmentary and degraded material survives from Paul's 1903 series.
27   J. H. Rivett-Carnac, *Many Memories of Life in India, at Home and Abroad* (Blackwood, 1910).
28   Nicolas' comment is quoted in Jay Leyda, *Kino* (Allen and Unwin, 1960), 69.
29   Urban's Durbar film ran 2 hours 30 mins, and attracted vast audiences, both at the Scala in London and around the UK. See Luke McKernan, *Charles Urban: Pioneering the Non-fiction Film in Britain and America, 1897-1925*. Exeter: Exeter University Press, 2013. Chapter 3, 'The Eighth Wonder of the World. 'The Eighth Wonder of the World'. Also online https://lukemckernan.com/2013/07/21/charles-urban/.
30   Samuel, 82.
31   John Grierson initially securing funding for documentary filmmaking from the 'Empire Marketing Board'. See feature on this at Colonial Film Database: http://www.colonialfilm.org.uk/production-company/empire-marketing-board.
32   Harold Innis, *Empire and Communications* (Oxford, 1950).
33   For a recent discussion of Innis' theories, see Megan Mullen, 'Space Bias/Time Bias: Harold Innis, "Empire and Communications"', *Technology and Culture*, Vol. 50, no. 1, 2009.
34   P. D. Morgan, 'Encounters between British and "indigenous" Peoples, c. 1500-c.1800', in M. J. Daunton and R. Hapern, eds., *Empire and Others* (Routledge, 1999), 68; quoted as an epigraph in Cannadine, vi.

20. Ancient Rome Revisited: Classical Subjects and Cinema's Expansion after 1910

1   Many of these painters were highly successful academicians, and reaction against them may have been fuelled as much by the Modernist revolt against academicism as by a disdain for their idealised and illustrative subject-matter. In the case of films based on popular 19th-century 'toga plays', these suffered the same derision as their sources, especially due to their association with mass evangelism. See David Mayer, *Playing Out the Empire* (Clarendon, 1994), 1-6.
2   Edward Thompson spoke of working against 'the enormous condescension of posterity' at the beginning of his groundbreaking recovery of English 'history from beneath', *The Making of the English Working Class* (1963). The idea of the properly 'cinematic' or 'filmic' emerges in film criticism around 1930, in such works as C. A. Lejeune, *The Cinema* (1931) and Rotha, *The Film Till Now* (1930).

3   Richard Abel, *French Film Theory and Criticism 1907-1939. A History/Anthology. vol. 1* (Princeton, 1988).
4   Robert Brasillach and Maurice Bardeche, *Histoire du Cinéma* (Denoël et Steele, 1935).
5   Letter from O'Neill to Beatrice Ashe, 7 October 1914, quoted in Richard Hayes, '"The Scope of the Movies": Three Films and their Influence on Eugene O'Neill', *The Eugene O'Neill Review*, vol. 25, no 1-2, Penn State University Press, 37-53, 2001.
6   The former belongs to a group of nine *vues historiques* made for Lumière in 1896 or 1897 by Georges Hâtot, which mark an exception in the Lumières' predominantly contemporary *vues*. Catalogue Lumière, cinquième liste, no. 747, *Néron essayant des poisons sur les esclaves*, in Georges Sadoul, *Lumière et Méliès* (Lherminier, 1985), 137.
7   Maria Wyke, *Projecting the Past* (Routledge, 1997), 150-86.
8   Lionel Lambourne, *Victorian Painting* (Phiadon, 1999), 294.
9   Michael Booth, *Victorian Spectacular Theatre 1850-1910* (Routledge, 1981), 72, quoting *The Times*, 4 April 1902.
10 Samantha Ellis, 'Ben-Hur, London, 1902', *The Guardian*, 8 October 2003.
11 Wyke 1997, 156-7. Paul began constructing his new studio in Muswell Hill in 1899, less than a mile from Alexandra Palace, which had by then presented 'Pain's Last Days of Pompeii' for at least a decade as part of its summer entertainment season.
12 Description in *The Era*, 28 June 1900, quoted in John Barnes (1997), 192.
13 Wyke 1997, 157, quoting from Mayer, *Playing Out the Empire*, 41-50.
14 See discussion of this in Chapter 19, 'Bringing the Empire Home'.
15 Rachael Low records that around 1912 'whether films should be accompanied by a lecturer exercised the showman', presumably on the basis of her close reading of trade journals. Low, *History of the British Film, Vol. 1* (Allen and Unwin, 1948), 17. However, the scale of lecturer accompaniment at this date and beyond is still far from clear.
16 Richard Abel, *The Ciné Goes to Town: French Cinema, 1896-1914* (California, 1994), 248
17 For an account and analysis of *Héliogabale*, see Abel (1994), 255-6.
18 See Chapter 14, 'Fumbling Towards Some New Art'.
19 *The Finchley Press*, 7 February 1912.
20 Low, *History of the British Film, 1914-1918, vol. 3* (Allen and Unwin, 1948), 26-7 quotes a range of British trade opinion, between 1915 and 1918, in favour of 'short pieces' and three-reel films, rather than the five-reelers that were becoming common. She suggests this may have reflected exhibitors' self-interest, since these films generally remained cheaper than the new 'super films' and allowed more shows to run during a day.
21 Low, *History of the British Film, 1906-1914, Volume 2*, 46.
22 Ivo Blom, *Jean Desmet and the Early Dutch Film Trade* (Amsterdam, 2003), 230 ff.
23 *The Bioscope*, 30 March 1911, 58.
24 *The Bioscope*, 23 February 1911.
25 *The Sketch*, 29 April 1914, 3.
26 Low, *History of the British Film, Volume 1*, 47.
27 *The Bioscope*, 16 March 1911, 59.
28 This information comes from a report in *The Times*, 13 May 1913, on 'holiday crowds at various places of recreation', which may be the first

time that a film presentation appeared alongside attendance figures for such venues as Hampton Court (120,000), Crystal Palace (60,000) and Alexandra Palace (30,000).

29 All quotes here are from *The Times*, 6 October 1913.
30 Three Zigomar films were made by Eclair in 1911-13 (directed by Victorin Jasset); five Fantômas serials were produced by Gaumont in 1913-14, followed by *Les Vampires* in 1915 (all directed by Louis Feuillade).
31 Glaucus, the hero of *The Last Days of Pompeii*, is a Greek living among the Romans of first century Pompeii and, while not a Christian (although Christianity is practised among the city's many cults), clearly embodies Christian values. The two other novels that would serve as key source-texts for later films set in the first century CE, *Ben-Hur* and *The Robe*, are both explicitly Christian apologetics.
32 Joseph Menchen's coloured 'lyricscope' screen version of the Vol. lmayer-Reinhardt spectacle had its world premiere at the Royal Opera House in London in December 1912, accompanied by a large orchestra playing Englebert Humperdinck's score, and ancillary staged elements, before touring widely and successfully.
33 Advertisement, *The Bioscope*, 6 September 1915.
34 *The Times*, 7 May 1913.
35 A copy from the Rink Picture Theatre, Aberystwyth, was digitised as part of Bibliografica Celtica, National Library of Wales.
36 *The Times*, 6 May 1913, 11.
37 *Evening Post*, Wellington, 17 July 1913.
38 *Ashburton Guardian*, 31 December 1913.
39 *The Times*, 24 September 1913.
40 *The Times*, 6 October 1913.
41 'Bulwer-Lytton and His Times', *The Times*, 1 November 1913.
42 All subsequent information in this paragraph comes from cinema advertisements in *The Finchley Press*.
43 See Chapter 13, 'The Lost World of Early North London Filmmaking'.
44 It is not clear what 1812 would have been, unless it was the Russian film of this title, directed by Vasili Goncharov, and possibly distributed internationally by Pathé.
45 *Bioscope*, 26 February 1914, 955.
46 Blom 2003, 229.
47 Blom 2003, 230
48 Blom 2003, 232
49 Skaff 2008, 46.
50 *The Times*, 9 April 1913, 11.
51 Von Hofmannsthal in Luft (2011), 115.
52 The film in question could be *Teodora imperatrice di Bisanzio* (1909, dir. E. M. Pasquali), the *Film d'Art Théodora* (1912, dir. H. Pouctal), or even a later memory of Ambrosio's post-war *Theodora* (1921, dir. L. Carlucci).
53 Prieur (1993), 182-3. Since C. B. DeMille's *The Ten Commandments* (1923) does not treat Moses' childhood, this could be a reference to Vitagraph's *Life of Moses* (1909, dir. J. S. Blackton).
54 Lewis (1955), 35.
55 Rotha (1930), 235. Rotha was born in 1907, and one wonders when – or even if – he had actually seen *Cabiria* at the time of writing his precocious overview. By comparison, the present writer recalls interviewing the Belgian

filmmaker Henri Storck, also born in 1907, who in the 1980s recalled vividly the impression that *Cabiria* had made on him as a child.
56 For example, David Robinson, *The History of World Cinema*, New York: Stein and Day, 1973; Eric Rhode, *A History of the Cinema From Its Origins to 1970*, New York: Hill and Wang, 1978.

21. A 'Theatre of Memory'? Screening Historic Literary London

1 Raphael Samuel, *Theatres of Memory* (Verso, 2012), xxi.
2 Although written by the novelist Graham Greene, *The Third Man* was an original screenplay, while *Lawrence of Arabia* was also an original script by the playwright Robert Bolt, after earlier attempts to adapt Lawrence's own memoir, *The Seven Pillars of Wisdom*, had failed to reach production.
3 Andrew Higson, 'Representing the national past: nostalgia and pastiche in the heritage film', in L. Friedman, ed., *British Cinema and Thatcherism*, London: UCL Press, 1993, 114. For an overview of the 'heritage cinema' debate, see Sheldon Hall, 'The Wrong Sort of Cinema: Refashioning the Heritage Film Debate', in Robert Murphy, ed., *The British Cinema Book*, 2nd ed. (BFI, 2001), 191-199.
4 Ibid./Higson, 'Representing the National Past', 114.
5 Typically, also, the German-born author of their screenplays, Ruth Prawer-Jhabvala, was left out of the equation, although the fact that this trio were none of them English might have been worth discussing
6 A typical dismissive review, though by a literary rather than a film critic, is Alan Hollingshurst's review of *A Room With a View*, in which he describes the novel as Forster's 'least interesting' and the Merchant-Ivory film as 'a spirited if simple-minded confection', 'Detached about Attachments', *Times Literary Supplement*, 11 April 1986, 375.
7 See, for instance, Claire Monk's argument that *A Room with a View* and *Maurice* are more radical in their portrayal of sexuality and gender than apparently more frank recent films such as *Carrington* and *Orlando*, 'Sexuality and the heritage', *Sight and Sound*, Vol. 5, no. 10 (NS), October 1995, 33-34.
8 'In the Merchant-Ivory films, where they make use of English settings, one wide shot says it all, and you really get a sense of who these people are'. Ian Christie and David Thompson, eds., *Scorsese on Scorsese*, 3rd ed., Faber, 2003, 187.
9 Raphael Samuel, *Theatres of Memory*, Verso, 1994. See also Carolyn Steedman, obituary of Raphael Samuel, *Radical Philosophy*, March-April 1997.
10 On the peculiar history of animosity by British critics towards British cinema, see, for instance: Victor Perkins, 'The British Cinema', *Movie*, no. 1, 1962; Ian Christie, *Arrows of Desire* (Waterstone, 1985/Faber, 1994); Julian Petley, 'The Lost Continent', in Charles Barr, ed., *All Our Yesterdays* (BFI, 1986); Alan Lovell, 'British Cinema: The Known Cinema?', in Murphy, ed., *The British Cinema Book*, 2nd ed., 200-205.
11 See for instance, the report *Stately Attraction: How Film and Television Programmes Promote Tourism in the UK*, 2007, reported in *The Guardian*, 27 August 2007.
12 Robert Stam, Robert Burgoyne, Sandy Flitterman-Lewis, *New Vocabularies in Film Semiotics* (Routledge, 1992), 142
13 Charles Affron and Mirella Jona Affron, *Sets in Motion* (Rutgers, 1995).

14 For elements of an overview, see Peter Ettedgui, ed., *Production Design and Art Direction* (RotoVision, 1999) and my essay 'Crafting Worlds: The Changing Role of the Production designer', in Steven Allen and Laura Hubner, eds., *Framing Film* (Intellect 2012). And a note on terminology: although the lead designer on a film is now called 'production designer', this role was known as 'art director' until the 1950s. Today, the 'art director' is the immediate subordinate of the production designer; and the field of work is ambiguously referred to as 'production design' and 'art direction'.

15 Following the FIAF Archives Congress at Brighton in 1978. For a brief overview, see Jan-Christopher Horak's blog: https://www.cinema.ucla.edu/blogs/archival-spaces/2018/06/08/fiaf-brighton-1978.

16 Ernest Lindgren, *The Arts of the Film* (Allen and Unwin, 1950), 47.

17 In fairness to earlier scholars, both Terry Ramsaye, in *A Million and One Nights* (1926), and Ernest Lindgren in *The Art of the Film* (1950) placed cinema in a larger context, especially that of literature.

18 Jay Bolter, Richard Grusin, *Remediation* (MIT, 2000).

19 Mikhail Bakhtin, *Speech Genres and Other Late Essays* (Texas, 1986), 5.

20 See Paul Langford, *Englishness Identified* (Oxford, 2000), Ch 3, with its opening section headed 'Barbarity'. See also, Christie, *Robert Paul and the Origins of British Cinema*, Chapter 3.

21 Paul's film is included in the BFI DVD *Collected Films of R. W. Paul*.

22 Richard Brown and Barry Anthony, *A Victorian Film Enterprise* (Flicks, 1999), 272.

23 *A Christmas Carol in Prose, Being a Ghost Story of Christmas* (usually known as *A Christmas Carol*), was first published in December 1843, with illustrations by John Leech.

24 Low, *History of the British Film 1906-1914*, 134.

25 See Jude Cowan Montague, 'Sixty Years a Queen (1913): a lost epic of the reign of Victoria', in Mandy Merck, ed., *The British Monarchy on Screen* (Manchester, 2016), 47-53.

26 See Chapter 20, 'Ancient Rome Revisited'.

27 Low, *History of the British Film*, 219.

28 Low, *History of the British Film, Volume. 2*, 190.

29 Sergei Eisenstein, 'Dickens, Griffith and the Film Today' (1944), published in Jay Leyda, ed. and trans., *Film Form* (Harcourt, Brace and World, 1949).

30 *The Bioscope*, 24. 9. 14, 1160; quoted in Low, *History of the British Film 1914-1918*, 54-55. Warwick Buckland appears to have been unconnected with Wilfred Buckland, DeMille's art director, and to have served as an all-round member of Hepworth's studio staff.

31 *KLW*, 1 March 1917, 23.

32 See Kristin Thompson, *Exporting Entertainment* (BFI, 1985).

33 Sir Hubert Herkomer RA, one of England's most distinguished painters, announced in 1913 that he was giving up painting to embark on a new career as a filmmaker, believing that 'the cinematograph is going to be the greatest educational force of the time'. Unfortunately, he died less than year later, leaving only a handful of completed films, none of which survive. See Lynda Nead, 'Paintings, Films and Fast Cars: A Case Study of Hubert von Herkomer', *Art History*, 25 (2), 2002) 240-255. See also Chapter 13, 'The Lost World of Early North London Filmmaking'.

34 On Bernhard's early film career, see Richard Abel, *The Ciné Goes to Town* (California, 1998), 313-316.

35 DeMille famously cabled to his financiers in New York that he had reached 'a place called Hollywood' where he proposed to begin filming his first production, *The Squaw Man*, in 1913. On DeMille's early career, see John Kobal, *The DeMille Heritage* (Giornate del cinema muto)

36 According to accounts of Buckland's relationship with DeMille, it was the former who insisted on integration and followed Belasco's precepts. See Léon Barsacq, *Caligari's Cabinet and Other Grand Illusions*, trans. and rev. Elliott Stein (New American Library, 1976), 200.

37 Adolph Zukor, 'Famous Players in Famous Plays', Motion Picture World, 11 7. 1914, 186; quoted in Sumiko Higashi, *Cecil B. DeMille and American Culture* (California, 1994), 8.

38 'Cashing in on Europe's War, 1916-18' is the title of a chapter in Kristin Thompson's invaluable study, *Exporting Entertainment* (BFI, 1985). The frontispiece is a 1917 trade paper cartoon captioned 'Zukor annexes Australia'.

39 Thompson, *Exporting Entertainment* (BFI, 1985), 63-64.

40 'Patriotism and Business' is the heading of an Ideal trade advertisement that insists these should not be confused, while arguing that its films successfully combine them. *KLW*, 22 March 1917.

41 See William Uricchio and Roberta E. Pearson, *Reframing Culture* (Princeton, 1993).

42 Marion Blackton Trimble's 'Personal biography by His Daughter' is certainly not always reliable, but her account of this dinner in 1920, which arose from shared interests in yachting, strikes a convincing note. J. Stuart Blackton (Scarecrow, 1985), 102-104.

43 *Restoration* (1995), adapted from a novel by Rose Tremain and directed by Michael Hoffman, is set in the reign of Charles II, and includes both the Plague and the Great Fire. Significantly, it won Eugenio Zanetti the Academy Award for production design.

44 Marion Tribble Blackton's account of the filming, in which she participated, is unfortunately entirely anecdotal (124-144).

45 Some art directors were emerging in the late 'teens, however, as is apparent from occasional articles in the trade press. See, for instance, a report on a talk by E. P. Kinsella, which included a contribution by 'Hayward Young… the first artist in this country to become an Art Director in the film studio', 'Kinsella on "Art in Production"', *KLW*, 12 December 1918, 59.

46 This and the subsequent quotation from his nephew's memoir, Michael Korda, *Charmed Lives* (Penguin, 1979), 99.

47 After the First World War, Wells campaigned for an international organisation, which led to the League of Nations, and wrote *An Outline of History* (1919-20) to spread popular awareness of the lessons of history. *The Shape of Things to Come* (1933), set in 1930, uses the conceit of a 'dream diary' based on the theories of J. W. Dunne, in which the hero foresees the following century.

48 The art director Edward Carrick wrote of Vincent Korda that, 'There is no distinctive personal touch about [his] sketches or finished sets', adding that, 'I think he is apt to look on films too much as a commercial product', *Designing for Moving Pictures*, The Studio Publications [n.d.], 39.

49 During the 1930s and much of the 40s, the Technicolor company stipulated that a representative had to be involved in each production using the process. This was usually Natalie Kalmus, wife of the founder Herbert Kalmus, and

she notoriously insisted on the maximum range and saturation of colour, to the irritation of many filmmakers and cameramen.

50 The Powell-Pressburger films that impressed many outside Britain were *A Matter of Life and Death* (1946), *Black Narcissus* (1947) and *The Red Shoes* (1948). On these and the course of British cinema history in the postwar period, see Ian Christie, *Arrows of Desire* (Faber, 1994, 2nd ed). See also Sarah Street, *British National Cinema* (Routledge, 1997).

51 *Major Barbara*, the last of Gabriel Pascal's ponderous Shaw adaptations, gave Bryan his first opportunity to work on a larger scale at Denham Studios, paving the way for his collaboration on the post-war Cineguild Dickens adaptations.

52 Ronald Neame, quoted in Kevin Brownlow, *David Lean* (Richard Cohen, 1996) 138-139.

53 See for instance the recurrent image of St Paul's in Humphrey Jennings' wartime documentaries, *Listen to Britain* and *Fires Were Started*, and in many newsreels of the period.

54 Among the Neo-romantics could be included the painters Graham Sutherland, John Piper and Cecil Collins, along with poets, musicians and filmmakers. See David Mellor, ed., *Paradise Lost* (Lund Humphries, 1987).

55 Gustave Doré and Blanchard Jerrold, *London* (Grant and Co., 1872).

56 The film was based on a recent biography of Friese Greene (1855-1921) which supported his claim to have devised practical moving pictures by 1899, although this remains unproven. But the film lives through Bryan's rich colour décor, Jack Cardiff's cinematography and an all-star cast, led by Robert Donat.

57 The 1927 Cinematograph Film Act obliged British exhibitors and distributors to meet a rising minimum quota of domestic productions throughout the 1930s, which encouraged many new companies to start making low-budget 'quota films'. Many of these were so impoverished that they earned the reputation of being 'quota quickies', although this has been applied too sweepingly to British production of the 1930s. The recent BFI set *Michael Powell: Early Works* showcases the range of production levels possible.

58 Bower had produced *Alexander Nevsky* as a radio play in 1941. See Ian Christie, 'Censorship, Culture and Codpieces: Eisenstein's Influence in England during the 1930s and 40s', in Al Lavalley and Barry P. Scherr, eds., *Eisenstein at 100* (Rutgers, 2001), 113-116.

59 On Box's career as a whole, Ian Christie, *The Art of Film* (Wallflower, 2009).

60 This Bond title was the only one not owned by the Saltzman-Broccoli partnership that had launched the Bond series with Dr No. It had become a Peter Sellers 'vanity project', with multiple actors playing Bond and up to six directors, described by Roger Ebert as 'a definitive example of what can happen when everybody working on a film goes simultaneously berserk'.

61 Fred Zinnemann, *An Autobiography* (Bloomsbury, 1992), 199.

62 Zinnemann, *Autobiography*, 199.

63 Films that feature the market include *Pygmalion* (Anthony Asquith, 1938); *The Red Shoes* (Powell and Pressburger, 1948), *My Fair Lady* (George Cukor,1964); and *Frenzy* (Alfred Hitchcock, 1972). In Dickens' novel, Oliver arrives in Barnet, and proceeds to Islington and Saffron Hill.

64 Doré and Jerrold, *London*, pl. 115.

65 See no. 4, 'The Tide of Business in the City', no. 23, 'A River-Side Street' and especially no. 130, 'St Pauls from the Brewery Bridge', *London* (Dover edition, 2004).
66 Sorenson juxtaposes a photograph from the Society for Photographing Relics of Old London, 'Old Houses in Fore Street', with part of Box's back-street set, *London on Film* (Museum of London, 1996), 104-105.
67 Pelham Crescent, SW7, for instance, was built in 1827-30. Another model might be Percy Circus, WC1.
68 There is a wider continuing debate on film's 'challenge to our idea of history', as the subtitle reads for Robert Rosenstone, *Visions of the Past* (Harvard, 1995). See also writings by Natalie Zemon David, Hayden White and Raphael Samuel.
69 On 18th-century imagery, see Sheila O'Connell, London 1753, catalogue of an exhibition in the Print Rom of the British Museum, The British Museum Peres, 2003. On mid-Victorian London illustration, see Lynda Nead, *Victorian Babylon* (Yale, 2000), especially Part 1, 'Mapping and Movement'.
70 Roy Porter observes, however, that Hogarth's print series, *A Rake's Progress* and *A Harlot's Progress*, are 'allegories but also literal journeys through the capital'. 'The Wonderful Extent and Variety of London', in O'Connell, *London* (1753), 17.
71 *The Art Journal*, 1872.
72 Affron, *Art Direction and Film Narrative*, 40-41.
73 As in such modern gangster classics as *Performance* (Roeg/Cammell, 1970) and *The Long Good Friday* (Mackenzie, 1980).
74 The theory of 'intertextuality', whereby various texts are seen in shifting relations to each other, without a presumed hierarchy of chronology or status, may be a firmer basis than 'adaptation' for considering the translation from verbal to audiovisual text. See Mikhail Iampolski, *The Memory of Tiresias*.
75 Matte paintings, often on glass, were used to extend built scenery in filmmaking throughout much of the 20th century, before the introduction of computer-generated imagery (CGI) during the 1970s. Many productions, however, use a combination of built scenery and practical effects, enhanced by CGI, to create an effective simulation. See, for instance, 'The CGI Magic of Harry Potter' (https://www.youtube.com/watch?v=2XshC_gAaPg).
76 Roger Ebert, *Chicago Sun-Times*, 26 January 1996.
77 Television's extended Dickens adaptations, such as the BBC's *David Copperfield* (1986-7, 10 episodes) or *Bleak House* (2005, 16 episodes), included much greater narrative and character detail than cinema versions, with correspondingly less emphasis on locations and architecture. The innovative 2015 series Dickensian took this to an extreme, with essentially only one 'street' set, in which its many Dickens characters interacted.
78 Grahame Smith, *Dickens and the Dream of Cinema* (Manchester, 2003).

22. Who Needs Film Archives? Notes Towards a User-Centred Future

1 The earliest national film archives date back to the 1930s. The Federation International des Archives du Film (www.fiafnet.org) was founded in Paris in 1938, and revived post-war. Based in Brussels, it now recognizes over 150 archives in 77 countries.
2 For a history of the international archive movement, see Penelope Houston, *Keepers of the Frame* (BFI, 1994).

3   Jullier and Leveratto, 'Cinephilia in the Digital Age', in Ian Christie, ed., *Audiences* (Amsterdam, 2012), 143-154.
4   Even the Library of Congress Motion Picture Division did not start active collecting until the early 1940s. See the American Memory range of online guides, tours, menus etc. developed by the Library of Congress.
5   Launched by Jacques Chirac, then mayor of Paris, as part of the new underground shopping and services hub at Les Halles/Chatelet.
6   See Frank Gray, 'Recovering a region's film history', *Film Studies*, Spring 1990, 92-94.
7   See Raphael Samuel's collected essays in *Theatres of Memory* (Verso, 1994), which recognized the value of many informal collecting practices; also the multi-author series *Lieux de memoire* (Gallimard, 1984-92), edited by Pierre Nora, which showed how popular traditions of commemoration create 'cultural sites' that include many media. An abridged translation of this was published by Columbia University Press as *Realms of Memory* (1994-96), while four volumes have been published by the University of Chicago Press, under the general title *Rethinking France: les lieux de memoire* (1999-2010).
8   *Their Past, Your Future*, a DVD produced by the London Screen Study Collection at Birkbeck College for London's Screen Archives: the Regional Network, drew heavily on the Pathe Newsreel Library, including a number of items never finalized for release.
9   This vast production by the Watch Tower Bible and Tract Society of Pennsylvania under the direction of Charles Taze Russell, the founder of the Bible Student movement (forerunners of the Jehovah's Witnesses), was considered lost until segments resulting from a private restoration project by Brian Kuscher began to appear on YouTube several years ago. A partial screening based on this restoration, was presented by the present author, place as part of the Derry/Londonderry City of Culture programme in November 2013. A major international study of the Photodrama is being coordinated by George Eastman Museum Rochester for publication in 2025.
10 The British Film Institute has operated up to nine mediatheques around the UK, offering casual or pre-booked access to curated selections, but currently (2024) operates only five, including the BFI Southbank Mediatheque. Wider access to its collections is via the BFI Player. The Australian National Film and Sound Archive, based in Canberra, has offered The Australian Mediatheque at the Australian Centre for the Moving Image in central Melbourne.
11 Film viewing in archives is generally carried out on a variety of 'flatbed' viewers, such as the Steenbeck, which allows film and sound elements to be combined, speed to be varied, and frequent stopping and starting.
12 Jacques Derrida, *Archive Fever* (Chicago, 1998), trans. Eric Prenowitz from *Mal d'Archive* (Galilée, 1995).
13 The Soviet archives had to be especially vigilant in both removing representations of politically censored figures, and is preserving these in case of subsequent rehabilitation. After Stalin's denunciation by Khrushchev in 1956, almost all filmic representations of Stalin disappeared from view, and were not seen again until the perestroika period of the later 1980s, some in copies preserved clandestinely by foreign archives.
14 Originally shortened for export versions in an attempt to court popularity, *Metropolis* has enjoyed a number of reconstructions – the most recent in 2010, following discovery of an original copy in Argentina.

15 At the British National Film Archive, in the 1970s, its technical officer, Harold Brown, devised ways of printing from shrunken and damaged film elements, which laid the basis for preserving many early films then in danger of ceasing to be reproducible. See obituary, Harold Brown RIP, Nov 2008, at http://thebioscope.net/2008/11/17/harold-brown-rip/. Even earlier, the US Library of Congress had engaged Kemp Niver to begin the process of transferring paper prints of its early copyright deposits so that these could generate new negatives, laying the basis for the Library's unique Paper Print Collection. See Kemp Niver, 'From Film to Paper to Film', *The Quarterly Journal of the Library of Congress*, Vol. 21, no. 4, October 1964, 248-64; also Paul C. Spehr, 'Some Still Fragments of a Moving Past', *The Quarterly Journal of the Library of Congress*, Vol. 32, no. 1, January 1975, 33-50.

16 Henri Langlois was notoriously cavalier in screening and storing rare prints, in contrast to Ernest Lindgren, the founding curator of Britain's National Film Archive, who always regarded conservation as the highest priority, irrespective of access requests. Although responsible for the loss of many elements through fire and poor record-keeping, Langlois was rewarded by an international campaign in his support in 1968 and by a continuing place in the legend of the Cinémathèque française as a cradle of future filmmakers. On controversy surrounding Langlois, see Roger Smither 'Henri Langlois and Nitrate, Before and After 1959', in Smither, ed., *This Film is Dangerous* (FIAF, 2002), 247-55.

17 This is the argument advanced in Ian Christie, *The Last Machine* (BBC/BFI, 1994) and in the accompanying BBC television series; also in various conferences marking the 'second birth of cinema' in 1910, reported in The Bioscope blog, at http://thebioscope.net/2010/06/18/the-second-birth-of-cinema/

18 This resulted in the collection edited by Pantelis Michelakis and Maria Wyke, *The Ancient World in Early Cinema* (Cambridge, 2013). Currently a new project is under way, coordinated by Wyke, Pantelis and Ivo Blom, *The Museum of Dream Worlds*, devoted to 'silent antiquity films in the BFI National Archive', funded by the UK Arts and Humanities Research Council, and based at University College London's Department of Greek and Latin.

19 Martin Loiperdinger, Uli Jung, eds., *Importing Asta Nielsen* (John Libbey, 2013). See also Chapter 16 here, which originally formed part of this book.

20 The British Film Institute's pioneering Museum of the Moving Image (1988-1999) was an early success as a visitor attraction, although closed by the BFI in favour of investing in a new IMAX cinema. However, a number of other film museums appear to be flourishing: notably the Fondazione Maria Adriana Prolo – Museo Nazionale del Cinema (Turin, Italy, since 2000); The German Film Archive – Museum for Film and Television (Frankfurt, Germany, since 2000); and The Museum of the Cinémathèque française at Bercy (Paris, France, since 2007).

23. 'A Very Wonderful Process': Queen Victoria, Photography and Film

1 John Plunkett, *Queen Victoria* (Oxford, 2003), 3.
2 Margaret Homans, 'Review: Queen Victoria: First Media Monarch', *Victorian Studies*, 46:3, Spring 2004, 520.
3 Bill Jay, 'Queen Victoria's second passion: royal patronage of photography in the 19th century' (1988). The date of her proposal is corroborated by

Christopher Hibbert in *Queen Victoria* (HarperCollins, 2000), 108-9, and other biographies, and in Victoria's journal, although this makes no mention of daguerreotypes.

4   Jay, 'Queen Victoria's second passion', 3.
5   Queen Victoria, Journals, 3 January 1854.
6   Charles Wheatstone, 'On some remarkable, and hitherto unobserved, phenomena of binocular vision', *Proceedings of the Royal Society*, 128, 1838.
7   Victoria records 'Stereoscope' in her draft journal entry for 25 August 1855, implying private time spent viewing stereographs while travelling in France.
8   Juan, Count of Montizon came to England after the uprisings of 1848 and was a founder member of the Photographic Society. After renouncing his claim to the Spanish throne, he lived for the rest of his life in Worthing and Hove. One of his London Zoo photographs, of a hippopotamus, illustrates his Wikipedia entry.
9   The Collodion process, invented by Frederick Archer in 1851, involved a glass plate being coated, exposed and developed within less than fi fteen minutes, often requiring a portable darkroom. It remained the preferred photographic process until the 1880s.
10 Jay, 'Queen Victoria's second passion', 5-6.
11 Jay, 7.
12 Her choice was apparently not the Gustav Mullins portrait taken on the day of the Jubilee, but an earlier image, which is now listed as 'photographer unknown'. Anne Lyden, quoted in interview by Barry Keevins, 'Picture pioneer: Queen Victoria's passion for photography', *Sunday Express*, 24 January 2014.
13 Keevins, 'Picture Pioneer'.
14 Jay, 'Queen Victoria's second passion', 7.
15 On Kahn's collection, see Teresa Castro, ' Les Archives de la planète,' *Jump Cut*, Winter 2006.
16 An attitude still apparent in much documentation of Victoria's photographic collecting. See for instance the online Diamond Jubilee Scrapbook, a website supported by the official British monarchy website: www.queen-victorias-scrapbook.org.
17 Cannadine quotes P. D. Morgan on the need to reach a 'synoptic view' of the imperial system in his *Ornamentalism: How the British Saw Their Empire* (Allen Lane, 2001). Philip D. Morgan, 'Encounters between British and "indigenous" peoples, c.1500-c.1800', in Martin Daunton and Rick Halpern, eds, *Empire and Others* (Routledge, 1999), 68.
18 See, for instance, Robert Paul's catalogues, 1897-1901, BFI Special Collections.
19 Jay records the earliest of these Royal Warrants as William Edward Kilburn being appointed 'Photographist to Her Majesty and His Royal Highness Prince Albert' in 1847, while later appointments were more specific, referring to 'Her majesty's photographer on paper' (Nicolaas Henneman, 1848) and 'Royal Photographer for Scotland' (George Washington Wilson, 1860). 'Queen Victoria's second passion', 5.
20 Prince and Princess of Wales Arriving in State at the Cardiff Exhibition (Northern Photographic Works [Acres], 40ft). Dennis Gifford, The British Film Catalogue, 1895-1985 (David & Charles, 1986), 6.
21 See the official website of the British Monarchy.
22 As reported in an article in the *Strand Magazine*, August 1896, 140.

23 *The Era*, 6 June 1896, 16.
24 *Illustrated London News*, supplement on the royal wedding, 1 August 1896.
25 Princess Maud's Wedding (Paul's Theatrograph, a two-part film of 80ft), released on 8 August. Gifford, *The British Film Catalogue*, 6.
26 Michael Pritchard, 'Downey' entry in John Hannay (ed.), *The Encyclopaedia of Nineteenth-Century Photography* (Routledge, 2013), 436.
27 Queen Victoria, Journals, 3 October 1896.
28 The printed programme is reproduced in John Barnes, *The Beginnings of the Cinema in England, 1894-1901, Vol. 1, 1894-1896*. Exeter: University of Exeter Press, 1998, 144.
29 Lady's Pictorial (December 1896), quoted in Barnes, *Beginnings*, 213-15
30 Queen Victoria, Journals, 23 November 1896.
31 This material was originally very unsteady, no doubt due to the improvised camera, but has been effectively stabilised and tinted by the BFI National Archive.
32 Queen Victoria, Journals, 23 November 1896.
33 Collette Piault, ' Films de famille et fi lms sur la famille', in Natalie Tousignant, ed., *Le Film de famille*, Brussels: Facultés universitaires Saint-Louis, 2004, 57. See also Roger Odin, ed., *Le Film de famille. Usage privé, usage public* (Méridiens-Klincksieck, 1999), 6. Odin insists that the family film, whatever its technical qualities, has a unique significance and adequacy for its subjects.
34 Barnes, Beginnings, 215.
35 The Balmoral film is now in the BFI National Archive, and has been included in documentaries. It has not proved possible to establish when it was first seen publicly.
36 There exists a good selection of photographs and illustrations of the Khodynka tragedy at www.alamy.com.
37 Jay Leyda recorded an account of the disaster, as told to him by Doublier, in his *Kino: A History of the Russian and Soviet Film* (George Allen & Unwin, 1960), 19.
38 For the most complete account of Matuszewski's somewhat mysterious career, see Magdalena Mazaraki, 'Boleslaw Matuszewski: photographe et opérateur de cinéma', *1895* 44, 2004.
39 Reported in *Le Figaro*, 'A travers Paris' (12 January 1898), 1-2, quoted in Mazaraki, 'Boleslaw Matuszewski'.
40 Boleslaw Matuszewski, *Une Nouvelle Source de l'histoire* ; *La Photographie animée*. Both published Paris, 1898.
41 Reminiscing about his early career as a film pioneer in 1936, Robert Paul recalled that 'in [the] year before the Jubilee, public interest in animated pictures seemed to be on the wane'. R. W. Paul, 'Before 1910: kinematograph experiences', *Proceedings of the British Kinematograph Society* 38, 1936, 5.
42 William M. Kuhn, 'Brett, Reginald Baliol', *Oxford Dictionary of National Biography*,
43 G. W. Steevens, 'Up they came', *Daily Mail*, 23 June 1897. The fullest account of the Jubilee and its filming is in Luke McKernan, 'Queen Victoria's Diamond Jubilee' (2012), accessible online: http://lukemckernan.com/wp-content/uploads/queen_victoria_diamond_jubilee.pdf.
44 For a survey of opinion on the Jubilee, see Niall Ferguson, *Empire* (Basic Books, 2008), 130-6.

45 Queen Victoria, Journals, 22 June 1897
46 Greg King, *Twilight of Splendor* (John Wiley, 2007).
47 Paul, 'Before 1910'.
48 *The Era*, 27 June 1896.
49 CPatricia Cook, *Slade's Electro-Photo Marvel: Touring film exhibition in late Victorian Britain*. PhD (2016), Birkbeck, University of London.
50 'Living pictures of the Queen', *Cassell's Family Magazine*, August 1897, 327.
51 Joseph Holloway, 'Diary', quoted in Kevin Rockett and Emer Rockett, *Magic Lantern, Panorama and Moving Picture Shows in Ireland, 1786-1909* (Four Courts, 2013), 231.
52 *Melbourne Herald*, 16 August 1897.
53 *Melbourne Herald*, 23 August 1897.
54 Queen Victoria, Journals, 23 November 1897.
55 Richard Brown and Barry Anthony argue that this was a deliberate strategy in their study, *A Victorian Film Enterprise: The History of the British Mutoscope and Biograph Company, 1897-1915* (Flicks Books, 2001), 57-8.
56 Ibid.
57 *Victorian Film Enterprise*, 59, 71n.
58 The films are also known as *Children of the Royal Family Playing Soldiers*, a title hardly suited to the second year of the Anglo-Boer War.
59 *Victorian Film Enterprise*, 59-60.
60 Surviving footage from this visit is in the British Pathé collection. This appears to show only the procession, although a man is seen on the road appealing to the waving crowd who occupy the foreground.
61 *Magic Lantern, Panorama and Moving Picture Shows in Ireland*, 235.
62 A man waving his hat and shouting at the crowd in a grandstand abruptly disappears, as a result of a jump-cut in the shot. This is most likely due to the fragmentary state of the film material, but could conceivably have recorded some disruptive behaviour at this moment in the ceremony, subsequently cut.
63 *Magic Lantern, Panorama and Moving Picture Shows in Ireland*, 235.
64 Cecil Hepworth, *Came the Dawn: Memoirs of a Film Pioneer* (Phoenix House, 1951), 56. A photograph of the moment described appears on page 24.
65 J. H. Rivett-Carnac, *Many Memories of Life in India, at Home, and Abroad* (William Blackwood, 1910), 410.
66 After this unconventional success, Urban would go on to play a leading part in organising the filming of both the Delhi Durbar and the coronation of George V.
67 Brown and Anthony, *A Victorian Film Enterprise*, 57.
68 The Harmsworth Magazine carried extensive coverage, with illustrations, of the making of Children of the Royal Family under the heading 'Our future king at play' in October 1900. Quoted in Brown and Anthony, *A Victorian Film Enterprise*, 59.
69 Such documentaries have included: *Royal Family* (1969), *Elizabeth R* (1992), *Windsor Castle – A Royal Year* (2005), *Monarchy: The Royal Family at Work* (2007).
70 On the aesthetics of procession films, and especially the stereoscopic effect of filming processions from an oblique angle, see Gerry Turvey, 'Panoramas, parades and the picturesque: the aesthetics of British actuality films, 1895-1901', *Film History*, 16:1, 2004.

71 David Cannadine has written of the 'interconnected pageants and mutually reinforcing ceremonials [with which], the British Empire put itself on display, and represented itself to itself ', in his *Ornamentalism*, 111. See my discussion of his thesis about the primacy of the 'ornamental' in Chapter 19 here.
72 Twain's eyewitness account of the Jubilee first appeared in two instalments in the *New York Journal* on 20 and 23 June 1897, and in a slender volume, privately printed in only 195 copies in 1910, entitled Queen Victoria's Jubilee 1897, subtitled 'The Great Procession of June 22, 1897,' reported both in the light of history and as a spectacle . The text is in Twain, *A Tramp Abroad, Following the Equator, Other Travels* (Library of America, 2010). See also discussion of this essay in Randall K. Knoper, *Acting Naturally: Mark Twain in the Culture of Performance* (California, 1996), 144-7.
73 Twain, *A Tramp Abroad*, 1051.
74 Victoria had sent a message to the American President in 1858, when the first transatlantic telegraph cable was successfully laid, after which telegraphic communication had become a major new communication medium, especially for Britain's global interests. See http://atlantic-cable.com/Books/Whitehouse/DDC/index.htm.

24. Thomas Edison: The Media Wizard of Oz

1 Strictly speaking, it appears that his very first laboratory was in the basement of his family home, as a child. And it was this he moved to a baggage car of the railway in 1859.
2 Edison didn't actually 'invent' the electric light bulb, a process that began over forty years before he registered his patents, in 1878-9. But he produced a practical, manufacturable version, as he would with many other 'inventions'.
3 Edison never considered the phonograph as primarily a device for entertainment, or even for preserving artistic aspects of aural culture – even though he maintained tight control over the repertoire of music recordings issued on his cylinder and later disc recordings. A museum in the remote Quebec town of Sainte-Anne de Beaupré, the Edison Phonograph museum (now closed), which I was able to visit in 2003, offered a remarkable display of his many versions of this key invention, including talking dolls and a range of office dictating machines.
4 This extraordinary cartoon was by George Du Maurier, artist and author, responsible for two influential novels, the Surrealists' favourite *Peter Ibbetson* (1891) and *Trilby* (1894). He was also grandfather to the writer Daphne du Maurier.
5 This was written before Skype, Zoom and giant domestic LED screens made its vision of the near future even more eerily prescient.
6 Edison built his first laboratory at Menlo Park, New Jersey, and encouraged use of the sobriquet 'the Wizard of Menlo Park'.
7 Yes, it's Villiers we have to thank for updating the term 'android', for his humanoid robot Hadaly in L'Eve future.
8 See my essay 'Early Phonographic Culture and Moving Pictures', in Richard Abel and Rick Altman, *The Sounds of Early Cinema* (Indiana, 2001), 3-12; also Tom Gunning's 'Doing for the Eye What the Phonograph Does for the Ear', in the same collection, and also given at the 1998 Domitor Conference in Washington DC.

9 By this time, Edison has moved to West Orange in New Jersey and built a larger laboratory complex, while he and his wife were living nearby in a grand mansion on the Glenmont Estate, the Victorian equivalent of a gated community intended for the very rich.

10 My visit to West Orange, which inspired this article, was part of the research undertaken for the BBC-BFI television series *The Last Machine*, which was transmitted on BBC2 in 1994 as an early part of celebrating the 'centenary of cinema'.

11 Speculation as to why Edison did not extend the Kinetoscope patent remains open. It appears that he was well aware of William Friese-Greene's 1889 patent. See Peter Domankiewicz's blog William Friese-Greene & Me at https://friesegreene.com/; also Vanessa Thorpe, 'Historian fights to establish William Friese-Greene as true father of cinema,' *The Guardian*, 2 May 2021.

12 This presentation was recreated by the Library of Congress' film music expert, Gillian Anderson in 1992.

13 See Chapter 17 here.

14 DeMille's *Carmen* has been recreated by Gillian Anderson, using DeMille's own tinted copy with newly recorded full-orchestra accompaniment.

15 See Ch. 20 here.

16 I have retained this from 1993, partly to show how wrong we can be about media prediction. In the 1990s, CD-ROMs really did seem to promise a new era in data storage and access, encouraging many optimistic futurists – such as Chris Marker – to invest in their creation. Most of this pioneering work is now inaccessible, as the era of 'physical media' on discs of all kinds appears to be precarious.

17 In 1993, I was happy to acknowledge how much this article owed to Gordon Hendricks' *The Edison Motion Picture Myth* (1961, now at the Internet Archive https://archive.org/details/edtisonmotionpic000796mbp); Charles Musser's *Before the Nickelodeon* (California, 1991) and Annette Michelson's article 'On the Eve of the Future' in *October*, no. 29, 1984.

27. New Windows on the World

1 The 34th Annual Congress of the International Federation of Film Archives was held on 29-31 May 1978 at the BFI's Brighton Film Theatre. The programme promised 'examples from over 1,000 fiction films' from 1900-1906, to be discussed by 'researchers from five countries', who included Noël Burch, Jon Gartenberg Tom Gunning, Jan-Christopher Horak and Charles Musser. David Francis, the organiser and then head of the BFI's National Film Archive, explained in a note ten years later that some 600 films were shown. https://www.academia.edu/36708855/The_FIAF_Brighton_Conference_1978_Ten_Years_After. For Chris Horak's account of the event, see https://www.cinema.ucla.edu/blogs/archival-spaces/2018/06/08/fiaf-brighton-1978.

2 An initial version of this essay was commissioned by Dartmouth College's Media Ecology Project (MEP) to introduce the online Early Cinema Compendium of Paper Print and Biograph materials, held by the US Library of Congress, and by EYE Filmmuseum in Amsterdam, plus a digitized version of the Biograph Exhibitors Catalog from The Museum of Modern Art. In its online version, the essay contains links to make of the films mentioned, as well as use of Dartmouth's Semantic Annotation Tool.

3 The idea of a 'Brighton School' of film pioneers was proposed by Georges Sadoul, a French historian, in his 1945 article 'L'Ecole de Brighton (1900-1905): Les Origines du Montage, Du Gros Plans et de la Poursuite', *Cinéma* 2, Paris: IDHEC (published in translation in *Hollywood Quarterly*, 1.3, 1946). Sadoul worked almost entirely from catalogues, since viewing copies were virtually inaccessible at this time; and he was preparing what would become his compendious *Histoire Général du Cinéma*, which would begin to appear in 1948.

4 The missing second shot of *Come Along, Do!* was animated by Edward Christie from stills in Paul's catalogue, with tinting added the first scene, reflecting Paul's offer of coloured prints at higher prices; and music by Stephen Horne comes from the BFI DVD of Paul's films.

5 See for instance, Ado Kyrou, *Le Surréalisme au Cinema*. Paris: Arcanes, 1953. The first edition of *The Shadow and its Shadow: Surrealist Writings on Cinema*, edited by Paul Hammond, BFI Publishing, 1978, had a still from *La Course des Potirons* on its cover.

6 See Chapter 11 here.

7 The Spanish-American War in Motion Pictures Collection at the Library of Congress.

8 Many of these can be viewed online at the BFI Player in 'The Brilliant Biograph: Earliest Moving Images of Europe (1897-1902)' at the BFI Player.

9 See Chapter 5 here.

10 See John Barnes, *Filming the Boer War*, volume 2 of *The Beginnings of Cinema in England 1894-1901* (Bishopsgate Press, 1992).

11 Stephen Bottomore, 'Filming, Faking, and Propaganda: The Origins of the War Film, 1897-1902', PhD, Utrecht, 2007.

12 'Cuban War Pictures,' *Phonoscope* 2, no. 4 (April 1898): 7, quoting from the *New York Journal*.

13 *Clipper*, 9 Apri 1904, 160, quoted in Charles Musser, *Before the Nickelodeon: Edwin S. Porter and the Edison Manufacturing Company* (California, 1991).

14 'Reproductions of Incidents of the Boer War', R.W. Paul catalogue, 1902. See also Chapter 5 in this collection.

15 See Christie, *The Last Machine* (BBC/BFI, 1994), 89-90.

16 See Chapter 14 here.

17 See Christie, 'Ponting's Polar "Monumentary": A Study in Film Footage Through Time', forthcoming in Elizabeth Watkins and Jeremy Murray, eds., *Polar Photography and Film: Archives of Exploration* (Royal Museums Greenwich/De Gruyter, 2025).

18 On Blok's missed appointment, see *The Last Machine*, 43, a quotation owed to Yuri Tsivian.

19 See Chapter 8 here.

20 See *The Last Machine*, 13. Also early studies of the adjustment to city life, such as Georg Simmel, 'The Metropolis and Mental Life' (1900).

21 Silver's film was based on Abraham Cahan's 1896 novella *Yekl: A Tale of the New York Ghetto*. Driven by poverty and persecution, some 2.5 million mainly Jewish immigrants came from Eastern Europe to the United States.

22 See for example Ben Brewster, 'Traffic in Souls: An Experiment in Feature-Length Narrative Construction', *Cinema Journal*, Autumn 1991, 37-56.

23 On Kozintsev and Trauberg's fascination with detective fiction, see Ian Christie, ed., *Eccentrism Turns 100: FEKS and the Early Soviet Avant-Garde* (2024).

24 This film from the Bamforth company is now thought to be *Women's Rights* (1899), although long known as 'Women's Skirts Nailed to Fence', and clearly a satire on militancy of the period, despite the pilloried women being played by men in drag.
25 According to the historian of scientific film Timothy Boon. See his note at http://www.screenonline.org.uk/film/id/1336505/index.html.
26 See Kristin Thompson, *Exporting Entertainment* (BFI, 1985).
27 Leonid Andreyev, 'First Letter on Theatre' (1911), in Taylor and Christie, eds., *The Film Factory: Russian and Soviet Cinema in Documents 1896-1939* (Routledge, 1988), 30-31.
28 Despite his being persecuted by cameramen trying to film him, Tolstoy maintained his enthusiasm for cinema in the final years of his life See Luke McKernan's *Picturegoing* blog (https://picturegoing.com/?p=4931) from a 1937 report on the subject from *The New York Times*.
29 See Chapter 4 here.
30 The Egyptian Theatre on Hollywood Boulevard in Los Angeles, an integral part of Hollywood's golden era, has survived as a showpiece cinema and currently (2024) has a partnership with Netflix, housing its merchandise store, as well as running an American Cinematheque repertory programme. In Britain, evangelical churches have played a leading part in maintaining such historic cinemas as the Gaumont State, Kilburn (now a Ruach City Church), and the former Finsbury Park Astoria (now headquarters of the Universal Church of the Kingdom of God).
31 McKernan's online anthology *Picturegoing* can be found at https://picturegoing.com with a book version, *Picturegoers: A Critical Anthology of Eyewitness Experiences* (Exeter, 2022).
32 Martin Loiperdinger and Uli Jung, eds., *Importing Asta Nielsen* (John Libbey/Indiana University Press, 2013).
33 See Chapter 16 here.
34 For online catalogue of the Bill Douglas Museum.
35 To explore the MDHL resources, see https://mediahistoryproject.org/#lantern-search.
36 Bill Morison, *Decasia* (2002) and subsequently *Dawson City: Frozen Time* (2016). Peter Delpeut, *Lyrical Nitrate* (1991), *The Forbidden Quest* (1993) and subsequently *Diva Dolorosa* (1999).
37 Virginia Woolf's essay 'The Cinema' appeared in several magazines, such as *Arts* (NYC), *The New Republic* (NYC), and *The Nation* and *Athenaeum*, with small but significant differences, during 1926. It can be found online at https://sabzian.be/text/the-cinema or at the website http://woolfonline.com.
38 Catherine Russell, *Archiveology: Walter Benjamin and Archival Film Practice* (Duke, 2018).
39 Jaime Baron, *The Archive Effect: Found Footage and the Audiovisual Experience of History* (Routledge, 2014).
40 The film was commissioned by NOW14-18, an arms-length arts programme for the First World War centenary, funded the National Lottery Heritage Fund, Arts Council England, the DCMS together with other public, voluntary and private supporters.

Index

Acres, Birt, 4, 25, 33-4, 36, 93, 95, 97, 104, 106, 155-56, 185, 270, 313-14, 332, 339, 342, 346, 358-9, 372, 401n, 404n
Affron, Charles and Mirella, on art direction and set design, 269, 292
Albert, Prince (Victoria's consort), 133, 243, 309-13, 317, 319, 323, 433n
Alexander Nevsky (Eisenstein, 1938), 286
Alexandra, Princess, wife of Albert, Prince of Wales, later Edward VII, 311
Alexandra Palace, 68, 155, 158, 162-65, 253, *255*, 424n
Alhambra Music Hall, 58-59, 62, 109, 147, 15-58, 172, 219-20, 223, 225, 235-36, 250, 314, 324, 340, 358-59, 366, 375, 419n
Allen, Robert, 171, 378
Alice in Wonderland (Hepworth, 1903), 362
Alma-Tadema, Lawrence, 48, 251, 253
Altick, Richard (*The Shows of London*), 42-43
Altman, Rick, 209, 213, 215, 217-18, 220
American Mutoscope and Biograph Company, 360
Anarchy in England (1909), 162
Andreyev, Leonid, on status of cinema, 376
Anglo-Boer War, 67-74, 222, 245-46, 322, 344, 363-65
Animatophone, 209
Anthony, Barry, 67, 145-46, 154, 322
Anthony and Cleopatra (Guazzoni, 1913), 259; in Netherlands, 264
Armat, Thomas, 332, 388
Arrest of a Pickpocket (Acres), 106, 270, 372
Arrivals as a genre, 236ff

Art direction, 269ff
As Seen Through a Telescope (Smith, 1900), 360
Assassination of the Duc de Guise, The (Film d'art, 1908), 228, *230*
Athenaeum magazine, 45
Atlantis (Blom, 1914), 363
Avatar (Cameron, 2009), 1, 3

Balmoral, film of Victoria with family members, 315-17
Balzac, Honoré de, 56
Barker, Robert, and his Panorama, 52-53, *54*-55,
Barker, Will, 180, 226, 271-72, 274
Barnaby Rudge (Hepworth, 1915), 228, 273-75
Barnes, John and William, 21, 37, 67, 69, 74, 96, 365
Baron, Jaimie, 384
Barrandov Studio, Prague, 293
Barry, Iris, 302
Bart, Lionel, 290-91
Battle of the Somme, The (1916), 228
Battle of Waterloo, The (Weston, B&C, 1913), 162, 228, 263
Barrie, J. M., 131, 166, 377, 410n
Baudelaire, Charles, 15-16, 28, 36, 101
Baugh, Christopher, 231, 407n
Baxendall, Michael, 111-12
Bazin, André, 21-21, 36
Beerbohm Tree, Herbert, 192, 194, 262, 271-72
Belasco, David, 276, 428n
Belfast, film of Queen Victoria greeted, 322-23
Bell, Alexander, 328
Belshazzar's Feast (Martin), *42*-44, *48*, 394n
Ben-Hur, novel by Lew Wallace, 188-*89*, 253, 408n
Ben-Hur (Kalem, 1908), 188-*89*

Benjamin, Walter, 4, 101, 112, 133-34, 199; *Arcades* project, 384-85
Berne Convention, 188-89
Bernhardt, Sarah, 194, 201, 416n; in *Queen Elizabeth* (1912), 276
Bible, The (Aquila, 1913), 260
'Big Ben' films (Pathé), 163-64
Bill Douglas Cinema Museum, Exeter University, 4, *13*, 21, 26, 387n, 392n
Biograph company, 335; films of New York: *Lower Broadway, What Happened on 23rd Street NYC, At the Foot of the Flatiron*, 370, *A Gesture Fight in Hester Street*, 370, *Levi and Cohen, the Irish Comedians*, 370, *Hot Mutton Pies, A Catastrophe in Hester Street*, 3 71; *Rube in an Opium Joint* (1905), 371; *The Downward Path* (1902), 372; 'athletic young woman' films: *The Athletic Girl and the Burglar* (1905), 374, *The Physical Culture Lesson* (1906), 374; *The Gibson Goddess* (1909), 374
Birkbeck College, 3, 78, 80, 387n, 419n, 421n, 431n
Bitzer, Bill, 371
Black Knight, The (Garnett, 1958), 287
Blackton, James Stuart, 137, 145, 408n; in Britain, 277-279; *The Haunted Hotel* (1907), 362
Blackfriars Bridge (Paul, 1896), 99-100, *102*, 106-108
Blackwood's Magazine, 41
Blok, Alexandr, 370
Boer War – see Anglo-Boer War
'Bogart or bacon', 92
Bohemian London, 286
Bolt, Robert, 287
Booth, Walter, 149, 151-52, 344, 407n
Bordwell, David, 23, 37-38, 170
Borelli, Lyda, and 'diva' films, 198, 201
Bottomore, Stephen, 132, 207, 412
Bower, Dallas, 286
Bowser, Eileen, 169-70
Box, John, 287-293
Boxing films, 367

Brewster, Ben, 237
Brewster, David, 13-17
Brighton, FIAF Congress (1978), 104, 157, 357, 379, 427n, 438n
British & Colonial film company (B&C), 160-63, 263
British Biograph, 343
British Board of Film Censors, 248
British Empire Exhibition, 249
British Film Institute, 1-3, 64,78, 92, 364
British Diorama (Royal Bazaar), 43, 57
British Institution, Pall Mall, 43
British Kinematograph Society, 92
British Museum, 113, 119, 183
British Mutoscope and Biograph, 146, 192; 1897 films of royal family, 321-22
Brown, Richard, 67, 145-46, 154, 183-85, 188, 322
Brown, Simon, 79, 149-50
Browning, Robert, 17
Bryan, John, 283-87, 290, 292-93
Buckingham Palace, 240, 318; 1907 Gaumont synchronised sound demonstration, 211
Bruno, Giordano, 10
Buckland, Warwick, 274-75, 426n
Buckland, Wilfred, 276, 279, 426n
Buffalo Exposition (1901), 322, 333, 367
Bulwer-Lytton, Edward, *The Last Days of Pompeii*, 253-54, 408n (see also *Last Days of Pompeii*)
Bunyan, John, 116
Burford, Robert – see Barker
Burrows, Jon, 59, 194, 227
Bushey, 164

Cabinet of Dr Caligari, The (Wiene, 1920), 279, 284
Cabiria, 77, 136-37, 159-40, *140*, 251-53, 258, 265, 335, 363, 395n
Café chantant, 358
Caillebotte, Gustave, 108
Came the Dawn (Cecil Hepworth memoir), 145, 150, 418n
Cannadine, David, *Ornamentalism*, 274, 353
Cape Town, 68

Car-boot sales, 305
Cardiff, Jack, 339, 429n
Careers of stars compared, 201
Carmen (De Mille, 1915), 276, 334, 436n; early films compared, 197
Carnon, Roy, 4
Carousel projector, 114
Carpentier, Jules, 20, 390n
Castle of Otranto, The, (Horace Walpole), 127, *129*
CERN, and creation of the World Wide Web, 119
Chamberlain, Joseph, 240, 246-47, 250, 318
Champs-Élysées (Lumière, 1896), 109
Chanan, Michael, 96
Chaplin, Charles, 164, 182, 194, 196, 277, 302; on tour for Karno, *351*, *City Lights*, 353; *Easy Street*, 361
Chaplin (Attenborough, 1992), 292, 352
Chase films, 360
Chirgwin, 'the white-eyed kaffir', 191, 210, 393n
Chomón, Segundo de, 136, 139, *140*
Christmas Carol, A, Dickens (filmed by Paul as *Scrooge; or, Marley's Ghost*), 226, 271, 362
Christus (Cines, 1916), 260
Chronophone (Gaumont), 192, 207-208, 210-13, 226, 414n, 417n (see also Gaumont)
Churchill, Winston, 282, 350
Cigarette cards, 38, 192, 200, 378
Cinema buildings, Grange Cinema (previously Gaumont
State) Kilburn, 59, *63*, 259; Grauman's Egyptian Theater, Los Angeles, 377; Tuchinski, Amsterdam, 377; Odeon Leicester Square, 377
Cinema Ritrovato festival, Bologna, 300, 302
Cinémathèque française, 4, 297, 301, 304, 392n, 434n
'Cinephilia 2.0' (Jullier and Leveratto), 296
Cinephone (Barker synchronisation system), 173, 208, 227, 412
Citadel, The (Vidor, 1938), 281

City Imperial Volunteers (CIV), 70, 225, 245, 398n
City of the Future (Keiller, 2008), 81
Clair, René, 103
CNC (*Centre nationale du Cinéma*), 2, 297
Codd, Irene, 432-33, 408n
Coe, Brian, 94, 346
Coffre enchanté, Le (Méliès, 1904), 121
Collins, Alf, 149
Collins, Wilkie, 134
Colosseum (Regent's Park), 57
Come Along, Do! (Paul, 1898),125, 159, 220, 222,340, *341*, 342, 360
Consequences of Feminism, The (Guy, 1906), 422
Constable, John, 48
Constable, William, Daguerrotypist, 350
Cooper, Merian and Ernest Schoedsack, *Grass* (1924), 417; *King Kong* (1933), 140-41.
Copyright, 207-214, 335, 340
Copyright Act (GB, 1842), 210
Copyright Act (US, 1870), 210
Cornell, Joseph, 435
Corrick concert-party, 88
Countryman's First Sight of the Animated Pictures, The (Paul, 1901), 142; remade as *Uncle Josh at the Moving Pictures*, 406
Covent Garden market, 329-330
Craig, Stuart, 332
Crary, Jonathan, 17
Cricks, G. H. and Howard, 105
Crowther, Bosely, 104
Crone, Bridget, 92
Cuarón, Alfonso, 333
Cunard Films, 183

Dagover, Lil, 201, 204
Daguerre, Louis (see also Diorama), 43, 45, 55, 57,
Dalla Vacche, Angela, 199
Danby, Francis, 41, 44
Daniel (Vitagraph, 1914), 260
Danish Film Archive, 304, 357
D'Annunzio, Gabriele, 251-52, 258
Daring Daylight Burglary, A (Mottershaw, 1903), 149, 360

Dauman, Anatole, 1
Davidson, I. B., film company, 162
Davison, Emily, Suffragette, 374
Day, Percy, 139, 408n
Day, Will, 87-9, 94, 97
Death of Chatterton, The (Wallis, 1856), 186-87
deCordova, Richard, *Picture Personalities*, 192, 378, 414n
Dee, John, 10
Deed, André, 194
Delhi Durbar, 74, 247, 249, 435n
Delpeut, Peter, 383, 440n
Demenÿ, Georges, 328, 339
DeMille, Cecil B., 38, 48, 140, 251, 334, 337, 425n, 427n, 428n, 437n; *Carmen*, 276
Departures as a genre, 238-47
Derby 1896, won by Persimmon, 219-20, 235, 314, 324
Derrida, Jacques, 78, *Archive Fever: A Freudian Impression*, 299
Deutsch, Gustav, 384
Descartes, René, 10
Desmet, Jan, and Dutch competitors, 263-64
Devant, David, 125, 191, 224
Dickens, Charles, 101, 107, 133, 159, 226, 255, 271, 273, 283-86, 290-93, 344, 382; *David Copperfield* (Bentley 1913 film), 273
Dickson, W. K. L., 33, 67, 69, 207, 330, 332, 334-35, 339; 68mm equipment, 321, 364, 379; *The Biograph in Battle*, 364
Dillon, Carmen, 386-87
Dixon, Bryony, 74, 80, 342
Diorama, 43, 45, 49, 55-57
Doctor Zhivago (Lean, 1965), 287
Domankiewicz, Peter, 94, 346, 402n
Domitor, 3, 207, 418n
Donat, Robert, 87, 89, 339, 429n
Donisthorpe, Wordsworth, 339
Doré, Gustave, 46, 108, 285, 290-91
Downey, William Ernest, prop. W&D Downey, 315
Doyle, Arthur Conan, 141, 164, 345
Dramatic Copyright Act (GB, 1843), 188
Dreyfus Affair, 367
Dr. Gar El Hama (Denmark, 1911), 372

Dr. Mabuse, the Gambler (Lang, 1922), 373
Drum, The (Korda, 1938), 283
Duncan, Francis Martin, 152, 375
Dupont, E. A., *Piccadilly* (1929), 318-319
Durgnat, Raymond, 96
Dyer, Richard, 191

East Finchley Picturedrome (now Phoenix), 262, 383
Eastman, George, 336
Edison, Mina Miller, second wife of Thomas Edison, 330, 335
Edison, Thomas, 2, 8, 9, 25, 27, 29, 30-31, 33-34, 79, 88, 91-94, 97, 105-106, 155-57, 172, 178, 183, 185, 187, 190-91, 207, 200-10, 213-14, 219, 228, 270-71, 275-77, 314, 327-39, 358-59, 361, 364-68, 370, 388n, 393n, 404n, 413n; Edison and MPPC, 91, 172, 178, 335, *336*; Edison Kinetophone, 209-10, 213-14, 335; fire at West Orange, 214; 'Telephonoscope', 328-329; 'Wizard of Menlo Park', 329; Home Projecting Kinetoscope, 336-36, *337*; X-ray venture, 338; films replacing books, 336; films of the Anglo-Boer War, 365
Egyptian Hall, 17, 42-43, 57, 125-26, 129, 219
Eidophusikon, 52-53, 217-18, 223, 229
Eisenstein, Sergei, on Dickens and Griffith, 273
Elephant Man, The (Lynch, 1980), 292
Eliot, T. S., 350, 354
Elsaesser, Thomas, 214-15
Elvey, Maurice, 162
Empire of India exhibition, Olympia, 156
Empire Theatre of Varieties, London, 122
Era, The, newspaper, 183, 320
Evans, Will, and Fred, 164
'Exclusive' renting terms, 179-80, 203, 257-58

Execution of Mary Queen of Scots (Edison, 1895), 361-62
Extraordinary Adventures of Mr West in the Land of the Bolsheviks (Kuleshov, 1924), 373
Eye Filmmuseum, Netherlands, 357, 364, 379
Ezra, Elizabeth, 122

Fallen Idol, The (Reed, 1948), 283
Fall of Troy, The (Pastrone and Borgnetto, Itala, 1911), 258, 263, 335
Fanny By Gaslight (Asquith, 1944), 284
Fantômas, 135-36, 160, 259, 263, 372
Faraday, Michael, 11
Farocki, Harun, 384
Faure, Félix, President of France, 317
Fechner, Gustav, 'psychophysics', 194, 414n
Féerie, 126, 128
FEKS (Factory of the Eccentric Actor) group, 373
Fenton, Roger, *310*, 311
Festival of Britain (1951), 4, 87, 97, 286
Fildes, Luke 102
Film d'Art company, 61, 193, 228
Film d'art, 190, 192, 194, 255, 275, 277
Filoscope, 35-38, 107, 393n, 404n
Finsbury Park Astoria (Rainbow), 62, 64, 397n
Finsbury Technical College, 59, 156
Fish Factory in Astrakhan (Pathé Russia, 1906), 375
Flaherty, Robert, *Nanook of the North* (1922), 369
Fool There Was, A (Theda Bara, 1915), 164, 180
Forestier, Laurent Le, 151-52
Forth, Muriel, 88, 93
Fox Talbot, William, 310
Frampton, Hollis, 2, 7, 21
French Dispatch, The (Anderson, 2021), 352
Freud, Sigmund, 18, 390n
Friese-Greene, William, 4, 87-98, 286, 339, 346
From the Manger to the Cross (Olcott, 1912), 228, 260
Funerals, of Nelson and Wellington, 237

Galsworthy, John, 377
Garrick, David, 52, 218
Gaudreault, André, 121, 184-85
Gaumont, 360-62, 369, 375, 424n, 442n
Gaumont British, 279, 281
Gaumont, Léon, 210-11; 341; chronophone and *phonoscènes*, 226, 378, 413n, 416-17n
Georgiades, Demetrius, 31, 155, 393n, 401n
Géricault, Théodore, 42, 57
Gérôme, Jean-Léon, 48, 251
Gibbons, Walter, 69-70, 183-85
Gide, André, 16
Gifford, Denis, 151, 173-75, 177, 409n
Gilbert, W. S., 126, 220; Savoy operas filmed, 211
Giornate del Cinema Muto, Pordenone, 207, 300
Glass painting, 43-44, 46, 48-49
Glorious Adventure, The (Blackton 1922), 278, *279*
Goaded to Anarchy (Paul, 1905), *180*
Golden Bowl, The (Ivory 2000), 268
Goodbye Mr Chips (Wood, 1939), 281
Gordon Highlanders, 236, 245
Gorky, Maxim, 109-11, 384, 404n
Gramsci, Antonio, 198-99, 415n
Great Exhibition, The, 1851, 243
Great Expectations (Lean, 1946), 284-85
Great Expectations (Cuarón, 1998), 293
Great Train Robbery, The Porter, 1903), 334, 360,
Griffith, D. W., 38, 48, 229, 251, 273, 275, 335, 371, 377; *Those Awful Hats* (1909), 359
Guinness, Alec, 286
Gunning, Tom, 2, 23-24, 35, 133-34
Guy, Alice, 207, 210, 341, 374
Guys, Constantin, 101

Hair's Breadth Escape of Jack Shepard, The (Paul, 1900), 271
Haggard, Rider, 377
Hale's Tours, 62
Hamlet (Hepworth, 1913), 61
Hamlet (Olivier, 1948), 286
Hamlet, Thomas, 43, 57
Hammond, Paul, 121
Hampton Court Palace, 288

Hardcastle, Ephriam, on the Eidophusikon, 218
Hardie, Kier, 318
Hardy, Oliver and Stan Laurel, 349, 352-53
Harper Brothers vs. Kalem Company and Kleine Optical (1908), 188
Harris, Augustus, 128-29
Harry Potter, 167, 293, 411n
Harryhausen, Ray 141
Hatton Garden, 4, 90, 92, 97, 148, 155-56, 346, 409n
Haunted Curiosity Shop, The (Paul, 1901), 122
Haydon, Benjamin, 41-43, 394n
Heard, Mervyn, 54
Héliogabale (Calmettes, 1910), 255, 424n
Hengler sisters, 191, *193*
Henley, W. E., 345
Henry V (Olivier, 1944), 286, *287*
Henry VIII (Barker, 1911), 180, 272
Hepworth, Cecil, 61, 145-46, 149-50, 154, 177, 181, 200, 202, 208, 226, 246, 271, 273-*75*, 277, 314, 323, 362; Vivaphone, 209-*10*, 226; recalling lantern/film performance, 223; filming Victoria's funeral, 323
'Heritage cinema', 267
Herkomer, Hubert von, 102, 164-65, 275, 427n
Hero of Alexandria, 11
Hester Street (Silver, 1975), 371
Highgate, Steerforth's house, 273
Hitchcock, Alfred, 61, 155; *Rope* and *Rear Window*, 269
Hoffmannstahl, Hugo von, 264
Hogarth, William, 291
Holloway Empire, 69, 73
Hornsey Journal, 73
Horse's Mouth, The (Neame, 1958), 286
How Green Was My Valley (Ford, 1941), 269
Howards End (Ivory, 1992), 267
Huaco, George, 202-203
Hugo (Scorsese, 2011), 87, 402n
Hume, David, 10
Hurley, Frank, *Endurance* (1919), 369
Huygens, Christiaan, 52, 395n

Ideal Husband, An (Korda, 1947), 283
Ideal production company, 166-67, 277; *The Vicar of Wakefield*, 274
I Know Where I'm Going (Powell/Pressburger, 1945), 139
Illustrated London News, 102, *130*, 236, *248*, 291, 314
IMAX, 29, 41, 64, 397n, 432n
IMDb, 96, 151
Imperial spectacle, 246-50
Incident at Clovelly Cottage, 104, 156
In the Hands of Imposters (Nordisk, 1911), 179, 258
India, under British rule, 246-49; 'Mutiny', 1857, 246; Durbar and Royal visits, 74, 246-49, 422n, 436n
Inferno, The (Milano, 1911), 258
Inn of the Sixth Happiness, The (Robson, 1958), 287
Innis, Harold, 67, 74, 250, 392n
Intertextuality (Bakhtin), 270, 430n
In the Hands of Imposters (Nordisk, 1911), 179, 258
Invaders, The (Clarendon, 179, 257
Ivanhoe (Bantock, Zenith, 1913), 164, 262-63
Ivanhoe (Brenon, IMP, 1913), 272

Jackson, Peter, manipulating archival film, 383-85
Jaquet-Droz, Pierre, 10
Jane Shore (Barker, 1915), 272, 274-75
Japanese-Chinese War, 1894-95, film, 366
Jay, Bill, 309, 312
Johnson, Samuel, 292
Jones, Inigo, 52
Jolly, Martin, 76, 83, 399n
Joyce, James, 17, 390n
Judgement of Paris (Pathé, 1902), 255
Julius Caesar, 260
Junge, Alfred, 279-80; *A Matter of Life and Death*, *The Red Shoes*, 281

Kahn, Albert, 'The Archives of the Planet,' 298, 313
Kaiser Wilhelm II, 192, 313
Kaleidopohone, 11
Kaleidoscope, 7, 11, 13-17, 21, 37, 387n
Karno, Fred, 188, 349-54; Karno's

London Comedians touring US, *351*; film produced, *Don't Rush Me* (1936), 354; and Crazy Gang, 354; and Will Hay, 354; Karno sketches: *Jail Birds*, 351; *Mumming Birds*, 188, 352; *A Night in an English Music Hall*, 352
Karno vs Pathé Frères (1908), 188
Keiller, Patrick, 81
Kempelen, Wolfgang von, 10
Keystone Cops, debut in *The Bangville Police*, 361
Kholodnaia, Vera, 201, 203
Kinemacolor, 59, 152, 249
Kinematograph and Lantern Weekly, launch of, 186
Kinematograph Manufacturers Association, 286
Kinetoscope, 4, 8-9, 20, 29-34, 36-7, 88-9, 92-3, 97, 102, 104, 145, 153, 155-56, 185, 191, 219, 313, 330, *331*, 332, 334, 336, *337*, 339, 346-47, 359, 362, 364, 367, 369n, 393n, 401n, 403n, 437n; *Arrest of a Pickpocket* (Acres and Paul), 106, 270, 372; Edison not patenting, 332
King Edward VII, 1903 coronation filmed, 249
King George V and Queen Mary, 248, 260
King John (British Biograph, 1899), 192, 271
Kipling, Rudyard, 74, 164, 235, 241, 245, 250, 350, 399n, 419n; *Mrs Bathurst*, 71, 238-40
Kircher, Athanasius, 52, 395n
Kiss, The (Edison, 1896), 157-158, 271, 359
Kitchener, Herbert, Field Marshall, as Sirdar and victor of Omdurman, 244-245, 250, 422n
Klee, Paul, 214
Kleine, George, 254
Koerber, Martin, 200
Korda, Alexander, 272, 279, 408n; *Things to Come*, 283, 347; *Thief of Bagdad*, 283
Korda, Vincent, 279, 282-84, 292; *Private Life of Henry VIII* (1933), 282. See also *Rembrandt*, *Things to Come*, *Thief of Bagdad, The*
Kovacs, Katherine Singer, 126
Kruger, Paul, 68, *73*, 74, 399n

Lady Windermere's Fan (Ideal/Fred Paul, 1916), 166-67, 274
Laemmle, Carl, IMP, 192
Lantern shows, 192, 222-23
Lantern slides, 113-19, 153, 222, 224, 227; 'life model' slides, 222, 270, 297, 315, 334, 365
Last Days of Pompeii – for novel see Bulwer-Lytton. For films see below.
Last Days of Pompeii, Pain's Fireworks Pyrodrama, 159, *255*
Last Days of Pompeii, The (Paul 1900), 159, 253, *254*
Last Days of Pompeii, The (Caserini & Rodolphi and Ambrosio versions, 1913), 61, 77, 136; at West End Cinema, 61; lecture by Bulwer-Lytton's grandson, 262
Last Days of Pompeii, The (Schoedsack and Cooper, 1935), 140
Last Machine, The, 2, 3, 23
Last of England, The (Ford Madox Ford, 1855), 237
Lauder, Harry, 192, 211-14, 378, 413n
Launch of H.M.S. Albion (Paul, 1898), *343*
Lauren, Stan, on Karno, 352
Lawrence, D. H., *The Lost Girl*, 229
Lawrence, Florence, 191-92, 194, 201, *Lawrence of Arabia* (Lean, 1962), 267, 287
Lean, David, 283-85, 287
Le Bargy, Charles and André Calmettes, *Societé Films d'Art* (1907), 193
Ledoux, Jacques, 302, 383
Leicester Square, London, 45, 53-55, 58-59, 61-62, 108-109, 157, 219, 235, 377
Leighton, Frederic, 251
Leno, Dan, 192
Le Prince, Louis, 90, 92, 94, 339

Lewis, C. S., on eroticism of ancient world fiction, 264-65
Library of Congress, USA, 2, 96, 183, 185, 295-96, 357, 363
Lieutenant Daring (1911), 161, 372
Life of Christ, The (Pathé, 1903), 362
Life Story of David Lloyd George, The (Elvey, 1919-1994), *166*, 167, 410n
Ligensa, Annemone, 133, 136
Linder, Max, 194, 414n
Lindgren, Ernest, 92-93, 302; *Art of the Film*, 272
Lindsay, Vachel, 229
Literary adaptation, 301ff
Living London, 78, *80-83*, 399n
Lloyd, Marie, 350, 354
Locke, John, 116
Loiperdinger, Martin, 192, 214, 303, 378
London (Keiller, 1994), 81
London Screen Archives Network, 298
London Screen History, 3, 80
Long, Chris, 79
Lord Chamberlain, theatre censorship, 350
Lost World, The (Hoyt, 1925), 141
Louthenbourg, Philippe de, 52, 217-18, 223, 229
Low, Rachael, 92-93, 165, 179-80, 209-10, 257, 271-73, 340-41
Lubin, Siegmund, 185, 187
Lucchi, Angela Ricci and Yervant Gianikian, *From the Pole to the Equator*, 384
Lumière, Louis and Auguste, 2, 8, 20, 25, 27, 33, 35, 59, 92, 99-100, 102-11, 122, 130, 150, 156, 171, 183, 192, 210, 223-24, 235-36, 313, 316, 321, 331-33, 339, 370, 377, 390n, 402n, 404n, 412n, 423n; musical accompaniment, 219; Victoria's Diamond Jubilee coverage, 240; coronation of Tsar Nicholas II, 317; *Sortie de l'usine Lumière, La*, *99-100*, 104, 107; *Train Entering a Station*, 358, 403n; Antoine, 106, 158.

Magic Box, The (Boulting, 1951), 87-*89*, 93-94, 96-97, 286, 339, 346
Magic Sword, The (Paul, 1901), 121-26, 131-31, 134, 159, 226, 344
Magritte, René, 160, paintings : *Le barbare* (1928), *Le retour de flamme* (1943), 373
Major Barbara (Pascal, French, 1941), 284, 428n
Man for All Seasons, A (Zinnemann, 1966), 287, 289-90
Mannoni, Laurent, 21, 36-37, 87
Marey, Etienne-Jules, 339
Martin, John, 41-49, 57
Martin, J. H., 149
Martinek, Ivy, and Henry Oscar Martinek, 161-63, 372
Marx, Karl, 15
Marx Brothers, 353
Maskelyne, Nevil, 17, 57, 125-26, 191, 219
Matthews, A. E., British Actors Film Company, 165
Matuszewski, Boleslaw, 317-18
Maurice, Clément, Phono-Cinéma-Théâtre (Paris 1900), 207
Maurier, George du, *329*, 435n
Mayhew, Henry, 58, 82, 101
Mazzei, Andrew, 279
McLaglen, Victor, 162, 278-79
McKernan, Luke, 3, 59, 67, 79-80, 152, 378
McKinley, President, assassination at Buffalo in 1901, 333, 367-68
McLuhan, Marshall, 25-26, 117-18, 250, 328
Media archaeology, 76, 96
Media Ecology Project, Dartmouth College, 358, 437
Media History Digital Library, 4, 379
Medium Exposed, The (Paul, 1907), 126
Meisel, Martin, 222
Melbourne, 76-77, 79; Victoria's Diamond Jubilee films shown, 242, 320-21
Méliès, Georges, 27, 57, 99, 121-22, 124-26, 134, 136, 151, 153, 159, 172, 324, 344, 362, 367, 402n, 407n; *A Trip to the Moon*

(1902), 362; *The Fantastic Voyage* (1904), *362*
Messiah, The (Pathé, 1913-14), 260
Messter, Oskar, 200, 214, 334; *Tonbilder*, 192; Biophon, 207-208
Metropolis (Lang, 1927), 300, 431n
Michelakis, Pantelis, 302
Milling the Militants (Clarendon, 1913), 374
Milton, John, *Paradise Lost*, 45-46, *47*, 52, 217
Miracle, The (Reinhardt, 1911), 260
Misérables, Les (Pathé, 1912), 262
Montaillou, Emmanuel Ladurie, 298
Moore, Annabelle, 330; filmed for Kinetoscope, 359
Morin, Edgar, 191
Morrison, Bill, 383
Motion Pictures Patents Company, 91, 172, 190, 275, 335, *336*,
Mottershaw, Frank, 149, 360
Moxey, Keith, 78
Moynet, Georges, 128
Münsterberg, Hugo, 194-98
Murch, Walter, 207
Museum of the Moving Image, 3
Music, incidental, accompanying plays and spectacles, 223-29
Music Halls, 350-51, 358
Music videos, 215
Musser, Charles, 2, 117, 365
Muswell Hill, 68, 70-1, 109, 122, 146, 148, 155, 158-59, 222, 340, 344-45.
Mutoscope and Biograph company, 192
Muybridge, Edweard, 328

Napoleon (Gance, 1927), 138, 383
National Film Preservation Foundation (US), *Treasures* box sets, 301
National Film and Sound Archive (NFSA), Canberra, 75, 79-80, 82-3; mediatheques, 289
Neame, Ronald, 284
Nederlands Filmmuseum (see also Eye), 2
Nekes, Werner, 21, 26, 37
Nero Trying Poisons on his Slaves (Hatot, 1897), 253

New Zealand, memorialisation of World War I, 384
Nick Carter, King of Detectives (Jasset, 1908), 160, 372
Nielsen, Asta, 191, 194, *195*, 200-204, 302-303, 374, 378, 414n
Nightingale, Sam, 75
Nora, Pierre, *Lieux de mémoire*, 298
Nordisk company, 179
Notting Hill (Michell, 1999), 292

O'Brien, Willis, 140
Odeon Leicester Square, 59, 61-62
Oliver! (Reed, 1968), 287, 290, *291*
Oliver Twist (Lean, 1948), 285, 290
Oliver Twist (Polanski, 2005), 293
Olivier, Laurence, 87, *89*, 97, 286, *287*, 346
O'Neill, Eugene, 137, 253, 264
Osborne House, 313, 323
Our New General Servant (Paul, 1898), 340
Owen, Wilfred, 385

Palace Theatre, London, 59, 244
Pantheon (Oxford Street, London), 58, 396n
Panofsky, Erwin, 292
Pantomime, 126-7
Pastrone, Giovanni, 137-*40*, 251, 263
Pathé, Charles, 153
Pathé Frères, 172, 177, 188
Pathé Vincennes studio, 152-*53*, 409n
Paul, Ellen (*née* Daws), 98, 146-47, 157-59, 339-348, 360
Paul, Robert, 2, 4, *18-19*, 20, 25, 33-34, 36, 53, 59, 68, 70-73, 87-93, 95-100, 102, 104, 106-109, 111, 119, 121-222, 124-26, 129-29, 131, 134, 145-51, 153-61, 166-172, 183-86. 190-91, 193, 210, 219-221, 223-226, 235-37, 241, 245-47, 253-55, 270-71, 313-14, 316-17, 319-20, 323, *331*- 332, 339-48, 358-60, 362, 364-66, 370, 372, 375-77, 390n, 393n, 398n, 399n, 401-402n, 404n, 406n, 408-11n, 418n, 421n, 423n, 434n, 437n; musical accompaniment, 225-26, 419n; 'illustrated songs', 225;

Prince's Derby at Alhambra, *221*; filming Diamond Jubilee, 240-43, 312, 318-21; *Robbery* (1897), 372; *His Brave Defender* (1900), 372; *Whaling Afloat and Ashore* (1908), 375-76
Paul's Animatograph Works, 146, *148-49*, *160*, 342, 410n
Pearson, George, 131, 164, 167, 372
Pepper, John (Pepper's Ghost), 58, 129-30.
Pepys, Samuel, 51-52
Perils of Pauline series (1914), 161, 372
Perrault, Charles, 126
Phantasmagoria, 54-54, 130
Philidor (Philipsthal), 53
Philipsthal, Paul de (see Philidor)
Phoenix Cinema, London, 262, 383
Phonograph, Edison's invention, *333*
Photo-Drama of Creation, 77, *299*
Photokinema (sound) system, 209, 215
Pickford, Mary, 191, 194, 201, 378, 414n
Pilgrim's Progress, *116*, 395n, 405n
Pirandello, Luigi, 194; *Si gira* [*Shoot!*], 198-99
'Pirating' films, 183, 185, 190
Planché, James Robinson (fairy extravaganzas), 126-27
Plunkett, John, 309
Poe, Edgar Allan, 101
Polanski, Roman, 293
Pollock's Toy Theatres, 127, 131
Polytechnic, London – see Royal Polytechnic
Ponting, Herbert, *The Great White Silence* (1924), *369*
Pope Leo XIII, 192, 364
Popple, Simon, 67-69
Porfirio Diaz, President of Mexico, 192
Porta, Giambattista della, 9-10, *12*
Porten, Henny, 199-201, 203-204
Porter, Edwin, 334, 359-60
Postcards, 200-202
Powdermaker, Hortense, 191
Powell, Michael, 139-40, 164, 281, 283, 408n, 428n, 429n
Precision Film Company, 162
Price, Derek, 10, 18
Prince Edward Theatre, 64
Prince of Wales (Albert Edward, 1841-1901), see Albert, Prince

Princess Maud's wedding, 1896, 235-36, 314
Prizma Color, 278-*297*
Programme music, 229
Promenade Concerts, London (films in interval), 224, 226, 419n
Promio, Alexandre, 240, 317, 319
Proust, Marcel, 17, 33, 390n, 393n
Pumpkin Chase, The (Gaumont, 1908), 360-*61*
Purcell, Henry, incidental music for plays, 218
Pygmalion (Asquith, Howard, 1938), 284, 429n
Pyke, Montagu, 59, 62, 227, 258, 412n.

'?' *Motorist, The* (Paul, 1906), 150, 345
Queen of London Counterfeiters (1914), *163*
Queen Victoria, 126, 129, 192, 246-47, 272; Diamond Jubilee celebration, 158, 240-41, 243; filming of, *315*; Victoria viewing Jubilee films, 321; reaction against film of her in Ireland, 322-23; filming her funeral, 323
Quo Vadis?, novel by Henryk Sienkiewicz, 253, 299
Quo Vadis?, 1913 film, 77, 136, *138*, 181, 228, *256*, 258-65, 271-2; 335, 377, 395n; sold by auction in Britain, 259; at the Albert Hall, 259-60; in New Zealand, 260-61; popularity in Britain, 259; competition over in Netherlands, 263

Ramsaye, Terry, 91, 93-94, 192, 346, 392n, 426n
Real Thing at Last, The (Barrie, 1916), 165
Reed, Carol, 290-*91*
Regional film archives, UK, 297-99
Remains of the Day, The (Ivory, 1993), 267-68
Rembrandt, 43
Rembrandt (Korda, 1937), 282-83
Remediation, theory of Bolter and Grusin, 64,111, 130, 270-71
Restoration (Hoffman, 1995), 293

Return of Ulysses, The (Calmettes, 1909), 255
Rhys, Jean, *Voyage in the Dark*, 264
Rivett-Carnac, J. H., 247-49, 323
Robert-Houdin, Jean-Eugène, 17
Robertson (Etienne-Gaspard Robert), 54, 396n
Robinson, David, 2-3, 96, 416n, 419n
Roget, Peter Mark, 11, 389n
Room with a View, A (Ivory, 1985), 267
Roosevelt, Theodore, on screen and filming, *Roosevelt in Africa*, 368
Rosenthal, Joseph, 152
Rossell, Deac, 96
Roth, Joseph, *The Antichrist* (1934) on 'a film about Moses', 264
Rotha, Paul, on *Cabiria*, 265, 425n
Rough Sea at Dover, 106, 156, 185, 332, 358-59
Royal Opera House, Covent Garden (film and slides, 1907), 224; *Glorious Adventure* premiere, 278
Royal Panopticon (later Alhambra), 58
Royal Polytechnic Institution (Regent Street Polytechnic from 1882), 57-59, 129-30, 156, 219, 223, 396n, 407n, 418n
Rube and Mandy at Coney Island (Edison, 1903), 370
Rubes in the Theatre (Edison, 1901), 370
Runaway Horse, The (Pathé, 1908), 360
Ruskin, John, 45, 116-17
Russell, Catherine, 384-85
Russell, Charles Taze, 77
Russo-Japanese War, 152, 344

St. Ann's Well, 146
St. Paul's Cathedral, 57, 290
Salt, Barry, 134
Salvation Army (Australia), 76
Samuel, Raphael, 75-76, 268; on 'orientalism', 238, 243; on *Cranford* (Mrs Gaskell), 238; *Theatres of Memory*, 267
Sapphire (Dearden, 1959), 286
Schoenberg, Arnold, 214
Scorsese, Martin, 87, 96, 403n; *The Age of Innocence*, 268, 370
Scott, Walter, 17, 42, 272

Scott of the Antarctic (Frend, 1948), 88, 96, 339
Sea Cave Near Lisbon, A (Paul/Short, 1896), 184-85; 223
Second World War in Colour, TV series 1999, 297
Secret Cinema, 64-65
Selig (Selig Polyscope), 152, 409n
Semiotic theory, 268-69
Sennett, Mack, 164, 335, 352, 359, 361, 409n
Seven Year Itch, The (Wilder, 1955), 370
Shaw, George Bernard, 284, 377, 428n
Shelley, Mary, 47-48, 329
Shelley, Percy Bysse, 48
Shepperton Studios, 288, 290-91
Short, Henry, 35-36, 97
Siddons, Mrs., 42
Sidney, Aurelio, 164
Sims, George, 81-82, 117, 157-58, 410n
Sixty Years a Queen (Samuelson, 1913), 272
Skladanowsky, Max and Emil, 339
Slade, William, 320
Smith, Albert, *Ascent of Mont Blanc*, 57
Smith, Albert, *Two Reels and a Crank*, 145
Smith, G. A., 59, 148, 152, 360
Smith, Grahame, 333, 293,
Smith, Jack, 149
Smith, Percy, 152; *The Acrobatic Fly, The Birth of a Flower* (Urban, 1910), *Secrets of Nature* series, 375
Soldier's Courtship, A, 109, 157, 220, 270, 342, 359-59, 409
Soldiers of the Cross, 76-77
Sorenson, Colin, *London on Film*, 290, 429n
Sorlin, Pierre, 199
Sound effects, 229
South Shields, Prudential Hall, 173, 411n
Spanish-American War, 363, 365, 368
Spiders, The (Lang, 1919-20), 373
Spottiswood, Raymond, 94
Staiger, Janet, 170
'Star system', 191
Starski, Alan, 293
Stationers Hall, 183-84, 412n
Stead, W. T., *The Maiden Tribute of Modern Babylon*, 82

Stereographs, *Death of Chatterton*, 186-*87*
Stereoscope, 15-17, 21, 38, 270, 311, 390n, 392n, 432n
Stereoscopic film, 105, 403n
Sternberger, Dolf, 17
Stevenson, Robert Louis, 29, 131
Stop Thief! (Williamson, 1901), 360
Story the Biograph Told, The (AM&B, 1904), 360
Story of the Kelly Gang, The, 78, 80, *81*
Strand magazine, 140
Street Dance in Drury Lane (Lumière, 1896), 108
Strike, The (Eisenstein, 1924), 373
Stroud Green Road, 74
Symbolist culture, 223
Synchronisation systems, 209-10
Talbot, Frederick, 89-90, 93, 123-25
Tale of Two Cities, A (Thomas, 198), 286
Tarquin the Superb (Capellani, 1908), 255
Ten Commandments, The (DeMille, 1923), 38, 140, 425n
Tennyson, Alfred, *Enoch Arden*, 238, 421n
Thirties in Colour, TV series, 2008, 297
Through the Keyhole (Zecca, 1901), 360
Tussaud, Marie, and wax museum, 54
That Hamilton Woman (Korda, 1941), 283
Theatre Royal, Covent Garden, 127
Theatre Royal, Haymarket, 126
They Shall Not Grow Old (Jackson, 2018), 383-85
Thief of Bagdad, The (Fairbanks, 1924), 139
Thief of Bagdad, The (Berger/Powell, 1940), 283
'Their Past Your Future', WW2 commemoration project, 298
Things to Come (Menzies, 1936), 321, 322
Thompson, E. P., 26; *Making of the English Working Class*, 298
Thompson, Kristin, 102: 'American hegemony' in distribution, 277
Third Man, The (Reed, 1949), 267, 283
Three-Fingered Kate film series, 161, 264, 372

Time Traveller: Robert Paul and the Invention of Cinema, 95, 97
Times, The (London), 92, 137, *140*, 157, 182, 251, 253, 261, 264-65
Tissot, Jacques, 48
To Be or Not to Be (Lubitsch, 1941), 283
Tolstoy, Leo, on potential of cinema, 376-77
Toys, 7-9, 15
Tour in Spain and Portugal, A (Paul/Short, 1986), 36, 72, 158, 184, 223
Trademark protection, 184
Trafalgar Square, 64, 78, 83, 127, 273
Traffic in Souls (Tucker, 1913), 372
Trajidis, George, 31, 155, 393n
Treasure Island (Haskin, 1950), 287
Trewey, Félicien, 108, 156, 358
Trick films, 51-52, 121-23, 126-31, 133-36
Trollope, Anthony, 101
'Trip to the Transvaal, A', 68, 222
Tsar Nicholas II of Russia, 192, 248, 315, 317, 333
Tudor London, in *A Man for All Seasons*, 287-90
Turner, J. W., 41
Turner vs Robinson (copyright case 1860), 186
Twain, Mark, 325, 435n
Two a.m.; or, The Husband's Return (Paul, 1896), 157, 271
Two Reels and a Crank (Albert Smith memoir), 145

Ultus thriller series, 164, 167, 372
Unexpected Return, The (Repin, 1888), 238
Unfortunate Policeman, The (Paul, 1903), 360
Upside Down; or, The Human Flies (Paul, 1899), 126, 149, 159, 382
Urban, Charles, 59, 79, 80-82, 146, 152, 170, 183-85, 249, 324, 343, 364, 366, 368, 400n; *The Unseen World* (1903), 375

Vampires, Les, 135, 259, 424n
Variety and vaudeville theatre, 3, 25, 32, 34, 59, 171, 191, 210, 213,

215, 219, 270, 277, 352, 358, 366, 377-78
Vaucanson, Jacques de, 10
Vaughan, William, 41, 49
Velle, Gaston, 121
Vengeance of Licinius, The (Pathé, 1912), 257
Verne, Jules, *The Carpathian Castle*, 330; *20,000 Leagues Under the Sea* (1916), 362
Vestal, The (Capellani), 255
Vidéothèque de Paris (later Forum des Images), 296-97
Villiers de l'Isle Adam, *Axel* and *L'Eve future*, 329
Visit to Peak Frean & Co's Biscuit Works, A (1906), 375
Vitagraph, 145, 172, 177, 181, 228, 235, 260, 277-78
Vivaphone, see Hepworth

Wagner, Richard, *Die Walküre*, 224, 419n; *Parsifal*, 333-34
Waif and the Wizard, The (Paul, 1901), 126
Walker, Alexander, 191
Walthamstow, 155, 162
Walton-on-Thames, 148, *160*
Walturdaw company, 177, 181, 203; Cinematophone, 208, 226; Highlights from *The Mikado*, 211
Warburg, Aby, *Mnemosyne Atlas*, *115*
Warburg Institute, 113-*114*
Warner Bros., 61, 166
Warwick Trading Company, 69, 146, 149, 183, 222, 245, 324
Way Down East (Griffith, 1923), shown in Peckham, 229
Webb, Beatrice, 318
Wells, H. G., 377; *Things to Come*, 282-83, 348; *When the Sleeper Wakes*, 347; *Story of the Days to Come*, 347; *The Time Machine*, 33, 48, 346, 393n; writing in *Nature*, 347.
West End Cinema, *60*-61, 259
Westinghouse industrial actualities, 375
Wheatstone, Charles, 11, 311
White, Chrissie, 150, 200-203
Wilde, Oscar, 166, 274
Windsor Castle, 310, 315, 317

Wizard of Oz (Baum), 338
Wood, Leslie, 89
Wood Green Weekly Herald, 69
Woolf, Virginia, 37, 103, 109, 111, 384, 394n
World War I, 383-85
Wyke, Maria, 253, 302
Wyld's Great Globe, 54-55

Yates, Frances, 10
YouTube, 2, 75, 99, 215, 298-99, 303, 345
Zanetti, Eugenio, 429, 427n
Za La Mort (Italy, 1914-24), 372
Zecca, Ferdinand, 152, 340, 360, 362
Zenith productions, 164, 262
Zigomar Contre Nick Carter, *136*, *138*
Zigomar the Eelskin, *137*
Zigomar, King of Thieves (Jasset, 1911), 134-35
Zinnemann, Fred, 288-89
Zukor, Adolph, as co-producer and distributor of *Queen Elizabeth*, 276

www.ingramcontent.com/pod-product-compliance
Lightning Source LLC
Chambersburg PA
CBHW060641160125
20431CB00007B/94